T0304246

The Canon in the History of Economics

The construction and the role of the canon, the accepted list of 'great works' and 'great authors', has been the subject of much recent literary and historical debate. By contrast, the concept of the canon has been largely dormant in the study of the history of economics, with the canonical sequence of Smith, Ricardo, Marx, etc. constituting the skeleton for most teaching and research. This important collection represents the first attempt at criticising the canon in the history of economics.

The papers in this volume address fundamental questions concerning the formation and perpetuation of the canon, and its interpretation and re-interpretation. A broad range of international topics are covered, spanning ancient to modern economic thought, that explore, define and question the relationship between the canon and the construction of the history of economics.

Michalis Psalidopoulos is Associate Professor at the Department of Sociology, Panteion University of Political and Social Sciences, Athens. He has written widely, in English, German and Greek, on the history of economic thought.

Routledge Studies in the History of Economics

The Canon in the History of Economics

Critical essays

Edited by
Michalis Psalidopoulos

Routledge
Taylor & Francis Group

LONDON AND NEW YORK

First published 2000 by Routledge
2 Park Square, Milton Park, Abingdon, Oxon OX14 4RN
Simultaneously published in the USA and Canada
by Routledge
711 Third Avenue, New York, NY 10017
Routledge is an imprint of the Taylor & Francis Group

© 2000 Michalis Psalidopoulos

Typeset in Baskerville by
Florence Production Ltd, Stoodleigh, Devon

British Library Cataloguing in Publication Data
A catalogue record for this book is available from the British
Library

Library of Congress Cataloging-in-Publication Data
Psalidopoulos, M. (Michalis)
    The canon in the history of economics: critical essays/
    Michalis Psalidopoulos
        p.   cm.
    Includes bibliographical references and index.
    ISBN 0-415-19154-8
    1. Economics—History.   I. Title.
    HB75.P79 2000
    330'.09—dc21   99–047824

ISBN 0-415-19154-8

Contents

vi *Contents*

List of tables and figures

Tables

Figures

List of contributors

Albert Arouh is Professor of Economics at the American College of Greece Deree College, Athens, Greece.

Louis Baeck is Emeritus Professor at the Catholic University Leuven, Belgium.

Mauro Boianovsky is Professor of Economics at the Department of Economics, Universidade de Brazilia, Brazil.

Michalis Hatziprokopiou is Professor of Economics at the Department of Economics, University of Macedonia, Thessaloniki, Greece.

Terenzio Maccabelli is Research Assistant at the University of Parma, Italy.

Terrence McDonough is Lecturer in Economics at the National University of Ireland, Galway, Ireland.

Thomas Moser is Researcher at the Institute for Business Cycle Research (KOF) at the Swiss Federal Institute of Technology (ETH) in Zurich, Switzerland.

Bert Mosselmans is Research and Teaching Assistant at the Free University of Brussels, Belgium.

Jan Peil is Lecturer at the Department of Applied Economics, Catholic University of Nijmegen, The Netherlands.

Henk W. Plasmeijer is Associate Professor at the Groningen State University, The Netherlands.

Michalis Psalidopoulos is Associate Professor at the Department of Sociology, Panteion University of Social and Political Sciences, Athens, Greece.

Peter Rosner is Professor of Economics at the University of Vienna, Austria.

Arild Saether is Professor at the Department of Economics, Agder University College, Kristiansand, Norway.

Evert Schoorl is Director of Graduate Studies at the Research School SOM of the University of Groningen, The Netherlands.

Kostas Velentzas is Associate Professor of Economics at the Department of Economics, University of Macedonia, Thessaloniki, Greece.

Acknowledgements

This volume consists of a selection of papers presented at the Third European Conference on the History of Economics (ECHE), held at Panteion University of Social and Political Sciences, Athens, 17–19 April 1997.

I would like to thank the following institutions for financial support: Panteion University of Social and Political Sciences, Greek Ministry of Culture, National Mortgage Bank of Greece, Agrotiki Insurance, Agrotiki Life, Bank of Greece, Société Générale.

I would also like to thank the other members of the Organizing Committee of ECHE 97, namely Jose-Luis Cardoso, Philippe Fontaine, Albert Jolink and Robert Leonard for our common sharing of this experience. The selection of papers and the editing of the present volume remains however my own responsibility.

I finally wish to thank all the participants of ECHE 97 for allowing me to host them at my University.

Michalis Psalidopoulos
Athens
2000

Introduction

The canon in the history of economics and its critique

*Michalis Psalidopoulos**

The construction and the role of the canon in the humanities have recently been hotly debated among literature and history scholars. In literary theory, for example, the role of the 'classics' has been challenged, either through fresh approaches that tend to undermine the role of authority, or through the study of previously neglected literary forms. The same is true of the historical disciplines where a traditional historiography that centred on careers and achievements of 'great men' lost ground to richer perspectives such as cultural history, oral history and feminist approaches.

This state of affairs could not leave the history of economics, a branch of the social sciences that has enjoyed a worldwide renaissance in research since the early 1980s at least, unaffected. Though still not an option in graduate studies programmes in economics, the history of economics has undergone a transformation in the last two decades of the twentieth century. An important aspect of this development has been the cooperation of historians of economics with methodologists, philosophers of science, historians and other social scientists, a cooperation that has led to a varied and diversified understanding of both the recent and more distant past of economics as a science.

It was therefore natural that the close investigation undertaken in literary criticism of the accepted list of great authors and great works that constitute the canon, would attract the attention of historians of economics. After all, every scholar of this discipline is familiar with Paul Samuelson's seminal paper (Samuelson, 1978) where he used the adjective 'canonical' (not the noun 'canon') to mean standardized or common features of growth theory shared by different writers in the classical tradition. It was, however, the favourable reception of Vivienne Brown's 1994 book, that made historians of economics aware of a new way of posing questions and undertaking investigations in the vast research area which the history of their subject constitutes. It was simply a matter of time before critical questions about the canon in the history of economics would emerge and be discussed (Mackie, 1998). These would include such questions as: how the canon is formed and perpetuated in the history of economics; how it is interpreted and re-interpreted; have certain perspectives or historiographical approaches been marginalised because of canonical authority; and others. A final problem for debate is whether the history of economics can approach these issues in the same manner as historians of science or literary critics approach their material.

It is however true that before one attempts to tackle these questions, one should start from basics, by posing the simple question about what the canon in the history of economics really is. This is important because the more a concept is being used without an exact definition, the more it loses its initial meaning and potential as a tool of analysis. According to the *Oxford Advanced Learners Dictionary of Current English* the word canon means 'a general rule, standard or principle by which something is judged, a list of sacred books or a set of writings accepted as genuine by a group or a particular author' (p. 165). According to the same source the concept of the canon also has roots in theology, as the expression 'canon law' of the middle ages reveals.

It is clear that in any given period there will be a mainstream orthodoxy of standard, accepted authors, texts and traditions followed by, perhaps, the vast majority of scholars in a field. If we take, for example, the most popular treatises in the history of economics (Schumpeter, Blaug, Spiegel, Ekelund/Hebert, Rima, Backhouse), to name more or less recent publications, we find a certain canonicity in exposure and sequence.

In other words the ideas of great economists of the past are usually described by following a specific mode of exposition. First, a problem gets identified and analysed by a certain author or authors. Certain codifications result, taking the form of text, essay or pamphlet. These are communicated to a larger audience, and if accepted as sound and valid by a majority of thinkers, are canonized. In our days, textbooks and treatises focusing on certain themes with the help of certain tools, reproduce canonically the standardized wisdom on a specific field of inquiry.

It is admittedly true that a lot of work is needed in order to concretely define the canon in the history of economics. Textbooks and treatises in the history of economic thought should be comparatively analysed, both qualitatively and quantitatively, and agendas of, as well as directions on, research should be used as means to identify the canon.

The essays in the present volume try to do exactly this: first, they attempt to identify the canon among some of the classical treatises in the history of economics; and second, they subject it to criticism. They try to analyse in a critical manner certain topics and themes from the whole spectrum of the history of economics, both chronologically and thematically.

Admittedly this procedure poses certain problems and weaknesses, as not all of the authors share the same ideas and beliefs; and neither do they subscribe to an agreed notion of what the canon in the history of economics is. The critical essays in the present volume are meant as introductory contributions to a discussion that will eventually lead to more analytical and synthetic approaches. For the present editor, the canon in the history of economics is not an obvious theoretical construct; it is itself a historically determined concept.

In the opening essay Louis Baeck criticizes the view that Aristotle can be regarded as an ancestor of modern economics. He shows that for Aristotle the ethical norms governing the *polis* had a priority over the profit seeking motives of traders. However, his analysis underwent a certain transformation in the works of Ibn Rushd, the Latin scholastics and the Italian humanists of the fourteenth century and as he became again a part of western thought, his texts were read without due attention to the environment he was living in; consequently new connotations were put on his wording. The outcome is that today, as Baeck demonstrates, canonical works portray a different Aristotle from the philosopher who taught the synergy of sociopolitical and ethical factors in economic development.

Thomas Moser discusses the typical canonic succession of classical Greek by medieval scholastic economic thought in textbooks and treatises, and observes, that this account neglects the Patristic literature between the first and the eighth century AD. His inquiry reveals that interest taking was not an issue in the early Christian writings, and, when it became one, the Church was very careful not to offend the political power, as the results of the Council of Nikaea, that Moser discusses, clearly show. Only when Charlemagne prohibited usury in the eighth century, under special historical circumstances, did the teaching of the church coincide with the decisions of the rulers. The lesson for the history of economics, according to Moser, is that without the political power to enforce the prohibition of lending at interest, the anti-usury dogma of the late middle ages might have not existed.

Arild Saether offers a narrative of how self-interest came to be an acceptable mode of human behaviour. Starting with Grotius' emphasis on man's inclination for society, and Hobbes' natural law teaching, Saether arrives at Pufendorf, whose synthesis influenced great Scots like Carmichael, Hutcheson and Smith. Saether's conclusion is not only that the propagation of self-interest was not an entirely Scottish invention, as most scholars would now agree, but that by admitting a marginal role to thinkers others than Smith on this issue, canonical works in the history of economics disengage economics from political philosophy, a potentially harmful consequence for both disciplines.

Jan Peil criticizes the tendency in canonical works to regard Smith as a predecessor of neo-classical economics. Drawing on recent Smith scholarship, Peil offers a hermeneutical interpretation of Smith's texts that portrays him as a eighteenth-century moral philosopher, who pleads for a 'good society' where men will no longer want to be patronized by authority. Thus according to Peil's reading, Smith supports the individual in society and not the economic man of today's mainstream economics.

Terenzio Maccabelli revisits Samuelson's seminal article of 1978 and assesses the validity of the canonical model of economic growth against the background of the Ricardo/Malthus debate. He finds that Malthus puts forward a different view of scarcity from Ricardo's. The motives underlying human behaviour in Malthus' system of thought bring him closer to an 'ethical' school of economics rather than an 'engineering' one of Ricardo. The outcome is that even if Malthus does not have a different growth theory from Ricardo, he cannot, according to Maccabelli, be regarded as part of a canonical classical economic growth model, since his entire approach to the subject is different.

Peter Rosner compares two contemporaries, Ricardo and Rau, and asks why, although Rau's ideas on value and welfare can be regarded as precursors of modern welfare analysis, canonical works do not appreciate his contribution as much as Ricardo's. This seems curious, since Ricardo's analysis is based on the labour theory of value, which has been abandoned by present-day mainstream economists. Rosner concludes that this state of affairs can be attributed to an admiration for Ricardo's achievements and the fact that he drew his economic policy propositions out of the premises of his theoretical framework. Rau's welfare propositions were 'insights', not necessary outcomes of his theoretical system. As long as economists view their science as a tool that analyses economic systems with a systematic theory guiding their economic policy prescriptions, the canonical valuation of Ricardo and Rau can be understood and explained.

Bert Mosselmans investigates in his essay W.S. Jevons' efforts to deconstruct the Ricardian canon that dominated British economic thought of his time, and to create a new one based on his own views. To do so Jevons tried to construct a new community of economists. He searched for forerunners, in order to find confirmation in history. He entered an alliance with foreign mathematical economists in order to create an international movement of new ideas. He finally wrote a new textbook. Jevons' deconstruction of Ricardo failed because of his untimely death, and Marshall's and J.B. Clark's contributions. However, as Mosselmans stresses, Jevons' approach was incorporated in the general canon of economics, not in place of the old one, but as an extension of it.

Terrence McDonough looks at J.K. Ingram, the Irish historian of economics, and asks if minority status for some economists and their ideas comes not because of their straightforward failure to achieve canonic status, but from their refusal of canonicity. McDonough explains Ingram's minor status because of his refusal to accept economics as a science independent of sociology. Ingram either would not understand or would not accept that the consolidation of the market economy made an analysis of the economy, as separate from the rest of society, conceivable. It was, therefore, usual for Ingram to be given minor status in the canonical histories of economics.

Mauro Boianovsky revisits G. Haberler's *Prosperity and Depression* in his paper, a book published almost simultanouesly with J.M. Keynes's *General Theory*, in order to determine whether the canonical history of macroeconomics has paid due respect to academics, researchers, men of affairs and cranks who contributed major insights on the upswings and downturns of the capitalist economy in the interwar period. Haberler's synthesis of these contributions was overshadowed by Keynes's conquest of the field of macroeconomics, until the mid 1970s when a reverse motion gave non-Keynesian explanations a new hearing.

Michalis Hatziprokopiou and Kostas Velentzas discuss the work of the Russian marxist E. Preobrazhensky, demonstrating that the exclusion from the canon of marxist economists and marxism in general, leads to serious flaws. This is more so because Preobrazhensky's theory of primitive socialist accumulation and its consequences for growth theory can be easily translated into mainstream economic language, and was in fact helpful to western development theorists in the 1960s and the 1970s. There is, in fact, a strong case for enriching the canon in the history of economics with neglected heterodox, undogmatic thinkers such as Preobrazhensky.

Albert Arouh tells the story of dominance and dissent in economics by using religion as a metaphor. In this framework, the canon is the 'true' faith, the orthodoxy, fighting against other heterodox faiths, in a never-ending struggle, for as time moves forward, different stories are told differently, in different settings, by different people.

Henk Plasmeijer and Evert Schoorl apply the concept of the canon in a national framework to analyse how, out of confessional traditions and ideological divisions during the interwar years, Dutch economics moved to a policy-oriented macroeconomics that united almost all economists in The Netherlands under the umbrella of the neo-classical synthesis. The authors discuss demand and supply factors in this process up to the recent past. The institutionalization of the collective bargaining economy led to a huge demand for policy-oriented economists with the knowledge and tools to reconcile partners in dispute. The neo-classical synthesis provided a basic consensus as to how and to what extent compromises should be reached, hence its canonical status in Dutch economics.

In all, the essays do not settle any unresolved issues. On the contrary, as is emphasized above, they are to be understood as efforts to criticize the canon in the history of economics and to open a most promising debate for future teaching and research.

Note

* I wish to thank Bob Coats and Stavros Ioannides for helpful discussion and comments.

References

Brown, V. (1994) *Adam Smith's Discourse. Canonicity, Commerce and Conscience.* London, New York: Routledge.

xvi   *Michalis Psalidopoulos*

Mackie, C.D. (1998) *Canonizing Economic Theory. How Theories and Ideas are Selected in Economics*. London, New York: M.E. Sharpe.
Samuelson, P.A. (1978) 'The canonical classical model of political economy', *Journal of Economic Literature*, 16: 1415–34.

1 The Mediterranean trajectory of Aristotle's economic canon

Louis Baeck

The broken life-cycle of canons

The history of ideas illustrates with ample evidence that canons, even the ones which enjoyed revivals, should better not be introduced and profiled as timeless universals. Like all human artifacts, even the most promising canons perish. Like all products of the human mind, they are up to a certain degree context-dependent and thus coded by the values, the norms, the paradigmatic modes of thought and the historical consciousness prevalent in the society from which they spring. Canons live a cycle of birth, growth and flourishing, followed by re-interpretation and decline. In this process some prestigious canons move through the ages and travel to other historical societies and cultures, as it was the case with Aristotle's economic primer. In the course of this trajectory to other societies and its concomitant translation into other languages, the original formulations and textualizations are received, absorbed and understood in a different way. Aristotle's original formulations were reshaped and attuned to the social, cultural and intellectual needs of the Mediterranean middle ages by different strands of Aristotelianism. Our paper traces the Mediterranean reformulations of Aristotle's economic canon only. Indeed, at the time when the Mediterranean culture lost its moral and intellectual gist, Western modernity took over the lead. In the wake of the Renaissance, Atlantic nations like Holland, England and France introduced a completely different canon of unending progress, utilitarianism and welfare maximization, all this driven by self-interest. Under the moral and intellectual impulses of the Enlightenment, modernity engendered an ideology that proclaimed a belief in the limitless growth of the economy. In the wake of the gradual economization of modern society and of its values and norms, economics became the queen of the social sciences. All this would have been anathema to Aristotle.

Today's Western societies and their mainstream notion of development have their roots in a system of thought and a related system of values quite different from Aristotle's. One of the major differences lies in their conception and valuation of the 'infinite' or the growth 'without end'. In

the paradigmatic world of the Socratic School and with Aristotle in particular, unlimited growth was unthinkable and the economization of society
and its values was seen as a corruptive trend and thus a sign of coming
decadence. It is our thesis that the economic canon of modern times is
positioned at the anti-pole of Aristotle's paradigmatic world. This means
that Aristotle's economic canon cannot be seen as a foundation of modern
economics.

In fourth century BCE Greece, the crisis of the city-state provoked an
intense wave of treatise writing, with a notable concentration in Athens.
After the catastrophe of the Peloponnesian War, Athens had lost the hegemony as the Aegean sea power and its masses were pressing for more
influence in public affairs and benefits for themselves, that is, for more
democracy and welfare programmes. Orators and essayists engaged in
petulant debates on a variety of subjects, but they all focused their attention on the problematic drift of events. Conservative establishment writers
raised the spectre of sociopolitical *hubris* or of an emerging tyranny of the
masses (*ochlokratia*); the Sophists denounced this conservative *patrios politeia*
mentality with a plea for a more efficient management of the economy
and technical progress; Isocrates pleaded for a panhellenist solution;
Xenophon published a financial rescue plan for the *polis* and a blueprint
for better management of the *oikos*; Plato came up with a philosophical
treatise on the ethical prerequisites for a virtuous or ideal republic. But
in political philosophy Aristotle was a richer source since he pioneered in
fundamentals without losing contact with reality. His most original contribution was the immanent, this is the natural law of development. He more
specifically thematized on a form of mis-development evolving under his
eyes, namely the ongoing deterioration of the *polis* into a commercial
society moved by a chrematistic spirit. Aristotle's primer on the novel
theme of the transition from *Gemeinschaft* to *Gesellschaft* are the strides of a
genius. For him, the development of a monied market economy that pros-
pers on commercial exchange between socially unrelated individuals and
that is moved by a chrematistic mentality, would adversely affect the traditional values of the community and gradually undermine the public spirit
of the *polis* and of its citizenry.

Aristotle's economic canon bears the mark from which it sprang, namely
his political philosophy and not from actual experience. In this paradigmatic scheme, household life and its *oikonomia* exist only for the sake of
the 'good life' in the *polis*. And the ethical norms of the *polis* had pride of
place over the pragmatic considerations and the profit seeking motives
of the business professionals. People engaged in the so-called *banausic* activities were held in low esteem and at first sight distrusted. In *Politics* (1258b
35) the occupations of the *banausoi* (slaves, craftsmen, merchants and
money-changers) were ranked as the meanest of society and consequently
they were refused the state of citizenship. For Aristotle the highest good
(*eudaimonia*) is to live well as a citizen in the *polis*. Felicity follows from

leading a flourishing life not so much in the productive sphere of the household but rather in the public space among the peers of the *polis*. This life of leisured self-expression excludes a too great involvement in production and exchange or in economic matters in general. The care of the household *(oikonomia)* is only a means to acquire the necessary material goods needed for the sake of the good life in the *polis*.

At the very moment that Aristotle was teaching his political and ethical theorems, Alexander conquered Syria, Persia and Egypt. Alexander's conquest and multicultural ambitions aimed at a symbiosis between Greek thought and the wisdom (salvation cults) of the East. And the Hellenistic philosophical schools that followed – Epicureans, Skeptics and Stoics – were also more concerned with the inner problems of the self, or with the therapy of desire, than with the flourishing in the public sphere. Consequently they left the canon of Aristotle's practical philosophy behind. In the Roman empire, a Latinized Stoicism had pride of place with Cicero and Seneca. However, Cicero, who was a gifted popularizer of complex issues and who translated Xenophon's *Oikonomikos* into Latin, had only a limited interest in Aristotle's theoretical theorems on the terms of trade and on the economy in general. With mild irony he remarked in *De Officiis* (book II, section 87) that 'this whole subject matter of making and investing money and spending it as well, is more appropriate for discussion by the worthy gentlemen who congregate around the Middle Janus, than by any philosopher, whatever school he may belong to'.[1]

When the Roman empire took over the reigns of power, whole armies stationed in Egypt and Syria became converts of Mesopotamian religions and the hellenized Isis–Osiris cult. But history took another and unexpected turn when emperor Constantine opted for the, until then underground, movement of the Christians. The cultural synthesis of their evangelical message with the Neoplatonic tradition of late antiquity, christened by the Cappadocian Church Fathers and reformulated by a converted Roman rhetor, namely Saint Augustine, became the spiritual thrust of the early middle ages in the Latin West.

In Byzantium the Neoplatonic tradition lived on undiminished for ages. Its exiled Chaldean Christians relayed the Neoplatonic synthesis of Plotinus, Proclus and Porphyry to the Magians of the Persian empire ruled by the Sassanids. They passed it to the invading Muslim ruling class and its intellectual elite. From the time of late antiquity, successive generations of scholars from different cultures took the Neoplatonic heritage of texts as a classical reference. This resulted in an impressive chain of translations: into Syriac, Persian, Arabic, Catalan, Latin and later into a great number of European languages. The revival of Aristotle's discourse on practical economic philosophy, however, had to wait for the late middle ages.

In the Andalusian part of the Islamic world, Aristotle's *Nicomachean Ethics* with its theorems on the terms of trade and the monetarization of the economy, underwent a spectacular revival in the trend-setting commentaries of the Arab scholar Ibn Rushd. Averroës, as he was called in the Latin West, sided with the political and religious reform movement against the traditional establishment and adapted the Aristotelian economic theorems to his own framework of thought.

For more than thousand years the Christian world had ignored Aristotle, but when he was rediscovered partially in the twelfth century and more fully in the thirteenth century, the Latin scholastics would estrange him from the sources from which he sprang and put other accents on his word-ings with the result of a significant change in their meaning. When our world entered the second millennium, a series of reform movements of the monastic rules, instigated by the great leaders of the Benedictine and Cistercian orders, initiated a new concept of development and of the proper place of man in God's creation. At the beginning of our millennium the Cluniac movement re-emphasized the maxim *ora et labora* or 'work and pray'. This meant that the vocation of the monks consisted not only in liturgical but also in productive activities. In the twelfth century the radical reform movement of the Cistercian orders would radicalize this rule. Under the spiritual and organizational leadership of Saint Bernard the new order conceived man as the active helper of God in this world to further devel-opment. God's creation had to be completed, not only by creatures leading a life of contemplation *(vita contemplativa)* but also by manual work and other worldly activities *(vita activa)*. This positive valuation of man's creative powers and activities in the new theology of work meant a complete break with the age-old contempt for manual labour. At the same time, the Latin translation of *energeia* in *actus* gave a new meaning to the concept. *Actus* which is etymologically rooted in *agere*, conveys the idea that man, not only nature as in Aristotle, is actively taking over the initiative of devel-opment. This novel Christian theology on the fulfilment of God's plan by the activity of man is translated in the commentaries on Aristotle's economic theorems of Albertus Magnus and Thomas Aquino. And thus the *Aristoteles Latinus* grows away from the original one. With the Latin scholastics the accent is clearly more on labour and on the productive effects of human activity in general, than in the original Aristotelian society (a slave society) and world view. The *animal laborans* of the Latin West grows further and further away from Aristotle's *zoon politikon* (political animal). In the succeeding commentaries by later scholastics this new view on development would be emphasized. This gradual paradigm shift prepared the view of the Italian humanists on the *homo faber*.

The Latin scholastics, more than preceding schools of moral philosophy, came to grips with the challenge of explaining the new and disturbing market forces in their feudal societies. The rhetoric schools of the Italian humanists re-interpreted Aristotle's political and economic thematizations from their own historical context. With a greater emphasis on utility and hedonism, the humanists produced significant hermeneutical shifts. In the re-workings of the *Quattrocento*, economic attitudes and humanistic culture met half way. The humanists announced the spirit of modern times, characterized by the assumption that human beings possess an innate self-interested and economic mentality. With the breakthrough of this modern mindset, Aristotle's concept of development went into decline. The Mediterranean adaptations of Aristotle's canon were in fact re-interpretations by commentators who lived in other societies and cultures. The Aristotelian tradition of the scholastics and the Italian humanists prepared the way for the complete break of post-Renaissance modernity away from Aristotle's concept of natural development. With Aristotle development flourishes according to a predetermined natural scheme; with modernity the scheme also changes. The *homo faber* and still more so modern man works not only for new actualities but also for new possibilities.

Aristotle's analytical and conceptual breakthrough

Since Aristotle's texts on the economy represent only a minor part of his writings they cannot easily be studied in isolation. The significance of the basic concepts and the keys to explanation used in these texts are defined and elaborated in his theoretical works, namely, in *Metaphysics* and in *Physics*. In Aristotle's conceptual world, development meant the realization of the inherent, natural virtualities and potentialities (e.g. of an individual, a society, an idea) into a state of maturity or actuality. The important point about this canon is that the natural goal *(telos)* of development provided the intrinsic norm or the immanent law of becoming: proper development is simply the becoming of the pre-given mature state. Nature is the intelligent artificer *(demiurgos)* and the intentional planner of the world and of its development. To describe this immanent process in more detail he used different terms, such as *becoming, unfolding, flourishing* and *flowering* into a pre-given, natural form towards completeness. In Aristotle's world however the concept *energeia* (actuality) was a much more passive notion than in later times. *Energeia* (the act of developing) designated all activities that do not pursue an end and leave no work behind, but exhaust their full meaning in the performance itself. With Aristotle, *energeia* or becoming (development) is more an appearing *(entelecheia)* of the virtuality, or the mature state of what was there already in embryonic promise (*Metaphysics* 1050a 22–35) than becoming something more or new as in modern times. Moreover, in Aristotle's scheme, the unfolding of the potentialities was not conceived to be a process that could go on infinitely or without end. In stark contrast to the infinite possibilities for progress and development proclaimed by modernity, he could not conceive, and still less confer, a positive value to an open-ended unfolding of virtualities into actuality. This world was that of the limited good. And the Socratic philosophers in particular frowned upon individuals and societies that might become victims of insatiable desire.

Aristotle's discourses on the politics and ethics of development were spread over two essays: in *Politics* (book I, chapters 8–11) the matter was looked upon from the perspective of the dichotomy *natural/unnatural* in the social context, while in *Ethica Nicomachea* (book V, chapter 5) it was analysed on the basis of the criteria *just/unjust* between individuals. In the many sociopolitical options operative in relation to the ends and means of development, Aristotle professed that political philosophy offers the ultimate guiding principles. Since man as a *zoon politikon* can only aim at a flourishing life in a community with others, political science is the most authoritative *(kuriotatès)* branch of practical philosophy. As such, it is able to provide the highest placed or overarching *(architektonikès)* principles and norms 'in accordance with which each and every one might do well and lead a flourishing life' *(Politics,* 1324a 23–25). This is a course of development that responds to the basic needs of the citizen and of the community. Moreover, the ideal course of development is a course that also ought to meet the criterion of justice. Only the harmonious community-ends of the *polis* that concomitantly comply with the criterion of justice guarantee a development course towards the highest good *(eudaimonia)*. Ethics enlighten us as to the best ends in order to achieve a just course. In a well-ordered praxis *(europrattein telos)*, that is, in a praxis oriented to the highest good in life, the instrumental and thus also the economic means are subordinated to the highest ordered ends. Since man is a social and political being, only an *eudaimonic* synergy of sociopolitical and ethical norms and ends can engender a harmonious course of development. This elitist view contrasted with popular views allegedly held by many people concerning, for example, the importance of wealth acquisition and the securing of commercial profit.

Aristotle's *Politics* was a synthesis of his research findings and lecture notes on the political regimes of the Aegean. The first chapters of book I, 8–11, open with a discussion on the basic difference and hierarchical relation between the superior art of politics and *oikonomikè,* the more instrumental art of household management. These chapters offer a penetrating discourse on the stages of transition from the natural and familial practice of household economy, governed by traditional social motivations, towards a market economy, in which unrelated individuals are animated by the profit motive and concentrate on commercial exchange.

Aristotle's text on the natural and unnatural forms of wealth acquisition is of extraordinary density since the discourse repeats the argument from different analytical perspectives: the historical, the functional and the motivational. One kind of acquisition is according to nature *(kata physin)* and as such is part of the household art, as long as it procures goods which are necessary for life and useful for the community of city or household *(Politics,* 1256b 30). But there is the unnatural kind of acquisition that is justly called so because in it there is thought to be no limit to riches and property *(Politics,* 1257a 1–5). The art of acquisition according to nature develops into an unnatural form of *chrèmatistikè* when wealth is pursued with a certain skill or art, for its own sake, motivated by a desire without limit. This happens when the securing of profit becomes the aim of wealth acquisition. The introduction of money as a medium in commercial exchange gives new impulses to the chrematistic spirit; money itself turns into an object of unlimited desire. The driving force of this monied mode of wealth acquisition (*chrèmatistikè ktètikè*) is the evolving dominance of the profit motive. The mis-development consists in the ruling of a misguided desire by which commercial exchange loses its function of natural need satisfaction and degenerates into purely speculative commerce (*chrèmatistikè kapèlikè*).

With remarkable subtlety, Aristotle analyses the operational and motivational changes of the economic agents in the course of the transformation from commercial exchange pursued to satisfy the natural needs of the household economy to a society which engages in commerce for pure profit. In the transition to a chrematistic stage of development money plays a key role. Originally money is merely a conventional intermediary or instrument of commercial exchange (*plouthos organon*), but in the chrematistic stage it changes nature and the accumulation of money (*plouthos nomismatos*) becomes the major objective of commercial and financial dealings. In chapter ten of book one, Aristotle introduces the most vicious form of trade and money-making contrary to nature, namely, the trade in money itself on the basis of charging interest. The literal meaning of 'interest' is *tokos* or offspring. Interest is money born from money: *tokos ginetai nomisma ek nomismatos* (*Politics*, 1258b 5–10). In Aristotle's view money is sterile as it is a mere intermediary of exchange; it cannot beget offspring under the form of interest. The philosopher's categorical stand against *tokismos* is a striking reaction against the more lenient position of influential orators such as Isocrates in his *Trapeziticum* and also by Demosthenes in his oration *Against Aphobus*. These two leading rhetors defended interest charges as a prerequisite of commercial development, on the condition that business be regulated by law to prevent usurious practices. Aristotle's paradigm on the sterility of money enjoyed a theoretical revival in the treatises of the Muslim and Christian scholastics. In their scriptures the Stagirite's stern position flowered into a canon.

In *Nicomachean Ethics*, book V, chapter 5 (*Nicomachean Ethics*, V, 5), Aristotle expounded his celebrated theorem on justice in exchange relations, where the law left a free hand. The thematization opens with the basic principle that in the social bond (*koinonia*) of the *polis*, originally constituted to meet the material necessity of natural need (*chreia*), the leading form of justice consisted in proportional reciprocity. The bond on which the *polis* is built can only function properly and be maintained in an orderly or just way then if exchange relations are conceived and realized, not on the basis of equality (*kat'isoteta*) but on the basis of proportional (*kat'analogian*) reciprocity (*Nicomachean Ethics*, 1132b 34–35). On account of the differences in the value of goods and services, and on the unequal quality of the producers who deserve dissimilar rates of reward (an hour of a doctor's services is worth more than a shoemaker's), the theoretical challenge consists in finding a comparable standard in order to solve the problem of commensurability. In his search for a common standard of measure, Aristotle muddles through three interwoven passages which continue to give commentators headaches. In the conceptual world of our *polis* theoretician, it is the common need (*chreia*) which has logical priority in the search for equitable or just exchanges. But, in reference to his discourse on economic development in *Politics*, he brusquely introduces money as a conventional middle term (*meson*) and measure (*metron*) in the process of exchange equalization. In the evolving commercialization and monetarization of the economy, money emerges as the conventional standard measure of all things. In the next step, Aristotle opens a new perspective on the nature and function of money; in due time it becomes the 'representative' of *chreia*. Money serves as an acceptable surrogate for the intrinsic or basic value measure: '*huppalagma tès chreias*' (*Nicomachean Ethics*, 1133a 29–30). In his view, money is not only a medium but, in due time, also becomes a value measure in exchange relations. Moreover, money serves as a stock of purchasing power for future transactions. Finally, since money is only a conventional instrument based on common agreement, its value is liable to fluctuations.

The chapter in *Nicomachean Ethics*, V, 5 on justice in exchange relations proved to be fundamental. In the scholastic economics of the Latin West variations on this theme were repeated as a refrain. The complexity of the Stagirite's thought and the subtlety of his arguments left some leeway for later commentators to interpret his texts from their own intellectual or their society's ideological needs. In the middle ages, the Aristotelian tradition of economics ramified like a river and flowed into several cultural beds.

The contribution of Ibn Rushd

From 750 to 1250 the Islamic civilization was hegemonic in the Mediterranean, culturally as well as materially. The revealed *shari'a* or the divine law was the binding element of the community of believers. Islam literally means submission to God's law. Consequently, the study and the application of law to changing circumstances became the master science of the Muslim world. The *shari'a* prescribes in great detail how believers should conduct their lives, how to submit to God, how to deal with their neighbour, how they ought to sell and buy at the market place, etc. The jurisprudential commentaries and the literature on commercial legislation (*hisbah*) offer a mine of information on the normative constraints of the economy. Their value resides not as much in the slender analysis they offer as in the empirical information they contain. The same is true of the other source of Islamic economic thought, namely *kalam* or scholastic theology. Since the revealed laws are of divine origin, it is only their interpretation by scholars that can be characterized as economic thinking in

Islam. The most noted authors in this field who offered valuable interpretative schemes are: Zaid bin Ali (699–738), Abu Ysuf (731–98),
al-Shaibani (750–804), al-Ghazali (1055–1111), Ibn Taimiyya (1263–1328)
and Ibn al-Quayyim (1292–1350). In this literature there is no trace of
Aristotle. The master work of Ibn Khaldun though (1332–1404) is less
theologically bound, that is, it shows signs of a somewhat more secular
view. He knew the Stagirite's work rather well, but he disagreed with him
on several points. Ibn Khaldun was without doubt the greatest social scientist of the Islamic world. More than any other medieval author, he was
attentive to the proper laws of the society at large and to its economic
dimension.

The Andalusian scholar Ibn Rushd (1126–98) became Islam's most brilliant commentator on Aristotle's philosophy. During his lifetime the
political and military conflicts between rulers of Berber and Arabic origin
became manifest. The Almohad dynasty headed a reform movement based
on a politico–religious doctrine of unity, with the assistance of open-minded
scholars. Ibn Rushd joined the chorus, but in his endeavour to harmo-
nize reason with faith the religious establishment forced him to lower the
flags. In keeping with his own theoretical focus and conditioned by the
Islamic context, the Andalusian sowed the seeds for the medieval tradition in Aristotelian economics. In the Muslim world he found no audience,
but some leading scholastics of the Latin West were influenced by what
came to be called Averroism. In the field of practical philosophy Ibn Rushd
wrote commentaries on Aristotle's *Nicomachean Ethics* (the text of *Politics* was
not in his possession) and on Plato's *Republic*. In his work on Plato's *Republic*
he analyses, in some detail, the conflicts of interest between the classes
engaged in politics and the money-making classes. In his view, the development and the outcome of the power struggle between the sociopolitical
and economic constituencies of the state are a determining factor for the
different types of political regime. Under a democratic rule the money-
making groups are more controlled and subdued; but if they gain more
power, the regime may result in a tyranny. In his commentary, however,
the Andalusian master proves to be more sympathetic to democratic rule
than to Plato.

The reading and the interpretation of his commentary on the *Nicomachean
Ethics* presents a problem since the original Arabic text is lost. Only the
Latin text and a Hebrew version are available. A comparative reading of
Aristotle's Greek text and the Latin version of Ibn Rushd's commentary
reveals that the Andalusian scholar elaborates Aristotle's discourse on ethics
rather faithfully, but in a more synthetic way than the original. The Stagirite
had not taken the time to rewrite his complex arguments into a compact
text. In the effort of systematization, Ibn Rushd was a notable interpreter,
followed in this by his disciples among the Latin scholastics. In some important parts of the discourse on the terms of exchange and on money
(*Nicomachean Ethics*, V, 5), the glosses of the Cordoban interpreter part

company with Aristotle's original text. In the passage (*Nicomachean Ethics* 1133b 18) where Aristotle, on metaphysical grounds, admits 'the impossibility for products so different to be rendered commensurable in the strict sense', Ibn Rushd elucidated the problem somewhat with an interpolation of his own. In his metaphysics (1052b 20) the Greek philosopher had also stated that each object to be measured 'should be measured by a unit of the same species'. The Arab philosopher added an important interpolation; his line reads: by the smallest unit of its kind '*sui generis minimo*'. In the analysis of exchange relations, where the pegging towards equivalence around a mean value may lead to a bargaining process of plus or minus, the perspectivation of measurement in terms of 'the smallest unit' could have opened the door to an original formulation of marginal calculus. But the Islamic world, as a highly developed commercial society, had long accepted the intermediary function of money and the Andalusian did not elaborate any further on barter marginalism in real terms, although he had provided the key to it.

In the Stagirite's discourse, money only had a footing in exchange relations as a convenient but artificial medium. It was considered to be no more than a surrogate of *chreia* (in Greek: *huppalagma*). The Andalusian scholar, however, who lived in a civilization where the monetarization of exchange relations had become an accepted and evident practice, did not have the same moral apprehensions against the development of commerce and its mediation by money as did Aristotle. In a clear style, the three functions of money are described: money is a medium of exchange (*instrumentum conegociandi*); it is a standard measure of commensurability between different things (*cognitio coequalitatis inter res diversas*); and it is also a reserve of purchasing power for the future (*tanquam fidejussor supplendi necessitatem futuram*). While the Stagirite professed a monetary nominalism based on pure convention, the Arab scholar recognized the mediating function of money in exchange relations as a legitimate and necessary practice.

To my knowledge, the German historian of monetary thought, C. Miller, was the first to discover Ibn Rushd's omission of Aristotle's line (*Nicomachean Ethics* 1133b 17) 'that the money standard itself is fluctuating like other commodities, since its purchasing power varies at different times'. Aristotle's statement is in fact ambiguous, for in that context he perceives money as a 'commodity' with changeable worth. How can a commodity with fluctuating value be a standard measure of commensurability? The Arabian scholar resolved the ambiguity by his option for an immutable standard. Instead of the Aristotelian locus on the fluctuating value of money, Ibn Rushd's paraphrase simply states that for the Greeks, money was liable to change according to convention and law; we quote '*El quum ista inveniatur in denario expone ut sit nomen legis apud grecos denominative sumptum a positione, nominatus est denarius in lingua greca nomine denominate sumpto a lege*' (in *Moralia Nicomachia Expositio*, chapter V, E: 241). The Arab scholar, living in a commercial civilization where the stability of the medium of exchange was an absolute prerequisite for its intrinsic quality of being money (*thamaniyah*: or money-ness), could neither subscribe to the Stagirite's hint of fluctuating commodity money nor to his monetary nominalism. As a judge in the Maliki tradition he was in favour of absolute stability for all measures, monetary standards included. From a metaphysical point of view, a fluctuating or changeable standard cannot serve as a measure to make things commensurable as exchange relations would then result in arbitrariness and indetermination. Aristotle was no doubt aware of this fact, which may well explain why he degraded money to a surrogate medium. In Ibn Rushd's world money figured as a fully-fledged medium. The rulers, however, did not always live up to this lofty principle. From the twelfth century onward, the princes of the Muslim world and of the West increasingly indulged in the practice of debasement. This fraudulent practice elicited a whole cycle of essay writing on the subject, which resulted in a deepening of monetary theory.

In the fourteenth century the Maghrebi historian and socioeconomist Ibn Khaldun wrote a masterly introduction to his *Kitab al-ibar*. In this prolegomena or *Muqaddimah*, he rejected both the extreme idealism of al-Farabi's *Virtuous City* and Ibn Rushd's rationalism. Ibn Khaldun had been a political activist in his early career and as such resonated more with Cicero's matter-of-fact Stoicism. His treatise was a masterpiece on the cycle of the rise, boom and decline of political regimes and societies. It was written in the genre initiated by Polybius, a Greek historian living in the second century BCE. On account of its comprehensiveness and in-depth analysis, Ibn Khaldun's development theory (*ilm al-umran*) far surpassed Aristotle's concept of the historical cycle of regimes (*anakuklosis politeion*). In contrast to the Stagirite's normative stand, the Arab scholar of the fourteenth century opted for political and economic realism. His approach was that of a social scientist rather than that of a political philosopher. In fact, his *Muqaddimah* was the first well-documented treatise on social and economic development, with an emphasis on historical dialectics.

The re-working of Aristotle's canon by the Latin scholastics

In the eleventh century, after an age-long rural slumber, the Latin West witnessed an urban and economic revival. And in the twelfth century the legacy of Greek science, already substantially commented upon by Islamic scholars, was translated into Latin from Arabic. This transfer in the West caused a sudden passion for the systematization of knowledge. Towards this effort a new scholastic genre of theology, based on the synergy between faith and reason, entered the scene. Practical philosophy and moral theology of the twelfth century continued to lean heavily on the Platonic–Augustinian tradition. However, they received a new methodological impetus through the study of Cicero's treatises, in particular, his *De Officiis*. Cicero's influence would keep the scholarly work of the twelfth century on politics, ethics and the economy within practical bounds, with only a trace of theoretical analysis.

In the thirteenth century, the study of practical philosophy and of moral theology took a radical turn towards a more theoretical orientation with the invasion of Aristotle's *Ethics*. The work of the Greek master reached the Latin West in the framework of Ibn Rushd's theoretical reformulations. Its intellectual impact provoked a break with the Augustinian tradition. After the direct translations from Greek into Latin had become available, an intellectual crisis was pending in which Albertus and his disciple Thomas played a crucial role. In the year 1247 Robert Grosseteste presented his *Translatio Lincolniensis* with the complete text of Aristotle's *Ethics* and a series of comments by early Greek exegetes. By the beginning of the 1260s William of Moerbeke had achieved the translation of the Stagirite's complete works, including *Politics* (up to chapter 1270a 30).

Albertus Magnus

Before we proceed to discuss Albertus' reading of the new material, a short reference to Moerbeke's rendering of some of the crucial Aristotelian terms is necessary. Indeed, they influenced Albertus' interpretative scheme on commercial activities and on usury. In Aristotle's original Greek version on the transition from a natural economy to a chrematistic misdevelopment, the key reference reads as follows: '*poristentos oun ede nomismatos*' (1257a 41). In Moerbeke's first version this line is translated as '*determinato igitur numismate iam ex necessaria commutatione altera species crimatistice facta est, campsoria*'. In his second version Moerbeke offers a slightly different wording: '*facto igitur iam numismate ex necessaria commutatione altera species pecuniativae facta est, campsoria*'. Plainly formulated: in its development course, the natural exchange of the *oikos* was overshadowed by another type of exchange, namely, monetarized trade for gain. Moerbeke rendered the notion of 'commerce for profit' into Latin as *campsor* and in other places as *campsoria*. In Latin, these terms refer to money-changers and bankers rather than to traders. The use of the word *campsor* or *campsoria* exclusively for commercial and monetary deals inspired by the profit motive indicates that Moerbeke reduced Aristotle's moral disapproval to only the money-changer's activity. This novel hermeneutical stance of the medieval translator was followed by the trend-setting commentators on the Stagirite's texts. Albertus picked up the line and gave the trading community a green light as long as the commercial activities responded to the needs of orderly community life and insofar as the merchants did not unduly profit from monopoly or scarcity situations. Conversely, the *campsoria* or the business of money-changers and commerce for pure gain '*ex cupiditate*' was sharply denounced.

In Albertus' early writings such as *De Bono* and in his commentary on Peter Lombard's text book *Super IV Sententiarium*, some brief references to the issue of justice in exchange are expounded in Ciceronian rhetorist fashion. But his trend-setting work in this field came in his two commentaries on Aristotle's *Ethica Nicomachea*. The first commentary, *Super Ethicam*, was written after his return from Paris University to Cologne (1250–2), and the second was completed in 1263. Albertus had a fair knowledge of Ibn Rushd's exegesis and felt free to depart from the original text in order to adapt it to his own historical context and outlook. This new technique of paraphrasing, *ex sensu supplevi*, was also applied in his treatment of book V, 5 of *Ethics* on justice in exchange. In spite of Aristotle's sometimes confusing analysis of the terms of exchange, which were somewhat clarified by Albertus' Arabian predecessor Ibn Rushd, Albertus' analysis emerged as a well-balanced discourse with new openings. The terms which Albertus substantially clarified were those of the *demand interpretation* and the *labour interpretation*. At the time when Albertus wrote his commentaries, the value of man's labour (also of manual labour) was already deeply anchored in the collective mind. It should be noted, however, that Albertus was the first scholar to upgrade the value of labour in the speculative tradition of moral philosophy. This entailed a scholastic departure from the Stagirite's formulation. In Aristotle's time manual labour was slave labour. This first full exegesis of Aristotle's exchange relation theorem by a Latin scholar became a historical benchmark in speculative, moral theology on economic matters.

In order to arrive at a just compensation in exchange for both sides, the equality should not be a quantitative but a proportional one (*secundum equalitatem proportionis*). In a further development, proportional equivalence in exchange is specified as the value of one packet of commodities over and against the value of another: '*secundum proportionem valoris rei unius ad valorem rei alterius*', and in a second line '*res in rem commutatur secundum valorem*'. Until this point, Albertus stays solidly within the crux of Aristotelian orthodoxy. When it comes to specifying the source of value, however, he parts company with his Greek model. Indeed, for the purpose of justice the exchangers should offer to each other an equivalent value '*in pretio secundum proportionem operis ad opus*'. In the first commentary, value does not stem from the status of the exchangers but from the worth of the products. The following lines leave no doubt that the norm for our Latin scholar is based on labour value or, more generally, on the cost of the inputs, as he repeatedly uses terms such as '*in laboribus et expensis*' and '*differentia secundum labores et expensae*'. This is illustrated in an Aristotelian fashion by a clear example: 'As the farmer is to the shoemaker in labour and expenses, thus the product of the shoemaker is to the farmer's product'. He concludes though that the norm of labour and material cost is not an absolute criterion of value. In order that exchange takes place, the exchanged products should respond to a need of the exchangers, that is, in response to each other's supply and demand: '*opus diximus esse usum vel utilitatem vel indigentiam*'.

In his second commentary his re-working of Aristotle's concept of *chreia* emerges more clearly. It refers not only to reciprocal need (*indigentia*), but also to *necessitas* and even to the more subjective notion of *utilitas*. Albertus did not elaborate on the value paradox inherent in this dualism. When he arrives at the difficult question of commensurability, he is perfectly aware of the problem raised by measurement to achieve equality between the things exchanged, as Aristotle himself was: '*Equalitas autem esse non potest sine commensuratione*'. In his commentary on Aristotle's *Metaphysics* X, 1, the Arab scholar Ibn Rushd had added the interpolation that an object's measuring rod had to be the *smallest* unit of its own kind. Albertus, a keen reader of the Andalusian philosopher, follows this line: '*quia sic unumquodque mensuratus sui generis minimo*', but he did not expand on this hint of marginalism. A few decades later the nominalist philosophers, with a greater sensibility for methodological individualism than the holism of Albertus, would break open the horizon.

In the discourse on the functions and value of money, Albertus comes very close to Ibn Rushd's metaphysical absolutism for measures. In its function of *mensura* or *regula*, the monetary medium serves as a valuation standard of different commodities and services as they are estimated *in the economic scale of values*. In the ideal situation, money should exhibit the quality of stability (*moneta certa*). A fluctuating '*mensura*' entails uncertainty and indetermination in exchange relations. This defect also diminishes the value of money as a stock of future purchasing power. In fact, money with a fluctuating value is an unreliable stock: '*non est fidejussor certus*'. But his feudal context induces him to a more political stand. With some hesitation he resignedly accepts the power of the prince to alter its course, according to the feudal concept of *valor impositus*. The Aristotelian thesis on the sterility of money is emphasized with a biological metaphor '*pecunia non parit*', that is, money cannot beget money. Albertus' *Super Ethicum* betokened a growth in the philosophical foundations of moral theology. His promotion of Aristotle's conceptual rationalism to the status of a privileged authority (etymologically *auctoritas* stems from the Greek *authentes*, or what can be trusted), prepared the way for a more radical wave, namely, Latin Averroism. The canonization of the Stagirite led to the decolonization of practical philosophy from the tutelage of theology, that is, towards its scientific autonomy. Whereas Ibn Rushd had been unable to consolidate a rationalist tradition in the scholarly world of Islam, Albertus was followed by generations of Latin disciples in Aristotelian tradition. The disciple Thomas Aquino who systematized this tradition into a canon became a celebrity in this field.

Thomas Aquino

The scriptures of interest to the historian of economic thought were all written in the mature age of Thomas. First there is his uncompleted treatise

on government *De Regno* (1207). This is followed by the more important
stream of his commentaries on Aristotle's practical philosophy, the *Sententia
Libri Politicorum* and the *Sententia Libri Ethicorum*, as well as the second volume,
second part of the *Summa Theologiae* (ST 2a, 2ae), all of which were written
during his regency as *magister* in Paris, from 1269 to 1272. In his sociopolitical opinions, Thomas positioned himself in retreat from the canonists'
sweeping formulations which conceived of the Church as a total society
on the principle of *plenitudo potestatis*. In his view, the natural and political
domains of man are to be considered in their own right, at least in the
first instance. Accordingly, the *doctor angelicus* sketches the characteristics
of an ideal state. The ideal state is endowed with a natural law-making
capacity, with a *potestas coactiva*. This is the case, for example, in the material
sphere where, in situations of monopoly prices or of undue fluctuations
in prices caused by commercial speculation, governmental authorities have
the capacity to intervene in order to regulate the gyrations of market
prices. The prince also has the capacity to fix the value of money, and of
seigniorage, expressed by the principle *valor impositus*. But even the ideal
state is no more than a useful stepping stone to the final end, since divine
law is of a higher order. All true or all authentic authority and power
therefore has a sacred character. In his teleological view, the Dominican
emphasized duties rather than rights, and the common good *(bonum
commune)* had priority over the individual.

His commentaries on the Stagirite's *Politics* and *Ethics* were developed
in the same vein as Albertus'. This should not come as a surprise as the
two worked studiously together during the formative years of Thomas.
This intellectual kinship is most clearly indicated in their comments
on exchange relations which, more than in Aristotle's case, developed into
a novel theory of economic value. Both emphasize that justice in exchange
relations is achieved when there is equality between the things exchanged.
Commercial exchange is an exchange of things for things. The value of
things does not derive from their worth in the natural order: 'a mouse
is of higher natural order than a jewel stone; a slave ranks higher than a
horse; but the stone and the horse may have a higher economic value'.
Value is also correlative with the functional worth in the spectrum of
utility: '*secundum relationem ad usum*'. Thomas, like his predecessor Albertus,
specifies the foundation of value with a clear distinction between production cost and *aestimatio*. This betokened a significant dualism of historical
impact. Value, monetarily expressed as price, is based on a conjunction
of the costs of production (expenses and labour) with the intensity of the
need *(indigentia)*.

The determination of need derives from the utility of the exchanged
thing *(res, opus)* to the buyers and sellers. At the moment of exchange
the subjective '*aestimatio*' influences the vectors of cost prices. In contrast
with nominalist and neoclassical conceptions of utility which are based on
methodological individualism, Thomas conceives of a social hierarchization

of need and utility according to the holistic constraint of *bonum commune*. In ST 2a, 2ae he admits that the just price cannot always be arrived at with precision: '*justum pretium rerum quandoque non est punctualiter determinatum*'. Therefore, in cases of *laesio enormis* the law of men has to intervene in order to bring about restitution; and if this is ineffective, market regulation must be established. Situations permitting disorderly exchange would destroy social intercourse with the result that the useful stream of exchange could dry up. Moreover, the measures of the commercial commodities are bound to be different in different places as these commodities are in such different supply everywhere. With this regional variety of situations it is the business of the state authorities to determine what are the just measures. Finally, since money expresses the price of commodities, the determination of its measuring capacity (*mensura*) belongs to the prince: '*valor impositus*'.

In the ST 2a, 2ae, more particularly in *questio* 77, article 4 on the problem 'is one entitled to make profits by selling for more than the purchase price', Thomas again departs from Aristotle's negative evaluation of commercial profits. By the thirteenth century, the social utility of the growing commercial middle class had already been recognized by the medieval legists and even by the leading canonists, the one condition being that profit-making stay within reasonable bounds. Within the clerical world of both canonist and moral theologians, however, the ban on the commerce of money for money with a profit (the *campsoria*) was maintained. And in his doctrine on usury, Thomas produced nothing new. Thomas of course was familiar with Aristotle's distinction between the natural monetized exchange of householders, linked to the unavoidable diversity of their consumption needs (*pecuniativa economica; ad domus sustentationem; unde laudatur*), and the exchange for pure profit '*ex cupiditate campsoria; et ideo iuste vituperatur*'. At the height of his intellectual powers, Thomas was ready to formulate his own view. In a burst of energy he engaged in the redaction of ST 2a, 2ae, written at about the same time, which resulted in a subtle discourse.

In a masterly show of interpretative skill and casuistry, he deliberates in a limpid style on the material context and the moral demarcation wherein a moderate profit is licit:

1   The first arguments, in recognition of the natural diversity of consumption needs, are still Aristotelian. Natural trade between householders and craftsmen is licit: *ad domus suae sustentationem*' and '*ad subveniendum indigentibus*'.

2   The following argument is already more aligned with Thomas' concept of the social good: '*propter publicam utilitatem*'.

3   Last but not least: '*lucrum licitum est, non quasi finem, sed quasi stipendium laboris*'. Thus, he conceives of profit as a compensation for the trader's efforts to improve the commodity in some fashion. As such

the justifiable profit is seen as a premium of the exchanger's work: '*premium sui laboris*'.

At the time when the two Dominicans lectured, the appreciation of manual labour often ascribed to both was no longer a novelty. The monastic tradition of the Cistercians, the glosses of the legists, some decretals of the canonists, and last but not least the heretical movements, had previously anchored the value of man's labour in the collective mind. It should be noted, however, that the two scholars were the first to introduce the concept of labour into the speculative tradition of moral philosophy. Under their influence, moral speculation on commercial exchange and the justification of a reasonable profit took a new turn. From a more general point of view, the schoolmen re-worked the Aristotelian concept of 'development'. Their terminology on the flowering from *dunamis*, in Latin *potentia*, towards *energeia*, in Latin *actus*, also initiated a shift in meaning. In the scholastic view, the transition towards actuality was conceived to be a more voluntary process, on the basis of which the productive activity of the economic agents began to be seen as directed towards less limited ends. In this area, the Franciscan scholars would take a new track a few decades later.

Limitation of space does not permit a detailed treatment of all the new waves that emerged in the course of the scholastic high tide of the thirteenth century. As time wheeled on, the commentators gradually re-interpreted Aristotle's economic theorems into novel forms; more specifically, by taking into account the differential value of skilled labour in the exchange equalization and by the new perception of money as 'capital'. All this led to an embryonic form of marginal analysis and to the emergence of new views on money and on interest as a legitimate surplus value on productive capital. The Franciscan scholar Petrus Olivi was one of the first scholastics to break with the principle of money's intrinsic sterility. In some commercial transactions the nature of money changes and turns into capital. With his dynamic vision on the productivity of money as capital and his emphasis on the economic value of 'time', Olivi departed from Aristotle's canon and created an opening leading towards modernity. The sixteenth-century schoolmen of Salamanca would pick up and develop this line of thought.

The re-working in the late middle ages

John Buridan was a moderate follower of Ockham's nominalism and became an enthusiast of empirical verification tests in his scientific research. He was, moreover, a noted philosopher of the arts faculty in Paris where he was elected rector of the university. The scriptures of interest for historians of economic thought are: *Questiones Johannis Buridani super decem libros Ethicorum Aristotelis ad Nicomachum* and the *Questiones Johannis Buridani super octo libros Politicorum Aristotelis*, both edited in Paris (1513). Buridan's treatment of Aristotle's *Politics* is an amalgam of traditional views, enriched by novel openings on commercial development and its monetary implications. In his more original comments on *Ethics*, he emerges as a benchmark in the development of marginalist calculus.

In *Ethics* questio 16 and 17, Buridan refers to Aristotle's passage on exchange relations but definitively goes his own way in both the definition of money and in the quantification of individual needs. Following the Greek philosopher, Buridan states that *indigentia* is the basic factor in exchange relations. In the search for equivalence between the things exchanged, however, his emphasis on the quantification of the subjective, inter-individual valuations of the exchangers betokens a theoretical departure from Aristotle's metaphysical and holistic approach. According to Buridan's methodological individualism, not the total but only the satisfaction deriving from 'the last' units of exchanged commodities plays a role in the measurement of needs. On this basis, the author's mathematical analysis of proportionality developed into a clear formulation of inter-individual valuation based on marginal calculus.

With the insertion of the metaphysical notion of the 'smallest unit' in the chapter on exchange in his commentary on *Ethics*, Ibn Rushd had already opened the door to a latent form of marginalism. But in the holistic vision of the Arab philosopher and of the great Dominicans, Albertus and Thomas, this shift in emphasis was left unexploited. Olivi's discussion on the hierarchical graduation of needs according to different scales of intensity was a first attempt towards a more explicit formulation of marginalism. This had, moreover, been exemplified in the Olivian theory on wage determination. There the differential quality of labour is introduced in a discussion on the just hierarchy of wages. Olivi's scriptures disappeared from sight for ages, while Buridan's quantitative approach immediately blossomed into a tradition. The affinity with the *Ethic* commentary of Gerald Odonis (± 1290–1349) is clear. Buridan was also at odds with Aristotle's monetary nominalism. As an advocate of commodity money, he took a different tack. In fact, Buridan was the first to introduce the metallist tradition into the philosophical constituency of the Latin West. His pioneering theoretical work inspired his contemporary Oresme to write a comprehensive treatise on money.

Oresme's translation of Aristotle's works into French was not the first in the field. Around 1305 a certain Pierre de Paris had rendered *Politics* in the vernacular. Just as Cicero had introduced the Greek philosophical legacy in Latin at a time when Rome became hegemonic, and just as Dante and Petrarca in Italy had introduced the vernacular in literature, the French humanists felt the need to render the scriptures of Antiquity in the nascent language of the mounting middle classes. The '*translatio studii*' from Latin, which had functioned as the transnational language of clerics and scholars for ages, into the language of the common people went hand in hand with the ambition of nation-building instituted by the French kings. According to Oresme, '(t)*ranslater telz livres en françois*' facilitated not only the transfer of ideas, but it also had seminal effects on the native language. On the basis of recent philological research it appears that Oresme's translation enriched the nascent intellectual idiom with a thousand new words. Like Moerbeke in his time, on several occasions Oresme was unable to find the correct word and proceeded to literal transliteration. Most of the time, however, his imaginative mind was alert enough to spawn new words and expressions. The reading of Oresme's charming medieval French is an intellectual spell in itself.

Oresme, unfamiliar with Greek, relied on Moerbeke's *translatio* of Aristotle's *Politics* with the well-known moral ban on *campsoria*. This term was rendered in the French text as *changeresse*. Moerbeke's version of the acquisitive spirit '*omnis eorum vita circa acquisitionem pecuniarum est*' becomes '*adonques touz telz mettent leur cure vers acquisition de pecunes*'. Accordingly, the counterfeiting of money by princes is compared to the usurious practice of money-changers. Indeed, the *changeresse* profited greatly from monetary instability on account of the higher transaction costs of financial and commercial dealings. It should be noted that the royal adviser's '*Sitz im Leben*' was very different from that of the Greek philosopher's. Moreover, Oresme's and Buridan's commentaries on Aristotle derived from a philosophical mindset different from that of the thirteenth century. In fourteenth-century France, the corporate interests of the bourgeoisie had evolved into a forceful social class to be seriously reckoned with in the political field. As a keen observer of the brooding conflict between the royal privilege of seigniorage and the sectional interests of the people, Oresme gives the *marchanderie* a solid footing in his texts. By the end of the fourteenth century, the Latin commentaries on Aristotle's theorems had passed their peak. And in the Muslim world Ibn Khaldun criticized him as an armchair philosopher who, in his conceptual framework, had idealized man and the *polis*.

The re-interpretation by the rhetoric tradition of the Italian humanists

The humanists of the Italian *Quattrocento*, still more than the scholastics, read the Athenian philosopher from a new historical perspective. For the medieval schoolmen, Aristotle was a canonized philosopher; for the humanists, he was a scholar who had to compete with the Stoics and the Epicureans of antiquity. More specifically, the Stagirite had to share intellectual influence with the Roman rhetor Cicero. In their political and philosophical thematizations, the humanists Leonardo Bruni, Matteo Palmeri, Leon Battista Alberti, Giannozzo Manetti and Lorenzo Valla questioned the moral restraint of the Aristotelian corpus as presented by the Latin scholastics.

In a reaction against the scholastic claim that the *vita contemplativa* is the highest good, the humanists emphasized that Aristotle was more concerned with human perfectibility and with civil virtue than with ascetics. In their more 'this-worldly' hermeneutics, they emphasized Aristotle's stance that human actions oriented towards a good living in this world are intrinsically valuable. Moreover, by means of a *vita activa* human action should be aimed at the flowering of natural capacities. The humanists rediscovered Aristotle's ideal of a flourishing life but gave it a Ciceronian twist. They argued that the material and bodily needs of man should be given more weight. The commentaries of the humanists were not only written in pure, classical Latin, but they also resulted in a hermeneutic adaptation of the original text to their own historical and cultural milieu. With several humanists, this reformulation resulted in a softening of some of the utterly idealistic accents taken over by Aristotle from his master Plato.

According to E. Garin, the cornerstone of the humanist cultural programme consisted in a combination of Aristotelian ethics with the Stoic tradition, enriched by Cicero's rhetoric and by the Epicurean spirit of their own historical perspective. Leonardo Bruni, who translated and commented upon Aristotle's practical philosophy, directed all his barbs against the so-called primitive Latin texts produced by the schoolmen and their medieval mentality. In his view the schoolmen, in their praise of the *vita contemplativa,* had over-emphasized the ascetic tone of the Stagirite's ethics. Bruni stood for the *vita activa* and introduced a more worldly Aristotle. He underlined Aristotle's dictum that a certain degree of wealth was a prerequisite for a virtuous life. Bruni also recognized the historical and cultural distance between the Stagirite's world view and the mindset of the *Quattrocento*. But in his final statement on *chrèmatistikè* Bruni concurred with the Stagerite that when man amasses more material goods *(divitiae)* than is necessary to meet the needs of one's family, the craving for wealth may become limitless. And in the purest Aristotelian tradition he warned: *nullus est terminus divitiarium* (without moral restraint) there is no limit to the desire for material goods.

The generation of humanists after Bruni went far beyond this balanced view on the acquisition and the accumulation of wealth. Palmieri proclaimed that capable men *(valenti huomini)* should have no moral qualms about the accumulation of worldly goods as long as they were the result of their own productive and creative labour. With the younger generation of humanists then, economic activity was morally and socially upgraded. It became a value in its own right. Alberti's dialogue *Della Famiglia* was one of the most kindly disposed towards the new economic spirit. In the historical transition experienced by Italian humanism, Alberti was a prestigious and leading rhetorician who advocated the efficient use of one's time in economic activities. He praised these as creative endeavours. With Xenophon's *Oikonomikos* as a model, Alberti's dialogue offers a penetrating analysis of the value conflict between the traditional mould and the modern business spirit. Alberti's message is well-balanced: enjoy the things of this world without being tied to them. In a more polemical style, Lorenzo Valla rejected the Aristotelian canon and opted for the Epicurean line of thought. With his hedonistic stance which he shared with Bracciolini Poggio, he proclaimed that *desiderare più del necessario é un fatto naturale*. The idea that it is natural to desire more than is needed, marked an open break with the Aristotelian concept of limited ends. Valla defiantly proclaimed that human virtue should not put too hard a brake on the human aspirations for worldly pleasure. In his view, the supreme achievements of man are not restricted to the cultural and intellectual domain only; they are also embodied in the entrepreneurial libido of the *homo faber*, manifesting himself in economic activities. This humanist advocate of pleasure, with the motto that *voluptas* represents the highest good, was an important turn of the tide.

The phasing out of Aristotle's economic canon

In the second quarter of the sixteenth century, the University of Salamanca became the centre of an important scholastic revival that spread to Seville, Valladolid, Coïmbra and Evora. In their comments on key concepts such as nature and natural change (development) in relation to the state, natural law and the economy, they referred to the teleological categories of Aristotle's *Physics* and *Metaphysics* rather than to the theses developed in *Politics* and *Nicomachean Ethics,* V. 5. This change of emphasis was but one of many significant departures from medieval Thomism. Moreover, their frequent reference to the historical contingency of basic concepts such as *utilitas, commoditas* and *necessitas et ratio rerun* was the mark of a more secularized view on social, political and economic processes. As a consequence of their philosophical stance, they became more conscious of the relative functional autonomy or of the intrinsic laws of the commercial and financial markets. Although in the first instance they were concerned with moral problems and with canonical norms, the intrusion of the market in the functioning of society was considered to be a natural phenomenon.

With the rise of Holland and England towards economic hegemony, a more radical break with Aristotle's economic canon was in the offing. A number of influential moral philosophers of the eighteenth and nineteenth century initiated a radical break with Aristotle's economic canon. They questioned his low-grading of the *banausic* activities and his political philosophy which held that the chrematistic spirit was unnatural and immoral. On the contrary, they valuated self-interest and the profit motive as positive incentives in the emergent commercial society. In the wake of this line of thought, the utilitarians affirmed that man is a bundle of appetites in search of satisfaction and that economic progress consisted in the most efficient way of maximizing this satisfaction.

From the twelfth century on the Latin scholastics followed by the humanists gradually de-Aristotelianize the Stagirite's economic canon. And
modernity brings a complete break. Consequently Aristotle cannot be
profiled as an ancestor or fundamental base of modern economics. As I
see it, Aristotle should rather be seen as a radical critique of modernity's
economization of society.

Note

1   'Sed toto hoc de genere, de quaerenda, de collocanda pecunia, commodius a
quibusdam optimis viris ad Janum medium sedentibus quam ab ullis philosophis
ulla in schola disputatur'. In Rome, the Middle Janus was the market place for
exchange. Thus, in Cicero's pragmatic view, commercial people were 'worthy
gentlemen'.

References

Aubenque, P. (1980) 'Politique et Ethique chez Aristote', *Ktema*, 5.
Baeck, L. (1994) *The Mediterranean Tradition in Economic Thought*, London: Routledge.
—— (1996) 'Ibn Khaldun's Political and Economic Realism', in *Joseph Schumpeter: Historian of Economics*, London: Routledge.
Baloglou, C. and Constantinidis, A. (1993) *Die Oekonomie des Aristoteles*, Frankfurt: Peter Lang.
Baron, H. (1988) *In Search of Florentine Humanism: Essays on the Transition from Medieval to Modern Thought*, Princeton, NJ: Princeton University Press.
Berman, L. (1978) 'Ibn Rushd's Middle Commentary on the Nicomachean Ethics in Medieval Literature', in *Multiple Averroës*, Paris: J. Vrin.
Berthoud, A (1981) *Aristote et l'argent*, Paris: Maspero.
Brams, J. and Vanhamel, W. (1989) *Guillaume de Moerbeke*, Leuven: Leuven University Press.
Cheneval, F. and Imbach, R. (1993) *Thomas von Aquin: Prologe zu den Aristoteles Kommentaren*, Frankfurt: Klostermann.
De Libera, A. (1990) *Albert le Grand et la Philosophie*, Paris: J. Vrin.
Dirlmeier, F. (1969) *Aristoteles Nikomachische Ethik*, Berlin: Akademie Verlag.
Finley, M. (1977) 'Aristotle and Economic Analysis', in J. Barnes (ed.) *Articles on Aristotle*, vol. 2, London: Duckworth.
Garin, E. (1961) 'La Fortuna dell'etica Aristotelica nell Quattrocento', in *La Cultura Filosofica dell Rinascimento Italiano*, Florence: Laterza.
Gillard, L. (1990) 'Nicole Oresme: Economiste', *Revue Historique*, vol. 279, pp. 3–39.
Houmanidis, L.T. (1982) 'Aristotle's Economic Ideas', *Spoudai*, vol. 32.
Jaeger, W. (1968) *Aristotle: Fundamentals of the History of his Development*, Oxford: Clarendon Press.
Karayiannis, A. (1988) 'Democritus on Ethics and Economics', in *Revista Internazionale di Scienze Economiche e Commerciale*, no. 4–5.
Koslowski, P. (1979) 'Haus und Geld: zur Aristotelischen Unterscheidung von Politik, Okonomik und Chrematistik', *Philosophisches Jahrbuch*, vol. 86.
Langholm, O. (1992) *Economics in the Medieval Schools*, Leyden: E.J. Brill.
Lapidus, A. (1993) 'Metal Money and the Prince: John Buridan and Nicolas Oresme

after Thomas Aquinas', paper presented at the 20th meeting of the History of Economic Society, Philadelphia, pp. 1–29.

Lowry, T. (1987) *The Archeology of Economic Ideas: the Classical Greek Tradition*, Durham: Duke University Press.

Manselli, R. (1983) 'Il Pensiero Economico del Medioevo', in L. Firpo (ed.) *Storia delle Idee Politiche, Economiche e Sociali*, vol. 2, Torino: Unione Tipografico.

Marchaise, T. (1992) *Les Grecs et Leurs Modernes: les Stratégies Contemporaines d'appropriation de l'Antiquité*, Paris: Seuil.

Meikle, S. (1979) 'Aristotle and the Economy of the Polis', *The Journal of Hellenic Studies*, 99, pp. 57–73.

Menjot, D. (1988) 'La Politique Monétaire de Nicolas Oresme', in P. Souffrin and A. Segonds (eds) *Nicolas Oresme*, Paris: Les Belles Lettres.

Miller, C. (1925) 'Studien zur Geschichte der Geldlehre', *Münchener Volkswirtschaftliche Studien*, no. 146, pp. 68–73.

Natali, C. (1980) 'Aristotele e l'Origine della Filosofia Practica', in C. Pacchiani (ed.) *Filosofia Practica e Scienza Politica*, Torino: Francisci Editori.

Nussbaum, M. (1994) *The Therapy of Desire: Theory and Practice in Hellenistic Ethics*, New Jersey: Princeton University Press.

Pellegrin, P. (1982) 'Monnaie et Chrématistique', in *Revue Philosophique*, no. 4.

Ruggiu, L. (1982) Aristotele e la Genesi dello Spazio Economico, in L. Ruggiu (ed.), *Genesi dello Spazio Economico*, Naples: Guida Editori.

Siegel, J. (1968) 'Leonardo Bruni and the New Aristotle', in J. Seigel (ed.) *Rhetoric and Philosophy in Renaissance Humanism*, New Jersey: Princeton University Press.

Spicciani, A. (1990) *Capitale e Interesse tra Mercatura e Poverta: Nei Teologi e Canonisti dei Seculi*, XIII–XV, Rome: Jouvance.

Urvoy, D. (1990) *Ibn Rushd (Averroes)*, London: Kegan Paul.

Verbeke, G. and Verhelst, M. (1974) *Aquinas and Problems of his Time*, Leuven: Leuven University Press.

2 The idea of usury in Patristic literature[1]

Thomas Moser

Introduction

In the history of ideas, there are only a few questions that have occupied human minds longer than the question of the justification of interest taking. While the theory of any factor price tends to touch upon the normative question of distributive justice, in the case of interest theory it was not just a question of the 'just price'. The question was if there should be a price at all. Furthermore, the answer to that question became a subject of religious beliefs with respect to both practice and doctrine. Judaism, Christianity, and Islam taught that money-lending for profit was a transgression against the command of God. During the middle ages, religious and secular laws prohibited the charging of interest and identified the practice as 'usury'.[2] In fact, the idea of usury became a 'central paradigm' of medieval society (Clavero 1986) and a canon of scholastic economics. It was not until the sixteenth century that 'usury' was redefined as high interest rates.

Although the medieval doctrine of usury has often been subject to research, Patristic literature rarely receives the attention it deserves. In the established 'history of economics canon', classical Greek is usually directly followed by medieval scholastic economic thought, thereby following the outline of Schumpeter's monumental *History of Economic Analysis*. However, it should be kept in mind that the 'Christian tradition' passed on to the middle ages as one of the foundations of Western culture was a Patristic conception. Not only did the Fathers of the Church select and transmit the authoritative texts in the form of the Christian Bible, but they also wrote commentaries and expositions which later gained an authoritative status. Since the condemnation of interest taking was part of the unanimous *consensus patrum*, it became a doctrine of medieval Christian tradition. To omit Patristic writings from the history of the usury controversy is to tell the story without paying attention to the construction of the canon of medieval economics. Furthermore, one misses a chance to study the interesting interplay of intellectual and economic history. For the longest time, the idea of usury was only a matter of the history of ideas. It did not become a matter of the economic history until the idea was enforced by political power.

The pre-Christian anti-usury traditions

While credit arrangements and the concept of interest go back to prehistoric times, the morality of interest taking became a subject of dispute almost at the same time in the ancient Hebrew, Greek, and Roman society.[3] As a result of this thematization two distinct anti-usury traditions emerged, one resting on religious–spiritual, the other on philosophical–rational grounds. Both of these traditions were later to exert a strong influence on the Christian canonization of the idea of usury.

The Hebrew legacy: the Septuagint

Since Christianity began as a movement within ancient Judaism, it goes without saying that it also adopted the Hebrew Bible. Much more astonishing is the fact that the early Church decided to maintain it as an integral part of its scriptures when the Christian movement finally separated from Judaism in the course of the second century AD. The *Septuagint* (LXX), as the Greek translation of the Jewish scriptures was called, played an important role in the Christian tradition, at first as *the* Testament and later as the *Old* Testament of the Bible. Therefore, it was a crucial fact that the Hebrew Bible displayed a clear condemnation of lending with interest and proclaimed three divine commandments prohibiting interest taking. Each of its three groups of books, according to the Jewish classification in (1) 'the Law' (*torah*), (2) 'the Prophets', and (3) 'the Writings', contained at least one statement of disapproval of the practice of interest taking. The three prohibitions in 'the Law' have the following reading:[4]

> If you lend money to any of my people with you who is poor, you shall not be to him as a creditor, and you shall not exact interest from him.
>
> (Exod. 22: 24[25])

> And if your brother becomes poor, ... Take no interest from him or increase, but fear your God; that your brother may live beside you. You shall not lend him your money at interest, nor give him your food for profit.
>
> (Lev. 25: 35–37)

> You shall not lend upon interest to your brother, interest on money, interest on victuals, interest on anything that is lent for interest. To a foreigner you may lend upon interest, but to your brother you shall not lend upon interest; that Yahweh your God may bless you ...
>
> (Deut. 23: 20[19]–21[20])

While the first two prohibitions seem to limit their application to poorer members of the Jewish community, the third prohibition includes all Jews with an explicit exception being made in the case of a foreigner. As a reason for the prohibition, the disapproval or approval of God is given, while Lev. 25: 36 adds 'that your brother may live beside you'. Among the books of 'the Prophets' we find a clear condemnation of interest taking only in the Book of Ezekiel. The just man who does what is lawful and right

> ... does not lend at interest or take any increase, withholds his hand from iniquity, executes true justice between man and man.
>
> (Ezek. 18: 8)

But a man who is a robber, a 'shedder of blood', who 'lends at interest, and takes increase; shall he then live? He shall not live . . .' (Ezek. 18: 13). And in his accusation against Jerusalem, Ezekiel has God say:

> If you men take bribes to shed blood; you take interest and increase and make gain of your neighbors by extortion; and you have forgotten me, says the God Yahweh.
>
> (Ezek. 22: 12)

In 'the Writings', Ps. 15[14] of the Book of Psalms asks: 'Yahweh, who will sojourn in thy tent?', and one of the answers declares:

> ... who does not put out his money at interest, and does not take a bribe against the innocent ...
>
> (Ps. 15[14]: 5)

And finally, in the Book of Proverbs one finds the more ambiguous statement:

> He who augments his wealth by interest and increase gathers it for him who is kind to the poor.
>
> (Prov. 28: 8)

The usury prohibitions in 'the Law' are based on a concept of solidarity: a Jew should treat his fellow Jew as a brother and do him a favor by lending to him interest-free. But the legitimacy of the concept of interest itself seems not to have been questioned, as can be seen by the permission to lend on interest to a foreigner (Deut. 23: 21[20]).[5] More important for further discussion is that the condemnation of interest taking in Ezekiel (and Ps. 15[14]) appears to rest on two certain aspects: (1) that interest taking is believed to have a bad effect on the debtor, and (2) that interest taking is believed to originate from an evil motive on the part of the creditor: profiting from the 'neighbor'.

The Graeco-Roman legacy: philosophy and politics

If we take a look at those philosophers who exerted greatest influence on Christian thought, it is crucial to observe that they all shared a negative view towards interest taking. In ancient Greece, both Plato (427–348 BC) and Aristotle (384–22 BC), who were critics of the democratic Athens that had transformed itself into a commercial center, condemned the concept of interest taking in their call for a return to the 'true ideals' of the self-sufficient city-state (*polis*).

Plato's vision of an ideal city-state is set out in *The Republic* and in a more practical form in the *Laws*. The *Laws* was Plato's last work and contains the fruits of his long experience and his most essential beliefs. Its dialogue is set in Crete, and the participants are three elderly men who concern themselves with the constitution for a new city-state to be established on a desert tract of land. One of the proposed laws for this ideal city-state is the prohibition of commercial money-lending at interest:

> No one shall deposit money with another whom he does not trust as a friend, nor shall he lend money upon interest; and the borrower should be under no obligation to repay either capital or interest.
>
> (*Laws* 5, 742c)[6]

In Plato's ideal state, there is no place for 'much of the vulgar sort of trade which is carried on by lending money' (*Laws* 5, 743d). Not even selling on credit was to be allowed, since

> . . . they shall exchange money for goods, and goods for money, neither party giving credit to the other; and he who gives credit must be satisfied, whether he obtain his money or not, for in such exchanges he will not be protected by law.
>
> (*Laws* 8, 849e)[7]

This last law, however, seems to contradict Plato's notion that interest may be allowed as a penalty for a delay in payment:[8]

> And let him who, having already received the work in exchange, does not pay the price in the time agreed, pay double the price; and if a year has elapsed, although interest is not to be taken on loans, yet for every *drachma* which he owes to the contractor let him pay a monthly interest of an *obol*.
>
> (*Laws* 11, 921c–d)

Plato's interest prohibition seems to be based on his belief that the practice of money-lending destroys the 'harmony' between the citizens of the state, which itself is equal to the prevalence of justice in the state. It gets disturbed – as Plato diagnosed in Book 8 of *The Republic* – by the growing inequality of wealth which is in turn a consequence of commercial enterprise. Those men who owe money and those who have lost their property are 'eager for revolution', while

> ... the men of business, stooping as they walk, and pretending not even to see those whom they have already ruined, insert their sting – that is, their money – into someone else who is not on his guard against them, and recover the parent sum many times over multiplied into a family of children: and so they make drone and pauper to abound in the State.
>
> (*Republic* 8, 555e–556a)

Plato's condemnation of interest taking is therefore based on the consideration of its supposed effects. But unlike Ezekiel, he is not concerned with an effect upon the individual debtor, but with an effect upon the society as a whole: the disturbance of the 'Platonic stationarity' (Schumpeter 1954, 56).

Aristotle's reasons are somehow different. Foremost, like Ezekiel he also condemns interest taking because of the money-lender's motive, which is according to Aristotle the making of money for its own sake. This again originates in the love of gain which is supposed to be unjust, for 'if a man makes gain, this is attributed to injustice but to no other evil habit' (*Nicomachean Ethics* 5, 1130a 31). To Aristotle, to make gain is to get more than one is due at someone else's expense:

> ... some exceed with respect to taking by taking anything and from any source, like those engaged in degraded occupations, e.g., pimps and the like and money-lenders who lend money for a short time and at high rates. For all these take from wrong sources and more than they should. What is common to these appears to be disgraceful gain, for all of them put up with a bad name for the sake of gain ...
>
> (*Nicomachean Ethics* 4, 1121b 32–1122a 3)

Subsequently, unlike the Old Testament and Plato, he condemns the concept of interest taking as unjust by its very own nature. In the *Politics* Aristotle – and later Karl Marx (1987 [1859], 121ff) and 1993 [1867], 161ff) – compared four different kinds of exchange: (1) goods for goods, (2) money for goods, (3) goods for money, and (4) money for (more) money (*Politics* 1, 1256b 40ff). The last two kinds, the exchange that seeks money-making as an end to itself (*chrêmatistikê*), he regarded as 'justly censured; for it is unnatural', whereby

> The most hated sort, and with the greatest reason, is usury, which makes a gain out of money itself, and not from the natural object of it. For money was intended to be used in exchange, but not to increase

at interest. And this term interest [*tokos*], which means the birth of money from money, is applied to the breeding of money because the offspring resembles the parent. Therefore of any modes of getting wealth this is the most unnatural.

(Politics 1, 1258b 1–8)

This argument against interest taking has become known as the 'Aristotelian concept of the sterility of money' (Langholm 1984): money should not 'breed' money. Apart from its defect of seeking gain, Aristotle regarded the exchange of money for (more) money as a perversion of the purpose for which money was invented (Schefold 1989, 40), namely to serve as a means of exchange in trading goods for goods. Therefore, independent of its motives, the practice of interest taking was to be condemned as being against the natural order – a powerful argument for an intellectual movement that was to become heavily influenced by the Stoic's ethical ideal of a 'life in agreement with nature'.[9] It should be noticed that the attitude of Plato and Aristotle towards interest taking were not commonly held in ancient Greece. This cannot only be seen by some of the private orations transmitted to us through the works of Demosthenes (383–22 BC) – especially *Against Phormio* 52–3 – but also by the fact that lending money for interest was not legally forbidden in ancient Greece.

Among the most influential Roman philosophers we can find a similar disapproval of the practice of interest taking. Cicero (106–65 BC) whose *De Officiis* was to have an immense influence on later Christian writers states that 'those means of livelihood are rejected as undesirable which incur people's ill-will, as those of tax-gatherers and usurers' (*De Officiis* 1, 42, 150). Furthermore, Cicero quotes Cato the Elder (234–149 BC) who, on being asked for his opinion on professional money-lending, replied: 'How about murder?' (*De Officiis* 2, 25, 89). Statements critical of lending on interest are also found among the writings of Seneca (4 BC–AD 65), especially *De beneficiis* 7, 10. But since the Roman philosophers did not contribute new arguments to the dispute, it is of more interest that we can find some negative attitudes towards interest taking in the legal practice and political history of the Roman Republic. This fact is often neglected by historians of economic thought since it does not complement the 'economic liberalism' usually (laudatively) attributed to Roman Law. But the Roman historian Tacitus (AD 55–117) tells us that '[t]he curse of usury was indeed of old standing in Rome and a most frequent cause of sedition and discord, and it was therefore repressed even in the early days' (Tacitus *Annals* 6, 6, 16). He then continues that the fifth century BC *Law of the Twelve Tables* set a maximum legal rate of *fenus unciarium* which most scholars believe to mean 1/12 part of the capital (see De Martino 1991 [1985], 169f).[10] In 347 BC this rate was reduced to *fenus semiunciarium* (Tacitus *Annals* 6, 6, 16; Livy *Ab urbe* 7, 27, 3) before in 342 BC a *Lex Genucia* prohibited the taking of interest on loans at all (Tacitus *Annals* 6,

16, 2; Livy *Ab urbe* 7, 42, 1). This seems to have been the very first legal prohibition of interest that was more than just an utopian idea.[11] We do not know how long this prohibition lasted, but the *Lex Sempronia* of 193 BC attests again to the existence of a maximum legal rate. In 88 BC a *Lex Unciaria* introduced the legal rate of *centesima usura* (12 per cent per annum).

Philo of Alexandria

The role that the Egyptian city of Alexandria played in the history of the Christian tradition can not be overestimated. Alexandria was one of the chief intellectual centers of the Hellenistic world since the *mouseion* with its huge library, founded by Ptolemy I in 280 BC and greatly expanded by Ptolemy II, attracted leading scholars of the time. Demetrius Phaleron (*c.* 354–283 BC), who was a member of Aristotle's *Lyceum* before he joined the court of Ptolemy I, seems to have exercised great influence on the organization of the *mouseion* and was an important, though not the only link between Aristotelian learning and the literary academy of Alexandria (see Lindberg 1992, 74). In this atmosphere of intellectual learning two important lines of thought were codified. In the third century BC a school of philology was developed that established the goal to protect or recover on a scientific level the purity of the Classical Greek texts. The works were then published in what were regarded as standard editions, together with separate treatises on the texts. The end product of this work was the 'Alexandrian canon of Classical Greek literature' (Assmann 1992, 277ff). Almost simultaneously, in the flourishing Jewish colony in Alexandria the Hebrew scriptures were translated into Greek. This translation, completed in the second century BC and later called the *Septuagint* (LXX), was to become the Bible of early Christianity. The first attempts to synthesize these two strains of traditions were undertaken not long thereafter, most remarkably and more importantly by the Jewish philosopher Philo of Alexandria (*c.* 15 BC–*c.* AD 40). His method of using Greek philosophy to interpret the Hebrew Bible laid the foundations for Christian theology. Early Christian thought took its main principles from Philo: (1) the allegorical method of interpreting scripture; and (2) the subordination of philosophy to scripture.[12] Concerning the idea of usury, Philo is the most important link in the chain that leads from Aristotle to Patristic literature.

Philo's treatise on the virtues (*De virtutibus*) was among the most read works by the Fathers. In his attempt to show that 'the Law' of the Hebrew Bible enjoins all the virtues of Greek philosophy, he mentioned the prohibition of interest as an example of humanity:

> He [Moses] forbids anyone to lend money on interest to a brother, meaning by the name not merely a child of the same parents, but

anyone of the same citizenship or nation. For he does not think it just to amass money bred from money as their yearlings are from cattle.

(*De virtutibus* 82)

Towards a person in need the best course would be to give free gifts, the second best to lend without demanding interest, for

> ... in this way the poor would not become more helpless, by being forced to pay more than they received, and the contributors would not be wronged though they recovered only what they spent.

(*De virtutibus* 84)

In the first statement, that it is unjust to amass money bred from money, we have the first attempt to reconcile the Aristotelian concept of the 'sterility of money' with the biblical prohibition of interest. In the second quotation, there are three elements worth mentioning. First of all, as in Ezekiel, interest taking is to be condemned, because it is supposed to lead to (a further) impoverishment of the borrower. Secondly, according to Philo, the reason for this impoverishment is the fact that the lender has to pay back more than he originally received. Hence, Philo declares interest as being unjust by its very own definition: the amount in excess of the capital. Aristotle had stated the principle that in any exchange justice demanded an equivalence in the things exchanged (*Nicomachean Ethics* 5, 1131b 25ff). Philo seems to apply this principle to intertemporal exchange, but in a strict sense: demanding interest violates equality since money seems to be exchanged for more money. Finally, it should be noted that Philo explains the fact, that the borrower is willing to pay back more than he received in the same manner as later Marxist economics will: the borrower is forced to do so. Philo also discussed the biblical prohibition of interest in his *De specialibus legibus*:

> Now lending money on interest is a blameworthy action, for a person, who borrows is not living on a superabundance of means, but is obviously in need, and he is compelled to pay the interest as well as the capital, he must necessarily be in the utmost straits. And while he thinks he is being benefited by the loan, he is actually like senseless animals suffering further damage from the bait which is set before him.

(*De specialibus legibus* 74)

And towards the money-lender he states:

> ... you who have lain in wait for the misfortunes of others, and regarded their ill-luck as your own good luck. Such a person may learn not to make a trade of other people's misfortunes and enrich himself in improper ways.

(*De specialibus legibus* 76–78)

Philo's argument, that somebody who borrows is necessarily somebody in need is very unfortunate but often stated in the context of interest prohibition, for a needy person is not the typical borrower. A needy person will not find a lender since that person's problem is not really the payment of the interest but the repayment of the loan itself. A loan is an (intertemporal) exchange and has to be distinguished from a donation. In the context of loan, 'to be in need' makes sense only in the event of temporary distress. But all in all, the argument – again – leads to the condemnation of interest taking for its effect on the borrower. A special feature of consequential ethics (i.e. an ethics which judges the 'goodness' of an act by its consequences) is that its statements at least in principle might be 'falsified' by empirical observations. Therefore, it is not surprising that the 'effect-argument' seems to have been the first argument that had to be defended against objections. Already Philo puts forward an auxiliary assumption contra the observation that the borrower expects to profit from the loan, since a loan contract based on a mutual agreement necessarily moves both parties – the lender and the borrower – to more preferred positions. Philo immunizes this objection by saying that the borrower misjudges his position and is unaware of the true effects of borrowing. Finally, Philo's comment directed towards the creditor seems to contain the 'motive-argument' against interest taking.

On the whole, it can be said that Philo mapped out the route for the Christian idea of usury. The main arguments for a rational defense of the biblical prohibition of interest are set out: money-lending for profit is to be condemned for its effects, its motive, and indeed for its very own nature. The last argument, which will be called the 'nature-argument', can again be subdivided into the Aristotelian sterility version (money should not breed money) and the equality version (interest makes the exchange unequal).

Usury and the early Church

If one considers the conformity between the Classical Graeco-Roman philosophy and the Old Testament in attitude towards lending at interest, it is somewhat surprising that interest taking was not an issue at all in the Christian writings of the first century AD. The New Testament, which contains the oldest surviving Christian documents almost contemporary with Philo of Alexandria, has nothing to say about usury. Lending at interest is mentioned only once, namely in the Parable of Talents (Matt. 25: 14–30; Luke 19: 11–27). If this passage contains a judgment about interest taking at all, it seems to be an approval, since the 'Lord' punishes his servant for not having brought the money to the bankers to gain some interest. But it is not only the authors of the New Testament that do not seem to have any problems with interest taking, the same is true for the earliest Christian writers in general, the Apostolic Fathers and the early Apologists. This fact that most historians of economic thought disregard calls for an explanation.

A possible answer could be the often stated opinion that the Christians of the first century were not interested in worldly matters. Unfortunately, the New Testament contains several judgments about 'worldly' matters, for instance the well-known phrase that 'the love of money is the root of all evil' (1 Tim. 6: 10) or Paul's prevailing theory concerning civil authority sanctioned by the grace and will of God (Rom. 13: 1–2), of which he makes even usage to justify the payment of taxes (Rom. 13: 5–7). It seems to me that the main reason for the astonishing silence about the biblical prohibition of interest can be explained by the fact that the relevance of the laws of the *torah* to the first Christians was far from certain.[13] What the most influential group of Christians and in particular Paul (Gal. 5: 3f; Gal. 4: 25) denied, was the significance of the observance of 'the Law' as a means of salvation. But at the same time, the Christians still regarded 'the Law' as a divine manifestation. Marcion (AD *c.* 160) and his efforts to reform the Christian Church by rejecting the *Septuagint* as having no validity for Christians forced the early Church of the second century to clarify its position toward the Hebrew Bible and to define what it accepted as the true canon of its teaching.[14] The Christian Church decided to defend the Hebrew God as the Christian God and to keep the Hebrew Bible as part of the Christian canon. Since Yahweh's position on the subject of interest taking was quite clear, it seems to be no accident that Christian literature took up the usury question for the first time in writings directed against Marcion's antinomism. Although this happened almost simultaneously in Greek and Latin literature, differences in the approach can be found. While Clement of Alexandria defended 'the Law' by showing its conformity with Greek philosophy, Tertullian attempted to demonstrate the harmony and continuity between 'the Law' and the Gospel.

The reinstatement of 'the Law'

As Alexandria was a major center of Greek learning, it is not surprising that there the first real scholarship within Christianity emerged. Clement of Alexandria (*c.*150–*c.*215), who became head of the Christian school in AD 190, was also the first Christian writer to make explicit mention of Philo of Alexandria. The issue of usury made its first appearance in Christian literature in Clement's *Paidagogos* (*c.* AD 197), an instruction for new converts on Christian conduct in daily matters. At that time, Alexandria was also the most important commercial center of the ancient world. Already Sommerlad (1903, 83) has pointed out that the beginnings of the Christian teaching against interest taking has to be placed against the background of a flourishing economy. Contrary to the commonly held

view, and in the same way as in ancient Israel and Greece, the Christian
anti-usury tradition seems to have originated more likely as a reaction
against economic progress than as an expression of economic depression.

Concerning the 'just man', Clement quotes Ezekiel: 'His money he will
not give on usury, and will not take interest'. 'These words', he then
concluded, 'contain a description of the conduct of Christians' (*Paidagogos*
I, 10, 95, 2), a clear statement that he regarded the interest prohibition
of the *torah* as binding on Christians.[15] The subject is taken up again some
years later in the second book of his major work *Stromateis*. Here Clement
makes on several occasions copious use of Philo's *De virtutibus* (see Runia
1993, 137). Arguing implicitly against Marcion, he adopts Philo's attempt
to show that the prescriptions of the Mosaic Law not only incorporate all
the virtues, but that they were also the 'source' of Greek moral teaching.
Concerning interest taking he states:

> Respecting imparting and communicating, though much might be
> said, let it suffice to remark that the law prohibits a brother from
> taking usury: designating as a brother not only him who is born of
> the same parents, but also one of the same race and sentiments, and
> a participator in the same logos; deeming it right not to take usury
> for money, but with open hands and heart to bestow on those who
> need. For God, the author and the dispenser of such grace, takes as
> suitable usury the most precious things to be found among men –
> mildness, gentleness, magnanimity, reputation, renown. Do you not
> regard this command as marked by philanthropy?
>
> (*Stromateis* II, 18, 84, 4f)

Although his arguments follow very closely Philo's words (*De virtutibus*
82f), Clement makes no use of the Aristotelian concept of the 'sterility of
money'.

Tertullian (*c.* 160–220) of Carthage discussed the problem of interest
taking in a book explicitly directed against Marcion (*Adversus Marcionem*).
The Christian Gospel, he argued, does not abolish 'the Law', but surpasses
it. The purpose of the law prohibiting the charging of interest was only
a preparation for the higher demands of the Gospel, i.e. not even to seek
the principal:

> Next, on the matter of lending at interest, when he puts this question,
> 'And if ye lend to them of whom ye hope to receive, what thank have
> ye?' run over what follows in Ezekiel on the just man above-mentioned:
> 'He hath not, it says, put out his money at interest, and will not accept
> any increase' – meaning the excess amount due to interest, which is
> usury. It was first necessary for him to suppress the return of interest
> on capital: by this means he would the more easily reconcile a man
> to the loss possibly even of the capital, when he had first been taught

to remit the interest on it. This is what I mean when I speak of the
function of the law in preparing for the gospel.

(*Adversus Marcionem* 4, 17, 1–2.)

Tertullian was the first to establish a connection between the interest prohi-
bition and a specific passage in the New Testament, namely Luke 6: 34.
But it should be noticed that he quite rightly did not claim that the New
Testament contained an interest prohibition.

In the middle of the third century AD the final stage of the reinstate-
ment of the usury law was reached with Cyprian (*c.* 200–58), bishop of
Carthage. His influential *Testimoniorum* (*Ad Quirinum*), a collection of biblical
texts arranged under subjects, was meant to serve as a compendium of
the moral and disciplinary duties of Christians. This work became very
popular as a reference book, cited under the subject *non faenerandum*, Ps.
15[14]: 5, Ezek. 18: 8 and Deut. 23: 20[19] as proof that interest taking
was prohibited (Test. 3, 48). Although Cyprian was the first to make direct
reference to 'the Law' (Deut. 23: 20[19]), it was his quotation of Ps. 15[14]
that was to become one of the main scriptural arguments against interest
taking.

After the Christian writers had clarified that the Old Testament interest
prohibition was also valid for Christians, ecclesiastical legislation was soon
to follow. In AD 306 the provincial Council of Elvira in Spain stated for
the first time a canonical prohibition of interest taking, and in a degree
of clarity and severity which was to remain unsurpassed during the Patristic
period, Canon 20 prohibited the practice of usury to all clerics and laymen
under penalty of excommunication. In AD 314 the first Council of
Arles representing all of the Western Church, forbade in canon 13 usury
only to clerics, but still under the penalty of excommunication. Finally, in
AD 325 the first general Council of Nicaea, valid for the entire Christian
Church, prohibited in its canon 17 the taking of interest, but only to clerics
and only under the penalty of removal from office. As Siems (1992, 508)
has mentioned, at the same time one can observe how the legal term for
interest, *usura*, slowly began to take over the meaning of 'shameful gain'
(*turpe lucrum*) in general.[16] Therefore, interest on money appeared just as
the main example of such an unjustified gain. The mildness of the Council
of Nicaea towards interest taking seems to lie in the fact that the Roman
Emperor Constantine (274–337) presided over the Council (as already over
the Council of Arles AD 314). Constantine, a month before the opening
of the Council, had declared a law that allowed as legal maximums interest
of 12 per cent per annum (*centesima*) on money and 50 per cent per annum
(*hemiolia*) on loans in kind (Codex Theodosianus 2, 33, 1). Nevertheless,
canon 17 of Nicaea, that founded its prohibition on the citing of Ps. 15[14]:
5, established parameters for all the following canonical usury prohibitions
of the Patristic period.

The law and its arguments

While the Christian writers of the third century saw their task basically as determining the validity of the Old Testament anti-usury law, the Fathers of the fourth century felt obligated to advance the prohibition not only on biblical but also on 'rational' grounds. The first Christian writer to do so was Lactantius (*c.* 250–325), an African teacher of rhetorics. Between AD 290–300 he was teaching at the court of Diocletian where he probably also taught the later Emperor Constantine. His writings make many references to Classical literature, while they are very meagre in their citation of the Bible, presumably limited to the use of Cyprian's *Testimonorium.* In his principal work, the *Institutiones Divinae* – a defense of Christian doctrine as a harmonious and logical system written between 304 and 311 – Lactantius referred to the prohibition of interest taking under a broader attempt to expose the Christian idea of justice. Referring to the duty of the rich to practice the virtue of liberality he states:

> ... whatever is given to those who are not in need, for the sake of popularity, is thrown away; or it is repaid with interest, and thus it will not be the conferring of a benefit. And although it is pleasing to those to whom it is given, still it is not just, because if it is not done, no evil follows. Therefore the only sure and true office of liberality is to support the needy and unserviceable.
>
> (*Institutiones Divinae* 6, 11, 26ff)

Arguing that lending at interest is not just, because 'without it no evil would follow', he seems to state an 'effect argument'. The sentence following the above quotation, that 'this is that perfect justice which protects human society', suggests that he had – like Plato – some social consequences in mind. Lactantius also seems to deal with an empirical objection against the effect argument. But unlike Philo, he does not question the rationality of the borrower, but the relevance of the borrower's utility. The subject of interest is taken up again a few chapters later, where Lactantius talks about the conduct of the 'just man' (obviously referring to Ezek. 18: 8):

> If he shall have lent any money, he will not receive interest, that the benefit may be unimpaired ... and that he may entirely abstain from the property of another. For in this kind of duty he ought to be content with that which is his own; since it is his duty in other respects not to be sparing of his property, in order that he may do good; but to receive more than he has given is unjust. And he who does this lies in wait in some manner, that he may gain booty from the necessity of another.
>
> (*Institutiones Divinae* 6, 18, 7–9)

Here we find the two additional arguments. Firstly, the nature argument in its equality version: usury is unjust, because it is to receive more than what is given. Secondly, the motive argument: usury is unjust, because the creditor tries to profit from the necessity of the borrower. The motive argument is also stressed in the *Epitome*, an extract of the *Institutiones Divinae* that Lactantius wrote some years later (see Epitome 59[64], 2[11]–4[13]).

After Lactantius, it takes almost half a century, until the task of giving 'rational' reasons for the biblical prohibition of interest is taken up again.[17] In a commentary on Ps. 15[14]: 5, Hilary of Poitiers (*c.* 315–67) made use of the motive and effect arguments. But more interesting is his subsequent argument, that 'idle money' should not bear a return:

> If you are a Christian, why do you scheme to have your idle money [*otiosam pecuniam*] bear a return and make the need of your brother, for whom Christ died, the source of your enrichment?
>
> (Tractatus in Ps. 14, 15)

Although this argument seems to hint at the question of the opportunity costs of money-lending, this line of reasoning was not developed until the scholastic period.

In the east, at the same time, the three Cappadocian Fathers entered into the usury debate: Basil the Great (*c.* 330–79), his friend Gregory of Nazianzus (*c.* 329–90), and Basil's younger brother Gregory of Nyssa (*c.* 335–94). The most interesting fact is that through the Alexandrian tradition they introduced the Aristotelian strain of argument into the Patristic writings on usury. Descending from a wealthy aristocratic family, both Basil and Gregory of Nazianzus received a thorough education in Classical literature, rhetoric and philosophy at different locations and became friends while they were studying in Athens. Gregory of Nyssa on the other hand seems to have obtained most of his education from his older brother Basil. Interestingly, the Cappadocian Fathers not only referred to the subject of interest taking, but indeed devoted entire writings to the matter. However, the usury treatments of both Gregory of Nazianzus and Gregory of Nyssa are strongly dependent on Basil's second Homily on Ps. 15[14]. In their writings, the motive argument and the effect argument received a comprehensive treatment, but more important is their approach to the nature argument. On the one hand, they all take up the Aristotelian line of thought by explicitly playing with the word *tokos*. Referring to the fertility of hares,[18] Basil states that money, although fruitless by its nature, breeds more offspring than any other living thing. But interest, he states, is an 'unnatural animal', since everything natural stops growing once it reaches its natural size, only the 'money of the greedy' grows without any limits (Homily on Ps. 14b, 3). Similarly, Gregory of Nyssa states:

What a misuse of words! 'Child' [*tokos*] becomes a name for robbery. What a sour marriage! What an evil union, which nature knows not, but which the vice of the covetous invented between inanimate parties! What intolerable pregnancies, from which such a 'child' is produced. . . . Among created things, only what is living can be divided into the male and the female. It was to them that God their Creator said, Increase and multiply, . . . but from what kind of marriage is the 'child' of gold generated? . . . This is that 'child' with which greed was in labour, and to which wickedness gave birth, and whose midwife is miserliness.

(Homily 4 in Eccles. 344, 15ff)

There is also an argument, taken from the statements of the Lord in the Parable of Talents, that seems to point into a new direction. As there should be no return on idle money, the idle creditor should not receive a wage for work he did not do. According to Gregory of Nazianzus, the usurer is 'gathering where he had not sowed and reaping where he had not strawed; farming, not the land, but the necessity of the needy' (Oratio 16, 18). Basil also deals with an objection against the effect argument: 'But many', he lets the money-lender say, 'grow rich from loans', to which he answers: 'But more, I think, fasten themselves to halters. You see those who have become rich, but you do not count those who have been strangled' (Homily in Ps. 14b, 4). According to Gregory of Nyssa, lending at interest can be called 'another kind of robbery or bloodshed without being far from truth', since there is no difference in 'getting someone else's property by seizing it through covert housebreaking' and 'acquiring what is not one's own by exacting interest' (Homily 4 in Eccles. 343, 10ff).

At nearly the same time, in the West, there was also a Latin Father who devoted an entire writing to the subject of usury. Ambrose of Milan (*c.* 339–97), like the three Cappadocian Fathers born into a noble family, received a thorough education in rhetoric and law to prepare him for a career in government. He is said to have been working as a lawyer before he became bishop of Milan in AD 373. Although some distance away from Alexandria, he was the Christian Father who made the most extensive and detailed use of Philo's writings.[19] His treatise on usury, *De Tobia*, was written AD 380. Since its first half is dependent on Basil's treatise and its second half on Philo's treatment of the subject, one can again encounter their arguments. It is therefore sufficient to concentrate only on the new elements. First of all, like any good lawyer, Ambrose is the first Christian writer to give an explicit definition of usury: 'whatever exceeds the amount loaned is usury' (*De Tobia* 14, 49). This is exactly the definition that Charlemagne and Gratian were later to employ in their laws. Second, Ambrose is the first Christian writer who referred thoroughly and in great detail to all of the three usury prohibitions in the Old Testament Law.

Third, he was therefore the first and only Father of the Church who felt obligated to give a reason for the allowance to lend at interest to a foreigner. In the eyes of the ancient Israelites, he argued, a 'foreigner' was always an enemy. Since Israelites – as we learn from the Old Testament – had the right to kill their enemies, they were also allowed to 'injure' them by means of usury. Therefore, the permission to take interest from a foreigner was some kind of a 'law of war' (*De Tobia* 15, 51). Further references to usury can be found in Ambrose's manual of ethics *De officiis ministrorum* (3, 3, 20), written in AD 390 and modeled on Cicero's *De Officiis*, as well as in *De Nabuthe* (4, 14) and *De bono mortis* (12, 56), where he sates that the money-lender will not attain eternal life.

The process of canonization

After the Cappadocian Fathers and Ambrose of Milan, the main idea of usury and the basic arguments against its practice were formulated and quickly incorporated into the Christian doctrine. John Chrysostom (*c.* 350–407), patriarch of Constantinople, who briefly treated usury in several of his sermons, uses almost exactly the same wording as his predecessors. A new feature in his approach is that he deals with an objection to the motive argument, which reveals some insight that money is not 'idle' and that there are opportunity costs of lending:

> 'But what do you require?' says one, 'that I should give another for his use that money which I have got together, and which is to me useful, and demand no recompense?'
>
> (in Matt. Homily 5, 5)

To which Chrysostom answers, in a quite original manner:

> Far from it: I say not this; yes, I earnestly desire that you should have a recompense; not however a mean nor small one, but far greater; for in return for your gold, I desire that you should receive heaven for usury.
>
> (in Matt. Homily 5, 5)

Chrysostom is the first to support his condemnation of usury with Roman Law. In AD 397 a law was introduced that prohibited senators from taking interest (Codex Theosiannus II 33, 3). It was set aside again by Arcadius in AD 405, allowing senators to lend at 4 per cent per annum. Referring to that law, Chrysostom stated, that even the Gentile lawmakers regarded the practice of usury as shameless, since

> . . . those, for example, who are in offices of honor, and belong to the great council, which they call the senate, may not legally disgrace

themselves with such gains . . . How then is it not a horrible thing, if you ascribe not even so much honor to the polity of Heaven, as the legislators to the council of the Romans.

(in Matt. Homily 56, 6)

The Latin father Jerome (*c.* 347–420) deserves some attention for an objection he brings forward against the interest prohibition. In his commentary on Ezek. 18, written *c.* AD 390, he gives the example of a 'usurer' that lends some grain to the debtor. At harvest time, the yield amounts to ten times the original quantity of the principal. Therefore, he lets the creditor argue, that it would be fair and just for him to ask for one and a half times the quantity of the principal in return, since this would leave the debtor a profit of more than eight times the quantity of the principal he received as a loan. This example is interesting because it clearly shows that the condemnation of interest taking was not limited to consumption loans, as it is sometimes stated. However, although Jerome clearly denies this justification for interest, his reasoning is somehow confusing:

Let the merciful usurer tell us briefly whether he gave to someone who had possessions or to one who did not. If to someone who had possessions, he should not have given to him at all, but he gave as if to someone who did not have anything. Therefore why does he demand more back as if from someone who had something?

(in Ezek. Hom. 6, 18)[20]

The fact, that towards the fifth century AD the idea of usury became more and more canonized, can also be seen by the manner in which Augustine (*c.* 354–430), one of the greatest Fathers of the Church treated the subject.[21] Even though he referred to usury several times, his interest in a more profound treatment was very limited. He largely repeated the already developed arguments:

What did you intend when you did lend on usury? To give money, and receive money; but to give a smaller sum, and to receive a larger.

(De consensu evangelistarum 4, 10, 36)

But Augustine is also a witness to the fact that money-lending at interest was widely practiced. 'Money-lending even has a profession' he remarks in his commentary on Psalm 55, 'money-lending also is called a science; a corporation is spoken of, a corporation as if necessary to the state, and of its profession it pays revenue; so entirely indeed in the streets is that which should be hidden'.

Pope Leo's (*c.* 440–61) letter written *c.* AD 443 (*Ut nobis gratulationem*) requires only brief mention here because it made its way into the *Dionysio-*

Hadriana, a collection of canons that Pope Adrian I presented to Charlemagne in AD 774. Much more important is the fact that another collection of canons written AD 700 in Ireland, the *Collection Hibernensis* (cap. 12, liber 33), for the first time founded the usury prohibition not only on the Bible (*Lex dicit*) and on canon 17 of Nicaea (*sinodus sancta*), but also on citations of Fathers of the Church (Siems 1992, 581). Towards the end of the eighth century AD this became a common practice. When finally Charlemagne, the Frankish founder of the Holy Roman Empire, in AD 789 prohibited the practice of usury to all inhabitants of his empire, he cited the following authorities: (1) the Council of Nicaea, (2) the above mentioned letter of Pope Leo I, (3) the *Canones Apostollorum*,[22] and (4) the Scripture. All relevant texts form part of the *Dionysio-Hadriana*. The prohibition was renewed at the Council of Nymwegen in AD 806, where an additional capitulary defined that usury occurs when 'more is demanded back than what is given'.

Notes

1 I have benefited from helpful comments by Kepa M. Ormazabal, from many conversations with Franz Ritzmann, and from valuable suggestions for improvement of an earlier draft of this paper made by Michalis Psalidopoulos.

2 The term 'usury' stems from the Latin term *usura*, which in Roman law denoted the payment for the use of a loan of any nonspecific good (*mutuum*). The modern term 'interest' evolved from the medieval Latin word *interesse*, a payment for damages arising to the creditor from default or delay in repayment (the *quod interest* of Roman Law).

3 For my thesis that the basis for the prohibition of interest is not found in the ethical prescription in a primitive society see Moser (1997 and 1999).

4 Translation according to the Revised Standard Version (RSV). Numeration according to the Hebrew Bible, numbers in full square brackets mark numeration according to RSV which follows the *Latin Vulgate*.

5 The term 'justice' also has a very specific meaning in the context of the Hebrew Bible. 'Justice' (*tsaedaeq*) refers to the contractual relationship between God (Yahweh) and 'his people' (Israel). It conveys the meaning of 'fidelity' or 'loyalty' towards the 'covenant'. To be 'just', means to fulfill the stipulations of this covenant which – for Israel – consisted of the divine commandments stipulated in 'the Law'.

6 It seems that the last part of the sentence stems from Plato's insight, that the development of commercial activity is dependent on legal protection of property rights. Compare this with his statement in *The Republic*, that there should be 'a general rule that everyone shall enter into voluntary contracts at his own risk, and there will be less of this scandalous money-making' (*Republic* 8, 556b). See further *Laws* 8, 849e.

7 It seems that the definition of exchanging money for goods and goods for money as the 'normal' or 'natural' case of exchange was first stated by Heraclitus (*c.* 550–480 BC), Frag. 90, 22.

8 This was to become the scholastic *interesse*. There are at least some hints that interest as penalty for a delay in payment might also have been allowed by the early Church. See for example cap. 11 in book 33 of the *Collectio Hibernensis*.

9 It has to be admitted that both arguments against interest taking attributed to Aristotle are somehow related since in his view the purpose (*telos*) of things is

subordinated to the *telos* of man. Therefore, money is thought to be a means of exchange to satisfy men's 'natural wants' and to strive for money for its own sake is to mistake the means for an end.

10 The Roman historian Livy (59 BC–17 AD), on the other hand, attributes this law to the *Lex Duilia Menenia* in 357 BC (*Ab Urbe Condita* 7, 16, 1).

11 Some modern historians have doubted the existence or contents of this law to preserve the 'canonic view' of the economic liberalism of Roman Law. I find it hard to call into question the unanimous report of two Roman historians, to whom we owe much of our knowledge about Roman history in general. The legal prohibition of interest is also confirmed by the Roman historian Appian (*ca.* 150 AD) (*Bella civilia* 1, 54), and the Roman lawyer Gaius (*ca.* 160 AD) mentions a *Lex Marcia adversus feneratores* (4, 23).

12 The Fathers of the Church were not only aware of this indebtedness to 'Philo Judaeus' but in general quite open about it. As Runia (1993, 31f) remarks, by the end of the Patristic period Philo had virtually achieved the status of a Church Father *honoris causa*.

13 The Greek-speaking Christians in particular had a different view about 'the Law', as can be seen from Acts 6: 8ff. Compare also the antitheses of the Sermon on the Mount in Matt. 5 (You have heard it said . . . but I say unto you) with the probably editorial Matt. 5: 17ff.

14 Marcion's main thesis, expounded in his *Antitheses*, was that the Hebrew 'God of Law' had nothing in common with the Gospel's 'God of Love'. He therefore created a 'New Testament' primarily based on Paul's writings, rejecting the Old Testament. Marcion was excommunicated, but he founded his own Christian Church that gained a large following.

15 That Clement was not biased against money or wealth in general shows his treatise *Quis dives salvetur*, an attempt to show that being rich does not necessarily disqualify from obtaining salvation.

16 Canon 17 starts with the remark that many clerics were avaricious and looking for shameful gain (*Quoniam multi sub regula constituti auaritiam et turpia lucra sectantur*), and at the end it makes clear that the prohibition also is valid for all other kinds of 'shameful gain' (*vel aliquid tale prorsus excogitans turpis lucri gratia*).

17 In the interim, there are three Fathers of the Church who take up the usury question, but they base their prohibition entirely on the scriptural argument: Athanasius of Alexandria (*c.* 295–373) in a commentary on Ps. 15[14], Cyril of Jerusalem (*c.* 315–86) in his *Catecheses* (4, 37), and the Persian Father Aphrahat (*c.* 340) in his *Demonstrationes* (14, 3 and 14, 26).

18 This analogy between interest on money and the procreation of hares was already drawn by Plutarch (*c.* AD 50–120). See Van Houdt (1996).

19 As Runia (1993, 292f) states, large sections of his writings are virtually translations from Philo's texts into Latin. At the same time, Ambrose mentions Philo's name only once – to criticize him.

20 Jerome, in Ezek. 6, 18: '*Respondeat enim nobis breviter foenerator misericors, utrum habenti dederit an non habenti. Si habenti, utique dare non debuerat, sed dedit quasi non habenti. Ergo quare plus exigit quasi ab habente?*'

21 An important exception to this statement about the fifth century AD is the *Opus imperfectum in Matthaeum* (Hom. 38). This text, that has been falsely attributed to John Chrysostom, developed some important new arguments against interest taking. But since those arguments do not stand in the tradition of the writings of the Fathers of the Church, they are not part of the Patristic idea of usury (see Moser 1997).

22 A collection of canons from the second half of the fourth century AD, although it seeks to give the impression of being Apostolic in its age. Canon 44 forbade usury to bishops and deacons.

References

Albrecht, M. von. [1992] (1994) *Geschichte der römischen Literatur von Andronicus bis Boëthius.* 2, verb. u. erw. Aufl., Nachdr. München: dtv Wissenschaft.

Altaner, B. and Stuiber, A. [1978] (1993) *Patrologie: Leben, Schriften und Lehren der Kirchenväter.* Freiburg i. Br.: Herder.

Assmann, J. (1992) *Das kulturelle Gedächtnis: Schrift, Erinnerung und politische Identität in frühen Hochkulturen.* München: Beck.

Baeck, L. (1994) *The Mediterranean Tradition in Economic Thought.* London and New York: Routledge.

Baldwin, J.W. (1959) 'The Medieval Theories of the Just Price. Romanists, Canonists, and Theologians in the Twelfth and Thirteenth Centuries'. *Transactions of the American Philosophical Society*, NS 49, Part 4, Philadelphia.

Clavero, B. (1986) 'The Jurisprudence on Usury as a Social Paradigm in the History of Europe'. *Historische Soziologie der Rechtswissenschaft*, E.V. Heyen (ed.) (Ius commune, Sonderheft 26). Frankfurt a.M.: Klostermann, pp. 23–36.

De Martino, F. [1980] (1991) *Wirtschaftsgeschichte des alten Rom* (Storia economica di Roma antica). 2 Aufl. München: Beck.

Dvine, Th.F. (1959) *Interest: An Historical and Analytical Study in Economics and Modern Ethics.* Milwaukee: Marquette.

Funk, F.X. (1876) *Geschichte des kirchlichen Zinsverbotes.* Tübingen: Laupp.

Gordon, B. (1975) *Economic Analysis before Adam Smith: Hesiod to Lessius.* London: Macmillan.

—— (1982) 'Lending at Interest: Some Jewish, Greek, and Christian Approaches 800 BC–AD 100'. *History of Political Economy*, vol. 14, pp. 406–26.

Langholm, O. (1984) *The Aristotelian Analysis of Usury.* Bergen: Universitets-forlaget.

Lesky, A. [1971] (1993) *Geschichte der griechischen Literatur.* 3, erw. Aufl.; Nachdr. München: dtv Wissenschaft.

Lindberg, D.C. (1992) *The Beginnings of Western Science: The European Scientific Tradition in Philosophical, Religious, and Institutional Context, 600 B.C. to A.D. 1450.* Chicago: University of Chicago Press.

Maloney, R.P. (1971) 'Usury in Greek, Roman and Rabbinic Thought'. *Traditio: Studies in Ancient and Medieval History, Thought, and Religion*, vol. 27, pp. 79–109.

—— (1973) 'The Teaching of the Fathers on Usury: An Historical Study on the Development of Christian Thinking'. *Vigiliae Christianae*, vol. 27, pp. 241–65.

Moser, Th. (1997) *Die patristische Zinslehre und ihre Ursprünge: Vom Zinsgebot zum Wucherverbot.* Winterthur: Schellenberg.

—— (1999) 'The Old Testament Anti-Usury Laws Reconsidered: The Myth of Tribal Brotherhood'. *Économie et Sociétés*, 4: 99, 28, pp. 139–50.

Runia, D.T. (1993) *Philo in early Christian literature: a survey* (Compendia Rerum Iudaicarum ad Novum Testamentum, Section 3). Assen: Van Gorcum.

Schefold, B. (1989) 'Platon und Aristoteles'. *Klassiker des ökonomischen Denkens*, J. Starbatty (ed.). München: Beck, pp. 19–55.

Schumpeter, J.A. [1954] (1994) *History of Economic Analysis*, ed. from manuscript by E.B. Schumpeter with a new introduction by M. Perlman. New York: Oxford University Press.

Sommerlad, T. (1903) *Das Wirtschaftsprogramm der Kirche des Mittelalters: Ein Beitrag zur Geschichte der Nationalökonomie und zur Wirtschaftsgeschichte des ausgehenden Altertums.* Leipzig: Weber.

Siems, H. (1992) *Handel und Wucher im Spiegel frühmittelalterlicher Rechtsquellen* (Monumenta Germaniae Historica, Bd. 35). Hannover: Hahn.

Van Houdt, T. (1996) 'Ut Lepus Superfetans: A Plutarchian Simile and its Functioning in the Early Modern Controversy about Interest and Usury'. *Plutarchea Lovaniensia: A Miscellany of Essays on Plutarch* (Studia Hellenistica 32), L. Van der Stockt (ed.), Lovanii, pp. 287–307.

3 Self-interest as an acceptable mode of human behaviour*

Arild Saether

Introduction

The science of political economy came into being as a result of philosophers struggling with the fundamental problem of how the individual pursuit of self-interest would lead to the highest social good. Canonical works on the history of economic thought generally credit Adam Smith with the honour of making self-interest an acceptable mode of human behaviour and take him as a point of departure for self-interest in economics (Spiegel 1983; Blaug 1985; Rima 1991; Ekelund and Hébert 1990; Landreth and Colander 1994). Most biographers and editors of his works have also tried to show that his ideas were of indigenous Anglo-Saxon growth and owed little, if anything, to outside sources (Stewart 1793; Rae 1895; Cannan 1904; Lerner 1937; Skinner 1970; Raphael and Macfie 1976; Stigler 1976). This is particularly the case with respect to his ideas of human behaviour. It is the purpose of this paper to give a narrative of how the pursuit of self-interest became an acceptable mode of human behaviour through accumulated influence from a narrow range of natural law philosophers who really fought to change prevailing attitudes.

The Reformation started a process that gradually released human reasoning from the chains of dogmatic theology, and broke down the secular power of the Universal Church over rigid social systems. It was no longer possible, in a time of liberating the intellect, to base any ideas on the dogmatic doctrines of the Church. Scholars tried to replace the old principles of authority with new universal principles. There was a move towards reason as the basis for the development of modern natural law theories away from revelation and theology. These new theories were independent of theology and found their basis in an investigation of human nature. However, it should be mentioned that many of their conclusions were not so different from the medieval thought of the scholastics. Thomas Aquinas, as the foremost representative of the scholastics, also distinguished between positive and natural law. Natural law was for him the earthly manifestation of divine law. This law was revealed through nature based on reason. Positive law was the law created by humans.

The new 'modern' natural law tradition maintained that knowledge of the natural order could be achieved through the discovery of the natural laws that governed not only the physical but also the social universe. These laws could be discovered with or without the existence of God. The scholastics maintained that following the natural laws would lead to happiness, which for the scholastics was Heaven. For the modern natural law philosophers, following the natural laws would lead not only to material prosperity and peace on earth, but since most of them also were true believers, ultimately to Heaven.

What is the nature of human behaviour?

The first of the moderns was the Dutchman Hugo de Groot or Hugo Grotius. In his main work *De Jure Belli ac Pacis* (The Laws of War and Peace) in three volumes published in 1625 he attempted to create a standard of international conduct in war and peace. He needed in this effort to go beyond the positive laws of each single nation and look for universal principles based on human nature. Natural law was defined as the dictate of right reason. This right reason could then be used to evaluate whether or not an act is in conformity with rational nature. If it is, it has in it a 'quality of moral baseness or moral necessity' and it would then be enjoyed by the Author of Nature, God. On the basis of this natural law he also created a law of nations.

According to Scott (1925: xliii) Hugo Grotius' work was 'the first systematic exposition, if, indeed, he is not the father of the system' of the law of nations. He is also considered to be the father of modern natural law. The term 'modern' emphasises the fact that natural law played an important role among the Greek and Roman philosophers of law. Their views were later adopted by the scholastics and the jurists of the Reformation. All of them used the term *jus naturae*. Grotius bypassed the jurists of the Church and found, like Aristoteles and Cicero, the source of what is right and wrong in human nature. He did mention that natural law also had its source in God but he carried out, according to Gihl (1932: 42), 'what one could call the dechristianisation or secularisation of natural law'. In the *Prolegomena* he stated daringly, although the language is in a mild form, that natural law would be the same if God did not exist. 'What we have been saying would have a degree of validity even if we should concede that which cannot be conceded without the utmost wickedness, that there is no God, or that the affairs of men are of no concern to Him' (Grotius 1646: 13).

His theory can be summed up as follows: Law and right is a purely human relation and it has its origin in human nature. We therefore have to understand what human nature is. According to Grotius it cannot be egoism since man has this in common with all living creatures. What is special with humans is their craving for intercourse with other people. Human reason will inform man how this craving can be satisfied, making it possible for man to decide what is right and what is wrong. Right is what is good for society and wrong is what hurts society. Once Grotius with logic abstraction had reached the source of law he deduced a system of natural and international law.

Grotius declared in his *Prolegomena* that man is an animal, but a social animal in need of association with others.

> Man is, to be sure, an animal, but an animal of a superior kind, much farther removed from all other animals than the different kinds of animals are from one another; evidence on this point may be found in the many traits peculiar to the human species. But among the traits characteristic of man is an impelling desire for society, that is, for the social life – not of any and every sort, but peaceful, and organized according to the measure of his intelligence, with those who are of his own kind; this social trend the Stoic called 'sociableness'.

From this, according to Grotius, it also follows that it cannot be stated as a universal truth; 'the assertion that every animal is impelled by nature to seek only its own good' (Grotius 1646: 11).

Man unites and forms societies which have need of laws in order not to disintegrate. Although man is an animal he is also an intelligent being. His law is therefore a product of his intelligence and the use of reason. Man has also been endowed with the faculty of knowing and of acting in accordance with general principles. Accordingly it follows that laws must be derived from the needs of men living together in society. Natural law is therefore as universal as society. The human instinct of sociability is its origin and the preservation of society is its objective. On this foundation Grotius built his law of nature and his law of nations.

Individual self-interest the driving force

The Englishman Thomas Hobbes (1588–1679) started his career as a political philosopher with the completion of his first book manuscript in the spring of 1640. In his dedication he described arrogantly his manuscript, which was entitled *Elements of Law, Natural and Politic*, as 'the true and only foundation' of such science. By the autumn of 1640 England was heading for civil war and Hobbes refused to risk Parliament's hostility towards those who had written for the King and fled the country. His book manuscript was therefore not published but circulated widely in copies. In 1649 and 1650 an incorrect copy of the manuscript was broken into two parts and published separately as *Human Nature* and *De Corpore Politico*, probably without Hobbes's participation (Goldsmith 1968: vi). *The Elements of Law* must be regarded as the first draft of *De Cive*, which was published in Paris in 1642, with a first English edition in 1651, and his most famous work *Leviathan* which also was published in 1651.[1]

Hobbes started his political theory, which he claims to be the founder of, with an analysis of human nature where he found the source of what is right or wrong. In several of his books, he described men as self-centred creatures who restlessly pursued their own good. The craving for intercourse between people is not the driving force but fear and pure egoism 'the disposition of men is naturally such that, except they be restrained through fear of some coercive power, every man will dread and distrust each other'. The basic views can be outlined as follows: Man is moved by appetites and aversions and the driving force is his own self-interest.

> And forasmuch as necessity of nature maketh men to will and desire *bonum sibi*, that which is good for themselves, and to avoid that which is hurtful; but most of all that terrible enemy of nature, death, from whom we expect both the loss of all power, and also the greatest of bodily pains in the losing; it is not against reason that a man doth all he can to preserve his own body and limbs both from death and pain. And that which is not against reason, men call RIGHT, or *jus*, or blameless liberty of using our own natural power and ability. It is therefore a *right of nature*: that every man may preserve his own life and limbs, with all the power he hath.
>
> (Hobbes 1640: 71)

Because of every man's right and drive to better his own position and to engage in an incessant struggle for power over others in the state of natural liberty men will live in a state of war.

> Seeing then to the offensiveness of man's nature one to another, there is added a right of every man to every thing, whereby one man invadeth with right, and another with right resisteth; and men live thereby in perpetual diffidence, and study how to preoccupate each other; the estate of men in this natural liberty is the estate of war. For WAR is nothing else but that time wherein the will and intention of contending by force is either by words or actions sufficiently declared; and the time which is not war is PEACE.
>
> (Hobbes 1640: 72–3)

If men seek intercourse then it is either because of fear or the belief that they can profit by it. In the natural state, everyone has the same equal and unlimited right to everything. This will, however, result in 'a war of all men against all men'[2] and will as a consequence lead to self-destruction. From self-interest it is therefore necessary for men to seek an agreement of cooperation or commonwealth with each other. But this commonwealth must be based on a covenant that each give up a part of one's unrestricted right to be able to keep the agreement that ultimately will secure peace. From this follows that with the opposite starting point Hobbes has reached the same result as Grotius.

The state of nature represented to Hobbes the hypothetical alternative to a civil society with peace and order. It is therefore a state of endless and oppressive insecurity, a war of all against all. Each has a right to everything and therefore nothing is anyone's with certainty. The notions of just and unjust have no place in this state. Men can only live together in peace if they agree to subject themselves to an absolute and undivided sovereign.

Hobbes took the same point of view as Grotius when he established the framework in which social inquiry was to take place. The foundation of these theories was human nature (Clark 1992: 156–7). With his thorough analysis Hobbes became one of the most famous thinkers of his time. His writings were widely read not only in England but also on the Continent. He exerted a powerful influence on his critics too – and they were many. However, his probing and confident writings expressing hard deterministic and materialistic views made him both famous and infamous and brought upon him a horde of angry, hostile attackers. He was accused of heresy and atheism by his clerical opponents and in these circles his name became a swear word. It was in particular his views on human behaviour that were hard to swallow both for the theologians and laymen of the church. They could not accept that self-interest and 'a war of all men against all men' were the only basis for human nature. Such a view was found to be in serious conflict with the words of scripture. To develop natural law and political theory on such a foundation was considered unacceptable not only by the Church establishment and their laymen but also by many universities. Already in 1653, Leviathan was investigated and nearly banned for blasphemy and in 1683, four years after his death, the University of Oxford condemned a number of Hobbes' works to the flames.

Self-interest and sociability

Samuel Pufendorf (1632–94) attempted in his works on jurisprudence and natural law to mediate between Grotius and Hobbes. He tried to unify Hobbes' natural law doctrine of self-interest with Grotius' natural law doctrine of 'man's inclination for society' and to integrate these new ideas with the scholastic methods of the sixteenth-century thinkers. His natural law is therefore based on the interactions between man's self-interest and man's existence as a social being. The result of these interactions will be a society in peace.[3]

A society cannot, according to Pufendorf, exist unless its members have a common feeling, basis or ideology about what is the proper way of conducting its affairs. In his first book on jurisprudence, *Elementorum Jurisprudentiæ Universalis* (The Elements of Universal Jurisprudence) published in The Hague in 1660, Pufendorf discusses the basis for human behaviour.

In an observation in book II called 'A man is destined by nature to lead a social life with men' he described the driving forces behind human actions (Pufendorf 1660: 233–8). The first force is self-interest. 'Man . . . loves himself most, is zealous to protect himself in every way, and strives to acquire the things which seem good to him, and to repel the evil.' According to Pufendorf this force is so strong that any attachment or devotion to other human beings has to submit itself to this force. Furthermore he rejects the possibility that people can act altruistically. If, for example, parents prefer to have transferred to themselves the pain which they see their children suffer 'this was done either because, as the result of an intimate relationship, they regarded the good or evil of others as their own, or else because, by that display of affection or fidelity, they were on the way to acquire some special good for themselves.' But the pursuit of self-interest is not the only driving force behind human action. Man has another inclination:

> Now, in truth, man would have been very little different from beast, nor would he be living a life much more civilised or comfortable than they, were it not that he had some other inclination also implanted by nature, namely that he enjoys living in association with his kind. This is so clear that it does not need to be set forth at length.

Why human beings have this inclination for living in association with their kind he explains in the following way:

> The weakness of human beings just born is greater than that of any other animal, and while in the case of others but a few days or months are sufficient to enable them to look out for their own food, in the case of men a number of years is hardly sufficient. Add that the earth has everywhere placed their food before beasts, but what suits man requires generally industry and cultivation. And yet the ability to gather food for the stomach is but a very small part in one's deserving the dignity the name man. Nay, we should not simply be the prey of beasts, but should also rage against one another mutually, in the manner of wild monsters, were it not that nature had altogether bidden us to unite to form a peaceful society.

The ultimate goal of human actions is then to establish a society where people live in peace.

How these two inclinations are balanced and why individuals unite to form a society Pufendorf explained in the following way.

> However, so that the reasons of those who undertake to deny matters as clear as the foregoing, may not, perchance, move one, it should be

known: (1) These two inclinations, by which man loves himself and seeks after society, ought, by the intention of nature, so to be tempered that nothing be lost to the latter through the instrumentality of the former. That is to say nature commended to man self-love, in such a way that he should, nevertheless, commit nothing because of it, which would conflict with his inclination to society, or injure the very nature of society. And when, through the exorbitance of his emotions, he neglects that, and seeks his own advantage together with some hurt to others, there arises whatever disturbance there be in which men conflict with one another. (2) That definite individuals unite to form a definite kind of society comes about either in consequence of a special harmony of dispositions or of other qualities, or else because they imagine that they can obtain some special end better with these persons than with those.

Man must, however, be educated to be able to act well in this society.

And so the sense of that trite saying, 'Man is by nature a social animal,' is this: Man is destined by nature to society with his like, and this is most suitable and useful to him; and man has been endowed with such a disposition that, by cultivation, he can receive a fitness for acting well in that society; nay more, this is perhaps the principal fruit produced by societies, namely, that the recently born, in whom no actual understanding of those things has been implanted by nature, may, within societies, be fashioned into suitable members of the same.

These two basic inclinations of human behaviour, pursuit of self-interest and inclination for society with others, are by Pufendorf transformed into the two fundamental laws of nature. In an observation entitled 'Right reason dictates that a man should care for himself in such a way that human society be not thrown into disorder' he states:

Now the fundamental laws of nature and those from which all the rest flow are two: (1) That any one whatsoever should protect his own life and limbs, as far as he can, and save himself and what is his own. (2) That he should not disturb human society, or, in other words, that he should not do anything whereby society among men may be less tranquil.

The interaction between these two laws is so close that they can be combined into one law. 'These laws ought so to conspire, and, as it were, be intertwined with one another, as to coalesce, as it were, into one law, namely, That each should be zealous so to preserve himself, that society among men be not disturbed.' And the result of carefully observing this law will be peace, 'which is the status best suited to human nature, and for the establishment and preservation of which the law of nature has primarily been implanted in man.'

This shows clearly that Pufendorf, in contrast to Hobbes' theory that the natural condition is a struggle of all against all, considered peace the condition best adopted by human society. It alone is in keeping with natural law. Written shortly after the Thirty Years War in a time of violence, turmoil and unrest, when peace was very much the exception, Pufendorf's writings were truly radical, if not revolutionary.

Pufendorf's fundamental view that man's pursuit of self-interest checked by his inclination of living in society with others would result in a society at peace was also the basis for his other two works on natural law. In his greatest work on jurisprudence, *De Jure Naturae et Gentium* (On the Law of Nature and Nations) in eight books published in 1672, he pointed out that the best and most direct way to learn the law of nature is through careful consideration of 'the nature, condition, and desires of man himself'. However, we must also observe factors outside man himself. 'For whether this law was laid upon man in order to increase his happiness or to restrain his evil disposition, which may be his own destruction, it will be learned in no easier way than by observing when man needs assistance and when he needs restraint' (Pufendorf 1672: 205). Pursuit of self-interest is man's first human attribute. 'In the first place man has this in common with all beings which are conscious of their own existence, that he has the greatest love for himself, tries to protect himself by every possible mean, and tries to secure what he thinks will benefit him, and to avoid what may in his opinion injure him' (Pufendorf 1672: 205). However, pursuit of self-interest is not only the first human attribute, it is also the strongest. And this love of each one for himself is always so strong that any inclination towards any other man yields to it' (Pufendorf 1672: 205–6).

Why self-interest is the strongest human attribute he answered in the following way:

> It should be observed, in this connection, that in investigating the condition of man we have assigned the first place to self-love, not because one should under all circumstances prefer only himself before all others or measure everything by his own advantage, distinguishing this from the interests of others, and setting it forth as his highest goal, but because man is so framed that he thinks of his own advantage before the welfare of others for the reason that it is his nature to think of his own life before the life of others. Another reason is that it is no one's business so much as my own to look out for myself. For although we hold before ourselves as our goal the common good, still, since I am also a part of society for the preservation of which some care is due, surely there is no one on whom the clear and special care of myself can more fittingly fall than upon my own self.
>
> (Pufendorf 1672: 207)

After this discussion of self-interest and self-love Pufendorf states that it is easy to find the basis of natural law because man also has another attribute or driving force.

> It is quite clear that man is an animal extremely desirous to his own preservation, in himself exposed to want, unable to exist without the help of his fellow-creatures, fitted in a remarkable way to contribute to the common good, and yet at all times malicious, petulant, and easily irritated, as well as quick and powerful to do injury. For such an animal to live and enjoy the good things that in this world attend his condition, it is necessary that he be sociable, that is, be willing to join himself with others like him, and conduct himself towards them in such a way that, far from having any cause to do him harm, they may feel that there is reason to preserve and increase his good fortune.
> (Pufendorf 1672: 207–8)

And to emphasise what he meant by being social he continues:

> For by a sociable attitude we do not understand here the particular meaning of a tendency to form special societies, which can be formed even for an evil purpose and in an evil manner, such as a banding together of highway robbers, as if it were enough for them to band together with any end whatsoever in view. But by a sociable attitude we mean an attitude of each man towards every other man, by which each is understood to be bound to the other by kindness, peace, and love, and therefore by a mutual obligation. And so it would be absolutely false to assert that the sociable attitude which we propose makes no distinction between a good and a bad society.
> (Pufendorf 1672: 208)

This human attribute has to be cultivated and it will then work for the welfare of society.

> For nature has not commanded us to be sociable, to the extent that we neglect to take care of ourselves. Rather the sociable attitude is cultivated by men in order that by the mutual exchange among many of assistance and property, we may be enabled to take care of our own concerns to greater advantage. And even though a man, when he joins himself to any special society, holds before his eyes, first of all, his own advantage, and after that the advantage of comrades since his own cannot be secured without that of all, yet this does not prevent his being obligated so to cultivate his own advantage, that the good of the society be not injured, or harm offered its different members; or at times to hold his own advantage in abeyance and work for the welfare of the society.
> (Pufendorf 1672: 214)

The question of what is the character of man or what motivates human activity is also discussed in an abridged version of his main work, 'a student edition', entitled *De Officio Hominis et Civis Juxta Legem Naturalem* (The Duty of Man and Citizen According to Natural Law) in two books published in 1673. In an early chapter entitled 'On natural law' (Pufendorf 1673: 17–21) he starts with the question; 'What is the character of the natural law, what is its necessity, and of what precepts it consists in the present state of mankind, are most clearly seen, after one has thoroughly examined the nature and disposition of man'. This fundamental question is answered with the following statement.

> Now man shares with all the animals that have consciousness the fact that he holds nothing dearer than himself, and is eager in every way to preserve himself; that he strives to gain what seem to him good things, and to reject the evil. This feeling is regularly so strong that all the others give away to it.

Man is thus compared to animals and is from birth found to be in a weaker position than all of those. Man is totally dependent on others and has to be cared or trained for by other men for a longer time than any animal is by its own kind.

> Thus then man is indeed an animal most bent upon self-preservation, helpless in himself, unable to save himself without the aid of his fellows, highly adapted to promote mutual interests; but on the other hand no less malicious, insolent, and easily provoked, also as able as he is prone to inflict injury upon another. Whence it follows that in order to be safe, he must be sociable, that is, must be united with men like himself, and so conduct himself toward them that they may have no good cause to injure him, but rather may be ready to maintain and promote his interest.

The laws of this sociability, which teach how a man should conduct himself, to become a good member of human society, Pufendorf then calls natural laws.

> So much settled, it is clear that the fundamental natural law is this: that every man must cherish and maintain sociability, so far as in him lies. From this it follows that, as he who wishes an end, wishes also the means, without which the end cannot be obtained, all things which necessarily and universally make for that sociability are understood to be ordained by natural law, and all that confuse or destroy it forbidden. The remaining precepts are mere corollaries, so to speak, under this general law, and the natural right given to mankind declares that they are evident.

Pufendorf's sociability is not benevolence in today's meaning of the word. In a chapter in book II 'On the common duties of humanity' he discusses what duties men have to others for the sake of the common sociability (Pufendorf 1673: 45–7). Here he introduces the concept of mutual benevolence which may be fostered among men. 'A man tends to promote the advantage of others indefinitely, if he thoroughly cultivates his own soul and body, so that useful actions may emanate from him to others; or if by ingenuity he finds the means of making human life better equipped.' It is therefore clear that Pufendorf found the cultivation of self-interest to be ethical as long as it is cultivated according to the law of nature. To make his readers understand the concept better he also discusses what he calls a higher form of humanity when men bestow something freely upon each other out of rare benevolence. The latter is more in accordance with today's interpretation of the term benevolence.

If men act in agreement with natural law peace will result. Peace accords most closely with the natural law; 'in fact peace itself is a state peculiar to man, as distinguished from the brutes' (Pufendorf 1673: 138).

With his integrated theory of natural law Pufendorf became famous all over Europe and in the New World. Natural law became a fashion and new chairs in this subject were created at many universities. Pufendorf's books were translated into most European languages. They were published in new editions and reprinted again and again. His abridged student edition could be found in the libraries of almost all 'learned' people throughout Europe. His natural law books were on the curriculum of almost all universities and Denzer (1987) tells us that students at some universities forced reluctant professors to accept Pufendorf on the curriculum. For more than one hundred years these books were among the most read academic books in Europe and the New World. His ideas became part of common knowledge to such an extent that it may partly explain why he is almost forgotten. Dufour (1982) shows that today's classics Jean Jacques Rousseau (1712–78), Charles Louis Montesquieu (1689–1755) and John Locke (1632–1704) had all studied Pufendorf's natural law works and that they considered these works to be both fundamental and necessary for the study of civil law and politics. They clearly built their own ideas on Pufendorf's. Furthermore Saether (1996) claims that there is ample evidence to support a strong connection between the basic premises of Physiocracy and Pufendorf's natural law works. We can therefore assume that all scholars who took part in the philosophical debate in the first half of the eighteenth century knew Pufendorf's opinion on the issues they engaged themselves in.

Pufendorf was also a controversial person in his time. His works created heated debates across Europe. However, his theory, founded on self-interest and sociability, contrary to Hobbes' theory based on self-interest and a war all against all, could be accepted as a starting point for a constructive scientific debate.

How natural law came to Scotland

The gospel of natural law was brought to Scotland by Gershom Carmichael (1672–1729). Carmichael, who lectured at the University of Glasgow, considered himself to be a disciple of Grotius, Hobbes and Pufendorf, and he introduced their ideas into Scotland. According to Hutchison (1988), he thereby played a vital role both in the history of Scottish philosophy and in the history of economic thought. The famous Scottish philosopher Sir William Hamilton (1791–1856) stated, according to McCosh (1875: 36), that Carmichael 'may be regarded, on good grounds, as the true founder of the Scottish school of philosophy'.

Carmichael used, according to Raphael and Macfie (1976: 24), Pufendorf's *De Officio Hominis et Civis* as a textbook in his course in moral philosophy, a discipline which he regarded as almost identical to natural jurisprudence. For the use of his students, he published in 1718 (revised 1724) with *Notes and Supplements*, one of the many editions of this book in Latin. Here he wrote that: 'There is no reason why we should distinguish between ethics or moral philosophy and natural jurisprudence.' What had up to then been termed natural law was from now on designated moral philosophy.

Pufendorf's strong emphasis on self-interest was not supported by Carmichael. He attached more importance to men's craving for intercourse with other human beings. In his *Supplements* he argues, as Stein (1982: 669) has noted, that 'man's ability to live with others in society depends on natural feeling of sympathy for others, which men could never have invented themselves and which must have been implanted in them by the supreme being'. This edition was also used as a textbook by his successor Francis Hutcheson.

Francis Hutcheson (1694–1746) who succeeded Carmichael as Professor of Moral Philosophy in 1729, based his early teaching upon Pufendorf and a 'compend' of his predecessor. According to Hutcheson (1747: i), Carmichael was 'by far the best commentator on that book'. His lecture notes were so good that they were 'of much more value than the text'. Hutcheson continued Carmichael's practice and he later based his works, *A Short Introduction to Moral Philosophy* (1747) and *A System of Moral Philosophy* (1755), on his own lecture notes and to a large extent on the works of Pufendorf. In his foreword 'To the Student in Universities' he admits explicitly that much of his work 'is taken from the writings of others, from Cicero and Aristotle; and to name no other moderns from Pufendorf's smaller work, De officio hominis et civis'. A comparison shows the strong influence of Pufendorf. Some chapters are almost directly copied.

Hutcheson was a reformer and a libertarian who believed that the world could, and should, be better organised by the application of reason. According to West (1976: 42–3), it was Hutcheson rather than Jeremy Bentham (1748–1832) who originated the famous phrase, 'the greatest happiness of the greatest number'. We know that Smith and David Hume (1711–76), also a friend of Hutcheson, had a very high opinion of their mentor and both were greatly influenced and inspired by him.[4] There is good reason to believe that Hutcheson made not only Smith but also all his students familiar with the works of the natural law philosophers in general and Pufendorf's works in particular.

But, although Hutcheson was an admirer of Pufendorf, he departed from him, followed Carmichael, and put his emphasis on man's passion towards altruism and cooperation which, he argued, are the major sources of society and of the capacity of human beings to live together amicably and constructively. He also maintained that human motivation, their self-interest and inclination to live together with others, and men's conception of right and wrong are innate and not acquired. This is in sharp contrast to Pufendorf who claimed that 'no actual understanding of those things has been implanted by nature'; man had to be educated to be able to act well in society.

Self-interest and sympathy

In 1737 Adam Smith (1723–90) entered, at the late age of fourteen, the University of Glasgow, a place which at that time drew students from all over Europe. Throughout the three years he studied there he was strongly influenced by several of his teachers, the most influential being Professor Hutcheson: 'It is certainly from him that our economist seems to have acquired the feeling and respect for "natural liberty and justice"' (West 1976: 42). However, Smith departed from his mentor and did not accept his views on human behaviour, that man on entering into the world was fully equipped to make correct moral decisions. Instead he embraced the ideas of Pufendorf, the author of his main textbook *De Officio Hominis et Civis*, a book used and praised but also criticised by Hutcheson.

Smith published his first book *The Theory of Moral Sentiments* in 1759. The book got in 1774 the subtitle *An Essay towards and Analysis of the Principles by which Men Naturally Judge Concerning the Conduct and Character, First of Their Neighbours and Afterwards of Themselves*. The fundamental question he asks in this book is how man, who is basically a creature that tries to pursue his own self-love or self-interest, can form moral judgements in which self-interest seems to be checked or transmuted to a higher plane? He starts the book with the opening sentence: 'How selfish soever man may be supposed, there are evidently some principles in his nature, which interest him in the fortune of others, and render their happiness necessary to him, though he derives nothing from it except the pleasure of feeling it' (Smith 1759: 9). This feeling for others, which he called sympathy, is to be found in all men. 'The greatest ruffian, the most hardened violator of the law of society, is not altogether without it' (Smith 1759: 9). The term is clarified in the following way:

Pity and compassion are words appropriated to signify our fellow-
feeling with the sorrow of others. Sympathy, though its meaning was,
perhaps, originally the same, may now, however, without much impro-
priety, be made use of to denote our fellow-feeling with any passion
whatever.

(Smith 1759: 10)

To explain how individual self-love is checked and brought down to
something that can be accepted by all men in society, Smith introduces
the concept of an 'impartial spectator', 'the man within the breast, the
great judge and arbiter of their conduct' (Smith 1759: 130), within each
individual and the concept of 'fair play' that governs the interactions
between all men in society.

Though every man may, according to the proverb, be the whole world
to himself, to the rest of mankind he is a most insignificant part of it.
Though his own happiness may be of more importance to him than
that of all the world besides, to every other person it is of no more
consequence than that of any other man. Though it may be true,
therefore, that every individual, in his own breast, naturally prefers
himself to all mankind, yet he dares not look mankind in the face,
and avow that he acts according to this principle. He feels that in this
preference they can never go along with him, and that how natural
soever it may be to him, it must always appear excessive and extrav-
agant to them. When he views himself in the light in which he is
conscious that others will view him, he sees that to them he is but
one of the multitude in no respect better than any other in it. If he
would act so as that the impartial spectator may enter into the principles of his conduct, which is what of all things he has the greatest
desire to do, he must, upon this, as upon all other occasions, humble
the arrogance of his self-love, and bring it down to something which
other men can go along with, They will indulge it so far as to allow
him to be more anxious about, and to pursue with more earnest
assiduity, his own happiness than that of any other person. Thus far,
whenever they place themselves in his situation, they will readily go
along with him. In the race for wealth, and honours, and preferments,
he may run as hard as he can, and strain every nerve and every
muscle, in order to outstrip all his competitors. But if he should jostle,
or throw down any of them, the indulgence of the spectators is entirely
at an end. It is a violation of fair play, which they cannot admit of.
This man is to them, in every respect, as good as he: they do not
enter into that self love by which he prefers himself so much to this
other, and cannot along with the motive form which he hurt him.
They readily, therefore, sympathise with the natural resentment of
the injured, and the offender becomes the object of their hatred and

indignation. He is sensible that he becomes so, and feels that those sentiments are ready to burst out from all sides against him.

(Smith 1759: 83)

Like Pufendorf, Smith claims that men are social beings, and social beings are dependent on each other: 'It is thus that man, who can subsist only in society, was fitted by nature to that situation for which he was made. All members of human society stand in need for each other's assistance, and are likewise exposed to mutual injuries' (Smith 1759: 85).

It is not possible for man to grow up to manhood 'in some solitary place'. When he is brought into society he is able not only to view his own passions, guided by the 'impartial spectator' but also to adjust and moderate these passions in accordance with the other members of society.

Bring him into society, and all his own passions will immediately become the causes of new passions. He will observe that mankind approve of some of them, and are disgusted by others. He will be elevated in the one case, and cast down in the other; his desires and aversions, his joy and sorrows, will now often become the cause of new desires and new aversions, new joys and new sorrows. They will now, therefore, interest him deeply, and often call upon his most attentive consideration.

(Smith 1759: 110)

From this it is also clear, according to Smith, that man is not endowed by nature with an innate moral sense. Man has to be educated, that is, brought into society with others.

The question concerning what motivates human actions is also discussed in Smith's *Lectures on Jurisprudence*, delivered and written in the early 1760s. In these lecture notes self-interest is looked upon as a general universal principle.

Whenever commerce is introduced into any country, probity and punctuality always accompany it. These virtues in a rude and barbarous country are almost unknown. Of all countries in Europe, the Dutch, the most commercial, are the most faithful to their word. ... This is not at all to be imputed to national character, as some pretend. There is no natural reason why an Englishman or a Scotchman should not be as punctual in performing agreements as a Dutchman, It is far more reducible to self-interest, that general principle which regulates the actions of every man, and which leads men to act in a certain manner from views of advantage, and is as deeply implanted in an Englishman as a Dutchman.

(Smith 1766: 538)

Adam Smith's most famous work *An Inquiry into the Nature and Causes of the Wealth of Nations* was published in 1776. In Ch. II, entitled 'Of the principle which gives occasion to the division of labour', he discusses his economic model and explains that the division of labour is a consequence of a propensity in human nature to truck, barter and exchange one thing for another.[5] This propensity is common to all men but not to be found in any other race of animals. He then stresses that man at all times and contrary to animals, which when they have grown up to maturity are entirely independent, and in their natural state have occasion for the assistance of no other living creature, is 'in need of co-operation and assistance of great multitudes'. He continues with one of his most famous statements:

> But man has almost constant occasion for the help of his brethren, and it is in vain for him to expect it from their benevolence only. He will be more likely to prevail if he can interest their self-love in his favour, and show them that it is for their own advantage to do for him what he requires of them. Whoever offers to another a bargain of any kind, proposes to do this, Give me that which I want, and you shall have this which you want, is the meaning of every such offer; and it is in this manner that we obtain from one another the far greater part of those good offices which we stand in need of. It is not from the benevolence of the butcher, the brewer, or the baker that we expect our dinner, but from their regard to their own interest. We address ourselves, not to their humanity but to their self-love, and never talk to them of our own necessities but of their advantages.
>
> (Smith 1776a: 14)

The view that individual pursuit of their own interest and only their own interest also promotes the public interest is expressed in the following way:

> As every individual, therefore, endeavours as much as he can both to employ his capital in the support of domestic industry, and so to direct that industry that its produce may be of the greatest value; every individual necessarily labours to render the annual revenue of the society as great as he can. He generally, indeed, neither intends to promote the public interest, nor knows how much he is promoting it. . . . [H]e intends only his own gain, and he is this, as in many other cases, led by an invisible hand to promote an end which was no part of his intention.
>
> (Smith 1776a: 423)

The question whether this explanation of human behaviour clashes with or complements his model of self-interest and sympathy in his first book has been debated for a long time. Raphael and Macfie (1976) should have ended this discussion when they, in their introduction to the last edition of *The Theory of Moral Sentiments*, wrote about *The Wealth of Nations*:

> It is largely, though by no means wholly, about economic activity and so, when it refers to motivation concentrates on self-interest. There is nothing surprising in Adam Smith's well known statement 'It is not from the benevolence of the butcher, the brewer or the baker that we expect our dinner, but from their regard to their own interest.' Who would suppose this to imply that Adam Smith had come to disbelieve in the very existence or the moral value of benevolence? Nobody with any sense. But this does not necessarily exclude scholars, some of whom have adopted the 'Umschwungstheorie', the hypothesis that the moral philosopher who made sympathy the basis of social behaviour in TMS did an about-turn from altruistic to egoistic theory in WN owing to the influence of the French 'materialistic' thinkers whom he met in Paris in 1766.
>
> (Raphael and Macfie 1976: 20)

There has never been any inconsistency between Smith's ethics and his economics. Carmichael and Hutcheson, and many contemporary English and Scottish writers with them, held the view that virtue and benevolence were interlinked and were one and the same.[6] According to this view an act was virtuous only if it was intended to benefit others. Benevolence was the guiding principle according to the Scripture and according to this view acts were virtuous only if they were intended to benefit others. Smith agreed that benevolence was the 'most graceful and agreeable of the virtues' but it was certainly not the only one. Men also had a moral duty to take care of themselves. He regarded prudence, the rational pursuit of one's own material well-being and happiness, as a cardinal virtue. Smith's basic principles, that self-interest is the primary force in the actions of man, that natural order exists, and that every individual's striving for his own best will also give the best result for society, therefore do not come from Hutcheson. This is also recognised by Cannan (1904: li) who writes:

> Adam Smith clearly believed that Hutcheson's system did not give a sufficiently high place to self-interest. . . . He may have obtained a general love of liberty from Hutcheson, but whence did he obtain the belief that self-interest works for the benefit of the whole economic community?

Cannan points to the notorious satirist Bernard de Mandeville (1670–1733) who, with his poem *The Fable of the Bees* in which the prosperity of society emerges through a complex interplay of individuals' egoism and self-interest, created a heated debate all over Europe. However, Smith had no patience with Mandeville's extreme emphasis on pure selfishness. His views in general, and in particular his views on benevolence, are clearly more in accordance with Pufendorf, who claimed in his discussion on the common duties of humanity that men 'should bestow such attention upon others, – or mutually exchange them, – that thus mutual benevolence may be fostered among men' (Pufendorf 1672: 45).

Smith agreed with Hutcheson that man has an ability to reach correct moral decisions. However he disagreed with his view that man at birth was fully equipped to make correct decisions. Man's moral decisions are not reached by any higher principle than by his common feeling of sympathy for others. This principle of sympathy enables man to adjust his actions to a level that is socially acceptable. Smith's views are more congruent with Pufendorf's view that our sociability with others will tell us how to make the right decisions.

Conclusion

From our discussion it follows that Hugo Grotius opened the 'modern' discussion on what is the driving force behind human nature. He himself claimed sociability, man's craving for intercourse with other people as the answer. Thomas Hobbes was the first who asserted that individual self-interest was man's main motivation. This was in direct conflict with basic religious belief. With his provocative writings Hobbes stimulated discussions and thereby exerted a powerful influence on the intellectuals of his time. However, because of his controversial writings, 'a war of all men against all men', he was accused of heresy and atheism and his name became a swear word.

Self-interest as a mode of human behaviour, therefore, did not become acceptable until Samuel Pufendorf made a synthesis of Grotius' and Hobbes' views in his natural law works. He claimed the individual pursuit of self-interest, checked by man's inclination to live in society with others, his sociability, as the driving force behind human behaviour. This behaviour would also lead to the best society, which for Pufendorf was a society at peace. The law of sociability teaches man how he should conduct himself to become a good member of human society. Pufendorf's sociability is not benevolence in today's meaning of the word. He introduces the concept of mutual benevolence which may be fostered among men. Here man tends to promote the advantage of others if he cultivates his own 'soul and body' so that useful actions may emanate from him to others.

Pufendorf's natural law works, written in Latin, were translated to most European languages and spread all over Europe and the New World. Like Hobbes, he also was a controversial person whose ideas created heated debates. But, being highly respected and the best known scholar in the eighteenth century, his natural law, founded on self-interest and sociability, could be accepted as a starting point for a constructive scientific debate. All serious scholars who wrote on moral philosophy in the first half of the eighteenth century were familiar with his ideas, irrespective of their acknowledgement of this fact or not.

The natural law philosophy of Pufendorf was brought to Scotland by Gershom Carmichael and Francis Hutcheson. Although they did not (dare?) support his strong emphasis on self-interest, they made his theories known to their students. Hutcheson, who attached great significance to man's passion towards altruism and cooperation, made his student Adam Smith study the works of the natural law philosophers in general and Pufendorf in particular. The fundamental question Smith asks is how man, who basically is a creature trying to pursue his own self-interest, can form moral judgements in which self-interest seems to be checked or transmuted to a higher plane? Smith finds, building on Pufendorf, the answer in the fact that men are also social beings dependent on each other. To explain how individual self-love is checked and becomes something that can be accepted by all men living together in society, he introduces the concept of an 'impartial spectator'. The impartial spectator enters into every man's conduct and lets him view himself in a light in which he is conscious of how others will view him. According to Smith man is not, by nature, endowed with an innate moral sense. We learn whether our behaviour and actions are good or bad by observing the behaviour and actions of others and their reactions to our behaviour and actions. In other words our concept of moral sense is determined through a process of social education. Man has to be educated, that is, brought into society with others. Smith's views are therefore in accordance with Pufendorf's natural law ideas based on self-interest and sociability, that man has to be educated to live in society with others.

Notes

* The financial support of the Bank of Norway's Fund for Economic Research and Professor Wilhelm Keilhau's Memorial Fund, both Oslo, is gratefully acknowledged.

1 The full titles of these books were Elementorum Philosophiae Secto Tertia De Cive, in English Philosophical Rudiments Concerning Government and Society, and Leviathan, or, The Matter, Form, and Power of a Commonwealth Ecclesiastical and Civil.
2 Philosophical Rudiments Concerning Government and Society Ch. I Sec. 12. 'If now to this natural proclivity of men, to hurt each other, which they derive from their passions, but chiefly from a vain esteem of themselves, you add, the right of all to all, wherewith one by right invades, the other by right resists, and whence arise perpetual jealousies and suspicions on all hands, and how hard a thing it is to provide against an enemy invading us with an intention to oppress and ruin, though he come with a small number, and no great provision; it cannot be denied but that the natural state of men, before they entered into society, was a mere war, and that not simply, but a war of all men against all men.'
3 New research into the connection and relation between Grotius, Hobbes and Pufendorf has lately put more emphasis on Pufendorf's dependence on Hobbes. See for example Palladini, Fiammetta (1990): *Samuel Pufendorf – Discepolo di Hobbes.*

Per una reinterpretazione del giusnaturalismo moderno, Bologna: Il Mulino, or a review of this book by Klaus Luig (1993) in *Zeitschrift für Historische Forschung*, Heft 3, Berlin: Duncker and Humblot.

4   Hutcheson's general influence as a teacher is reviewed in W. Leechman's preface to the posthumously published *System of Moral Philosophy* (1755). Hutcheson 'spread such an ardour for knowledge, and such a spirit of enquiry every where around him, that the conversation of the students at their social walks and visits turned with great keenness upon subjects of learning and taste, and contributed greatly to animate and carry them forward in the most valuable pursuits' (Leechman 1755: xxxvii)

5   Ch. II is almost identical to pp. 20–5 (570–2) in 'Early Draft' of Part of The Wealth of Nations from 1759 in *Lectures on Jurisprudence*.

6   See for example Myers (1983).

References

Blaug, M. (1985) *Economic Theory in Retrospect*, Homewood: Richard D. Irwin.

Brown, M. (1988) *Adam Smith's Economics. Its Place in the Development of Economic Thought*, London: Croom Helm.

Cannan, E. (1904) Editor's Introduction to Adam Smith, in A. Smith (1776) *An Enquiry into the Nature and Causes of the Wealth of Nations*, 5th edn, reprinted New York: Random House, 1937.

Clark, C. Michael Andres (1992) *Economic Theory and Natural Philosophy*, Aldershot: Edward Elgar.

Clark, J.M., Douglas, P.H., Hollander, J.H., Morrow, G.R., Palyi, M. and Viner, J. (1928) *Adam Smith, 1776–1926. Lectures to commemorate the sesquicentennial of the publication of 'The Wealth of Nations'*, Chicago: The University of Chicago Press.

Denzer, H. (1987) *Pufendorf (1632–94)*, in 'Klassiker des Politischen Denkens, Zweiter band von Locke bis Max Weber'. Hans Maier, Heiz Rausch and Horst Denzer (eds). 5th edn, München: Verlag C.H. Beck.

Dufour, A. (1982) *Pufendorfs Ausstrahlung im französischen und im anglo-ameriknischen Kulturraum*, in K.Å Modéer, (ed.) *Samuel von Pufendorf 1632–1982*, Stockholm: A.-B. Nordiska Bokhandeln.

Ekelund, R.B. and Hébert, R.F. (1990) *The History of Economic Theory and Method*, New York: McGraw-Hill.

Evensky, J. (1987) 'The Two Voices of Adam Smith: Moral Philosopher and Social Critic', *History of Political Economy* 19: 3, Durham, NC: Duke University Press.

Gihl, T. (1932) 'Samuel Pufendorf och Jus Naturae et Gentium', *Nordisk Tidsskrift for Internasjonal Ret*, no. 2, Stockholm.

Goldsmith, M.M. (1968) *New Introduction to Hobbes*, in Thomas Hobbes (1640–60) *English Works of Thomas Hobbes of Malmesbury*, 11 vols, and *Opera Philosophica (Latin Works)*, 5 vols; reprinted Oxford, 1961.

Grotius, H. (1646) *On The Law of War and Peace Three Books*. Wherin are set forth the law of nature and of nations. Also the principles of public Law. New Edition With the annotations of the author. Now much enlarged in consequence of his last revision before his death. Whereto have been added also Notes on The Epistle of Paul to Philemon. Amsterdam, Johan Blaeu 1646. (First edition 1625.) Oxford: Clarendon Press, 1925.

Heilbroner, R.L. (1982) 'The Socialization of the Individual in Adam Smith', *History of Political Economy* 14: 3, Durham, NC: Duke University Press.

—— (ed.) (1986) *The Essential Adam Smith*, New York: W.W. Norton and Company, Critical Notes by Ferdinand Tönnies. (1st edn 1889), 2nd edn 1984, with a new introduction by M.M. Goldsmith, London: Frank Cass.

Hobbes, Thomas (1640–60) *English Works of Thomas Hobbes of Malmesbury*, 11 vols, and *Opera Philosophica (Latin Works)*, 5 vols, Sir William Molesworth (ed.) London 1839–45; reprinted Oxford 1961.

Hollander, S. (1973) *The Economics of Adam Smith*, London: Heinemann Educational.

—— (1987) *Classical Economics*. New York: Basil Blackwell.

Hutcheson, F. (1742) *An Essay on the Nature and Conduct of the Passions and Affections*, 3rd edn 1969, Gainsville, Florida: Scholars' Facsimiles & Reprints.

—— (1747) *A Short Introduction to Moral Philosophy, in three books; containing the Elements of Ethicks and the Law of Nature*. Collected works vol. IV, Hildesheim 1969: Georg Olms Verlagsbuchhandlung.

—— (1755) *A System of Moral Philosophy*. Collected works vols V and VI, Hildesheim 1969: Georg Olms Verlagsbuchhandlung.

Hutchison, T. (1988) *Before Adam Smith. The Emergence of Political Economy, 1662–1776*. Oxford: Basil Blackwell.

Johnsen, E.A.J. (1937) *Predecessors of Adam Smith. The Growth of British Economic Thought*. New York: Prentice-Hall.

Kaye, F.B. (ed.) (1924) *Bernard Mandeville: The Fable of the Bees: or, Private Vices, Publick Benefits*. 6th edn 1732, Oxford: Clarendon Press.

Khalil, E.L. (1990) 'Beyond Self-Interest and Altruism. A Reconstruction of Adam Smith's Theory of Human Conduct', *Economics and Philosophy*, vol. 6. no. 2, Cambridge.

Krieger L. (1965) *The Politics of Discretion. Pufendorf and the Acceptance of Natural Law*. Chicago and London: The University of Chicago Press.

Landreth, H. and Colander, D.C. (1994) *History of Economic Thought*, Boston: Houghton Mifflin.

Leidhold, W. (1986) 'Einleitung. Liebe, Moralsinn, Glück und Civil Gouvernment. Anmerkungen zu einigen Zentral-begriffen bei Francis Hutcheson', in *Francis Hutcheson Eine Untersuchung über den Ursprung unserer Ideen von Schönheit und Tugend Über moralisch Gutes und Schlectes*, Hamburg: Felix Meiner Verlag.

Lekachman, R. (1959) *A History of Economic Ideas*. New York: McGraw-Hill.

Lerner, M. (1937) 'New Introduction to Smith', in A. Smith (1776) *An Enquiry into the Nature and Causes of the Wealth of Nations*, 5th edn, reprinted New York: Random House, 1937.

McCosh, J. (1875) *The Scottish Philosophy, Biographical, Expository, Critical, From Hutcheson to Hamilton*, London: Macmillan.

MacFie, A.L. (1967) *The Individual in Society. Papers on Adam Smith*, London: George Allen and Unwin.

McReynolds, P. (1969) *An Introduction to Francis Hutcheson: An Essay on the Nature and Conduct of the Passions and Affections*, Gainesville, Florida: Scholars' Facsimiles & Reprints.

Mandeville, B. (1714) *The Fable of the Bees: or, Private Vices, Publick Benefits*. 6th edn 1732, F.B. Kaye (ed.), Oxford 1924: Clarendon Press.

Modéer, K.Å. (ed.) (1986) *Samuel von Pufendorf 1632–1982*. Ett rättshistorisk symposium i Lund 15–16 januari 1982, Stockholm: A.-B. Nordiska Bokhandeln.

Monroe, D.H. (1987) 'Self-interest', in Eatwell, J., Milgate, M., Newman, P. (eds) *The New Palgrave Dictionary of Economics*. vol. 4, London: Macmillan.

Myers, M.L. (1983) *The Soul of Modern Economic Man. Ideas of Self-Interest Thomas Hobbes to Adam Smith*, Chicago and London: The University of Chicago Press.

Pufendorf, S. (1660) *Elementorum Jurisprudentiæ Universalis Libri Duo* (The Elements of Universal Jurisprudence), vol. I Photographic Reproduction of the Edition of 1672 with a List of Errata which refers to the first edition of 1660; vol. II The Translation of the 1672 Edition by William Abbot Oldfather, Oxford 1931: Clarendon Press.

—— (1672) *De Jure Naturae et Gentium Libri Octo* (On the Law of Nature and Nations), vol. two. The translation of the edition of 1688 (with references to the first edition of 1672 by C.H. and William Abbot Oldfather, 1933, reprinted 1964, New York: Oceana Publications and London: Wiley and Sons.

—— (1673) *De Officio Hominis et Civis Juxta Legem Naturalem Libri Duo* (The Duty of Man and Citizen According to the Natural Law) vol. I. A Photographic Reproduction of the Edition of 1682 with a List of Errata that refers to the first edition of 1673. vol. II. A Translation of the Text by Frank Gardner Moore. New York 1927: Oxford University Press.

Rae, J. (1895) *Life of Adam Smith*. London: Macmillan: Reprinted with an introduction by Jacob Viner. New York 1965: Augustus M. Kelley.

Raphael, D.D. and Macfie, A.L. (1976) *Introduction to Adam Smith's The Theory of Moral Sentiments*, Oxford: Clarendon Press.

Rima, R. (1991) *Development of Economic Analysis*, Homewood: Richard D. Irwin.

Saether, A. (1996) *Physiocracy Yesterday and Today*, Cracow: Cracow Academy of Economics School Publications.

Scott, J.B. (1925) 'Introduction to Hugo Grotius', in H. Grotius (1646) *On the Law of War and Peace Three Books*, reprinted Oxford: Clarendon Press, 1925.

Scott, W.R. (1900) *Francis Hutcheson. His Life, Teaching and Position in the History of Philosophy*. Cambridge: The University Press.

—— (1937) *Adam Smith as a Student and Professor*. Glasgow: Jackson.

Simmons, W. (1933) *Introduction to Samuel Pufendorf's De jure naturae et gentium libri octo*. The translation of the edition of 1688 (with references to the first edition of 1672), New York: Oceana Publications, and London: Wiley and Sons.

Skinner, A. (1970) *Introduction to Adam Smith The Wealth of Nations Books I–III*, Harmondsworth: Penguin.

Smith, A. (1759) *The Theory of Moral Sentiments*. Glasgow, sixth edition (1790) D.D. Raphael and A.L. Macfie (eds), printed 1976 reprinted 1991, Oxford: Oxford University Press.

—— (1766) *Lectures on Jurisprudence, Report of 1762–3 and Report dated 1766 together with an Appendix containing the 'Early Draft' of the Wealth of Nations from the 1760s*, Meek, R.L., Raphael, D.D. and Stein, P.G. (eds), printed 1978 and reprinted 1987, Oxford: Clarendon Press.

—— (1776a) *An Inquiry into the Nature and Causes of the Wealth of Nations*. Edinburgh, 5th edn, 1789, Edwin Cannan (ed.) 1904, reprinted with an additional introduction by Max Lerner, New York: Random House, 1937.

—— (1776b) *An Inquiry into the Nature and Causes of The Wealth of Nations*. Edinburgh, 5th edn, 1789, Edwin Cannan (ed.) 1904, reprinted with a new preface by Stigler, G.J., Chicago: The University of Chicago Press, 1976.

Spiegel, H.W. (1983) *The Growth of Economic Thought*. Durham: Duke University Press.

Stein, P.B. (1982) 'From Pufendorf to Adam Smith: The Natural Law Tradition in Scotland', *Europäisches Rechtdenken in Geschickte und Gegenwart*, Festschrift für Helmut Coing,. Munich.

Stewart, D. (1793) *Account of the Life and Writings of Adam Smith*, LL.D. From the
    Transactions of the Royal Society of Edinburgh. An addition to Adam Smith
    Essay on Philosophical Subjects, Indianapolis 1982, I.S.Ross (ed.).
Stigler, G.J. (1976) 'New Preface to Adam Smith', in A. Smith (1776) *An Enquiry
    into the Nature and Causes of the Wealth of Nations*, 5th edn; reprinted Chicago: The
    University of Chicago Press, 1976.
Taylor, W.L. (1965) *Francis Hutcheson and David Hume as predecessors of Adam Smith*,
    Durham, North Carolina: Duke University Press.
Werhane, P.H. (1991) *Adam Smith and His Legacy for Modern Capitalism*, New York:
    Oxford University Press.
West, E.G. (1976) *Adam Smith The Man and His Works*. Indianapolis: Liberty Press.

4 Deconstructing the canonical view on Adam Smith

A new look at the principles of economics

Jan Peil[1]

Introduction

Canonical works in the history of economic thought (Schumpeter et al.) tend to picture Smith as an anticipator of (neo)classical economics. Recent developments in economics plus the discussion around the bicentenary, however, promote a new reading of Smith. In this paper the canonical view on Smith will also be challenged. It will be argued that a new reading of Smith's discourse on wealth, virtue and the commercial society is of relevance for today's rethinking of the principles of economics.

Contemporary schools of economic thought (e.g. new classicals, new Keynesians, post-Keynesians, neo- and new institutionalists, and (neo)-Austrians) show an uneasiness with conventional modern dichotomies such as the individual versus society, the market versus the state, positive versus normative economics, causal explanation versus historical *verstehen*. A new reading of Smith in a hermeneutical model of interpretation reveals that these dichotomies were no part of his frame of reference. So, in re-interpreting Smith we may find suggestions for new relational interpretations of the aforementioned twin concepts.

This paper on Smith and the principles of economics consists of four sections. The first section focuses on the question: why re-read Smith and according to what model of interpretation? The second section deconstructs the canonical interpretation of Smith's economic thought as a misinterpretation, because it is anachronistically framed in modern (neo)classical economics. The third section of the paper presents a new look at the principles of economics by reinterpreting Smith as a moral philosopher. Or more precisely, as a moral philosopher who was critical of the old doctrine that free, self-interested economic exchange was dangerous to the *bonum commune*, and whose views were also at odds with the new modern philosophies that explained wealth and its distribution by deduction from the behaviour of calculating atomistic individuals. The fourth section concludes this paper with a brief summary of the relevance of re-reading Smith for today's debate on the principles of economics.

Re-reading Adam Smith

Economists who look upon their science as a process of research and debate, progressing towards ever better knowledge of the basic economic laws, are probably puzzled as to how re-reading Smith may contribute to solving problems of present day economics. In the view of those economists Smith is history: he was important in founding economic science, but with the development of economic thought his work became obsolete in the nineteenth and twentieth century.

Of course, in comparison with publications in, say *The American Economic Review* or *The Journal of Political Economy*, Smith's *The Wealth of Nations* is outdated in terms of the technical skills used. This, however, does not mean that Smith's texts may not be of interest for discussions about principles. Today's Adam Smith renaissance offers proof to the contrary. Titles such as *The Market and The State*, *Wealth and Virtue* and *Markt, Staat und Solidarität* indicate that this new interest in Smith's work is inspired by the same issue on which economists have been severely divided since the 1960s: the relevance of the (neo)classical view of the production and distribution of wealth.[2]

There have been disputes about this issue before, but the present day crisis is singular in its kind. After the dispute in the 1960s and early 1970s on the relevance of the concept of the self-coordinating market economy, the subject of the dispute shifted with the decline of Keynesian economics in the late 1970s to its conventional (neo)classical interpretation.

A similar change can be observed in the reception of Adam Smith's work. Up to the 1970s Smith was celebrated and criticized as a founding father of modern economics because his *The Wealth of Nations* effected the breakthrough of the concept of the (free) market economy. For example, Schumpeter's *History of Economic Analysis*, the book of reference in the 1960s and 1970s, qualifies chapter vii of book I of *The Wealth of Nations* as *by far the best piece of economic theory turned out by A. Smith* because of its *rudimentary equilibrium theory* that *points towards Say and, through the latter's work, to Walras*.[3] In accordance with such an interpretation Smith was, until recently, generally referred to as a founding father whose work was outdated thanks to progress in the general equilibrium analysis.

However, the reception of Adam Smith's work has radically changed since the 1970s. In line with the change in the disputes on the principles of economics there is a re-interpretation of Smith going on. The conventional separation of Smith's economic analysis and his discourse on ethics and jurisprudence is under discussion. Questions have risen with respect to the conventional laissez-faire interpretation of Smith's view on economic policy, and – most important of all for an economist – with respect to the general equilibrium interpretation of Smith's concept of the self-coordinating market economy.

Economists who look upon economic science as a process that will progress continuously to ever better representations of the laws of economic life, are probably wondering at the noise about Smith and the decline of

Keynesian economics. Eliminating errors is a characteristic of sound science, they might say. Of course this is true, but is that really what is at stake in the Adam Smith re-interpretation and the disputes between schools of economic thought?

Economists of conflicting schools have criticized each other on concepts, logic and aim of research. However, the effects have mostly been cancelled out because they do not understand each other. They are talking in different frames of reference. When, for example, new classicals criticize (neo-) Austrians for lack of mathematical rigour in their analysis, it would be a mistake to see this as just a dispute about more or fewer mathematics in economics. It may be true that new classicals are well-trained in mathematics and that (neo-)Austrians lack even elementary mathematical skills. But a look at (neo-)Austrian economics will clearly show that it is their view on economic processes or more generally their *Weltanschauung* and not their incompetence with respect to mathematics that makes their economics different.[4]

A dispute like the one between the new classicals and the (neo-)Austrians is in the end a rivalry between different frames of reference. This view on disputes between schools differs radically from the traditional view of schools debating on the performance of theories in representing an objectivistically given economic world. In contrast to this positivistic view, in the present paper the rivalry between schools is viewed as a rivalry between different concepts of the economic world, produced by professionals – i.e. economists – on behalf of the existential need of man to give meaning to experience.

The model of interpreting Smith in this paper fits in this view of economic science and its periodical disputes on principles, i.e. the dialogue is the interpretation model of this paper. The aim of re-reading Smith is not to correct the old interpretation in the sense of getting nearer to the intrinsic meaning of his texts. Re-reading Smith according to the hermeneutical interpretation model of this paper means re-opening the dialogue with the author about the interpretation of ideas like the (free) market economy and the price mechanism.

In line with the new Smith literature this paper supports a re-introduction of Smith in the discussion of the conceptual framework of economics. As pointed out before, present day rivalry between schools of economic thought differs from crises earlier in the nineteenth and twentieth century. The conceptualization of the economy as a market economy is no longer a subject of dispute. Now the rivalry between schools of economic thought relates to differences in interpretation of that market economy. So it may be better not to talk of the crisis of vision *in* modern economic thought as Robert Heilbroner and William Milberg do, but of a crisis *of* modern economic thought.[5]

Heilbroner and Milberg are right when they say that in modern economic thought there is an absence of a set of widely shared political and social preconceptions after the collapse of the Keynesian view in the 1970s.[6] But there is more. Since the 1980s the crisis *in* modern economic thought has deteriorated to a crisis *of* modern economic thought.

In contrast to the disputes of the 1960s and 1970s the market economy is today the leading idea in almost every school of thought. However, discussions of hysteresis, ergodicity, rule-governed behaviour, rational expectations, systems of belief and institutions indicate a discontent with the modern dichotomies on which the conventional (neo)classical interpretation of the market economy is based.

In discussing these subjects, economists of various schools reflect an uneasiness with the antipodal interpretation of twin concepts, such as the individual versus society, the market versus the state, the economic system versus history, positive versus normative economics. This is very peculiar in comparison with earlier disputes.

In the 1960s and 1970s schools of economic thought were still divided along antipodes such as the individual versus society or the market versus the state. The disputes of the 1980s and 1990s about new interpretations of the market economy, however, reflect a struggle to overcome these traditional antipodal interpretations of basic economic concepts. This change may be called *a postmodern revolution in economics*, in accordance with similar trends in philosophy and other social sciences.[7]

Today's Smith renaissance distinguishes itself by the same interest for new relational interpretations of, for example, the autonomy of the individual or the influence of social values and institutions on the behaviour of the individual.[8] However, many an economist is still used to the modernistic reading of Smith, exemplified in Schumpeter's general equilibrium interpretation, the canonical interpretation of the last forty years. This means that the discussion about Smith and the principles of economics is hampered from more than one side. There is not only the problem of different interpretations, but also a more serious one: the discussants are using different models of interpretation.

Re-interpreting Smith and criticizing the canonical interpretation in a hermeneutical model of interpretation is easily misunderstood as an interpretation in the traditional modernistic model, especially when a critique of the traditional interpretation refers to Smith's intentions. These references are often misunderstood, as if the interpreter is still calling upon the author to certify his interpretation as the correct representation of the meaning of the text.

In the hermeneutical dialogue model an interpretation does not have the connotation of a representation of the author's intended meaning. Interpreting a text means producing a meaning in dialogue with the author. So, when in the next paragraph the dichotomies of the conventional interpretations are criticized with reference to Smith's intentions, these references call attention to the author's horizon.

In the hermeneutical model of interpretation re-reading Smith means re-opening the dialogue with Smith on the market economy and the price mechanism. Re-opening that dialogue means at the same time decanonizing the conventional interpretations of Smith.

One of the most compelling arguments for decanonizing an interpretation like Schumpeter's general equilibrium interpretation is that in such an interpretation Smith's oeuvre is full of contradictions and dichotomies. Many of them are as old as modern economics. Remember for instance Cliffe Leslie's discourse in the 1870s on the dichotomy between Smith's historical and mechanistic natural law approach.[9] Best-known, of course, are the discussions around the turn of the century of the so-called Adam Smith Problem, i.e. the contradiction between the altruistic view of man of *The Theory of Moral Sentiments* and the selfish view of man of *The Wealth of Nations*.[10]

These dichotomies and contradictions indicate, with reference to Smith's intentions concerning his texts, that interpretations like those of Cliffe Leslie and Schumpeter are misinterpretations. According to Smith, *The Theory of Moral Sentiments* and *The Wealth of Nations* should be read as parts of a comprehensive study of man and society. So general laws and historical evolutions for instance, are both part of his discourse.[11]

Such a reference to Smith, used as an argument to re-open the dialogue with Smith can, however, easily be misunderstood, as comment by Vivienne Brown on the 'Introduction' of the editors of *The Theory of Moral Sentiments* illustrates.

> The editors of TMS, . . . argue in their Introduction that TMS and WN must be consistent because the 'same man' wrote both works and because, in the [i.e. Smith's] Advertisement to the sixth edition of TMS, Smith's words may be understood to mean that he, Smith, conceived of his work as one single, albeit unfinished project. . . . But this kind of argument assumes that Smith's personality and his own understanding of his writings are definitive in interpreting the meanings of the texts and in assessing the overall structural thematicity of his works.[12]

At first sight a reference to Smith's intentions might suggest, as it did to Brown, that interpreting a text is erroneously understood as a search for the *originary meaning . . . bestowed there by the author*.[13] Is this the one and only interpretation of such a reference?

Brown supports a new reading of Smith in line with today's new awareness of the significance of rhetoric for reading and understanding a text. Referring to recent literature in the field of the philosophy of language Brown argues in favour of laying aside the traditional assumption that the author imbues the text with meaning and that close reading intends to reproduce that meaning. She proposes to see meaning as produced by reading.[14] We agree with this view on meaning without accepting that any reference to the author's own words about his texts is without meaning.

A written text naturally differs from spoken words in the sense that writing involves an 'emancipation' of the text from the author. But as there is no emancipation without marks of the hand that gave birth to the text, why ignore these marks?

Not only does the meaning of a text interpretation depends on the interpretation model, the same is true for the meaning of a reference to the author's intentions. If such references in the conventional modernistic model are used as corroborating evidence for an interpretation, such will not be the case in the hermeneutical model used in this paper. The remarks of Smith about *The Theory of Moral Sentiments* and *The Wealth of Nations* in the *Advertisement* will be interpreted as a serious appeal by the author to read these publications not as separate but as complementary texts.[15] The contrast between these remarks and the results of the conventional interpretations – e.g. The Adam Smith Problem – will be interpreted as an indication of an unperceived conflict between the author's and the reader's frame of reference.[16]

Brown proposes first to interpret each text separately, i.e. in its own terms, and only afterwards to comment on Smith's discourse as a whole by putting the separate readings together. Why should Smith's texts first be read separately, when the object is to read his *discourse on commercial society* as part of the contending discourses on the Enlightenment?[17] There is no such thing as the evidence of the text, neither with respect to the meaning nor with respect to the discursive frame of the text.

Reading Smith is a dialogue with Smith about the commercial society. So when Smith declares that his publications are integral parts of that discourse, we should not first interpret them separately in order to get a picture of the whole afterwards. Proper reading of Smith's discourse on the commercial society presupposes a reading of the parts – the texts – in relation to each other with reference to the whole, i.e. the discourse on the commercial society. We will only get a good picture of Smith's discourse, if we look at the various texts from the start in relation to that discourse.[18]

In this paper the phrase *referring to the author* will be interpreted according to Gadamer's view on hermeneutics: *Verstehen, die Kunst sich etwas sagen zu lassen.*[19] It expresses our recognition that interpreting a text is a play of two contexts or horizons: the context of the author and the context of the interpreter, i.e. contexts that fuse in a proper interpretation. When we speak of a deconstruction of the canonized interpretation of Adam Smith, we use that expression in a Gadamerian way too. This means that we want to re-open the dialogue with Smith to get, in an encounter with Smith, a richer understanding of our own commercial society, in particular its economy with its free market exchange.

Deconstructing the canonical view on Smith

Thanks to economists like Walras, Pareto, Debreu and Arrow we know that under certain conditions a situation of general equilibrium is feasible in a free market economy. The proof of the existence of general equilibrium was a milestone in modern economic analysis. It was the first time that economists delivered a systematic presentation of what could be achieved when people coordinate their economic behaviour by free market exchange. Adam Smith gave us a glimpse of this in his stories of the invisible hand. Not until general equilibrium analysts like Arrow and Debreu did so, could economists specify their ideas of the well-ordered market economy in a mathematical model.

There was a drawback to the great success of the general equilibrium analysts for those economists to whom economics is not just an academic game. The analysis explicated very clearly that the idea of a self-regulating market economy was inconceivable in the case of atomistic individuals, unless conditions of dubious realism prevailed. The results of the analysis with respect to the dynamics of that self-regulating economy were even more dramatic, for self-regulation appeared only to be conceivable in the absence of truly free exchange. That is, in the general equilibrium perspective the individual actors do not set the rules and terms of trade themselves in the process of exchange.

The analysis of the existence and dynamics of general equilibrium is not about an economy regulated by free exchange, for the individuals are not truly free with respect to action and motivation. In the models used, the individuals act like actors in a play. They are just playing the part the producer has arranged for them. In Walras' auction model the individuals have to play the part of buyer or seller at an auction. That is, they must act according to a priori rules, institutionalized in the figure of the auctioneer and the calculus of efficient rationality. In new classical models the players are still rational atomistic individuals, but the a priori rules of the external director – i.e. the auctioneer – are now replaced by a priori knowledge of the basic laws of the economy. The individual is supposed to act according to these laws because of the mechanism of rational expectations. So in all these models the conditions of general equilibrium, including the corresponding dynamics, are not only of dubious realism. They do not even reflect what it is all about in a real-world market economy. In other words, these models of general equilibrium analysis offer no understanding nor any explanation of the market economy as a possible and desirable project of the commercial society, i.e. a society founded in free commerce of its members.

With these results of the general equilibrium analysis in mind, it is remarkable that it was not until the end of the 1970s that a discussion arose on the interpretation of the concept of the market economy. In the 1960s and 1970s there was a heated dispute between several schools in favour or against the so-called neoclassical framework of economics. However, this did not affect mainstream economics, probably because of its loose adherence to the general equilibrium framework.

Since the end of the 1970s the situation has dramatically changed. After the echec of Keynesian macroeconomics and a revival of the traditional ideas of free market economy, there is now a growing awareness that the conventional neoclassical interpretation of the market economy, exemplified in the general equilibrium theory, is inadequate.[20] The debate on economic policy is no longer directed simply at deregulating the economy to restore free competition on markets. Policies of re-regulation are reflecting a new awareness of the relevance of rules and institutions in constituting a flourishing free market economy.

So today the concept of free market economy in itself is no longer a bone of contention. The disputes concerning the principles of economics are now about different interpretations of that concept. In such a context it is obvious that the conventional neoclassical interpretation of Smith's economics is also being put to the test.

As Tobin said before, Smith gave us the idea of the invisible hand but after the best minds of the profession such as Walras, Pareto, Hicks, Samuelson, Debreu and Arrow gave rigour and precision to it, we can no longer use this idea for its original purpose: understanding the self-regulating capacity of free commerce in real-world economies.[21] Tobin was right, this is bad news indeed about the modern general equilibrium version of the invisible hand.[22] But is it also bad news about Smith? What Tobin described as giving rigour and precision was at the same time an interpretation of the invisible hand. So any re-reading of Smith's oeuvre, motivated by doubt or discontent with respect to the modern version of the invisible hand idea, is at the same time an exercise in deconstructing the conventional modern interpretation of Smith as a misinterpretation.

The traditional way of interpreting Smith is to elucidate the meaning immanent to his texts with the hindsight of later developments in economic analysis. Schumpeter, to whom Tobin and other economists still refer, reads Smith in retrospect of the *magna charta of economics*: the Walrasian general equilibrium analysis.[23] The attention Schumpeter pays to other parts of Smith's oeuvre rather than the economic–theoretical ones is also a priori framed by the modern disciplinary view of economists on economic thought.

In Schumpeter's reading there is no hermeneutical wonder with respect to the author's horizon. Referring to the Walrasian general equilibrium theory Schumpeter declared:

> The rudimentary equilibrium theory of Chapter 7 [of *The Wealth of Nations*, book I], by far the best piece of economic theory turned out by A. Smith, in fact points toward Say and, through the latter's work,

to Walras. The purely theoretical developments of the nineteenth century consist to a considerable degree in improvements upon it.[24]

But is there any evidence that Smith's horizon is identical to that of a modern economist, exemplified by Say or Walras? No, on the contrary.

There are at least indications that Smith does not fit the framework of modern economics. The analysis of the market economy in both *The Theory of Moral Sentiments* and *The Wealth of Nations* is related to ethico-political theories of contemporary commercial societies. Smith's economic discourse is not yet separated from other discourses on man and society like modern economics from other social sciences on the one hand and public debates on economic policy on the other. The so-called self-interested man in *The Theory of Moral Sentiments* as well as in *The Wealth of Nations* is an individual *in* a society, who wants to exchange, to persuade, to be honoured. This means that he is not yet an atomistic actor driven by a rationalistic pain and pleasure calculus. Smith deals with the market economy as part of the historical evolution of European feudal societies into commercial societies. So Smith's theory about the market economy is not yet an ahistorical theory about universal laws concerning human economic behaviour.

Economists who read Smith as a modern economist, are confronted over and over again with another Smith who contradicts the image of the modern economist. For example: Smith who interprets economic situations and processes in historical perspective beside Smith who explains with reference to universal economic principles or laws, or Smith who interprets man and society from the sympathy-perspective beside Smith who explains the interaction on markets from the self-interest perspective.[25]

The conventional solution in such situations is earmarking such a contradiction as a dichotomy and choosing for that side of the dichotomy which most resembles the modern economic framework. This solution is, however, highly questionable. Why is it more reasonable to interpret Smith's economic thought as infant modern economics, suffering from growing pains, than to read him as an author whose frame of reference was different from that of nineteenth and twentieth century modern economists?

Of course, an advertisement of 1790, in which the author confirms a statement from 1759 that his publications are complementary, or in which he makes it clear again that general laws and history do not oppose each other, cannot be used as corroborating evidence against the Smith interpretation of modern economics.[26] But if we regard interpreting a text as a dialogue between the author and the reader, and if we consider Smith as a competent and honest partner in dialogue, we will not accept an interpretation such as the modern economic one, based without convincing argument on the assumption that the author mixed up various contradictory stories. Such an interpretation should be looked upon as nothing but a warning that the horizons of the author and interpreter do not go together.

A dialogue with Smith about the market economy leads to Babel when the economist–interpreter considers it a dialogue between modern economists. Nineteenth or twentieth century modern economics was not Smith's frame of reference. Smith was an eighteenth-century moral philosopher. This means that we should read his texts as a philosopher's contribution to the public discourse on the *bonum commune* in a world in which men no longer want to be patronized by church and king.

Like Hobbes, Pufendorf, Locke, Mandeville, Hutcheson, Hume and many other writers of the Enlightenment, Smith was participating in a discourse that reflected the sixteenth, seventeenth and eighteenth century struggle in Europe for free commerce by its urgency to understand, explain and explore the world with nothing but man's own faculties. It is with reference to that discourse – more precisely: with reference to his particular position in that discourse – that we have to read Smith, if we really want to understand his theory of the market economy.

Smith lectured and wrote successfully on many subjects of moral philosophy, but he became most famous for his analysis of the problems of wealth, self-interest and individual freedom in the perspective of self-regulating free commerce. Referring to the self-regulatory aspect of free commerce, Smith delivered the first systematic critique of the conventional Aristotelian–scholastic doctrine, according to which curtailment of self-love by moral or political law was a *conditio sine qua non* for a prosperous and peaceful, morally sound society.[27]

Smith's theory of the market economy shows how economic processes and relations could be understood as elements of an all-encompassing system of self-regulating markets. His concept of the market economy made it possible to think of free commerce as a mechanism which, in a situation of fair competition, stimulates and directs the self-interest of the individual actors to an unintended growth of the wealth of everyone. However, Smith's theory of the market economy was not only critical of the traditional defense of curtailments of free commerce. Smith criticized also the tendency in the new moral philosophy, still alive in today's mainstream economics, to analyse man and society against the background of an atomistic and rationalistic interpretation of man.[28]

This has never been fully recognized, perhaps because the readers of Smith's work missed the quintessence of his critique.[29] Ironically, Smith became a victim of what he himself exposed as *some confused misapprehension of the system of sympathy*.[30] *The Theory of Moral Sentiments* was, so to speak, a project intended to expose that misapprehension, to generate by dialogue a new understanding of *sympathy* and to re-interpret, explain, and evaluate the evolving commercial society as a system of (mutual) sympathy. *The Wealth of Nations* was, as Smith himself stressed repeatedly, an extension of that discourse to the tasks of the *statesman or legislator* with respect to *police, arms and revenue* in such a society.[31]

A reinterpretation of Smith's economic discourse

In the seventeenth and eighteenth century there was a tendency to interpret man as an atomistic individual. Man's thought and behaviour, including the societies man was part of, were explained by deduction from innate faculties or propensities.[32] As a scholar of the Scottish Enlightenment, Smith stressed the autonomy of the individual too. However, his interpretation of that autonomy differed profoundly from the atomistic interpretation of man. He himself stressed this most explicitly by his re-interpretation of *sympathy* in *The Theory of Moral Sentiments*.[33]

In all his texts – but most expressly in *The Theory of Moral Sentiments* – Smith applies the dialogical trope, usually in combination with examples from everyday life. A common explanation of this style is that Smith's publications are to a large extent transcriptions of lectures for students who were of the age of secondary schoolboys today.[34] According to this interpretation the dialogical style seems no more than a relic of the rhetorics Smith had used in his lectures to interest his pupils in the subject. The dialogical style may be of great help to a professor in kindling the interest of the audience, but only in situations suitable for that style. For, in contrast to the monologue, the dialogue is attuned to generating and legitimizing meaning and knowledge in the intersubjectivity of the communication with someone else. This idea – i.e. that meaning, systems of belief, and (self)consciousness are of an intersubjective, discursive nature – is central to Smith's oeuvre and in particular to his discourse on sympathy in *The Theory of Moral Sentiments*.

So the dialogical style of Smith's texts is more than a relic of his classes in Edinburgh or Glasgow. It reflects the view that understanding, explaining and exploring the world with nothing but man's own faculties has no foundation but the intersubjective concurrence of dialogical communication. In Smith's texts we may even find warnings against the illusion of modern science that there is an absolute truth, waiting out there in nature to be discovered by the faculty of reason or sense.[35] So Smith warns us, as it were, not to substitute the fallacy of the old absolute truth of the church and the king for a new fallacy of absolute truth discovered by philosophy or science.

As we said before, the dialogical style is used most expressly in *The Theory of Moral Sentiments*, particularly in the discourse on sympathy. That discourse is the most important part of *The Theory of Moral Sentiments*. Sympathy is the key concept of Smith's general theory of man and society, of which *The Wealth of Nations*'s theory of a self-regulating market economy is a special one, as it is about the economy of a commercial society. Smith even called his theory of man and society a *system of sympathy*.[36]

The discourse on sympathy in *The Theory of Moral Sentiments* is a dialogue between Smith and his readers to communicate the experience of an a priori longing for praiseworthiness in a context of values and beliefs shared in dialogue. Smith calls it *mutual sympathy*, knowing that his use of the notion *sympathy* differs from conventional interpretations.

> Pity and compassion are words appropriated to signify our fellow-feeling with the sorrow of others. Sympathy, though its meaning was, perhaps, originally the same, may now, however, without much impropriety, be made use of to denote our fellow-feeling with any passion whatever.[37]

At first sight it probably seems that Smith only broadens the meaning of the notion *sympathy*.[38] This is, however, not the case. In the opening lines of *The Theory of Moral Sentiments* Smith already indicates that it is a new interpretation in the context of a new view on man and society.

> How selfish soever man may be supposed, there are evidently some principles in his nature, which interest him in the fortune of others, and render their happiness necessary to him, though he derives nothing from it except the pleasure of seeing it.[39]

In his discussion of self-love, benevolence, self-command, self-interest, and utility Smith makes clear that he does not dispute the relevance but the conventional interpretation of such concepts in understanding and explaining human behaviour and social phenomena. Smith opposes the naturalistic model of knowledge according to which explaining individual behaviour or social phenomena is synonymous with tracing these explanations back to a priori known human faculties or propensities. In accordance with his re-interpretation of sympathy, Smith argues that the interpretation and explanatory use of concepts like self-love and benevolence are always related to the belief systems and social value patterns man lives in.

With his re-interpretation of sympathy in mind it is not difficult to imagine why Smith called his theory of moral philosophy: *system of sympathy*. Those of us who share Smith's re-interpretation of sympathy, experience an inclination to interpret and model the world as a system according to the principle of sympathy, as Smith did in his discourses on law, customs and fashion, utility and producing and distributing wealth.[40] Interpreting sympathy as an a priori need of man to share values and beliefs as well as to be respected in reference to these social patterns of values and beliefs, goes hand in hand with modelling the world as a system of overlapping communication patterns, which structures life but exists only 'virtually' in the process of persons acting individually.

Smith's re-interpretation of sympathy and the corresponding 'system of sympathy' does not just marginally differ from the trend in new philosophy. Smith's approach is truly different and special: it meets the common daily life experience that an individual is always an individual in relation to a society.[41] The sympathy approach does not force the interpreter of individual behaviour or social phenomena to choose between the well-known opposing methodological assumptions: methodological individualism versus methodological collectivism. Instead of arguing for the methodological device of deducing social phenomena from the behaviour of individuals, or vice versa, Smith's sympathy approach points to a third way beyond that modern framework of perceiving the world in dividing contrasts.

Smith's sympathy approach is a sort of refusal to look at the individual as an isolated or atomistic individual who contrasts with society, interpreted as an entity of his own. He also did not break with the premodern tradition of perceiving the individual in relation to his society. Smith gave the relational approach a new interpretation. In combination with his reinterpretation of sympathy the individual and society became two sides of what we called earlier the intersubjective concurrence of dialogical communication.

In Smith's view, man is – in his longing for praiseworthiness – constantly engaged in real or imaginary processes of dialogical communication, in which common values and beliefs are created, refuted or confirmed. That is, in Smith's sympathy approach the behaviour of the individual and social phenomena, such as conventions, rules, laws, and other institutions, are both manifestations of the processes of dialogical communication, focused on sympathy.

So Smith points to the relevance of social communication patterns in explaining both the behaviour of the individual and social phenomena. It is by means of this that he suggests interpreting the behaviour of the individual and the social order by analogy with language. Initially, on the one hand the individual is guided by the language pattern (the language speaks in me), but on the other hand the individual gives just as much shape 'later' to this language by speaking the language in his own way.[42]

In Smith's well-known metaphor of the *invisible hand* this view of man and society is expressed most concisely. However, that notion is misinterpreted just like Smith's *system of sympathy*. Whereas Smith used the notion of the *invisible hand* to indicate that free commerce is well-ordered because of the social communication patterns in which the plans and actors are embedded, that same notion became synonymous with the mechanistically and naturalistically interpreted price mechanism of (neo)classical economics.

The contrast with Smith's view of the auto-coordination of the market economy becomes even more distinct when the difference in interpretation of utility is taken into consideration. In economics the notion *utility* refers to the satisfaction of needs which an individual expects from the use of a certain commodity. It indicates a quality of a strictly subjective nature according to the proverb *de gustibus non disputandum*. From Smith's perspective this interpretation is a misinterpretation because it distracts from what people commonly experience in wanting conveniences, wealth or prestige: a longing for praise(worthiness) in the context of shared beliefs and values.

Smith devoted a special part of *The Theory of Moral Sentiments* to discussing the meaning of *utility*, or more precisely *The Effect of Utility upon the Sentiment of Approbation*.[43] In a nutshell Smith wants to make two points. The first point is – in Smith's own words –

> ... That the fitness of any system or machine to produce the end for which it was intended, bestows a certain propriety and beauty upon the whole, and renders the very thought and contemplation of it agreeable, is so very obvious that nobody has overlooked it. ... But that this fitness, this happy contrivance of any production of art, should often be more valued, than the very end for which it was intended; and that the exact adjustment of the means for attaining any conveniency or pleasure, should frequently be more regarded, than that very conveniency or pleasure, in the attainment of which their whole merit would seem to consist, has not, so far as I know, been yet taken notice of by any body. That this however is very frequently the case, may be observed in a thousand instances, both in the most frivolous and in the most important concerns of human life.[44]

The second point Smith wants to make, is that it is not the exact adjustment as such which motivates mankind

> to cultivate the ground, to build houses, to found cities and commonwealths, and to invent and improve all the sciences and arts, which ennoble and embellish human.[45]

It is the expected admiration or sympathy of his fellow-men for the exact adjustment which motivates the individual to take part in the

> race for wealth, honours, and preferments, [to] run as hard as he can, [to] strain every nerve and every muscle, in order to outstrip all his competitors ... in fair play.[46]

So wealth, honour and preferments as well as the way they are attained, are in Smith's interpretation not the effect of rationalistic calculations by the subjects to gain ease or pleasure and to avoid discomfort or pain.[47] Smith even warns against such an interpretation of human behaviour.[48] According to his sympathy approach behaviour, even acting from self-interest reflects the values of society, interpreted by the actor in his own personal way. It is because of these social value patterns that we can expect good offices for instance from the butcher and the baker. They do not offer meat and bread because of some benevolence, Smith argues in *The Wealth of Nations*, but because we as the demanders persuade them to behave in that way by reference to these value patterns.[49]

Now it is also easy to understand that Smith's discourse on natural and market prices is no invitation to conceive economics as a mechanics of self-interest.[50] It is no longer necessary to refer to nineteenth or twentieth century economic theories, in particular the Walrasian general equilibrium theory, in order to make sense of this discourse on self-coordination in real-world market economies. As soon as it has been acknowledged that Smith's frame of reference was different from that of later modern (neo)classical economics, the traditional problems of economists with Smith's texts disappear. Remarks on supposed contradictions in the discourse or other weaknesses, characteristic to theories *in statu nascendi*, are out of order.

Smith's theory of natural prices and market prices is about real-world economies. In accordance with real economic life Smith discusses prices as part of a social–economic order that is organized and functions as a communication pattern in a way similar to the language pattern. The pattern as a system of rules exists only 'virtually' in the process of persons acting individually. Real market prices are 'oscillating' around the natural – i.e. normal – prices, because in the perspective of sympathy individual behaviour is not rigid 'law-governed' behaviour but flexible 'rule-governed' behaviour, that demands a personal (self-interested) interpretation of these rules.

The notion *natural prices* refers to the normal – i.e. guiding – values of the economic process. As a participant in the economic process the individual is so 'familiar' with these values that he acts accordingly by his 'own' will and on his 'own' initiative. So, the real market prices are continuously moving up and down as if gravitating towards some 'average', which is known as the normal or the natural value.[51]

It is important to notice that the analogy of gravitation is used here in the sense of an *analogia proportionalitatis*. That is, in the perspective of man's longing for praiseworthiness – i.e. the principle of sympathy – the market prices fluctuate 'similarly' to the movement of bodies seen in the perspective of the principle of gravitation. Economists misinterpreted the gravitation analogy as an *analogia proportionis* when they took the analogy as an encouragement to conceive economics, in the words of Jevons, as a *mechanics of self-interest*.[52]

This, however, does not mean that Smith was averse to any attempt to present the production and distribution of wealth as a system. The opposite is true, as both *The Theory of Moral Sentiments* and *The Wealth of Nations* abundantly show.[53] Smith's interpretation of the notion 'system' was, however, profoundly different from the objectivistic interpretation by later economists. Smith even had a totally different view on philosophy or science than the ideas economists would adhere to in the nineteenth and twentieth century.

Smith did not discuss systems or theories as representations of the basic structure of an objectivistically perceived world, as economists did after Smith. In an unpublished early manuscript, usually called *History of Astronomy*, Smith deals with philosophy or science in the perspective of man's existential need to give meaning to experiences and phenomena.[54] Philosophy or science is interpreted as a product in accordance with that need experienced in a context of prosperity, order and, above all, trust in man's power to control life and environment. *Systems* or *theories*, scientific or not, are discussed as systems of belief, reflecting the need of people to understand the world as a well-ordered system according to the experience in prosperous and well-organized societies that man has control over his world.[55]

This interpretation of *system* or *theory* in combination with the discussions of the nature and causes of wealth in *The Theory of Moral Sentiments* and *The Wealth of Nations* indicates that (neo)classical economists did not develop the economic science Smith had in mind. In Smith's interpretation of philosophy and science the object of economics is not to reveal the basic structure of an objectivistically perceived economic world. The object in Smith's frame of reference is to contribute in a professional way to the discourse on understanding the social processes of producing and distributing wealth as a well-ordered meaningful system. Interpreted in that way, economics is neither positive nor normative economics in the conventional sense.

Economic systems of theories, in Smith's sense, are of relevance in guiding man in the real processes of producing and distributing wealth in society.[56] So they also have to be evaluated with respect to that relevancy. In particular with respect to that relevancy, *The Wealth of Nations* criticizes two systems of political economy influential in Smith's day.[57] According to Smith, neither system – i.e. the mercantile and the agricultural system – was suited to an adequate understanding of the economic revolutions of the contemporaneous commercial societies.

Smith criticized both systems with reference to his own system: the self-regulating market economy. Both the mercantile system and the agricultural system impeded a proper discussion of producing and distributing wealth in the context of a commercial society, because their organizing principles did not coincide with the principle of an encompassing commercial society. In Smith's perspective of sympathy the commercial society is a system in which the individuals are free to act according to their personal (self-interested) interpretation of the value pattern of their society. So an economic system that did not reflect in all respects that *natural system of perfect liberty and justice*, hampered the discussion about the production and distribution of wealth in a commercial society.[58]

Smith emphasized, however, that this so-called *natural system of perfect liberty and justice* had to be interpreted as a *utopia*, as a normative frame of reference in understanding and transforming the real market economy towards a market economy that is regulated by an unobstructed concurrence of individuals longing for mutual sympathy.[59] According to Smith, this means a transformation sustained by contemporary opinions and values. A withdrawal of old institutional impediments to a free market exchange is only allowed when society is ready for it.

In Smith's view a government should be severely criticized if it tried to enforce the transformation to the free market economy, ignoring the values and beliefs of society in this respect.[60] On the other hand he also indicates that a market economy only functions properly when the economy does not systematically exclude or hinder individuals from participating in society's game of sympathy.[61] A government policy that is not directed towards social cohesion and inclusion distorts the production and distribution of wealth, because it can endanger society and human identity.

This warning concerns in particular the commercial society and its market economy, as their institutional arrangements are ever more accommodated to a direct regulation of man's life and society by the games of sympathy. Notice Smith's stress on the need for an exact administration of justice, since without that exact administration the games of sympathy will be frustrated and, with it, society will *crumble into atoms*. Furthermore it is important to note that Smith indicates in both *The Theory of Moral Sentiments* and *The Wealth of Nations* that a prospering society can only endure when people are fit to participate in the games of sympathy. This does not only concern the competence to play but also the expectations of the players about the results.[62]

A new look at today's debate on the principles of economics

Re-reading Adam Smith in a hermeneutical interpretation model deconstructs the canonical interpretation of *The Wealth of Nations* as a misinterpretation. Re-constructing Smith's frame of reference in a hermeneutical way as *premodern/modern* and our contemporary frame as *modern/postmodern* reveals the interpretation of an author like Schumpeter as an inadequate modernistic one.

The Wealth of Nations was Smith's contribution to the discourse on wealth in the emerging commercial societies in eighteenth-century Western Europe. According to Smith the production and distribution of wealth is self-regulating for the benefit of everyone involved, when the individual actors are free to compete fairly and when accompanied by concurrence in the patterns of behaviour. Smith criticizes every curtailment of self-interest beyond the basic rules of justice and fairness, but his interpretation of self-interest, justice and fairness refers to the *individual in society* and not to the atomistic *economic man* of nineteenth and twentieth century economics.

Smith conceptualizes the production and distribution of wealth as a self-regulating system of interrelated markets. However, his interpretation of this system and its principle of regulation differs profoundly from the modernistic interpretation of nineteenth and twentieth century economics. In Smith's interpretation there is not yet an opposition between the individual and society, between market and government, between positive and normative economics, between the system approach and historical interpretations of economic phenomena. In Smith's perspective the individual, for example, is just an individual in relation to his society.

This reinterpretation of Smith's economic thought sheds new light on the recurrent debate on the principles of economics. It supports today's change from disputing the principles without discussing the accompanying modernistic frame of reference to reinterpreting the principles according to today's growing uneasiness with that framework. From Smith's point of view economics is a science and as such a very important part of the social discourse on meaningful systems of producing and distributing wealth.

The Wealth of Nations was Smith's contribution to the search for a new understanding of the production and distribution of wealth in evolving commercial societies. Consistent with his *system of sympathy* Smith was an advocate of the free market economy, because such a system is best accommodated to the basics of a truly human life, i.e. to live a free life in society in accordance with the a priori longing for praiseworthiness of one's fellowmen. Much new research on Smith and economics has been done in the last twenty years, but re-thinking economics in Smith's sympathy perspective has begun only recently.

Notes

1 I would like to thank Martin Plattel for the stimulating conversations on modernism and hermeneutics, and Gerhard Clever, Harry Garretsen and Michalis Psalidopoulos for comments on an earlier version of this paper. Any errors remain my own responsibility. In this paper all references to Smith's work are based on *The Glasgow Edition of the Works and Correspondence of Adam Smith*, Oxford.
2 Wilson, T. and A. Skinner (eds), *The Market and The State, Essays in Honour of Adam Smith*, Oxford, 1976; Hont, I. and M. Ignatieff (eds), *Wealth and Virtue. The Shaping of Political Economy in the Scottish Enlightenment*, Cambridge, 1983; Kaufmann, F.X. and F.G. Krüsselberg (eds), *Markt, Staat und Solidarität bei Adam Smith*, Frankfurt am Main, 1981. Also Trapp, M., *Adam Smith – politische Philosophie, und politische Ökonomie*, Göttingen, 1987; Werhane, P.H., *Adam Smith and His Legacy for Modern Capitalism*, Oxford, 1991; or Muller, J.Z., *Adam Smith in his Time and Ours: Designing the Decent Society*, New York, 1993.
3 Schumpeter, J., *History of Economic Analysis*, New York, 1954, p. 189.
4 Cf. Hoover, K.D., 'An Austrian Revival', in *The New Classical Macroeconomics. A Sceptical Inquiry*, Aldershot, 1992, pp. 231–57.
5 Heilbroner, R. and W. Milberg, *The Crisis of Vision in Modern Economic Thought*, Cambridge, 1995.

6 Ibid., pp. 68–96.
7 See for example Appleby, J. et al. (eds), 'Postmodernist Thought' and 'Responding to Postmodernism', in *Knowledge and Postmodernity in Historical Perspective*, New York, 1996, pp. 385–554.
8 See for example Young, J.T., 'Natural Price and the Impartial Spectator: A New Perspective on Adam Smith as a Social Economist', *International Journal of Social Economics*, 1985(12), pp. 118–33; Werhane, P.H., *Adam Smith and His Legacy for Modern Capitalism*, Oxford, 1991; or Muller, J.Z., *Adam Smith in his Time and Ours: Designing the Decent Society*, New York, 1993.
9 Leslie, T.E. Cliffe, 'The Political Economy of Adam Smith'. *Fortnightly Review*, November 1870, also published in Leslie, T.E. Cliffe, *Essays in Political and Moral Philosophy*, London, 1879, pp. 216–42.
10 See for example Morrow, G.R., *The Ethical and Economic Theories of Adam Smith. A Study in the Social Philosophy of the 18th Century*, New York, 1923/1973 and 'Introduction' in Raphael, D.D. and A.L. Macfie (eds), *The Theory of Moral Sentiments*, Oxford, 1976/1991, pp. 20–25.

11 In the last paragraph of the first Edition of the present work, I said, that I should in another discourse endeavour to give an account of the general principles of law and government, and of the different revolutions which they had undergone in the different ages and periods of society; not only in what concerns justice, but in what concerns police, revenue, and arms, and whatever else is the object of law.

(*The Theory of Moral Sentiments*, Advertisement, p. 3)

12 Brown, V., *Adam Smith's Discourse: Canonicity, Commerce and Conscience*, London, 1994, p. 20.
13 Ibid., pp. 12–13.
14 Ibid., p. 5.

15 In the last paragraph of the first Edition of the present work, I said, that I should in another discourse endeavour to give an account of … In the *Enquiry concerning the Nature and Causes of the Wealth of Nations*, I have executed this promise; at least so far as concerns police, revenue, and arms. What remains, the theory of jurisprudence, which I have long projected, I have hitherto been hindered from executing, by the same occupations which had till now prevented me from revising the present work. Though my very advanced age leaves me, I acknowledge, very little expectation of ever being able to execute this great work to my satisfaction; …, I have allowed the paragraph to remain as it was published more than thirty years ago, when I entertained no doubt of being able to execute every thing which it announced.

(*The Theory of Moral Sentiments*, Advertisement, p. 3)

16 When in earlier publications we called The *Adam Smith Problem* a 'pseudo-problem', by that expression we meant that it is a problem created by the readers themselves, when they read Smith's texts in a context, different from Smith's own context, in the belief that they were just elucidating the meaning immanent to these texts. See for example Peil, J., 'A New Look at Adam Smith', *International Journal of Social Economics*, 1989 (16), pp. 52–72, reprinted in Blaug, M. (ed.), *Adam Smith (1723–1790), Pioneers in Economics*, part II, Aldershot, 1991, pp. 279–99.
17 Brown, V., *Adam Smith's Discourse: Canonicity, Commerce and Conscience*, London, 1994, p. 20.

18 See also Peil, J., 'A New Look at Adam Smith', *International Journal of Social Economics*, 1989 (16), pp. 52–72, and *Adam Smith. A Reconstruction of His Economic Thought*, Research Memorandum 8802, Economic Institute KUN, Nijmegen, 1988.

19 Safranski, R., *Hans-Georg Gadamer erzählt die Geschichte der Philosophie, part 6: Verstehen. Die Kunst sich etwas sagen zu lassen*, Köln/Rome, 1996.

20 Remember, for example, the discussions about fix or flex prices and about rules or discretion, or look at today's discussions about institutions and systems of belief in market economies.

21 Tobin, J., 'Theoretical Issues in Macroeconomics', in Feiwel, G.R. (ed.), *Issues in Contemporary Macroeconomics and Distribution*, London, 1985, pp. 105–106.

22 Ibid.

23 Schumpeter, J., *History of Economic Analysis*, New York, 1954, pp. 242 en 827.

24 Ibid., p. 189.

25 For example, Seligman, B.B., 'Philosophical Perspectives in Economic Thought', in Samuels, W.J. (ed.), *The Methodology of Economic Thought*, New Brunswick, 1980, pp. 245–68; and Clark, Ch. M.A., 'Adam Smith and Society as an Evolutionary Process', *Journal of Economic Issues*, 1989 (24), pp. 825–44. See also Schumpeter, J., *History of Economic Analysis*, New York, 1954; and Hutchison, T.W., '*Positive Economics' and Policy Objectives*, London, 1964, concerning the so-called problematic relation between Smith's positive and normative economics.

26 See notes 11 and 15.

27 Even Schumpeter, whose opinion was that *The Wealth of Nations* did not contain any really novel ideas, recognized the importance of Smith's *mastering the unwieldy material that flowed from many sources and . . . subjecting it, with a strong hand, to the rule of a small number of coherent principles: the builder who built solidly, regardless of cost, was also a great architect.* Schumpeter, J., *History of Economic Analysis*, New York, 1954, p. 185.

28 For instance *The Theory of Moral Sentiments* I.i.1–2, II.ii.3.5, VII.1.1–4, VII.iii.2.5–9, VII.iii.3.4, *The Wealth of Nations* I.ii.1–2, *Lectures on Jurisprudence*, Report of 1762–1763 (LJ(A)) vi.56 and LJ(B) 221–2.

29 Even scholars like Morrow, Macfie and Skinner who have always stressed that Smith's view on man was truly different from the conventional atomistic and rationalistic view on man in economics, have neglected to re-interpret Smith's theory of the market economy in the light of that different view on man. See for instance Morrow, G., *The Ethical and Economical Theories of Adam Smith. A Study in the Social Philosophy of the 18th Century*, New York, 1923/1973; 'Adam Smith: Moralist and Philosopher' in Clark, J.M. (ed.), *Adam Smith, 1776–1926: Lectures to Commemorate the Sesquicentennial of the Publication of 'The Wealth of Nations'*, Chicago, 1928, New York, 1966, pp. 156–79; Macfie, A.L., *The Individual in Society. Papers on Adam Smith*, London, 1967, 'Introduction' in Raphael, D.D. and A.L., Macfie (eds), *The Theory of Moral Sentiments*, Oxford, 1976/1991, pp. 1–52; Skinner, A., *A System of Social Science: Papers Relating to Adam Smith*, Oxford, 1979; 'Adam Smith' in Eatwell, J., Milgate, M. and P. Newman (eds), 'The Invisible Hand', *The New Palgrave*, London, 1987/1989, pp. 1–42.

30   That whole account of human nature, . . ., which deduces all sentiments and affections from self-love, which had so much noise in the world, but which, so far as I know, has never yet been fully and distinctly explained, seems to me to have arisen from some confused misapprehension of the system of sympathy.

(*The Theory of Moral Sentiments* VII.iii.4)

31 *The Theory of Moral Sentiments*, *Advertisement* and *The Wealth of Nations* IV.1–2.

32 For a brief outline see for example Myers, M.L., *The Soul of Modern Economic Man. Ideas of Self-Interest. Thomas Hobbes to Adam Smith*, Chicago, 1983.
33 *The Theory of Moral Sentiments* I and VII, especially *The Theory of Moral Sentiments* I.i.1.5, VII.iii.1.4, VII.iii.2.8–9 and VII.iii.3.
34 See for example 'Introduction' in Raphael, D. and A. Macfie (eds), *The Theory of Moral Sentiments*, Oxford, 1976/1991, pp. 4–5.
35 For example *Essays on Philosophical Subjects* Astronomy, IV.67 and IV.76.
36 For instance *The Theory of Moral Sentiments* VII.iii.1.4 and VII.iii.8–17.
37 *The Theory of Moral Sentiments* I.i.1.5.
38 Cf. the editors' comment on *The Theory of Moral Sentiments* I.i.5 in the *Glasgow Edition*: Smith's unusually wide definition of 'sympathy' needs to be noted because some scholars, more familiar with his economics than with his moral philosophy, have mistakenly equated sympathy with benevolence and have inferred that *The Theory of Moral Sentiments* deals with the altruistic side of human conduct and *The Wealth of Nations* with its egoistic side.
39 *The Theory of Moral Sentiments* I.i.1.1.
40 *The Theory of Moral Sentiments* II.iii, IV.1–2 and V.1–2.
41 See for example *The Theory of Moral Sentiments* III.1.3 and *The Theory of Moral Sentiments* IV.2.12. Macfie already stressed that the individual in Smith's view on man and society is not an atomistic individual but an individual in society. One of his most important publications on Smith is even called *The Individual in Society. Papers on Adam Smith*, London, 1967.
42 See also Peil, J., 'Is it all in Adam Smith?', *Working Paper 8701*, Institute of Economics, Nijmegen, 1987.
43 *The Theory of Moral Sentiments* IV.
44 *The Theory of Moral Sentiments* IV.1.1 and IV.1.3.
45 *The Theory of Moral Sentiments* IV.1.10.
46 *The Theory of Moral Sentiments* II.ii.2.2.
47 *The Theory of Moral Sentiments* IV.1.8 and IV.2.3.
48 For example *The Theory of Moral Sentiments* VII.iii.1.1–4 and VII.2.1–7.

49   It is not from the benevolence of the butcher, the brewer, or the baker, that we expect our dinner, but from their regard to their own self-interest. We address ourselves, not to their humanity but to their self-love, and never talk to them of our own necessities but of their advantages.

                                                              (*The Wealth of Nations* I.ii.2)

50 For example Letwin, W., *The Origins of Scientific Economics*, London, 1963, p. 225: It was Smith who taught Bastiat to speak of the 'social mechanism', Cairnes to analyse Ricardo's work as an exercise in mechanistic explanation, and Jevons to describe the science of economics as the 'mechanics of self-interest'.

51   The natural price, . . ., is, as it were, the central price, to which the prices of all commodities are continually gravitating. Different accidents may sometimes keep them suspended a good deal above it, and sometimes force them down even somewhat below it. But whatever may be the obstacles which hinder them from settling in this center of repose and continuance, they are constantly tending towards it.

                                                              (*The Wealth of Nations* I.vii.15)

        There is in every society or neighbourhood an ordinary or average rate both of wages and profit in every different employment of labour and stock. This rate is naturally regulated, partly by the general circumstances of the society, their riches or poverty, their advancing, stationary, or declining condition; and partly by the particular nature of each employment.

There is likewise in every society or neighbourhood an ordinary or average rate of rent, which is regulated too, . . ., partly by . . ., and partly by . . .

These ordinary or average rates may be called the natural rates of wages, profit, and rent, at time and place in which they commonly prevail.

When the price of any commodity is neither more nor less than what is sufficient to pay the rent of the land, the wages of the labour, and the profits of the stock employed in raising, preparing, and bringing it to market, according to their natural rates, the commodity is then sold for what may be called its natural price.

(*The Wealth of Nations* I.vii.1–4)

52 See note 50.
53 For example *The Theory of Moral Sentiments* VII.iii.1.4, VII.iii.3.13 and *The Wealth of Nations* IV.vii.c44 and IV.ix.51.
54 The unabridged title of the manuscript which Smith did not want to be destroyed after his death, is *The Principles Which Lead and Direct Philosophical Enquiries; illustrated by the History of Astronomy.*
55 *Essays on Philosophical Subjects* Astronomy, Intro, I, II, and III, especially II.7–12 and III.1–5. See also *The Theory of Moral Sentiments* V.2.9.
56 *The Theory of Moral Sentiments* IV.1.11, *The Theory of Moral Sentiments* VII.iii.1.2 and *The Wealth of Nations* IV.Intro.1–2, *The Wealth of Nations* V.i.g.14.
57 *The Wealth of Nations* IV.
58 With respect to the *natural system of perfect liberty and justice* see *The Wealth of Nations* IV.vii.c.44, IV.ix.17 and IV.ix.51.
59 For example *The Wealth of Nations* IV.ii.43.
60 See for example *The Theory of Moral Sentiments* VI.ii.2.16.
61 For example *The Theory of Moral Sentiments* I.iii.2.8, *The Theory of Moral Sentiments* II.ii.1.8, *The Theory of Moral Sentiments* II.ii.3.4.
62 *The Theory of Moral Sentiments* I.iii.2.1, *The Theory of Moral Sentiments* I.iii.2.8, *The Wealth of Nations* V.i.g.12 and *The Wealth of Nations* V.i.f.48–61.

References

(a) The Glasgow Edition of the Works and Correspondence of Adam Smith

Bryce, J. (ed.) (1983) *Lectures on Rhetoric and Belles Lettres*, Oxford.
Campbell, R., Skinner, A. and Todd, W. (eds) (1976/1979) *An Inquiry into the Nature and Causes of the Wealth of Nations*, Oxford.
Meek, R., Raphael, D. and Stein, P. (eds) (1978/1987) *Lectures on Jurisprudence*, Oxford.
Mossner, E. and Ross, I. (eds) (1987) *Correspondence of Adam Smith*, Oxford.
Raphael, D. and Macfie, A. (eds) *The Theory of Moral Sentiments*, Oxford, 1976/1991.
Skinner, A. and Wilson, T. (eds) (1975) *Essays on Adam Smith*, Oxford.
Wightman, P., Bryce, J. and Ross, I. (eds) (1980) *Essays on Philosophical Subjects*, Oxford.

(b) Secondary sources

Appleby, J. et al. (eds) (1996) 'Postmodernist Thought' and 'Responding to Post-modernism', *Knowledge and Postmodernity in Historical Perspective*, New York.

Brown, V. (1994) *Adam Smith's Discourse: Canonicity, Commerce and Conscience*, London.

Clark, Ch.M.A. (1989) 'Adam Smith and Society as an Evolutionary Process', *Journal of Economic Issues*, vol. 24, pp. 825–44.

Heilbroner, R. and Milberg, W. (1995) *The Crisis of Vision in Modern Economic Thought*, Cambridge.

Hont, I. and Ignatieff, M. (eds) (1983) *Wealth and Virtue. The Shaping of Political Economy in the Scottish Enlightenment*, Cambridge.

Hoover, K.D. (1992) *The New Classical Macroeconomics. A Sceptical Inquiry*, Aldershot.

Hutchison, T.W. (1964) *'Positive Economics' and Policy Objectives*, London.

Kaufmann, F.X. and Krüsselberg, F.G. (eds) (1981) *Markt, Staat und Solidarität bei Adam Smith*, Frankfurt am Main.

Leslie, T.E. Cliffe (1879) 'The Political Economy of Adam Smith', *Fortnightly Review*, November 1870, in Leslie, T.E. Cliffe, *Essays in Political and Moral Philosophy*, London.

Letwin, W. (1963) *The Origins of Scientific Economics*, London, 1963.

Macfie, A.L. (1967) *The Individual in Society. Papers on Adam Smith*, London.

Morrow, G. (1966) 'Adam Smith: Moralist and Philosopher' in Clark, J.M. (ed.), *Adam Smith, 1776–1926: Lectures to Commemorate the Sesquicentennial of the Publication of 'The Wealth of Nations'*, Chicago, 1928, New York, pp. 156–79.

Morrow, G.R. (1923/1973) *The Ethical and Economic Theories of Adam Smith. A Study in the Social Philosophy of the 18th Century*, New York.

Muller, J.Z. (1993) *Adam Smith in his Time and Ours: Designing the Decent Society*, New York.

Myers, M.L. (1983) *The Soul of Modern Economic Man. Ideas of Self-Interest. From Thomas Hobbes to Adam Smith*, Chicago.

Peil, J. (1987) 'Is it all in Adam Smith?', *Working Paper 8701*, Institute of Economics, Nijmegen.

—— (1988) *Adam Smith. A Reconstruction of His Economic Thought*, Research Memor-andum 8802, Institute of Economics KUN, Nijmegen.

—— (1991) 'A New Look at Adam Smith', *International Journal of Social Economics*, 1989, vol. 16, pp. 52–72, reprinted in Blaug, M. (ed.), *Adam Smith (1723–1790)*, Pioneers in Economics, part II, Aldershot, pp. 279–99.

—— (1995) *Adam Smith en de economische wetenschap: een methodologische herinterpretatie*, Tilburg.

Recktenwald, H. (1978) 'An Adam Smith Renaissance *anno* 1976? The Bicentenary Output – A Reappraisal of His Scholarship', *Journal of Economic Literature*, vol. 16, pp. 56–83.

Safranski, R. (1996) *Hans-Georg Gadamer erzählt die Geschichte der Philosophie, part 6: Verstehen. Die Kunst sich etwas sagen zu lassen*, Köln/Rome.

Schumpeter, J. (1954) *History of Economic Analysis*, New York.

Seligman, B.B. (1980) 'Philosophical Perspectives in Economic Thought', in Samuels, W.J. (ed.), *The Methodology of Economic Thought*, New Brunswick, pp. 245–68.

Silverman, H. (1991) 'Gadamer and Hermeneutics', *Continental Philosophy IV*, New York.

Skinner, A. (1979) *A System of Social Science: Papers Relating to Adam Smith*, Oxford.

Skinner, A. (1987/1989) 'Adam Smith', in Eatwell, J., Milgate, M. and Newman, P. (eds), 'The Invisible Hand', *The New Palgrave*, London, pp. 1–42.

Tobin, J. (1985) 'Theoretical Issues in Macroeconomics', in Feiwel, G.R. (ed.), *Issues in Contemporary Macroeconomics and Distribution*, London, pp. 105–6.

Trapp, M. (1987) *Adam Smith – politische Philosophie, und politische Ökonomie*, Göttingen.

Werhane, P.H. (1991) *Adam Smith and His Legacy for Modern Capitalism*, Oxford.

Wilson, T. and Skinner A. (eds) (1976) *The Market and The State, Essays in Honour of Adam Smith*, Oxford.

Young, J.T. (1985) 'Natural Price and the Impartial Spectator: A New Perspective on Adam Smith as a Social Economist', *International Journal of Social Economics*, vol. 12, pp. 118–33.

5 The 'canonical' model of economic growth in the debate between Ricardo and Malthus

*Terenzio Maccabelli**

Introduction

This paper tries to address the question of 'canon' from the point of view of 'growth economics'. As we know, in the history of economic analysis the genesis of the growth theory is usually associated with the name of Roy Harrod. From his work of 1939, 'An Essay in Dynamic Theory', stems the modern concept of growth (Backhouse 1985: 318), despite the initial terminological hesitation between 'dynamic', 'development', 'progress' or 'growth' (Schumpeter 1986: 1160). As I shall try to argue later, growth models developed after Harrod's seminal contribution were eventually incorporated within a sort of 'canon' of growth, at least for some important common features that seem to be widely accepted. The differences between neo-Classical, Keynesian and neo-Ricardian approaches do not prevent the convergence toward an abstract, axiomatic and formalised conception of 'dynamics', from which is excluded any questions about motivations of economic agents.[1]

It is very important, in the light of this paper, to use 'canonical growth models' in the history of economic analysis, as tools for the retrospective reconstruction of classical 'dynamics'. If Blaug, thanks to the Harrod equation, tries to prove Malthus inconsistent as a growth theorist (Blaug 1985: 168–76), other scholars have pointed out the analytical coherency of the classical system. Paul Samuelson, for instance, introduced one of the best-known interpretative 'canons' in the history of economic analysis, namely his *Classical Canonical Model of Political Economy*. Samuelson's 'canon' rests on the assumption that 'Adam Smith, David Ricardo, Thomas Robert Malthus, and John Stuart Mill shared in common essentially one dynamic model of equilibrium, growth, and distribution', at whose centre lies the principle of decreasing returns in the agricultural sector. 'The same canonical classical model', Samuelson continues, recurs in Karl Marx 'when the limitation of land and natural resources is added to his system' (1978: 1415).

The aim of this paper is to assess the validity of the canonical model against the background of the debate on economic growth between Malthus and Ricardo. As I shall attempt to argue, the 'classical canon' identified by Samuelson is only a special case of the wider notion of dynamic economics that has gained ground in the 1930s. In other words, Samuelson's proposal to define the classical economic growth model as 'canonical' might be amended, considering that *first* a 'canon' of growth arose, *and then* the classical system was assessed according to that 'canon'. The question I wish to address is whether Malthus and Ricardo really contributed to pave the way for a method of investigation such as that developed by 'canonical' growth theorists. Unlike Ricardo, whose approach shows certain similarities, the Malthusian system often appears incompatible with the 'canonical' notion of economic growth. While in Ricardo's model the shortage of land is the chief and only limit to growth, in the Malthusian system it becomes an essential component of what he labelled the 'progress of wealth'. In order to explain these different theoretical and methodological perspectives on growth economics, I shall attempt to shed light on the different significance of decreasing returns in each system and to evaluate their translatability into the analytical framework of 'canonical growth'.

'Canonical growth'

It is well-known that classical economists did not use the term 'economic growth', as they preferred the now outdated phrase 'progress of wealth' (or 'progress of opulence' in Smith's work).[2] This theme forms the core of the classical system, for which value and price theory is always instrumental. Despite the different definition of political economy suggested by Ricardo and Malthus, both authors were in fact concerned with the issues of economic dynamics.[3] Many of the issues discussed in the paragraphs and chapters devoted to the progress of wealth are very similar to those subsumed by the phrase 'economic growth', even if – especially in Malthus's case – the different language reflects at times a different methodology. However, these alternative terms do not generally challenge the prevailing dynamic approach to economic themes within the classical system.

On the other hand, the phrase 'economic growth' took a long time to establish itself in economic discourse, partly because the marginalist revolution not only overturned the classical system's foundations but also helped to move the focus of economic debate from dynamics (the progress of wealth) to statics (the allocation of scarce resources that have alternative uses). The process of refinement and improvement of analytical tools – i.e. marginal concept, mathematical formulation, interdependence of the whole pricing system – was accompanied by a loss of interest in dynamics. As Harrod observes, not only the leading marginalist economists but Marshall himself, who even attempts to bridge the gap with the classical tradition, seldom show 'any trace of that dynamic theory which occupied at least half of the attention of the old classical school' (1948: 15). Things changed partly thanks to Keynes, whose opposition to the neo-classical system was insufficient to bring about an immediate recovery of the dynamic notion of economics. Overall, Harrod concludes that between 1870 and the early 1900s, dynamic theory 'passed into disfavour'. Classical dynamic theory 'was crude, in part untenable as universal law, and in part untenable altogether. But nothing has been put in the place of this theory' and 'the corpus of the theoretical economics that we teach today right up and including Keynesian doctrine remains almost exclusively static. The idea that Keynes is more dynamic than Ricardo is the exact opposite of the truth' (1948: 18).

As we know, the access to dynamic economic analysis was re-opened by Harrod's seminal contribution in 1939, a consequence of his 'insistence on the need for a theory of growth as general in application and as abstract in character as that of general equilibrium' (Shackle 1967: 7). The rise of a new disciplinary area that replaced the classical theme of the 'progress of wealth' created of course certain terminological difficulties. Harrod's dynamics was immediately renamed economic *growth* by some authors, while the understanding of words such as *development* and *progress* became more complex. Harrod later emphasised this linguistic ambivalence in an article of 1960:

> There has been some terminological hesitation between the use of 'dynamics' and 'growth theory' in relation to certain matters. I believe that a distinction can be made, and that it would be convenient to use 'dynamics theory' for the relations between the rates of increase (or decrease) of certain magnitudes in a growing economy. The theory of economic growth would have a wider ambit, including dynamic theory in this narrow sense. It would comprise also such matters as the sociological effects of the impact of economic progress, the contribution of the social pattern to it, the contribution of education, both general and technological, the need for political security, the usefulness of greater or less governmental intervention in successive phases, the development of moral codes, etc. . . . In fine, growth economics would then constitute the 'political economic' of growth, while dynamic theory would be its pure economics.
>
> (Harrod 1960: 277–8)

The need to keep these two methodological approaches separate, reflects the split that had developed in growth studies. While pure dynamics became increasingly abstract and formalised, some authors preferred not to abandon an institutional and sociological approach to the problem of economic growth. In linguistic terms, however, the road taken by most economists followed only in part Harrod's expectations. The broader tasks that the English economist associated with growth theory are attributed to a field of studies termed 'development economics', while the terminological difference between 'dynamics' and 'growth', both used to define 'pure' growth economics, is gradually lost. Hahn and Matthews's famous 1964 review in the *Economic Journal* helps to sanction the use of 'growth theory' as a synonym of 'dynamics'. The two authors of this article reconstruct and compare a wide range of growth models which, since Harrod's key contribution in 1939, have greatly enlivened the economic debate. Harrod's challenge wields a heavy blow to the 'static' foundations that still prevailed in the two main theoretical orientations. On one hand it provides the Keynesian tradition with suitable tools to develop dynamic themes in disagreement with the neo-classical school, embodying the blend of neo-Ricardism and neo-Keynesianism that typifies the Cambridge school;[4] on the other hand, it forces the neo-classical school to make a theoretical effort and integrate the dynamic conceptual framework.[5] Nevertheless, the differences between these research traditions do not prevent the development of analytical means with significant common features. *Abstract, axiomatic* and *formalised* models (Hicks 1965: 55) became the main analytical tool to tackle growth problems. Such models, forming a body of mathematical relations that connect the growth rates of economic magnitudes, are usually 'be made up of a number of building blocks' and 'require to specify functions relating to the supply of labour, saving, investment, production, technical progress and distribution of income, to name only the most important'. For each of these functions there are 'numbers of possibilities' differently suggested by authors belonging to the neo-classical and Keynesian traditions (Hahn and Matthews 1964: 780) yet without undermining the common analytical framework (interpreted as a 'toolbox'). Indeed, despite the dichotomy between Keynesian and neo-classical growth models, they are all characterised by the 'extreme level of abstraction employed and the very artificial nature of the problem considered', according to Harrod's rationale of 'pure economics' of growth (where realism can aspire at most to describe what Kaldor calls 'stylised facts'). The purpose of these models is generally 'to illustrate how an economy *would* move on certain assumptions, in the hope that understanding of the laws of motion of their imaginary world might cast light, even if only by analogy, on the laws of motion of the infinitely more complex world of reality' (Hahn and Matthews 1964: 894–5).

Between 1939 and 1964 the words 'dynamic' and 'economic growth' thus acquired their *canonical* nature, in terminology and substance.[6] In their canonical form, growth models have failed to investigate matters such as the relation between society and economy, historical aspects and political–institutional constraints, now targeted by 'development economics' (i.e. the 'political economy of growth' in its wider context, to use Harrod's terms). From a methodological point of view we can say that 'growth economics' belongs to what Sen has termed the 'engineering' approach to economics, as opposed to the 'ethical' school of thought whose principal aim is to produce an economic analysis based on human

motives.[7] In other words, 'engineering' approaches conceptualise economic growth by means of 'closed' models, where the separation between
'open' and 'closed' models reflects the different attitude toward cultural
variables such as 'motivations', 'taste', 'mental and social institutions' and
'historical–environmental factors of production'. A closed model generally
'stems from certain assumptions and, by a sequence of logical-causal
steps, reaches a deterministic conclusion. The heuristic sequence employed
is lines, it moves from premise to conclusions' and account only for 'events
linked by logical ties'. Even the notion of time loses its 'historical' quality
and becomes a logico-mathematical concept. The expansion of an
economic system depends exclusively on the quality of predefined functions, with a logico-causal process leading inescapably from assumptions
to conclusions. Conversely, the use of open models seeks a representation
of the economic world that accounts not only for 'externality and feed-
back effects' occurring in historical times but involves also the motives
and 'irrational' acts of individuals, all variables often 'appearing as
"external" data and frozen by the *ceteris paribus* formula in close models'
(Bianchini 1982: 410–12).

The division into closed and open models – which is comparable to
Sen's distinction between an 'engineering' and an 'ethical' approach to
economics – may serve to understand the differences in Ricardo and
Malthus's concept of economic growth. Closed models are not only able
to grasp the essential features of 'canonical' economic growth models,
but display also unique similarities with Ricardo's reasoning. Instead, the
attempt to extend the growth 'canon' to Malthus's system clashes with
the 'open' nature of his view of economic development.

Progress of wealth, decreasing returns and corn laws

The reappearance in this century of a dynamic approach to economic
issues could only lead to a re-examination of classical economics, in the
light of new theoretical tools. It is not surprising that the most active theorists at the frontline of the new dynamic paradigm – namely Samuelson,
Pasinetti and Morishima, among others – were also the most keen to
reinterpret the classical theme of 'progress of wealth' as 'growth theory'.
As recently argued by Costabile and Rowthorn, two interpreters of Malthus
as a growth theorist, 'many writers have produced models of economic
growth based on the theories of Classical Economists, but reformulated
with the aid of the modern techniques of economic analysis. These writers
have mostly concentrated on Ricardo's theory, and many mathematical
models of the Ricardian system are now available. However, in more
recent times, Malthus's theory of growth has also been the object of this
kind of analytical approach' (1985: 418). Not only Samuelson, therefore,
but also other scholars have tried to force the classical system within the

boundaries of 'canonical' growth. The Ricardian system, in particular, soon appeared an ideal testing ground for the new analytical tools, both from a neo-classical and a Sraffian–Keynesian point of view.[8] More recently, since Samuelson's construction of a 'classical canonical model', there have been attempts to extend the growth 'canon' also to the Malthusian system.[9] Despite the inevitable differences in key areas, this interpretative effort made by authors working on different theoretical paradigms, involves a common conceptual outlook – at least as regards the analytical tools employed to revisit classical economic dynamics.

From this view point, it is worth noting that underlying all 'canonical' growth models is an aggregate production function 'expressing the dependence of total output on the amounts of capital and labour employed' (Green 1960: 57). The definition of the production function is the starting point of every canonical model of economic growth and if land scarcity is assumed – as in the classical model – it shows decreasing returns. Most interpreters of Ricardo have opted for an aggregate production function, while others – more faithful to the Ricardian scheme – have preferred a disaggregate function, in accordance with the different nature of manufacturing (with constant returns) and farming (with decreasing returns).[10] But for all versions of the Ricardian framework, the key role is played by land scarcity, which forces the introduction of decreasing returns at least for the production function in agriculture. Constraints on natural resources cause a gradual erosion of the rate of profit, and this in turn – given the lack of technical progress, which Ricardo considers exogenous – leads necessarily to a stationary state.[11] Despite the different theoretical paradigms employed by interpreters, as seen chiefly in their reading of Ricardo's notion of wages,[12] the 'canonical' growth models can therefore only transfer to the analytical plane a development path characterised by decreasing returns, until the complete exhaustion of accumulation.

This outcome of economic growth is a direct consequence of decreasing returns. Of course, as Caravale observes 'it is not possible to grasp the essential nature of the problem [of growth], or to discover 'many important truths' about it', without reference to decreasing returns and consequent rent theory (1985a: 129). It is equally true, however, that the main aim of Ricardo's model is to show the possibility of avoiding decreasing returns. In fact, the model used by Ricardo to represent 'stationary state' should be considered a theoretical device rather than a real life possibility,[13] first of all because technological progress might progressively alter its scenario and second – this is the main point – because Ricardo advocates free trade and the abolition of corn laws in order to overcome scarcity. Stationary state is one of the famous Ricardian 'strong cases', a way of illustrating 'what *might* happen to profits in a closed economy, one that was forced to rely on its own high-cost producers of food' (Winch 1996: 368). But diminishing returns due to the limited availability of land can be avoided, 'by abandoning domestic agriculture and importing agricultural products from countries and colonies where land is abundant and agriculture is not subject to diminishing returns' (Morishima 1989: 126). In this manner, domestic farming would have favoured more competitive lands, leaving the international market to meet the increased requirement of corn.[14] Therefore the decision to import corn in favour of manufacturing, where constant costs prevail, would have further delayed the prospect of stationary state, thus permitting accumulation to proceed without variation in the rate of profit.[15]

What becomes then the 'canonical' model of economic growth, which – as mentioned earlier – usually hinges on the assumption of a production function with decreasing returns? To answer this question one should consider that Ricardo openly subscribes to the idea of two separate phases in the development process: a first phase characterised by the opportunity to produce agricultural goods at constant returns, given the ample availability of farmland, and a second phase characterised conversely by the extension of corn production to less fertile soils. During the first phase, where rent is absent (Ricardo 1951, I: 69), the process of economic growth depends entirely on the distribution of wages and profits. Ricardo assumes an initial wage rise, as the population growth proves unable to keep up with capital increase (Ricardo 1951, I: 98, 101–4). Subsequently, population growth could exceed the rate of capital increase, which in turn would lower wages. As the two trends occur at a distance of fifteen to twenty years, it is arguable that economic growth would be marked by cyclic phases of increasing wages and decreasing profits and vice versa, but always along a growth path. This cyclic pattern may cease, however, when the variation rate of labour supply begins to approximate the variation rate of capital, thus enabling economic growth in a state of dynamic equilibrium (with '*steady* real-wage and profit rates').[16] In this manner, the Ricardian system would closely resemble simpler models of economic growth such as those with constant technology and constant returns to scale, where – as Pasinetti observes – 'the growth of the economic system is entirely determined by the rate of growth of population (and thus of the labour force). This growth ... remains constant over time, and economic growth simply means that the economic system expands all its sections at the same percentage rate, while the structure of the economic system (its relative composition) remains constant over time'.[17] This growth is precisely what, according to Ricardo, the importation of corn would have caused, by avoiding decreasing returns on less fertile land.[18]

What should be stressed here is the rationale underlying Ricardo's model, which does not differ from that of canonical growth models. The system's movement is simply a result of the 'mathematical' quality attributed to economic variables: namely the production function, the propensity for saving and investment, demographic trends, assumptions on the labour market, etc. Any externality that implies changes in the initial premises does not affect the system's operative rationale. The repeal of tariffs on imported corn reflects an exogenous change demanding a review of the production function, because its 'wage-profit frontier' would be pushed up. After liberalisation, the economic system would return to function as during the phase of constant returns, when there was yet no shortage of fertile land. In other words, the Ricardian model is typically reversible, as the passage from one stage of economic development to the other involves no further change, if not in the production function.

Overall, this schematic description of the Ricardian model implies a rationale very similar to that associated here to 'canonical' (or 'closed') models of economic growth. The question then is whether the claim can be extended to Malthus. As I shall try to demonstrate, the Malthusian concept of economic growth cannot be easily placed within a system of functions regarding production, saving, etc. Although Malthus helped to account for the nature of rent as a consequence of the permanent scarcity of fertile land, his notion of decreasing returns separates him sharply from Ricardo. Unlike the latter, Malthus believes that decreasing returns are a fundamental 'stimulus' for the 'progress of wealth', and not the main constraint on economic growth. This different view of scarcity is one of the main obstacles to a mathematical translation of the production function representing the Malthusian approach to economic growth.

In his *Principles* Malthus provides a dynamic theory of profit very similar to Ricardo's, which has made Hollander, among others, declare that Malthus's model of economic growth is the same as Ricardo's.[19] This common theoretical framework, however, is impaired by the divergence on the effects of the shortage of fertile land. Malthus is not particularly concerned that decreasing returns, strengthened by the preservation of corn laws, lead to a gradual fall in profit rate. Indeed, he did not believe that repealing the corn laws would be beneficial for growth, even though he contributed to promote a theoretical explanation of differential rent. It is very difficult to translate this different perspective on decreasing returns into a 'canonical' model. Even emphasising, in Keynesian terms, the role of effective demand, it would be impossible to explain 'analytically' Malthus's opposition to the abolition of corn laws.[20]

Alternatives to the canon: 'stimulus' and 'motives to produce' in the Malthusian system

The problem of economic growth is addressed by Malthus in the final chapter of his *Principles*, entitled 'On the Progress of Wealth'. At a glance, the variables considered seem to match perfectly those used by canonical growth theorists: population growth, saving and accumulation, soil fertility, and technological advancement. A closer reading, however, reveals that for the Malthusian approach such factors are inadequate to explain the 'progress of wealth', since they fail to include human motives among stimuli to growth. The inquiry posed by Ricardo 'about the *effects* of accumulation' is 'replaced by the prior and separate question of *motives* for accumulation' (Winch 1996: 368).

Malthus is not prepared to accept the straightforward motives postulated by Ricardo to account for production and consumption. Ricardo's human motives are rather simple and easily defined. His theory always implies a boundless desire for consumption in economic agents. The famous 'homo œconomicus' – although the term was not yet used by Ricardo – always opts for more rather than less.[21] This simple assumption enabled Ricardo to regard the rate of profit as the only motive for production and the keystone of his growth model.[22] Malthus, on the other hand, found a starting point in the notions of 'stimulus' and 'motives to produce'. These features make it so difficult to identify a production function capable of expressing the Malthusian approach in mathematical terms. Eltis, who was among the earliest interpreters to formalise the Malthusian theory of economic development, openly acknowledged that 'Motivation is central to Malthus's account of economic development'. He therefore theorised a production function that contained, as well as traditional inputs, an index representing the 'state' of human motives. But Eltis is also forced to admit that 'any attempt to encapsulate the factors to which Malthus attributed the motivation to develop an economy in algebraic form is likely to miss much that is significant' (1980: 31–2).

The stimuli considered by Malthus, but ignored altogether by Ricardo and by growth theorists in general, point in the direction of anthropology and psychology (cf. Maggioni 1976). They concern first of all basic human needs, followed by higher needs which, as they originate from rentiers, motivate and stimulate the economic system to extend its action beyond the strict necessities of biological life. This range of motives includes individual 'irrational' behaviour and cannot be modelled on a principle of economic rationality. By discussing human stimuli and motives, Malthus moves away from the rationale of closed economic growth models. His overall approach to the issue seems far closer to the one taken by open models, since variables such as 'tastes', 'mental and social institutions' and the cultural constraints of society are not exogenous to the model but form instead the core around which Malthus constructs his representation of the economic world. Its starting point is the notion of 'want', which provides the initial stimulus for wealth production:

> It is unquestionably true – argues Malthus – that wealth produces wants; but it is a still more important truth, that wants produce wealth. Each cause acts and re-acts upon the other, but the order, both of precedence and of importance, is with the wants which stimulate to industry; and with regard to these, it appears that, instead of being always ready to second the physical powers of man, they require for their development, 'all appliance and means to boot'. The greatest of all difficulties in converting uncivilized and thinly peopled countries

into civilized and populous ones, is to inspire them with the wants
best calculated to excite their exertions in the production of wealth.
(Malthus 1989: 470)

Malthus clearly aims to emphasise the non-universal nature of the link
between need and desire for wealth. Most human societies possess only
so-called 'lower' needs, as they lack a mechanism capable of stimulating
individuals to produce more than is strictly necessary. The desire for wealth
and the need to produce more than required for mere biological life are
stifled by idleness, a fundamental anthropological trait typical of human
nature. 'It is an important error to take for granted [Malthus writes] that
mankind will produce and consume all that they have the power to produce
and consume, and will never prefer indolence to the rewards of industry'.[23]
Malthus claims that the exclusion of this aspect from the guiding factors
of human behaviour, assuming that man always tends to prefer wealth, is
a mistake common to many economists, including Ricardo himself:
'Another fundamental error into which the writers above mentioned
[Ricardo, Mill, Say] and their followers appear to have fallen is, the not
taking into consideration the influence of so general and important a principle in human nature, as indolence or the love of ease' (1989: 358).

The removal of indolence involves a slow historical process assisted
largely by the shortage of fertile land and the rent creation thus produced.
This process, however, is not related entirely to a logico-mathematical
account (which underlies growth models with decreasing-return production functions) as in Ricardo's case. For Malthus, the transition from a
phase of abundant fertile land to a phase of prevailing scarcity is a process
set in 'historical times', with major consequences on the economical–social
plane. On one side, the overall majority of the working population experiences greater uncertainty, as it is forced to change its habitual indolence
into productive drive – if only to achieve that strictly necessary for survival.
On the other side, decreasing returns produce rents and leisured classes
whose more refined lifestyle and needs bring about, in economic terms, a
new type of demand for so-called luxury goods. As Malthus explains, these
needs – embodied by landowners – are the result of a slow and uncer-
tain evolutionary process: 'an efficient taste for luxuries and convenience,
that is, such a taste as will properly stimulate industry, instead of being
ready to appear at the moment it is required, is a plant of slow growth,
the history of human society sufficiently shows' (1989: 359).

Such passages reveal a key feature of Malthus's approach to the issue
of economic progress: that productive effort stems from the creation of
needs which do not develop easily (Maggioni 1976: 320). Only the interaction of needs and stimuli enables the creation of 'motives to produce'.
Such phenomena constitute the fundamental mechanism driving economic
development and are the result of a historical process caused by the prevalence of decreasing returns, which depends ultimately on the shortage of

land.[24] For Malthus, the advanced countries are those with the least productive soil, while the better farming conditions of less developed countries encourage man's natural tendency to idleness:

> It appears then, that the extreme fertility of these countries, instead of affording an adequate *stimulus* to a rapid increase of wealth and population, has produced, under the actual circumstances in which they have been placed, a degree of *indolence* which has kept them poor and thinly peopled after the lapse of ages. Though the labouring classes have such ample time to work for conveniences and comforts, they are almost destitute of them.[25]

'Hence his criticism of Ricardo for overlooking this aspect of human nature, and his formulation of the central question at issue between them as whether, without the unproductive expenditure of landowners and other with surplus incomes, indolence might not be preferred to luxury, thereby bringing growth to a standstill' (Winch 1996: 367). The behaviour of social class of capitalists is also connected to the problem of 'stimulus' and 'motives to produce'. The desire for wealth, or 'passion for accumulation', are not universal for Malthus. These stimuli would not work without competition with the upper classes, whose status middle classes strive to reach.[26] Social stratification is indeed a factor that deeply affects, in Malthus's view, both the behaviour and motives of economic actors. Unlike Ricardian economic theory, which assumes indiscriminate behaviour of economic agents, the social hierarchy activates the main propeller of economic acts among individuals: namely a desire to improve – or the fear to lose – their standing in society.

The array of arguments mobilised to uphold the function of 'stimuli' and 'motives to produce' helps to explain the controversy on corn laws between Malthus and Ricardo. For the latter, rent creation following decreasing returns is a 'logical' and 'reversible' process without effects on the functioning of the economic system (interpreted as a change of behaviour in economic agents). If decreasing returns were avoidable, for instance by the importation of corn, then the economic system described by Ricardo could proceed again along the path of 'stationary growth'. It is not relevant whether Ricardo was really attracted by the prospect of the disappearance of rentiers; there is no doubt, however, that the 'economy' derivable from his theoretical framework is more adequate and likely to grow without them (cf. Ricardo 1951, II: 223). The Malthusian view of economic growth appears instead in a very different light. Rent creation is a historical–evolutionary process involving changes in the behaviour of economic agents, whether leisured or working classes. It cannot therefore be considered a 'logical' process as that inherent in models where rent is explained merely as a function of decreasing returns. The opportunity to acquire food at better conditions would involve important 'qualitative' effects, and not only a change in the system's external conditions. The removal of decreasing returns would indeed produce retroactive effects by altering entirely the premises on which the economic system functions:

> to infer that the greater is the facility of procuring food, the more abundantly will the people be supplied with conveniences and luxuries would be one among the many rash and false conclusions which are often made from the want of due attention to the changes which the application of a proposition may take in the premises on which it rests.
>
> (Malthus 1989: 378–9)

Within the 'open model' theorised by Malthus, decreasing returns cannot simply be viewed as exogenous to the system. In principle, without agricultural protectionism, there would be no landowners, as there would be no decreasing returns, and the economic system would consist only of capitalists and workers. This would raise the issue of 'effective demand', yet without the 'Keynesian' traits so often attributed to it. The greater productive potential of a system without decreasing returns would be offset by the qualitative structure of demand, unable (even if it had the capacity) to express the tastes and will necessary to purchase the whole production. In other words, the population would revert to the experience of inferior needs and less-developed tastes associated with an economy still below the stage of scarcity and decreasing returns. Market saturation and the ensuing lack of real demand would be due entirely to the people's dearth of needs.[27] Without the needs originated by a leisured class, the demand for luxury products would drop dramatically, with the threat of market saturation. 'A large body of manufactures and merchants [writes Malthus] can only find a market for their commodities among a numerous class of consumers above the rank of mere workmen and labourers' (1989: 431). Moreover, the prerequisite of an expanding economy, i.e. the stimulus arising from competition between producers to promote product innovation, could not develop without the *tastes* and *needs* required to appreciate new consumer goods:

> It will be readily allowed that a new commodity thrown into the market, which, in proportion to the labour employed upon it, is of higher exchangeable value than usual, is precisely calculated to increase demand; because it implies, not a mere increase of quantity, but a better adaptation of the produce to the *tastes, wants* and consumption of the society. But to fabricate or procure commodities of this kind is the grand difficulty.
>
> (Malthus 1989: 356, my emphasis)

'Needs', 'stimuli' and 'motives to produce' are therefore the fundamental concepts in Malthus's notion of 'progress of wealth'. In my view, his conception differs strongly from the notion prevailing among 'canonical' growth theorists, who arguably comprise – for their somewhat similar economic rationale – even Ricardo. It is not surprising therefore that there is a total lack of communication and understanding between Malthus and Ricardo on such themes, as shown by various letters – dating from the period immediately after the publication of Malthus's *Principles* – devoted to the discussion on stimuli and motives.

> I fear [writes Malthus on 7 July 1821] I must have expressed myself very clumsily throughout the whole of my long final chapter in my last work, as both in your notes and conversation you appear quite to have misunderstood me. You constantly say that is not a question about the *motives to produce*. Now I have certainly intended to make it almost entirely a question about *motives . . . By inquiring into the imme-diate causes of the progress of wealth I clearly mean to inquire mainly into motives.*
> (Ricardo 1951, IX: 9–10, my emphasis)

Ricardo's answer confirms his narrow reading of Malthus's chapter: 'You are right in supposing that I have understood you in your book not to profess to enquire into the motives for producing, but into the effects which would result from abundant production' (Ricardo 1951, IX: 15). Ricardo essentially interprets Malthus's chapter on the factors of economic progress in the light of his own theoretical framework, which – in terms of stimuli to produce – lays importance on the rate of profit and the opportunity to produce without decreasing returns. Malthus's concern that a lack of stimuli on demand side may lead to overproduction and a fall in the rate of profit is therefore unwarranted: variations in quantity, price and distribution rates were to bring the system to a new state of equilibrium:

> I acknowledge there may not be adequate motives for production, and therefore things will not be produced, but I cannot allow, first that with these inadequate motives commodities will be produced, and secondly that, if their production is attended with loss to the producer, it is for any other reason than because too great a proportion is given to the labourers employed. Increase their number, and the evil is remedied. Let the employer consume more himself, and there will be no diminution of demand for labour, but the pay of the labourer, which was before extravagantly high, will be reduced.
> (Ricardo 1951, IX: 16)

This debate on the content of the last chapter of Malthus's *Principles* contains, in my opinion, some of the clearest evidence of the fundamental difference between the two approaches, and also of the authors' partial inability to communicate with each other. While Malthus's question was largely 'how to sustain economic motivation', a problem which he 'regarded as being crucial and constant, not merely in poor and what would later be called underdeveloped economies' (Winch 1987: 85), the role of motives and stimuli to produce has no place at all in Ricardo's theory. According to Ricardo, in a country like Britain – 'with a dense population abounding in capital, skill, commerce, and manufacturing industry, and with tastes for every enjoyment that nature, art or science will procure' (cf. Winch 1996: 368) – there aren't any questions about motivations. On the other hand, in Malthusian economics, human motives are complex and changeable, and only in certain conditions does *a part* of society take on the role of *homo œconomicus* and act under the spur of a 'passion to accumulate'. This can only occur, however, after a slow evolutionary process has, on one hand, overcome man's natural indolence and, on the other hand, engendered higher needs which only the leisured classes can convey.

Conclusions

The axiomatic, formalised economic growth models established in this century – referred to here as 'canonical models of economic growth' – are important interpretative tools for understanding the work of classical economists. They include of course various interpretations, reflecting the different theoretical paradigms (neo-classical, neo-Ricardian, and post-Keynesian) of recent growth theory. In general terms, however, such interpretative schemata share certain notable features. The present paper does not discuss which of these theoretical frameworks has proved most adequate to interpret the classical outlook on the 'progress of wealth'. It only aims to understand whether the controversy between Ricardo and Malthus provides evidence of the type of reasoning made famous by Samuelson's canonical model of economic growth.

My conclusion is that Ricardo may be fully regarded as a 'canonical' growth theorist. Ricardo addresses the question of dynamics relying on a logico-causal representation of economic events (Hollander 1987: 309, 319) which can easily be translated, despite all its unsolved interpretative problems, into a coordinated set of functions concerning production, labour supply, saving, investment, income distribution, etc. I believe that the same approach does not apply to Malthus. The focus of Malthusian theory appears distant from this attempt to build a model divided into a set of functions. Malthus is interested chiefly in the motives underlying human behaviour: a feature that makes his approach closer to the taxonomy of 'open models' and to the 'ethical' school of economics, and opposed to the 'engineering' approach of Ricardo and modern growth theorists models with no interest in 'what *motivation* lies behind the action of economic agents' (Sen 1987: 18). Therefore when Malthus refers to the 'progress of wealth', he is only partly concerned with issues related to the sphere of 'economic growth'. This does not imply in fact a *different* growth theory, but an entirely different approach to the whole subject.

Notes

* I'm grateful to Marco Bianchini, Marco Guidi and Pier Luigi Porta for their helpful comments on earlier versions of this work.

1 On the growth economics in historical perspective, see Kurz and Salvatori (1993, 1997) and Rostow (1990).
2 I try to discuss this problem in Maccabelli 1987.
3 The apparently static task that Ricardo assigns to the economy should not be misunderstood. The overall structure of his work shows – as observed, for example, by Harrod – that the issue of distribution should be interpreted 'in a dynamic sense, the economist's first task being not only to determine how the produce will be apportioned among the factors at one time but how progress successively reapportions the product among the factors' (Harrod 1948: 16).
4 Cf. Robinson (1956), Kaldor (1957) and Pasinetti (1962).
5 Cf. Samuelson and Solow (1953), Solow (1956), Meade (1961), and Morishima (1964).
6 As argued also by Hahn and Matthews, the real division within such models is between the 'formal models which do and those which do not take account of learning by doing', which seems 'the most important dichotomisation which could be made' (1964: 894–5). From now on, I shall refer only to the former as canonical models.
7 'The engineering approach is characterized by being concerned with primarily logistic issues rather than with . . . human behaviour'. 'It has also had the effect of ignoring a variety of complex ethical considerations which affect human behaviour and which, from the point of view of the economists studying such behaviour, are primarily matters of fact rather than of normative judgement' (Sen 1987: 4, 7).
8 Since Pasinetti's (1960) seminal article, among the first to translate Ricardo's growth economics into current models, there have been various interpretations, seeking to connect his position to dominant (neo-classical and Sraffian/ Keynesian) paradigms. A collection of such contributions appears in Caravale (1985b). Other important re-interpretations of Ricardo's growth theory are in Eltis (1984), Kurz and Salvatori (1993 and 1997), Morishima (1989) and Rostow (1990).
9 See, among others, Eltis (1980), Costabile and Rowthorn (1985), and Waterman (1993).
10 See, in particular, Morishima (1989: 125).
11 Cf. Ricardo (1951, I: 110–11,115,120,145–6) and (1951, IV: 14).
12 It is well known that the theoretical disagreement centres on a different interpretation of wages. For the 'New View' of the Ricardian model see Hollander (1987, 1990) and Casarosa (1985). On the notion of 'dynamic natural wages', a concept that overcomes the old idea of fixed wages at a subsistence level, cf. Caravale (1985a) and Tosato (1985).
13 On the stationary state as a theoretical construct rather than a view of reality, see Kolb (1972) and Mosselmans (1997).
14 'We manufacture commodities, and with them buy goods abroad, because we can obtain a greater quantity than we could make at home' (Ricardo 1951, I: 295); cf. also Ricardo (1951, IV: 180): 'there would always be a limit to our greatness, while we were growing our own supply of food: but we should always be increasing in wealth and power, whilst we obtained part of it from foreign countries, and devoted our own manufactures to the payment of it' (quoted in Kolb 1972: 178).

15 Cf. Ricardo (1951, II: 288): 'Instead of supposing that all the corn this pros-perous and commercial city required was imported let us suppose that three fourths of that quantity was imported, and that no land remained in cultivation but such as afforded so abundant a supply that the farmer could afford to sell it at the low price of importation and obtain the current rate of profits . . . Mr. Malthus would probably then agree with me that profits could not fall whilst we could import corn at the same price because till it rose no worse land could be cultivated.'

16 Hollander (1990: 738) and (1984: 395).

17 Pasinetti (1981: 59). This is also the so-called Robinsonian 'golden age', i.e. 'a process of growth where all goods and factors grow at the same constant rate' (Robinson 1956 and Little 1957).

18 'The richest country in Europe is yet far distant from that degree of improve-ment, but if any had arrived at it, by the aid of foreign commerce, ever such a country could go on for indefinite time increasing in wealth and population, for the only obstacle to this increase would be the scarcity, and consequently high value, of food and other raw produce. Let these be supplied from abroad in exchange for manufactured goods, and it is difficult to say where the limit at which you would cease to accumulate wealth and to derive profit from its employment' (Ricardo 1951, IV: 179, cited in Kolb 1972: 178). See also Ricardo (1951, I: 126).

19 Differences concerning the relationship between wage change and population dynamics are not meaningful in Hollander's opinion, because the 'theoretical' process of economic growth leads – for Ricardo as well as Malthus – to a 'stationary state' (cf. Hollander 1987: 202). In his *Principles* Malthus does in fact describe the dynamics of profit in 'Ricardian' terms (see 1989: 295), and in other contexts he also presents the idea of a dynamic balance between wages and profits (Malthus 1989: 297). On the matter see Hollander (1984: 400).

20 The 'Keynesian' reading of Malthus's growth model has emphasised the possible lack of coordination between investment decisions made by profit earners and saving decisions made by capitalists as well as landowners. Only certain levels of profit and wages ensure equality of aggregate demand and supply. This is the only feature capable of showing in formal terms the difference in Ricardo's and Malthus's approach to the theme of economic growth (cf. Costabile and Rowthorne 1985; Eltis 1980; Hollander 1984).

21 'While there is no limit to the desire of 'convenience, ornaments of building, dress, equipage, and household furniture', there can be no limit to the capital that may be employed in procuring them' (Ricardo 1951, I: 294).

22 'While the profits of stock are high, men will have a motive to accumulate. Whilst a man has any wished-for gratification unsupplied, he will have a demand for more commodities; and it will be an effectual demand while he has any new value to offer in exchange for them' (Ricardo 1951, I: 290–291).

23 Cf. Malthus (1989: 359, see also 458).

24 'It is the want of *necessaries* which mainly stimulates the labouring classes to produce luxuries; and were this stimulus removed or greatly weakened, so that the necessaries of life could be obtained with very little labour, instead of more time being devoted to the production of conveniences, there is very reason to think that less time would be so devoted' (Malthus 1989, 2: 69).

25 Malthus (1989: 384); see also 382: 'if the facility of getting food creates habits of indolence, this indolence may make him prefer the luxury of doing little or nothing, to the luxury of possessing conveniences and comforts; and in this case, he may devote less time to the working for conveniences and comforts, and be more scantily provided with them than if he had been obliged to employ more industry in procuring food.'

108   *Terenzio Maccabelli*

26 'The mercantile classes would either be induced to moderate their *exertions* in the acquisition of wealth, from the absence of the *motive* of competition with the landlords' (Malthus 1989: 438).
27 On this issue compare Rashid (1977).

References

Backhouse, R. (1985) *A History of Modern Economic Analysis*, Oxford: Basil Blackwell.
Bianchini, M. (1982) 'Modo di produzione', entry in *Enciclopedia Einaudi*, vol. 15, Turin: Einaudi.
Blaug, M. (1985) *Economic Theory in Retrospect*, Cambridge: Cambridge University Press.
Caravale, G. (1985a) 'Diminishing returns and accumulation in Ricardo', in G. Caravale (ed.) (1985) *The Legacy of Ricardo*, Oxford: Basil Blackwell.
—— (ed.) (1985b) *The Legacy of Ricardo*, Oxford: Basil Blackwell.
Casarosa, C. (1985) 'The "New View" of the Ricardian theory of distribution and economic growth', in G. Caravale (ed.) (1985) *The Legacy of Ricardo*, Oxford: Basil Blackwell
Costabile, L. and Rowthorn, B. (1985) 'Malthus's theory of wages and growth', *The Economic Journal*, 95: 418–37.
Eltis, W. (1980) 'Malthus's theory of effective demand and growth', *Oxford Economic Papers*, 32: 19–56.
—— (1984) *The Classical Theory of Economic Growth*, London: Macmillan.
Green, H.A.J. (1960) 'Growth model, capital, and stability', *Economic Journal*, 70: 57–73.
Hahn, F.H., Matthews, R.C.O. (1964) 'The theory of economic growth: a survey', *Economic Journal*, 74: 779–892.
Harrod, R.F. (1939) 'An essay in dynamic theory', *Economic Journal*, 49: 14–33.
—— (1948) *Toward a Dynamic Economics*, London: Macmillan.
—— (1960) 'A second essay on dynamic theory', *Economic Journal*, 70: 277–93.
Hicks, J. (1965) *Capital and Growth*, Oxford: Oxford University Press.
Hollander, S. (1984) 'The wage path in classical growth models: Ricardo, Malthus and Mill', *Oxford Economic Papers*, 36: 200–12; reprinted in J.C. Wood (ed.) (1986) *Thomas Malthus. Critical Assessment*, Beckenham: Croom Helm, 3: 392–405.
—— (1987) *Classical Economics*, New York: Basil Blackwell.
—— (1990) 'Ricardian growth: a resolution of some problems in textual interpretation', *Oxford Economic Papers*, 42: 730–50.
Kaldor, N. (1957) 'A model of economic growth', *Economic Journal*, 67: 591–624.
Kolb, F.R. (1972) 'The stationary state of Ricardo and Malthus: neither pessimistic nor prophetic', *Intermountain Economic Review*, 3: 17–30; reprinted in J.C. Wood (ed.) (1986) *Thomas Malthus. Critical Assessment*, Beckenham: Croom Helm, 3: 174–95.
Kurz, H.D. and Salvadori, N. (1993) 'Von Neumann's growth model and "classical" tradition', *The European Journal of the History of Economic Thought*, 1: 129–60.
—— (1997), 'Theories of "Endogenous" Growth in Historical Perspective', forthcoming in the conference proceedings of the Eleventh World Congress of the International Economic Association.
Little, I. (1957) 'Classical growth', *Oxford Economic Papers*, 9: 152–77.
Maccabelli, T. (1997) *'Il progresso della ricchezza'. Economia, politica e religione in T.R. Malthus*, Milan: Giuffrè.

Maggioni, G. (1976) *La sociologia di Malthus*, Milan: Giuffrè.

Malthus, R.T. (1989) *Principles of Political Economy*, 'Varium Edition' edited by J. Pullen, Cambridge: Cambridge University Press.

Meade, J.E. (1961) *A Neo-Classical Theory of Economic Growth*, London: Allen and Unwin.

Morishima, M. (1964) *Equilibrium Stability and Growth*, London: Oxford University Press.

—— (1989) *Ricardo Economics*, Cambridge: Cambridge University Press.

Mosselmans, B. (1997) 'Reproduction and scarcity: the population mechanism in classicism and in the Jevonian revolution', Unpublished paper.

Paglin, M. (1961) *Malthus and Lauderdale. The Anti-Ricardian Tradition*, New York: Kelley.

Pasinetti, L. (1960) 'A mathematical formulation of the Ricardian system', *Review of Economic Studies*, 27: 78–98.

—— (1962) 'Rate of profit and income distribution in relation to the rate of economic growth', *Review of Economic Studies*, 29: 267–79.

—— (1981) *Structural Change and Economic Growth*, Cambridge: Cambridge University Press.

Rashid, S. (1977) 'Malthus' model of general gluts', *History of Political Economy*, 9: 367–83.

Ricardo, D. (1951 ssq.) *The Works and Correspondence of David Ricardo*, edited by P. Sraffa, Cambridge: Cambridge University Press, 11 vols.

Robinson, J. (1956) *The Accumulation of Capital*, London: Macmillan.

Rostow, W.W. (1990) *Theorists of Economic Growth from David Hume to the Present*, Oxford: Oxford University Press.

Samuelson, P.A. (1978) 'The canonical classical model of political economy', *Journal of Economic Literature*, 16: 1415–34.

Samuelson, P.A., Solow, R.M. (1953) 'Balanced growth under constant return to scale', *Econometrica*, 21: 412–24.

Schumpeter, J.A. (1986) *History of Economic Analysis*, London: Allen and Unwin.

Sen, A. (1987) *On Ethics and Economics*, Oxford: Basil Blackwell.

Shackle, G.L.S. (1967) *The Years of High Theory*, Cambridge: Cambridge University Press.

Solow, R.M. (1956) 'A contribution to the theory of economic growth', *Quarterly Journal of Economics*, 70: 65–94.

Tosato, D. (1985) 'A reconsideration of Sraffa's interpretation of Ricardo on value and distribution', in G. Caravale (ed.) (1985b).

Winch, D. (1987) *Malthus*, Oxford: Oxford University Press.

—— (1996) *Riches and Poverty. An intellectual history of political economy in Britain, 1750–1834*, Cambridge: Cambridge University Press.

Wood, J.C. (ed.) (1986) *Thomas Malthus. Critical Assessment*, Beckenham: Croom Helm.

6 In defence of a traditional canon

A comparison of Ricardo and Rau

Peter Rosner

I Introduction

If one looks at standard history of economics courses one would probably find a subset of the same authors covered – the pre-modern mercantilists and physiocrates, the classics Smith and Ricardo, the marginalist revolution, the macroeconomic revolution of the 1930s, and finally the general equilibrium theory. The authors looked at such standard textbooks comprise the canon of the history of economics. Most of the other authors are relegated to footnotes or into chapters on interesting side paths such as, for example, Karl Marx. The history is presented as if there were a straight road from earlier authors to later ones, as if each author had learned from his predecessors. This is somehow true. In Smith we can read in which way his theory is different from that of the mercantilists and physiocrates. Karl Marx extends this story to Smith and Ricardo. Marshall called himself a neo-classic precisely because he thought that he could build on some of Ricardo's principles. These authors laid open what they had learned from earlier theories.

On the other hand, if one looks at a journal on the history of economics or listens to the contributions in specialised seminars and meetings on the history of economics, one gets a completely different picture. There are many outsiders and precursors whose ideas can be seen as earlier contributions to some important theories. However, for one reason or the other these authors did not manage to get access to the Olympus of economists. Usually it is not an argument about 'who published first', as it was the case, for example, in the dispute about the Swedish school versus Keynes. Some of the authors discussed in the journals or at conferences are simply forgotten, others did not publish in English, therefore they were not known in the centres of the development of economics and remained of only regional significance. The latter point is particularly important, as before modern means of communication allowed a rapid exchange of ideas across great distances, local traditions had great impact. This is not surprising because economics is related to the political and social discourse of a society.

In the light of all the research in the history of economics, should we forsake the canon? Can we supplant it with a new outline of all the knowledge dug up in the last decades? Or should we give up altogether the idea that there is something like a 'history of economics' which can be summarised in a textbook, and have instead a huge number of precursors of different ideas not to be assembled in any systematic development, similar to the canon usually presented? The answer to these questions depends very much on what one wants to know from the history of economics.

One possibility would be simply to find out who published which idea first. For example one could find out who was the first to have the idea of the money multiplier – perhaps Joplin, or who was the first to argue the principle of differential rent due to decreasing marginal product of land – West, Ricardo, or Malthus. But it is doubtful whether this type of history of economics is very interesting. It would bring honours to dead authors, like awarding them the Nobel Prize posthumously, but it does not tell us much about the development of economics.

First, economics does not progress merely by finding new theories. The publication and the acceptance of the published ideas are necessary as well, because science advances through communication between scientists. Merely developing a theory, or publishing it in such a way that hardly anybody reads it, cannot be seen as a contribution to the development of economic theory. Therefore one justification of a traditional canon could be to prove that the authors of the canon learned from each other. The canon mentioned above, or the canon to be found in Blaug's guidebook (Blaug 1978), can be defended on this basis. They give accounts of a development; they are not the construct of later historians. Though unknown precursors may be interesting to read, they are not important as they did not influence the development of economic theory.

Second, those who read older economic texts are often surprised to find propositions and arguments in these texts long before they became accepted knowledge within the profession. For example, there are arguments for expansionary monetary policy to be found in the economic literature of the post-Napoleonic crisis (e.g. Attwood 1817; Sinclair 1820; Blake 1823).[1] Some of these arguments would still make sense. Should we count these ideas as early contributions to current knowledge? Should it be an important task of the history of economics to uncover all these earlier contributions?

In this paper I pursue these questions by comparing Ricardo and Rau, both having published in the first third of the nineteenth century. In part II, I present the theoretical question. In part III, I point to the aspects in Ricardo's work which are still part of main stream economics. In part IV, I will do the same for Rau. Whereas it suffices for the argument in this paper to call on the theories of Ricardo, because they are generally known, the section on Rau has to be longer, as most readers will not be familiar with Rau's theories. In part V, I pursue the main proposition of my paper, namely the reasons for giving Ricardo a more prominent place in the pantheon of economists than Rau.

II History of what?

There is probably no history of economics text covering the first half of the nineteenth century which does not contain a central chapter about Ricardo. But there are many which do not mention Rau. Furthermore, Ricardo gets published again and again, and has been translated into all major languages, whereas Rau was hardly republished after his textbooks stopped being used for teaching. Neither have his works been translated. To know something about Ricardo is a must for a well-educated economist, but Rau is read only by the specialists. In this paper I do not question the validity of this judgement, I rather want to reflect on it. The question is, can we argue by any objective standard why Ricardo is generally considered to be the more important economist when compared with Rau.

It is clear why neo-Ricardians or Marxists will put Ricardo above Rau. They consider his theory of value to be of prime importance. They use the theory they consider to be a 'good' theory as a standard of evaluation. Ricardo has contributed to their economic 'knowledge', as they consider their theory of value to be a relevant theory. They claim that Ricardo made a very important contribution to their theory. However, these economists comprise only a small part of those who will consent to this valuation. So why do mainstream economists who usually do not accept a labour theory of value subscribe to this valuation as well? Clearly, they also need a standard to evaluate the theories of Ricardo and Rau, and this standard has to be a theory for which one can say that Ricardo had contributed more than Rau did.

If on the other hand one would restrict the question of the contributions of Ricardo and Rau to Marxist or neo-Ricardian economic theory, the history of economics would be divided into many histories – for each school a different history. This surely is legitimate, yet it would put economics in the same situation as, for example, philosophy: there are different philosophies, each one with its own history. But economics as it exists today is *not* in the same situation. There exists a mainstream:[2] The similarity of curricula all over the world, the use of the same textbooks, the identity of the technical language amongst professional journals all show that there exists a core of methodological rules and technical instruments which provide generally accepted positive results in pure economic theory and which are used for empirical economic research. This core cuts across different economic schools.

It is therefore legitimate to take the current mainstream as a measuring rod when one evaluates older theories. We can ask whether they can be seen as contributions to the development of current economic theory. This is not a normative proposition, it only makes explicit the perspective for the history of economics. We are interested in earlier theories in their relation to existing theories. We want to know in which way earlier economists contributed to current economic theory, as this is the question of their contribution to current knowledge. Under 'knowledge' I understand the set of research strategies, theories, and empirical propositions which are considered to be true. The problem of evaluating the contributions of Ricardo and Rau turns into the question: in which way did Ricardo contribute more to modern mainstream economics than Rau?

III Ricardo

What did Ricardo know which is still considered to be true? What did he discover which is considered to be valuable knowledge today? To be a little more precise, which of the propositions put forward by Ricardo are still taught? The theory of value, a cornerstone of his theory, definitely does not belong to that part of the propositions which are considered to be true. One aspect of this theory still gets high credentials, namely his theory of rent. This theory can be considered as a precursor to the idea of marginal product which is absent in earlier theories of differential rent, namely that of Smith. However, Smith's theory of rent is in one aspect more in line with modern economic theory than the theory of Ricardo. The idea that marginal land never earns a rent, which is a logical conclusion in the labour theory of value, would be contradicted today. Probably the most important part of his theories valued today is the theory of comparative advantage, which is still one of the cornerstones of the theory of foreign trade. Any modern textbook about foreign trade will mention it, and quite a lot of research on foreign trade, both theoretical and empirical, uses this theory as a framework. The theory of comparative advantage is most definitely a lasting contribution, though it was argued within the framework of the labour theory of value.

Ricardo's verdict on public debt is probably another important proposition which is still part of the knowledge of economists. As this is called 'Ricardo's equivalence', we can assume that Ricardo somehow 'discovered' it. His statements in the 'Principles' about the payment of interest on the national debt (Ricardo 1817, p. 244), his thought experiment about buying back the national debt (ibid., p. 246) can be regarded as the relevant propositions. This does not imply that it is generally accepted to be true that the Ricardian equivalence theorem is empirically valid. I merely suggest that it is accepted to be true that this proposition holds under certain conditions. It provides a framework for economic research.

What about his predictions concerning future development? As it was shown by Blaug (1956) his predictions not only did not come true, but this could already have been known by the existing material in the decades immediately after the publication of the 'Principles'. de Marchi (1970), although more hesitant than Blaug when attacking Ricardo and Mill, mentions '. . . a generally recognised gap . . . between the abstract analytical propositions of Ricardian economics and the concrete truth implicit in their use by contemporaries as guides to legislative action'. (p. 257) However, today nobody interested in long run tendencies of development will turn to Ricardo. This is not surprising as we cannot expect a rejected theory to deliver propositions which can be accepted to be empirically true – his theory of value which is the basis of his theory of accumulation is largely rejected. Current interest in Ricardo only concerns his pure theory.

Of course, many economists will find something in Ricardo which they, as members of a particular school, consider to be important. These economists may include the already-mentioned Marxists and neo-Ricardians and also those economists who, for example, consider technical progress to be a hindrance to full employment, or those who are convinced that monetary policy cannot be used to increase aggregate demand. These positions are a result of some modern economic theories as well, but it cannot be claimed that they are generally accepted to be true. The former is negated by most economists, and for decades the latter proposition was considered to be wrong by at least a sizeable number of economists. When Blaug published his 'Economic Theory in Retrospect' in 1962 the mainstream favoured monetary policy as a means to regulate aggregate demand (Blaug 1978). However, the high estimation of Ricardo as a theoretician is not due to new macroeconomic theories which entertain the same opinions concerning monetary policy as Ricardo had done. It is not a *renewed* interest in Ricardo due to new theories, or due to new fashions which puts Ricardo on reading lists in courses in the history of economics. He was always there.

IV Rau

Taking the immediate impact and measuring it by publications Rau was probably more important. His textbook on political economy (Rau 1826; 1828; 1837) went through many editions. It was used for economic education in Germany, first of all in the curricula for those who entered the civil service, until it was supplanted by the books of Roscher. It was the first German textbook which had the concept of political economy in its title, whereas older textbooks – for example that of Sonnenfels – dealt with economic subjects under the title of *Kammeralwissenschaft*, pursuing the questions of good economic governance. His classification of the subject into economic theory, economic policy and public finance has remained in the German and Austrian curricula up to the present day.

The new title was important. Using the word 'political economy' was a declaration of sympathy for the British theories – namely those of Smith and Ricardo. This sympathy did not imply that Rau was an adherent to the labour theory of value, to the theory of comparative costs, or to Ricardo's equivalence. The sole aspect of Ricardo's theory which Rau accepted was the theory of rent. But it implied a sympathy for the liberalism of the British school, particularly that there is no higher purpose for the economy as the well-being of the people – the strength of the state or its glory is of no concern whatsoever. Rau was a liberal in the field of politics and economics.

Rau on theory

Rau's book on theory contains, besides an introduction on methods and history of the subject, five chapters: production of wealth, distribution of wealth, consumption of wealth, and the productive industries. In the first, very short, chapter Rau discusses what is to be understood by wealth and how it can be estimated. The problem was how the goods owned by the members of a society can be aggregated into a number.

To determine the amount of wealth he relates the existing goods to welfare, namely 'the size of the wealth depends on the amount of the advantages [*Vortheilen*] this wealth grants' (Rau 1826, p. 40).[3] This advantage determines the value of the goods. He states: 'That degree of advantage which a good bestows upon its proprietor determines its value in a general sense. It [the value] is based on the acceptance of the usefulness for human purposes.' (ibid.) In a footnote he remarks that some authors call this *Nützlichkeit* [utility], *utilité*. Although the value of a good is not the same as its price, the value of a good has special importance. 'The amount of sacrifice one is prepared to accept in order to obtain a good depends on its value, if there is no easier way to get it. Therefore the value of a good is one of the circumstances which determines its price.' (ibid., p. 42.)

Rau obviously had the idea that the utility a good causes is important for its value. His concept of value corresponds to the modern concept of the reservation price. For Rau the importance of the concept of value was the possibility of distinguishing between wealth and welfare. The problem which haunted the authors of that time – Smith, Ricardo, Say, Lauderdale, Storch – was that by identifying the price of a good with its value a person could increase its wealth by monopolising its supply. It was a widely held opinion that thereby the aggregate wealth evaluated at market prices could increase, while welfare will decrease.[4] This was one of the reasons why Ricardo rejected the idea that value may have anything to do with welfare, or as he called it 'riches' (Ricardo 1817, pp. 273ff). For Rau, however, the distinction was important. It is justified to say that Rau's ideas of value and welfare are precursors of concepts of modern welfare analysis, a topic completely absent in Ricardo.

Furthermore, the formulations of Rau were similar to those Carl Menger later used for his theory of value.[5] The valuation of goods is made by individuals.

The value presupposes not merely a certain quality, but a judgement of people about its relation to his scopes. One cannot speak about the value of a single good, as one can only assign to it a usefulness but not a degree of it; only in comparison with other goods an idea of its value can be reached. It size depends

(1) on the place which the next purpose for which a good can be used has in the totality of human purposes . . .'

(Rau 1826, p. 46)

He distinguishes between the truly individual value, which may be due to special idiosyncrasies, and a general value which conforms to a general judgement concerning the quality of goods in a rational living. The value of goods may change when the judgement concerning the quality of goods changes, and he links these changes to the process of civilisation (ibid., p. 47; p. 251). Fifty years later, both aspects were important for Menger (Rosner 1992). Taking account of the subjectivity of all values an estimation of the wealth of a nation cannot be given (Rau 1826, p. 48).

The production costs of a good are only important for the value of a good, as a person supplying a good can regain it by producing it. In that case s/he will not lose if s/he sells it at production costs (ibid., p. 111).[6] On the other hand, a person who desires a good is not prepared to give more for it than necessary (ibid., p. 112). However, the production costs of a good set a limit to its demand: 'The value a good has for us determines the maximum sacrifice we are prepared to accept in order to get it.' (ibid., p. 110).

The theory of rent which Rau takes from Ricardo fits perfectly into this idea (ibid., p. 163ff). The difference between the value of a good and its costs is the gain of exchange (ibid., p. 114). As it is the difference between what a person is prepared to pay and what the person has to pay, the gains from exchange can be seen as an earlier notion of consumer rent.

The welfare approach of Rau remains topical throughout the book. The supply of labour depends not only on the income the person might get by working – therefore the remuneration should be related to output – but on the needs of the labourers as well. These needs are not fixed as cultivated labourers refine their needs (ibid., p. 75). Labour supply will not decrease when wages increase.[7]

Concerning the supply of capital Rau describes the situation of a wealthy person making a choice between current consumption and using the wealth as capital. This is done without the moralistic overtones which are to be found, for example, in Smith. By using wealth as capital a person foregoes current advantage in favour of a future income. Without remuneration for this postponement there will be no inducement for it. Therefore capital has to bear interest (ibid., p. 101). There must also exist a certain relation between industrial profits and the rate of interest, because the supply of entrepreneurial activity depends on the relation between these two incomes (ibid., p. 181). Rau conceptualises the distinctive roles of the capitalist and the entrepreneur which became very important in the marginalist revolution, as it makes possible a theory of the money rate of interest in relation to profits. In Ricardo's theory nothing equivalent is to be found.

The welfare approach is also used for the determination of the maximum amount of consumption. In the classic theory, given the product, the smaller consumption is, the higher is the increase of capital. A growing capital is favourable as more people can be set to work. In Smith this is not really clear, as he distinguishes between employment of productive labour by capital accumulation and employment of unproductive labour by consuming. However, Smith does not claim that the amount of employment depends on accumulation. He rather uses moral and sociological arguments in favour of employing productive labour. Ricardo simply assumes the benevolent aspects of increasing capital. Rau returns to the expression of Smith, namely of productive and unproductive consumption, but the moral overtone against unproductive consumption which is prevalent in Smith is completely absent in Rau. In line with his welfare ideas he writes:

> The using up, the most frequent and most important way of consumption, is useful for an economy, if the reduction of goods is not bigger than the advantage the society gets from it.
>
> (ibid., p. 252)

Of course this is not a rule for optimal saving; however, by taking into account the welfare aspects of accumulation, it shares an important aspect with current growth theory which is absent in the maximum accumulation rule of Smith and Ricardo.

He also pursues the question whether a market system where goods only are supplied when one can make profits will safeguard an appropriate amount of basic goods. He writes:

> Because each person cares so much for his urgent needs, therefore one can count on it that normally the purchasers direct with their desire the production into the most useful direction, and no goods of lesser value will be produced as long as there is deficiency of more valuable goods. The distribution of wealth must be very uneven for to exist a productive consumption profitable for the entrepreneur but resulting in a loss to the economy as a whole, as long as there is freedom.
>
> (ibid., p. 254)

In the footnote he mentions the possibility that the lower classes are so poor that they cannot pay to safeguard the supply of goods which are necessary for them – in which case redistribution can bring a remedy according to the second theorem of welfare economics.

Rau on policy

His book on economic policy is encompassing as it covers all subjects falling into the realm of economics in a wider sense. It reads as a 'how to do book', namely how do you run a state in such a way that the society progresses economically. Empirical material from different countries and different times are relegated to the footnotes to each paragraph. The arguments he provides for particular measures or against them are always in accordance with economic theory. Economic policy is nothing but applications of the propositions of theory. Therefore his book on policy follows the same pattern as modern applied economics when arguing for or against a specific policy.

Naturally he lacks the modern reference point for economic policy, namely that a specific policy is only advisable when it will lead to a Pareto-improvement. His reference point is whether the people of a state may become richer if the government follows a specific policy. His methodological approach to evaluate specific measures is the same as that of most modern applied economics, namely that the state should not interfere unless there is a specific economic reason to do so. The burden of proof is always with those who argue for state intervention, never on the side of a free-market-policy. Economic theory can say when and under which circumstances the working of the market will not safeguard an optimal result. One of the main purposes of his books on economic policy and public finance is to restrict the state to the functions it can fulfil better than the market. The general presumption is that markets can do better, exemptions have to be argued.

This methodological liberalism of Rau is in line with his opinion, namely that the incentives provided by a free market system will bring about a good result – namely people will supply labour and capital, entrepreneurs will invest and produce the goods whose demand is most urgent. In his book on policy Rau is more specific about it. He mentions a couple of times three important conditions for this result: (i) agents in the market have the necessary information; (ii) it is difficult for the government to collect the information necessary for the administration of a good policy;[8] and (iii) competition must be sufficiently fierce.

The first two conditions concern first of all two subjects which are still important, namely the licensing of professions and crafts and the control of the quality of goods and services. The reason why, according to Rau, government interference can be kept to a minimum is that customers can judge for themselves. All the traditional regulations of the guilds which limit the range of economic activities of agents are harmful to the supply of goods. The traditional argument in favour of such regulations, namely that they are necessary to protect the consumers is contradicted. As a result of regulation, quality might even be too high if one considers economic welfare:

> For the production of simple and cheap goods, which satisfy the needs of the poorer people, there is less skill necessary [then safeguarded by the mastersystem of the guilds], as would be necessary for the more artificial goods.
>
> (Rau 1828, p. 191)

Furthermore, if the quality of goods is difficult to establish, people will be particularly careful when choosing the supplier of a good or service (ibid.).[9] Therefore all public regulation and public control of the training of craftsmen is unnecessary. If there is a danger that unskilled labourers will bring damage to other suppliers – an external effect – an examination system is advantageous; however, it should be left free for each producer whether s/he undergoes the examination or not. The consumer can then make his/her choice (ibid., p. 190). In general the incentives provided by the market will safeguard the acquisition of skills.

Concerning the third point, Rau in line with his theory advocates competition 'Such circumstances in which the freedom of the individual must be restricted because of the general welfare are fortunately very rare, they are exceptions' (ibid., p. 4). The guild system reduces the supply and increases the price of products (ibid., p. 184), the buyers will get cheaper and better products without it (ibid., p. 192). Foreign trade should be left free (ibid., p. 332), and protection of infant industries is explicitly rejected (ibid., p. 218): it will hinder trade to take its natural course.[10] Of course, when Rau published his book all this was 'common knowledge' amongst like-minded economists, however he advocated interference into the economy for two reasons.

One was that the state should do everything to further competition. This included the abolition of all legal restrictions to free entry – in the German states before 1850 this was an important agenda. As already mentioned, consumer protection was no reason for Rau to impose any restriction. However, furthering competition included the technical means to create a unified market, namely the reduction of all kinds of transaction costs: a unified system of weights and measures (ibid., p. 260ff), a unified currency system, the creation of a network of transportation – roads, railways, canals, ports.[11] He saw it as a duty of the state to contribute to the organisation of markets. Their existence should not be taken for granted – at least historically.

The second reason for state interference, more interesting from the point of view of the development of economics, was that he thought that there are circumstances in which free markets may not result in a 'good' solution. Of course, he could not have argued that state interference can bring about a Pareto-superior solution as is usually done in literature on market failures nowadays. However, the examples he gave would fit into this type of theory today. For example, he is generally against price regulation, because the incentives markets provide make this unnecessary. But he notes the following exemption:

> In the case of bread, meat and beer there is the further consideration that these items cannot be transported, wherefore the vendors living on a specific area who are in the first two cases the producers as well, have the advantage that there are less competitors from other areas in comparison with most other goods.
>
> (ibid., p. 328)

If there is a local monopoly which for technical reasons cannot be abolished, price regulation may be beneficial. Local natural monopolies and thin markets are again mentioned in connection with special labour supply (ibid., p. 362) and the markets for loans (ibid., p. 367). Whenever the number of suppliers is restricted such that they can form a cartel, price regulation can be advantageous. In relation to loans, price regulation may be beneficial, if the debtor is not able to plan for a long period of time – maybe due to the urgency of the need for the loan. His/her situation could be exploited.

A further reason for state intervention to be beneficial are external effects, particularly against future generations:

> It is not to be underestimated that there are circumstances which obliges the government to reduce the freedom of the individual in respect to the general welfare, namely. [. . .] second, if for the immediate benefit which private agents have in their mind, some disadvantages for the future may emerge.
>
> (ibid., p. 4)

In the footnote to this paragraph Rau notes 'harmful clearing of woods, ruinous exploitation in mines'. The problem of common resources is mentioned in connection with clearing of woods (ibid., p. 157) and mining (ibid., p. 37) as well. The most important positive external effect he considers are that of training and education – the state should provide general public education (ibid., p. 23), schools for mining (ibid., p. 145), schools for agriculture (ibid., p. 145), technical schools (ibid., p. 229), school for shipping industry (ibid., p. 315).

A special reason for state intervention according to Rau is that of high set-up costs. They are prevalent in the provision of infrastructure, roads and railways[12] and of utilities (e.g. the postal service, ibid., p. 250) and they may hinder the development of irrigation schemes. However, high set-up costs are not considered to be a cause for market failures today.

Concerning public goods, the market failure comes from the inability of the demanders to put their demand prices into a common pool so that a supplier can find it worthwhile to supply the public good under consideration. Today the flexibility of capital markets allows a privately organised supply of even the greatest projects, if they can make profits – at least in the long run. Only if capital markets do not function properly, namely if there is rationing, then high set-up costs can result in a market failure. However, in the German states in the first half of the nineteenth century, capital markets were surely far from working efficiently. Rationing must have been prevalent.

There was another topic dealt with in the volume on politics, namely how the state should regulate private contracts. This topic comes up the first time in connection with agriculture,[13] but it is also present in the chapters on trade and industry. He discusses this topic from the economic point of view. That means: law should facilitate production. He asks whether people would work efficiently, would monitor quality, would collect information, would protect themselves against losses, etc. He generally assumes that information is not centrally available. To put it into the language of modern economics, all regulations, whether they are general law or private contracts, should be 'incentive compatible' on the condition that private information exists.

In a similar way he discusses in the book on public finance commercial activities and monopolies of the state. He asks whether the state should produce the goods itself which should be provided publicly, again taking care of the incentives for quality production, if information is private. He also discusses privatisation of state property and favours auctions for doing this.

V Insights and theory

Although there is nothing in Rau's work comparable to 'Ricardo's equivalence' there are many propositions in his work which can be argued within the framework of modern analysis or propositions which are closer to results of modern economics than the relevant propositions in Ricardo. Particularly, somebody interested in economics for the sake of organising a state efficiently will probably find much more in Rau than in Ricardo. And though some of Rau's results may be found already in earlier authors, many of them are his own. For example, his ideas that utility is important for the value of a good is much closer to certain aspects of modern analysis than any formulation of this idea by Say or by the German advisor to the Russian throne Storch (Rosner 1997).

Be that as it may, looking merely for results of the analysis, in the sense 'what was known' after an author had published his/her work (equating having published a specific proposition with the knowledge of this proposition), there would be no reason to concentrate the history of economics during the first half of the nineteenth century to Ricardo and to relegate

Rau to one of those who also ran. If the purpose of economic analysis and economic research were to consist in delivering definite results, it would make sense to value the contributions of an author by the positive results such as can be found in the work of Rau. This standard is often used in the history of science. For example, when one wants to appraise Einstein's contributions to physics, one has to look at the difference between the theories published shortly before and some time after Einstein's publication. It is then an empirical question, whether the change is due to the merits of Einstein or whether somebody else – perhaps a woman in his entourage – should be credited with this merit. But for the development of physics it is unimportant who was the particular person with the important ideas of relativity. However, we can say, that before Einstein's publications it was considered to be true that Newton's laws provided a valid description of movements of objects even with high speed, whereas a few years after these publications this was accepted to be wrong.

My claim is that economics hardly proceeded in this way, although economists and a wider interested public as well always look for such results. As an example, Ricardo's equivalence may serve. If we accept this theorem as the result of a discovery, why is Barro's paper, 'Are Government's Bonds Net Wealth' so often quoted? Ricardo's book was widely read all through the decades, and this proposition was never forgotten (Blaug 1978, p. 140). Therefore Barro's paper cannot be considered as an independent rediscovery. Ricardo's proposition concerning the relation of public debt to taxes was obviously accepted to be true.[14]

Therefore, one might wonder, what was new in Barro's paper. If something is discovered and then becomes generally known through publication and circulation, a later publication of the same proposition is hardly considered to be an important contribution to scientific knowledge. Of course, new arguments for a well known proposition or new evidence supporting a proposition are very common, they are part of daily life for scientists, but they hardly qualify for seminal papers, as surely Barro's paper in 1974 did.

There are important differences between Barro's formulation and Ricardo's – e.g. rational expectations, intertemporal allocation etc. But taking into account all these aspects and crediting Barro with a really important contribution to the stock of economic knowledge, can we still say that Ricardo knew about the relation of tax financing and debt financing of public expenditure? Looking back from Barro's paper, Ricardo's proposition can be seen as an insight. However, his proposition was not put forward as a conjecture, like Goldbach's conjecture or the Great Fermat. In these cases, it was clear that proof was needed. But as Blaug showed, Ricardo's arguments for the proposition was always accepted by the profession.

The difference between the proposition of Ricardo and of Barro is the way in which they are argued. Whereas Ricardo could not even use the fully developed concept of a market equilibrium, because the concepts of supply and demand schedules were not developed at his time, Barro argued the proposition of the neutrality of the way of financing public expenditure with the help of the concepts available in the 1970s. He could make precise what in the earlier statements remained vague. The concepts have become clearer since then; it is stated explicitly what has to be assumed empirically. Whereas for Ricardo the proposition about the equivalence of tax financing and debt financing was simply true, thereby mixing empirical propositions and theoretical concepts, Barro by arguing this theorem within the theoretical framework of economics of his time put his theorem into the typical 'if–then' condition: If specific assumptions about economic behaviour are fulfilled, then a certain economic result will come about. This is the form of economic theorems as one can find them today in textbooks, monographs and journals, namely if the conditions a, b, c, . . . are valid, then the statements x, y, z are descriptions of the economy.

It is an important aspect of scientific progress in economics to argue earlier insights in a systematic way.[15] This new argumentation is developed within a generally accepted theoretical framework. It consists of conclusions from certain premises of the theory which therefore have to be accepted. That is of particular importance if the propositions under consideration are politically controversial, as is the case with Ricardo's equivalence. Of course, Barro did not prove that this theorem is part of a description of an existing economy, as its if-clauses are empirically controversial, however he gave a framework to discuss it.

If one accepts the difference between propositions as 'insights' and propositions argued within a theoretical framework one gets a key to evaluate the contributions of former authors. For example, concerning the problem of safeguarding quality of products Rau argues against the guild system:

> Industrial enterprises are better equipped through technological and mercantile knowledge compared to the craftsman, therefore one can leave the decision, whether and how he will get acquainted with scientific knowledge and mechanical appliances to the industrialist, who will be forced to exact deliberation, *because of jeopardising the capital.*
>
> (Rau 1828, p. 188, my emphasis)

Rau obviously considered fixed capital a means to guarantee quality, because otherwise the industrialist will make a loss. As it was posited by Rau, one could believe it or not. The obvious counterargument is that by making easy profits when supplying low quality, a firm can make higher profits. In the 1970s and 1980s there was a discussion about this topic. Based on the modern theory of risk it was shown to what extent one can rely on market forces when one is concerned with the problem of quality of products (e.g. Klein and Leffler 1981). Somewhere else Rau argues that an insurance contract should never replace the whole loss, because of negligence of people buying insurance. Modern theory argues that in a principle–agent setting the agent has to take *some* risks even if the principal is less risk averse than the agent. These propositions were simply stated by Rau. They were presented as insights, not as logical conclusions which follow from a theory. Today many of these insights can be presented as logical conclusions in modern theory.

If we look to what extent an author argues his propositions systematically within a theory, there is a fundamental difference between Rau and Ricardo. Rau's new aspects of the theory, namely his new formulations of the utility principle, have nothing to do with his propositions on economic policy. Discussing economic policy with him could be done without taking his theory into account. On the other hand Ricardo's equivalence theorem, his theory of rent and the theorem of comparative costs were systematically argued within a theory developed by Ricardo himself. They were logical conclusions. If one wanted to discuss with Ricardo his political conclusions, for example the idea that it does not matter whether public expenditure is financed by a loan or by raising taxes, one would have had to discuss his theory. The limitations of the validity of this theorem could also be discussed on the basis of Ricardo's theory – for example one could point to the empirical assumptions which one has to make to get the result. But that is what we expect a theory to deliver, namely the means to discuss economic policy.

This leads to the final question of this paper: How could the theoretical basis of Ricardo, namely his labour theory of value, provide a framework for the discussion of economic policy, which could deliver results theoretically supported by modern theory? Rau's theory which in some aspects is closer to the modern theory could not provide such a framework. An answer can be found by distinguishing between the substantive content of the value theory – labour value or based on utility – and the formal aspects of the theory.

Ricardo's theory works with the idea of equilibrium, although the concept of supply and demand function were not yet developed. However, aggregate income equals aggregate costs and supply price is independent from demand.[16] It is therefore an equilibrium theory. In this formal sense his theory is much closer to modern price theory than Rau's theory, albeit the fact that today most economists would reject not only a labour theory of value but any purely cost-based theory. Rau could not use his ideas on value being dependent on utility to form a price theory with the same formal structure as Ricardo – namely aggregate income equals aggregate costs and the supply price of goods being independent of demand. Ricardo's theory is not only an elegant theory apt to be formalised, it also allows political conclusions to be drawn as necessary inferences. It is theory in the emphatic sense of the word. As long as we see economics as a science to analyse economic systems with a systematic theory, the traditional valuation of Ricardo and Rau can be defended.

Notes

1 Actually these authors had a much better understanding of aggregate demand in the context of a money economy than Malthus who was credited by Keynes to have, if not a better theory, however, better working plain sense (Rosner 1995).
2 This is pure factual statement without any normative implication.
3 All quotations of Rau were translated by the author.
4 It is clear that nominal income cannot rise in such a case if neither the amount of money nor the velocity of circulation changes.
5 The major difference is that Rau does not speak of a the utility of a specific good in a specific situation (e.g. the value of bread for me when I am hungry in a specific place at a specific time) but of the utility of a good of a specific character (bread for nourishing people). The former principle lead to marginalism (cf. Rosner 1992).
6 Ricardo's labour theory of value is discussed and repudiated as it is shown that relative prices must change if wages change (Rau 1826, p. 156).
7 For centuries this was considered to be an important problem. It was claimed that whenever the price of corn is low due to a bumper harvest the supply of labour decreases, whereas in the case of a crop failure labourers work assiduously. Adam Smith was one of the first authors who explicitly denied that this is the case (cf. Furniss 1920; Rosner 1981).
8 For example, 'When the government applies different methods to further trade there is always the danger that it will do more harm than it will be helpful, if it does not have the most precise information of the circumstances and needs' (Rau 1828, p. 242). When he discusses the advantages of a publicly fixed minimum size for farming plots to guarantee the possibility of survival of the farmer he notes that such a minimum must depend on the size, the type of product grown, etc. Furthermore other activities of the particular farmer must be taken into consideration when fixing a minimum. Therefore the state should abstain from such regulations altogether (ibid., p. 81). The difficulties Rau describes are basically the same which arise when fixing an individualised poll tax.
9 The trade run by peddlers and haberdashers seemed to Rau an exemption to this rule. This type of trade, mostly to be found outside cities, should be regulated as there are too many swindlers active. Public licensing is therefore advantageous (ibid., p. 324).
10 Later Rau wrote a small book arguing against the nationalist economic system of List who advocated customs with the infant industry argument (Rau 1843).
11 When Rau wrote his books Germany was still divided into many kingdoms, duchies and principalities.
12 The discussion of railways and the telegraph system is found in later editions only.
13 At that time agricultural producers in some German states still owed duties due to feudal laws.
14 Actually Ricardo was not convinced that it is empirically true. In his contribution to the *Encyclopaedia Britannica* on the 'Funding System' he recapitulates his theoretical insight about the equivalence of taxes and loans to finance the war with an appropriate thought experiment, but then continues: 'but the people who pay the taxes never so estimate them, and therefore do not manage their private affairs accordingly. We are apt to think, that the war is burdensome only in proportion to what we are the moment called for it in taxes, without reflecting on the probable duration of such taxes. It would be difficult to convince a man possessed of 20 000 l, or any other sum, that a perpetual payment of

50 1 per annum was equally burdensome with a single tax of 1000 1 . . . This argument of charging the posterity with interest of our debt, or of relieving them from a portion of such interest, is often used by otherwise well informed people, but we confess we see no weight in it' (Ricardo 1820, p. 186).

15 For a discussion of scientific progress in the Keynesian revolution see Rosner, 1996.

16 That is the reason why rent on marginal land has to be zero and profit is only a residual. In Smith value theory demand has a much greater role to play as profits depend on demand and on the rent of marginal land as well.

References

Attwood, T. (1817) *A Letter to the Right Honourable Nicholas Vansittart on the Creation of Money and its Action upon National Prosperity*, Birmingham.

Barro, R. (1974) Are Government's Bonds Net Wealth, *Journal of Political Economy* vol. 81, pp. 1095–117.

Blake, W. (1823) *Observation on the Effects provided by the Expenditure of Government during the Restriction of Cash Payments*, London.

Blaug, M. (1956) The Empirical Content of Ricardian Economics, *Journal of Political Economy*, vol. 44, pp. 41–58.

—— (1978) *Economic Theory in Retrospect*, Cambridge University Press.

Furniss, E.S. (1920) *The Position of the Laborer in a System of Nationalism*, New York: August M. Kelley Reprints of Economic Classics, 1965.

Klein, B. and Leffler, K.B. (1981) 'The role of market forces in assuring contractual performance', *Journal of Political Economy*, vol. 89, pp. 615–41.

de Marchi, N.B (1970) 'The Empirical Content and Longevity of Ricardian Economics', *Economica* vol. 37, pp. 257–76.

Rau, K.H. (1826) *Grundsätze der Volkswirtschaftslehre*, Heidelberg.

—— (1828) *Grundsätze der Volkswirtschaftspflege*, Heidelberg.

—— (1837) *Grundsätze der Finanzwissenschaft*, Heidelberg.

—— (1843) *Zur Kritik über F. List's nationales System der politischen Ökonomie*, Heidelberg.

Ricardo, D. (1817) 'On the Principles of Political Economy and Taxation', in Sraffa, P. (ed.), *The Works and Correspondence of David Ricardo*, vol. 1, Cambridge University Press, 1970.

—— (1820) 'Funding System', in Sraffa P. (ed.), *The Work and Correspondence of David Ricardo*, vol. 4, Cambridge University Press, 1970, pp. 149–200.

Rosner, P. (1981) *Arbeit und Reichtum*, Frankfurt: Campus.

—— (1992) 'Was heißt "subjektive Schätzung" in der österreichischen Schule', in Schefold, B (Hrsg.), *Studien zur Entwicklung der ökonomischen Theorie. Schriften des Vereins zur Sozialpolitik*. Bd.115/XI Berlin: Duncker and Humblot, pp. 301–21.

—— (1995) 'Say's law and the post-Napoleonic crisis', *History of Economic Ideas*, III/3, pp. 35–64.

—— (1996) 'Can we Consider the Keynesian Revolution to be Scientific Progress?', *History of Economics Review*, no. 25, pp. 32–44.

—— (1997) 'Reichtum und Wohlfahrt – über einige Schwierigkeiten früher deutscher Ökonomie mit theoretischen Gundbegriffen', in Priddat, B. (ed.), *Wert, Meinung, Bedeutung*, Marburg: Metropolis, pp. 191–216.

Sinclair, J. (1820) *The Creed of Improved Circulation*, London.

7 Cracking the canon
William Stanley Jevons and the deconstruction of 'Ricardo'[1]

Bert Mosselmans

Introduction

Most textbooks present the history of economic thought as a succession of names and theories. This results in a 'Whig history', a canon in which an older theory (and author) is replaced by a newer one because of 'obvious' rational reasons. Kenneth Boulding argued that this approach may be harmful to a student's perception of the history of economic thought:

> The student first learned what was wrong with Adam Smith and all the things in which he was wrong and confused, then he went on to learn what was the matter with Ricardo, then what was the matter with John Stuart Mill, and then what was the matter with Marshall. Many students never learned anything that was right at all, and I think emerged from the course with the impression that economics was a monumental collection of errors.
>
> (Boulding 1971: 232)

The canon in the history of economics is not an 'obvious' theoretical framework, it is historical itself. In his recent editorial for the HES mailing list J. Daniel Hammond discusses the role of 'Taxonomy in History of Economics'. He argues that pressing taxonomies on the history of economic thought may be dangerous. By abstracting and simplifying of economic theory, taxonomy allows analysis and understanding. However 'good taxonomy requires critical attention to both the definition and application of categories and their labels'. Good taxonomy pays attention to biographical circumstances, published writings and the unpublished record of drafts, notes, and correspondence.[2] Postmodern historiography argues that history is a language game which develops contextually its own standards of truth. The historian produces his or her own construction out of a virtually unlimited content and mediated by other historians. Since more than one construction is possible, the reader should deconstruct the text and examine for whom it was written. Every 'stream' in history defines itself, which implies that a methodology should be reflexive. Jenkins (1991) argues that we should analyse how texts were written in the past, and that we need methodological reflexive studies about how history is written in the post-modern world. In this paper we apply the reflexive notion of historiography to the theme of this book: the canon in the history of economics. We argue that the historical process of de- and reconstruction of a contemporary canon may illuminate the thought of historical authors. They make *their* taxonomy, categories and labels visible in their description of 'the' canon. The study of this process should pay attention to biographical circumstances, writings and correspondence of historical authors.

We direct our attention to the so-called 'marginal revolution', which changed the outlook of the canon of economics until today. We will not provide an overview of the 'marginal revolution', because Steedman (1997: 43–52) recently wrote a brief survey. Steedman (1997: 61–2) argues that abstractions made in the study of the history of economic thought may be useful, but cannot replace the lecture of original texts. In his case, reading the *Theory of Political Economy* reveals that Jevons' economics are a complex mixture of 'classical' and 'neo-classical' elements. We should take the *Theory of Political Economy* seriously. Jevons' economic thought stands on its own, and should not be pressed in categories which are too narrow. In this paper we investigate the development of Jevons' deconstruction of the 'Ricardian' canon and the establishment of a new framework.

The first section describes the Ricardo–Mill canon as Jevons found it. We argue that the classical framework can be described as a reproductive system with internal scarcity, as contrasted to the neo-classical framework of non-reproductivity and external scarcity. Whereas in a reproductive environment scarcity results from the misbehaviour of certain individuals (and therefore can by avoided by an alteration of behaviour), in a non-reproductive system scarcity is determined externally. External scarcity cannot be avoided by an alteration of human behaviour, which implies that we can only redistribute the externally given scarce means in order to minimize the harmful effects of external scarcity. The second section describes several biographical elements that influenced Jevons' perception of the economic system. We argue that the 'railway boom crisis' of 1847/8 forms a first 'external shock' in Jevons' life: it led him to the experience that the economic system is not harmonious, but determined by outward events. We will identify traces of this external shock in his writings. A second 'external shock' is the death of his father in 1865, which leads Jevons to a reflection on 'selfishness'. This reflection shifts his attention from the natural towards the social sciences. Society is depicted as a huge mechanical system governed by outward causes. We argue that *The Coal Question* forms a significant work, because it leads to an externalization of scarcity which cannot be avoided through an alteration of human behaviour. We describe Jevons' depiction of the non-reproductive economy as a mechanical system which is determined by outward causes, objective mechanisms and external scarcity.

The third part describes how Jevons criticizes and 'translates' 'Ricardian' reproductive concepts into the new, non-reproductive framework. Jevons' repudiation of the classical wages fund theory provides a good example. The last parts are devoted to the *Theory of Political Economy* as the outcome of Jevons' reasoning. The work did not receive much attention. We describe how Jevons tried to construct a new canon to rest his *Theory* on: by searching library catalogues in order to find 'forerunners'; through the establishment of an 'international alliance' of mathematical economists; and even by rewriting *The Wealth of Nations*. The deconstruction failed, due to authors such as Marshall and Clark, but certain authors were discovered and became incorporated in the general canon of economics. We describe the most interesting case: Hermann Heinrich Gossen. We conclude that studying how a canon has been constructed in the past may offer some significant insights about the constructors of this canon. In Jevons' case, the replacement of the Ricardo–Mill canon by a new framework is accompanied by a transition from a reproductive towards a non-reproductive economic framework.

The Ricardo–Mill canon according to Jevons

Elsewhere, I deal extensively with the 'classical' framework of reproduction with internal scarcity (Mosselmans 1998a). According to Malthus scarcity is the result of a natural process – the fact that the power of population is indefinitely greater than the earth's power to produce subsistence. This evil cannot be blamed on the Deity – if man follows reason, no misery emerges. Human moral perfection grows in the process of overcoming the evil (the 'growth-of-mind' theodicy). The growth of moral perfection towards God cannot possibly come to an end, which implies that the 'stationary state' can only be a temporary stop. All this implies that scarcity is the temporary result of a natural process; it comes from within and is caused by ignorant men putting unmaintainable beings into existence.[3] Malthus' population theory should thus be located within *a reproductive framework with internal scarcity*. The economy is reproductive, because growth itself is good but should be balanced; the scarcity is internal because it is not due to external circumstances, but to the misbehaviour of human free will (Malthus 1798: 8–9, 1826: 12–13, 1826: 467–89).

A similar scenario can be found in Ricardo. The stationary state, the outcome of a theoretical growth model, could be avoided through free trade, as it changes the situation of permanent land scarcity. In this sense, the situation of ultimate scarcity can be avoided through the adoption of free trade; and in this sense, guilt is laid upon persons unwilling to pursue this policy (Kolb 1972). This all means that Ricardo's scarcity scenario remains internal (at least to a certain extent), because it can be avoided through importation of foreign corn.[4] What prudential restraint is to Malthus, is free trade to Ricardo: human actions directed towards the avoidance of general scarcity. Ricardo's system remains within the reproductive framework, because he stresses the importance of economic growth and capital accumulation. He is not pessimistic, as his 'stationary state' can be seen as a theoretical tool in his struggle for free trade. But even this stationary state remains reproductive: the economy is reproduced on the same level, without improvements in the quantity and quality of provisions (Ricardo 1821: 67–84, 1820: 179, 1816–18: 271). The classical, reproductive economy is also described clearly by John Stuart Mill (1848: 73–4):

> To return to our fundamental theorem. Everything which is produced is consumed; . . . The greater part, in value, of the wealth now existing in England has been produced by human hands within the last twelve months. A very small proportion indeed of that large aggregate was in existence ten years ago; . . . and even these would not in most cases have survived so long, if fresh labour had not been employed within that period in putting them into repair. . . . Capital is kept in existence from age to age not by preservation, but by perpetual reproduction . . . The growth of capital is similar to the growth of population.
>
> (Mill 1848: 73–4)

In Mill, capital is identified with the perpetual reproductive process, because it is perpetually reproduced by human labour. Mill (1848: 746–51) is even optimistic regarding the stationary state: since the economy remains reproductive, the stationary state does not exclude further moral and social progress. 'I cannot, therefore, regard the stationary state of capital and wealth with the unaffected aversion so generally manifested towards it by political economists of the old school. I am inclined to believe that it would be, on the whole, a very considerable improvement on our present condition' (Mill 1848: 748).

Biographical influences

We argue that the disintegration of this 'classical', reproductive framework can be seen in Jevons' biography. In his youth Jevons encountered a first 'external shock'. Hutchison (1953: 33–4) argues that the 'railway boom crisis' of 1847–8 had lasting effects on Jevons, since it meant the bankruptcy of the family firm. The railway crisis was a result of the pressure of the increasingly vast accumulations of capital for profitable investment (Hobsbawm 1968: 110–15). The capital glut encouraged bad investments, so the production of capital absorbing railways was growing at a high rate. When profits remained absent, railway production was checked and the demand for iron, which had grown during the 'railway boom', fell dramatically. The Jevonses were among the unfortunate iron merchants that were driven into bankruptcy. According to Keynes (1936: 110), Jevons had 'good hereditary cause' for not overlooking the phenomenon of commercial fluctuations. Indeed, his father, his grandfather Roscoe, his grandfather Jevons and two uncles had been bankrupted due to commercial crises (Könekamp 1972: 11).

Jevons certainly did not overlook the phenomenon of business fluctuations. We can find traces of this 'external shock' in his writings. In the *Theory*, he states 'we often observe that there is abundance of capital to be had at low rates of interest, while there are also large numbers of artisans starving for want of employment' (Jevons 1871: 268). In the *Lectures* we find the same argument: 'we know there is such a thing as depression of trade when the banks are overflowing with money but they can't get anybody to spend it' (Black 1977d: 62). In a letter to the Editor of *The Times*, dating from December 1866, Jevons elaborates on depressions: 'It is apparent that the price of bar iron was very high during the periods of years 1845, 1847, and 1853–7, when much capital was in course of investment in railway and other fixed works. The revulsions of both 1847 and 1857 were followed by considerable depressions of price' (Black 1977b: 142). In this quotation, explicit reference is made to the 'railway boom crisis', which affected Jevons' life drastically. The crisis partly motivated Jevons to accept a post as an assayer at the Australian Mint, because the large salary would be of great assistance to the family (Könekamp 1972: 16–18, Schabas 1990: 13–14, Peart 1996a: 2).

During his stay in Australia Jevons received the news of the sudden death of his father. We argue that this 'second external shock' shifts Jevons' attention from the natural to the social sciences. A study of his diary reveals that, once in Australia, Jevons' spare time is filled with natural science and meteorological observations. The entry of 4 November 1855 concerns exclusively his work on botanics, natural philosophy, molecular philosophy and metereology (Black and Könekamp 1972: 113–15). Schabas (1990: 15) states that Jevons' interest in economics did not arise from one day to another; reducing this interest to his reading about the railway controversy is a huge oversimplification.[5] After the death of his father, 'Jevons found in the social sciences a means to vent his "love of man"' (Schabas 1990: 16). Before the death of his father, Jevons seems not to be very interested in economics; thereafter his interest in the subject gradually rises.

We can illustrate this evolution through a study of Jevons' published diary and letters. On 6 January 1856, Jevons starts reading *The Wealth of Nations*, but on 21 January he has still only read the very first chapters on 'value' (Black 1981: 115). At first, Jevons seems not to be very interested in the subject. On 14 February he receives the message of the sudden death of his father, and he starts writing letters to Lucy and to Henrietta (Black 1973: 208–14). His thoughts are almost entirely concerned with the 'sad subject'. In his letter of 15 February, these thoughts are related to morals:

What a pleasure it is to know that he received & read some letters of mine in Rome [where his father died], and how I could wish that those letters had been expressions of all the love I bore for him, & which, unlike the rest of you, I had no means of showing since I left but by letters or by actions that would prove it.

One finds a trace of selfish feeling in these which are the first few thoughts that struck *me*, & would I dare say most others also for themselves. I feel quite conscious that I should be more pleased by knowing that I had pleased him, myself than that the same amount of pleasure had been given by others whom I ought in unselfishness to love & esteem before myself. This however is no more than takes place with all our thoughts & motives which never seem to spring from a perfectly pure source.

(Black 1973: 212, original emphasis)

Jevons' thoughts are filled with 'the sad subject': on 17 February he rearranges the different letters he received from his father (Black and Könekamp 1972: 115–23). His reflections on selfishness, caused by the death of his father, lead him to read the novel of Bullwer-Lytton (finished on 29 July), and undoubtedly encourage him to visit Woolley's lecture (the week before 13 September).[6] Both the novel and the lecture are concerned with selfish motives and morals, a 'good' subject 'and of interest' to Jevons (Black 1973: 132).

His reflections on selfishness drove him into the arms of economics – the science concerned with selfish motives. Mirowski's (1989: 258–9) statement that Jevons' writings should be seen as 'direct extrapolations from the energetics movement of the later nineteenth century', is not very convincing. Jevons' references to the conservation of energy concern the physical properties that were understood well before 1860 (Peart 1996a: 40–1). Moreover, Jevons writes in August 1858 that he must give up physics (Black 1973: 334, Schabas 1990: 16). Instead, his interest in economics rises gradually. On 25 March Jevons finishes reading *The Wealth of Nations*; and already in 1856 he plans to write a work on 'Formal Economics'. In 1857 Jevons reads the *Principles* of Mill (which he dislikes, because he reads many parts 'but carelessly');[7] he gets engaged in the Land and Railway Policy questions; purchases Lardner's *Railway Economy*; he commences reading of Malthus' *Population* which he regards as a 'great & useful work'; (Black 1981: 115–19). The 'external shocks' Jevons encountered shifted his attention to the study of economics as a 'sort of vague mathematics which calculates the causes and effects of man's industry, and shows how it may best be applied', as he states in a letter of February 1858 (Black 1973: 321).

Jevons depicts the economy as a mechanical system governed by objective psychological forces (pleasure and pain) and disturbed by outward events. These 'objective psychological forces' are the outcome of his reflections on selfishness after the death of his father;[8] the 'railway boom crisis' showed that the economy seems to be disturbed without reason by outward events. The development of Jevons' thought can be seen as a quest for these outward events. In 1860 he commences a work on political economy, in which value is 'to be established on the basis of labour' (Black 1981: 120). Only two weeks later he arrives at 'a true comprehension of *Value*' and drops the labour theory of value altogether (La Nauze 1953, White 1991a). The economy becomes a non-reproductive system, and reproductive, classical concepts are translated into the new framework.

In 1864 Jevons is 'undertaking the Subject of the exhaustion of Coal in England' which he regards as 'a serious matter'. White (1991b) remarks that Jevons' theoretical works did not receive much attention, so he began to write on practical subjects. Indeed, Jevons states that 'A good publication on the subject would draw a good deal of attention' (Black 1977a: 52). But this cannot be the whole story, since Jevons is looking upon it as 'the coming question' (Black 1977a: 58).[9] As I argue in Mosselmans (1998a), the work amounts to a 'translation' of the Malthusian principle of population into the new, non-reproductive framework. The reference to a Malthusian 'geometrical increase' is made quite explicit in a letter from Jevons to Cairnes:

> A matter which has been taken most of my attention lately is the possible exhaustion of our Coal Mines. I have lately completed an essay directed to clearing up the popular ideas on the subject, and showing that it is physically impossible for our industrial progress to be long continued (a few generations) at our present rate of geometrical increase. The consequences must be of a serious character.
>
> (Black 1977a: 65)

The basic subsistence material is no longer food or land, as in Malthus and Ricardo, but coal. Because a mine is not reproductive, and the available coal resources cannot be augmented by human actions, Jevons portrays the economic system as non-reproductive with external scarcity. The decline is inevitable: Malthusian 'prudential restraint' or Ricardian free trade cannot illuminate the coal question. This implies that attention should no longer be directed towards production in itself, but to the rational use of the produced goods, and therefore to consumption.

Mill's optimism regarding the 'stationary state' disappears in Jevons, because the result of the coal question will be a large-scale emigration with negative, instead of zero, growth rates. Jevons' scheme cannot be located within a reproductive framework: in a mine there is no reproduction. Jevons' *Coal Question* should be located within *a non-reproductive framework with external scarcity*. Jevons' preoccupation to determine outward, external influences on the economic system is also visible in the establishment of his 'sun spot theory'. In 1875 Jevons feels uncomfortable with Mills' description of the cycles as caused by 'mood fluctuations'. Instead,

Jevons seeks *external* or *outward* explanations, and finds them in his famous but often ridiculed 'sun spot theory' (Peart 1996b: 144–6). The similarity with *The Coal Question* is striking; both times it concerns an external engine responsible for economic development. After all, coal is nothing else than 'sunshine bottled up', as Jevons remarks in 1878: 'now it is among the mere common places of science that all the motions & energies of life, whether it be that of the windmill, the waterwheel, the steam engine, the beast of burden, or the human operative, are directly or indirectly derived from the sun' (Black 1981: 97).

The repudiation of the classical wages fund theory

Jevons' 'translation' of 'classical', reproductive concepts into the new non-reproductive framework is especially visible in his repudiation of the wages fund theory, as we will argue in this section. Jevons (1871: 268–9) criticizes the classical wages fund theory:

> Another part of the current doctrine of Economics determines the rate of profit of capitalists in a very simple manner. The whole produce of industry must be divided into the portions paid as rent, taxes, profits and wages. We may exclude taxes as exceptional, and not very important. Rent may also be eliminated, for it is essentially variable, and is reduced to zero in the case of the poorest land cultivated. We thus arrive at the simple equation – Produce = profits + wages. A plain result also is drawn from the formula; for we are told that if wages rise profits must fall, and *vice versâ*. But such a doctrine is radically fallacious; *it involves the attempt to determine two unknown quantities from one equation.*
>
> (Jevons 1871: 268–9)

According to White (1991a), the remaining output should be divided between profits and wages, but the basic classical distribution framework is unsatisfactory because the output level cannot be taken as exogenous in a value and distribution theory. Therefore White suggests that the two 'unknown quantities' are produce and profits. One unknown quantity is certainly profits, because the equation mentioned should determine 'the rate of profits of capitalists'. The second unknown quantity is wages, and not produce as White suggests. Jevons grants that 'if the produce be a fixed amount, then if wages rise profits must fall, *and vice versâ*. Something might perhaps be made of this doctrine if Ricardo's theory of a natural rate of wages, that which is just sufficient to support the labourer, held true' (Jevons 1871: 269). The following paragraph is concerned with the refutation of this 'Ricardian' doctrine. Jevons therefore states that, *even with a given produce*, the equation is indeterminate, because we cannot determine two unknown quantities (profits and wages) from this one equation.

The 'mathematical functions' Jevons wanted to establish departed from the labour of one labourer, working on a land with a given fertility. As the fertility of the land is given and rent may be eliminated as a surplus which is reduced to zero in the case of the poorest land cultivated, and because the labour of the individual labourer forms the starting point of the analysis, we arrive at a relation between individual labour on the one hand and the division of the produce of this labour between wages and profits on the other hand. Jevons directs his attention towards the classical wages fund theory in order to determine the unknown quantity of wages. The question to be answered becomes the determination of the wages fund. Indeed, Jevons states:

> The whole question will consist in determining how much is appropriated for the purpose; for it certainly need not be the whole existing amount of circulating capital. Mill distinctly says, that because industry is limited by capital, we are not to infer that it always reaches that limit; and, as a matter of fact, we often observe that there is abundance of capital to be had at low rates of interest, while there are also large numbers of artisans starving for want of employment.
>
> (Jevons 1871: 268)

The equation 'produce = profits + wages' is indeterminate, because the wages fund cannot be presupposed, and this because past experience shows that 'capital may be laid by'.[10] In the first part of this paper we argued that this insight can be traced back to Jevons' first 'external shock', the railway boom crisis. The fact that 'capital may be laid by' indicates that the economy is not a harmonious, reproductive system; it can be affected drastically by outward events. Jevons (1871: 271–3) still uses the wages fund theory, because it 'acts in a wholly temporary manner'. He translates it into the new non-reproductive framework: at first the wages fund theory is in operation (the capitalist advances maintenance to the labourers), but after a certain number of years the conditions will be completely different. Capitalists will learn and change their investment decisions.

Peart (1996b) emphasizes the role of investment decisions and 'errors' in Jevons' economic thought. Although individuals are on average good decision-makers, there is certainly room for mistakes and education is required in order to promote correct decisions. Capital may be laid by, and investment decisions may change over time due to outward events, insecurity and a lack of knowledge. The result of Jevons' perception of the non-reproductive economy is that he translates classical, reproductive concepts, like the wages fund theory into the new, non-reproductive framework.

The deconstruction of the 'Ricardo–Mill' canon

The Theory of Political Economy forms the result of Jevons' reasoning. Its disappointing reception leads him to deconstruct the contemporary canon and to establish a new canon to found his work on. The reception of Jevons' economic theory is described adequately by Black (1962). His *Notice of a General Mathematical Theory of Political Economy*, read before Section F of the British Association at Cambridge in 1862, does not receive much attention. The first edition of *The Theory of Political Economy* gives rise to 'only a small trickle of correspondence', with Shadwell, Brewer and G.H. Darwin. In 1874–5, the *Theory* becomes known on the continent. Jevons exchanges ideas with continental economists like Walras, d'Aulnis, Pierson and Falbe Hansen. This correspondence leads to an 'international alliance' of mathematical economists, since they promote and even translate each others' works. In this process the prevailing canon becomes deconstructed, since all 'evil' Ricardian elements have to be eliminated; and new 'predecessors' are discovered and put into the limelight.

In his *Brief Account* Jevons argues that Ricardo made an 'erroneous simplification . . . when he assumed that all labourers have a certain uniform power', and he quotes Mill's definition of capital and establishes a 'much simpler one' (Jevons 1866: 308, 311–12). However, it is remarkable that Jevons refers to Anderson's theory of rent, and not to Ricardo's. In a letter to Foxwell in 1875, Jevons states that Ricardo does not have 'the slightest claim to the theory, as it was quite as well stated by Malthus if not by Anderson long before' (Black 1977b: 146). This priority claim can also be found in Mill's *Principles*: 'This is the theory of rent, first propounded at the end of the last century by Dr. Anderson, and which, neglected at the time, was almost simultaneously rediscovered, twenty years later, by Sir Edward West, Mr. Malthus, and Mr. Ricardo' (Mill 1848: 425). Since Jevons read Mill's *Principles* in 1857, it is probable that he found Anderson's claim on the rent theory in Mill; but Jevons seems to be more hostile about this priority claim.

Jevons did not like Mill's *Principles* very much, since he read 'many parts but carelessly and rapidly' (Black 1981: 117); but he had 'respect for Mill's straightforward & zealous character' (Black 1977b: 167). Jevons was opposed to the methods of the 'Ricardo–Mill' school, but his criticism was mainly directed towards the 'followers' of this school who were unwilling to consider alternative accounts of political economy. de Marchi (1973) argues that this 'unwillingness' is undeniable, but there was no monolithic 'Mill faction' which 'sought to influence appointments in a manner which suggests that they placed a man's orthodoxy above every other quality'. After all, Mill mentioned *The Coal Question* during a speech in the House of Commons, and Jevons wrote a letter to Mill to thank him for it; moreover, Mill recommended Jevons in a very positive testimonial (Black 1977a: 119, 94–5, 120). Thus, the 'deconstruction' of the canon was not due to an aversion towards Mill or Ricardo. In the preface to the first edition of the *Theory*, Jevons describes this generally accepted canon.

> I believe it is generally supposed that Adam Smith laid the foundations of this science; that Malthus, Anderson, and Senior added important doctrines; that Ricardo systematized the whole; and, finally, that Mr. J.S. Mill filled in the details and completely expounded this branch of knowledge.
>
> (Jevons 1871: v)

Jevons continues by questioning Mill's claim that 'our conception of Value is perfect and final', and he criticizes 'the so-called Wages Fund Theory' (see above) (Jevons 1871: vi). The refutation of the 'Ricardo–Mill school' amounts to the claim that it does not keep the complexities of the economic system in mind: labour cannot be treated as a homogenous commodity bought up by capitalists; and the Ricardo–Mill definition of 'capital' is inadequate since it neglects the possibility that 'capital may be laid by'. Jevons' 'hereditary causes' lead him to depict the economy as a non-reproductive system with external scarcity, in which no 'natural rates' exist. The starting-point for economic analysis should be the individual, since a priori generalizations about 'the system' cannot be made any longer. This implies that the diversity of individuals is a fact to start with, and economic theory should form a mathematical system in which the diversities are equalized through the establishment of a rate of exchange. The Ricardo–Mill school, on the contrary, started with 'erroneous simplifications' which a priori equalized the differences by a reduction of complex to simple labour or through the existence of a natural wage rate. Ricardo's 'erroneous' abstractions are replaced by Jevons' 'erroneous' reductionism which implies the depiction of 'bodies' as individuals.[11]

Constructing the canon

The disappointing reception Jevons' ideas received lead him to establish a more solid ground to rest his theory on: a new canon. In 1873, Jevons starts searching catalogues and bibliographies in order to find some previous attempts to apply mathematics to political economy, but without success (Black 1977b: 3). New 'forerunners' are discovered in the process of correspondence between the different members of the 'international alliance' of mathematical economists. The most interesting of these is Gossen. On 14 August 1878 Adamson writes to Jevons that he found a notice on Gossen's work in Gyula Kauntz's *Theorie und Geschichte der National-Ökonomie*. It took him some effort to find the book, but he finally succeeded. Adamson offers a brief abstract of this 'remarkable' work to Jevons (Black 1977b: 267–9). A week later, Jevons writes to his younger brother:

> Within the last few days I have had rather a disagreeable incident in
> the discovery, by Adamson of Owens College, of an unknown German
> book, by a man called Gossen, containing a theory of political economy
> apparently much like mine. There are, in fact, a whole series of books,
> hitherto quite unknown, even on the Continent, in which the prin-
> cipal ideas of my theory have been foreshadowed. I am, therefore, in
> the unfortunate position that the greater number of people think the
> theory nonsense, and do not understand it, and the rest discover that
> it is not new.
>
> (Black 1977b: 272)

Jevons obviously informs T.E. Cliffe Leslie about Gossen, since Cliffe
Leslie writes, on 28 August, that he does not know the book and that it
is not mentioned in Roscher's work on the history of German political
economy (Black 1977b: 272). A few days later, the same written conversation occurs between Jevons and Pierson (Black 1977b: 279–80). Jevons'
unfortunate position described above is slightly changed, since the discovery
of Gossen reinforces Jevons' claim that he developed a 'true theory' of
political economy.

> A remarkable book by a German writer named Gossen, published at
> Brunswick in 1854 has just come to my knowledge for the first time.
> To a great extent it anticipates my Theory of Pol. Economy, but my
> want of knowledge of German prevented my ever hearing of the book
> before, nor do I find that any other economists are acquainted with
> it. The coincidence is however very remarkable as regards the results
> especially, & goes far to prove the truth of the theory.
>
> (Black 1977b: 279–80).

Jevons informs Walras about the existence of Gossen's book on 15
September (Black 1977b: 281–2). Walras replies that he will try to find a
copy of it, and he plans to write an essay in order to 'révéler à ces Messieurs
les allemands qui savent tout, un livre lumineux, publié chez eux et dont
ils n'ont nulle connaissance' (Black 1977b: 289). Walras succeeds in finding
a copy, describes the work as 'remarquable' and undertakes a translation,
assisted by one of his colleagues (Black 1977c: 21). Jevons holds Gossen
in the highest regards, since he plans to include 'the best abstract I can
get of Gossen' in the second edition of his *Theory* (Black 1977c: 22). Indeed,
in the preface to this second edition much attention is paid to Gossen's
theory. Jevons states:

> Under such circumstances [the fact that Gossen did not attract any
> attention, even in Germany] it would have been far more probable
> that I should discover the theory of pleasure and pain, than that I
> should discover Gossen's book, and I have carefully pointed out, both

in the first edition and in this, certain passages of Bentham, Senior, Jennings and other authors, from which my system was, more or less consciously, developed. I cannot claim to be totally indifferent to the rights of priority; and from the year 1862, when my theory was first published in brief outline, I have often pleased myself with the thought that it was at once a novel and an important theory. From what I have now stated in this preface it is evident that novelty can no longer be attributed to the leading features of the theory. Much is clearly due to Dupuit, and of the rest a great share must be assigned to Gossen. Regret may easily be swallowed up in satisfaction if I succeed eventually in making that understood and valued which has been so sadly neglected.

(Jevons 1871: xxxvii–xxxviii)

The unfortunate and discouraging aspect of the matter is the complete oblivion into which this part of the literature of Economics has always fallen, oblivion so complete that each mathematico–economic writer has been obliged to begin almost *de novo*. It is with the purpose of preventing for the future as far as I can such ignorance of previous exertions, that I have spent so much pains upon this list of books.

(Jevons 1871: xliii)

The new canon is ready: Ricardo and Mill 'shunted the car Economic science on to a wrong line', and previously unknown authors like Gossen, Thünen, Cournot, Dupuit, etc. receive a proper place in this new construction.

When at length a true system of Economics comes to be established, it will be seen that that able but wrong-headed man, David Ricardo, shunted the car of Economic science on to a wrong line – a line, however, on which it was further urged towards confusion by his equally able and wrong-headed admirer, John Stuart Mill. There were Economists, such as Malthus and Senior, who had a far better comprehension of the true doctrines (though not free from the Ricardian errors), but they were driven out of the field by the unity and influence of the Ricardo–Mill school. It will be a work of labour to pick up the fragments of a shattered science and to start anew, but it is a work from which they must not shrink who wish to see any advance of Economic Science.

(Jevons 1871: li–lii)

Jevons does, however, retain the central position of Adam Smith, the 'founder of economic science', in his canon: 'I am beginning to think very strongly that the true line of economic science descends from Smith through Malthus through Senior while another branch through Ricardo to Mill has put as much error into the science as they have truth' (Black 1977b: 146). Jevons' comments are very favourable regarding *The Wealth of Nations*: he describes it as 'an excellent, though rather old book' (Black 1973: 280) and states that 'it contains probably more truth & less error than any other book on the same subject, altho' it still contains a considerable amount of error' (Black 1977d: 3). This opinion amounts to the claim that 'it is all in Adam Smith', a view which can also be found in Macleod (Black 1977b: 115–16). Since the book 'still contains a considerable amount of error', it should be revised. Indeed: Jevons undertakes a project to write an 'abridged' edition of *The Wealth of Nations*, but he never completes it. In a letter to MacMillan, he states:

> It seems to me that the Wealth of Nations particularly requires abridgment; it was from the first rather a collection of treatises and disgressions than a single connected whole, and large parts of the work are either obsolete or of inferior interest. . . . These notes [which would be mostly selected from the best writers on pol.econ.] would enable me to some extent to fill up the gaps in Smiths doctrines . . . I should endeavour to make the work neutral ground and while passing over doctrines which seem false, I would confine myself to presenting in the original language the best established facts of political economy.
>
> (Black 1977b: 218–19)

Therefore the new canon starts with a revised *Wealth of Nations*, and descends from classical authors, clarified from 'Ricardian errors', and newly discovered mathematical economists, to the 'international alliance of mathematical economists'. The newly discovered economists still have a place in the generally accepted canon: there is no textbook on *HOPE* which does not mention Gossen.

However, the attempts to withdraw Ricardo from the canon failed, since he was 'picked' up again by authors such as Marshall, Clark, Walker and Hobson. Marshall states: 'There are few writers of modern times who have approached as near to the brilliant originality of Ricardo as Jevons has done. But he appears to have judged both Ricardo and Mill harshly, and to have attributed to them doctrines narrower and less scientific than those which they really held' (Marshall 1890: 673). In the 1891 volume of *The Quarterly Journal of Economics*, three articles on 'Ricardian' rent by Clark, Hobson and Walker appeared. Explicit reference is made to Ricardo, but none to Jevons. Clark writes

> The law of rent has become an obstacle to scientific progress: it has retarded the attainment of a true theory of distribution. Yet it is itself capable of affording such a theory. The principle that has been made to govern the income derived from land actually governs those derived

from capital and from labor. Interest as a whole is rent; and even wages as a whole are so. Both of these incomes are 'differential gains' and are gauged in amount by the Ricardian formula.

(Clark 1891: 289)

We repeat Jevons' statement on rent, which is very similar to Clark's, although Ricardo's name is not mentioned: 'I would especially mention the Theories of Population of Rent, the latter a theory of a distinctly mathematical character, which seems to give a clue to the correct mode of treating the whole science' (Jevons 1871: vi).[12] Although the resemblance between Jevons and Clark is striking, Clark refers to Ricardo, but not to Jevons. This implies that Jevons' attempt to exclude Ricardo from the canon failed. However, the discovery of previously unknown authors, the most interesting being Gossen, changed the outlook of the canon until today. A canon is de- and reconstructed by every generation out of the perception of the actual economic environment. In Jevons' case, the deconstruction failed, and his reconstruction was absorbed by a new canon in which Ricardo and Mill were honoured for their contributions.

Conclusion

In this paper we defend the view that a reflexive approach towards the historiography of ideas should give rise to an examination of how the canon is constructed in the past, in order to make the intellectual framework of earlier authors visible. The different 'external shocks' Jevons encountered during his lifetime led him to depict the economy as a non-reproductive system with external scarcity. Classical, reproductive concepts were translated into the new, non-reproductive framework. The canon should be cleared from 'Ricardian' vices: *The Wealth of Nations* should be rewritten, the Ricardians should become excluded from the canon, and the importance of new 'forerunners' should be emphasized. The deconstruction failed, due to authors such as Marshall and Clark; but newly discovered 'forerunners' remained in the canon until today. We described the most interesting case of Hermann Heinrich Gossen. This paper also illustrates that the use of biographical information may be more useful than the application of abstract taxonomies.

Notes

1 This paper is based on 'Cracking the Canon: Jevons' Repudiation of the Classical Wages Fund Theory', paper presented at the *European Conference on the History of Economics*, '*Constructing the Canon*', Athens, 16–20 April 1997. I would like to thank my discussant, Samuel Hollander, for his most valuable comments. I am also very indebted to Dirk Frantzen, Sandra Peart and Paul Wendt for their remarks on earlier versions. Remaining errors are, of course, mine.

2 Hammond's Editorial, as well as some comments, are available at http://www.cica.es/ehnet/Archives/hes/may-97/.

3 Malthus altered his 'theodicy' in the second edition of 1803, but Waterman (1991: 136–50) argues that these changes did not make difference to the body of 'economic analysis'. They include a rejection of the 'growth-of-mind' theodicy. In the first edition of the *Essay*, postponing marriage implied a trade-off between vice and misery. In the second edition, Malthus argues that postponing marriage allows the accumulation of a margin above the subsistence level. The result will be fewer, but maintainable, children in the future; but also economic development. Self-love reinforces the duty of moral restraint. The 'negative polemic' (the impossibility to achieve Godwin's utopia) is saved by a device which actually strengthens the 'positive polemic' (the possibility of establishing improvement). Therefore the *Essay* of 1803 is no more and no less optimistic than 1798, but it has been brought more into line with the requirements of contemporary orthodoxy.

4 We can compare Ricardo's 'optimism' with Jevons' 'pessimism'. Ricardo argues that import of foreign corn leads to a situation in which the stationary state is out of reach: 'it is difficult to say where the limit is at which you would cease to accumulate wealth and to derive profit from its employment' (Ricardo 1820: 179). Jevons, on the contrary, argues that free trade cannot illuminate the coal question, and states that 'we cannot long continue our present rate of progress' (Jevons 1865: 11). According to Jevons, the situation with negative growth rates is within reach.

5 The influence of Lardner's *Railway Economy* on Jevons has been investigated by some scholars. White (1982) stresses the influences of Pell, Woolley and Whately and refutes the *primordial* influence of Lardner; Hutchison (1982) re-emphasizes the influence of Lardner, on which he receives a response by White (1984); Hutchison's (1984) rejoinder summarizes both views, since he acknowledges that both Lardner and Pell are important; Bostaph (1989) finally tries to reinforce Hutchison's opinion concerning Lardner's central influence, and stresses the importance of Bulwer-Lytton's *My Novel*.

6 See note 5 for some references on Woolley's lecture and Bullwer-Lytton's novel.

7 He does not mention Ricardo's *Principles*, which suggests that he knew Ricardo through the eyes of Mill, at least until 1858.

8 See White (1994) for Jennings' role in the establishment of Jevons' mechanical metaphors.

9 White also argues that Jevons used a 'Millian framework' in *The Coal Question* as an opportunist, since he rejected it earlier. In Mosselmans (1998a), I reject this opinion by arguing that the concepts used in *The Coal Question* do not deviate from those in *The Theory of Political Economy*.

10 Davanzati (1995: 34–42) argues that Jevons' criticism relies upon a very short-run tautological interpretation of the classical wages fund doctrine. According to Steedman (1972: 46–8), Jevons' theory of wage determination (in the 'Concluding Remarks' of the *Theory*) is only comprehensible if the supply of capital is taken as given. Indeed: profits are the part to be first determined, and the 'amount of capital will depend upon the amount of anticipated profits' (Jevons 1871: 272). In the determination of wages, the supply of capital is given because the investment decision of the capitalist comes first. However we agree with Steedman's criticism that Jevons' theory of capital does not determine the rate of interest, which leaves everything undetermined.

11 This topic is investigated in Mosselmans (1998b).

12 We therefore agree with Steedman's (1997: 62) characterization of Jevons' economics: 'in the second edition Preface of 1879 he was in effect outlining a

comprehensive marginal productivity theory of all the forms of income from production, in which the traditional theory of rent was to be extended to cover also wages and interest – which is not, of course, to say that Jevons could ever have filled in that outline in a logically watertight manner.'

References

Black, R.D.C. (1962) 'W.S. Jevons and the Economists of His Time.' *Manchester School of Economics and Social Studies* 30(3): 203–21.

—— (ed.) (1973) *Papers and Correspondence of William Stanley Jevons Volume II. Correspondence 1850–1862*. London and Basingstoke: Macmillan.

—— (ed.) (1977a) *Papers and Correspondence of William Stanley Jevons Volume III. Correspondence 1863–1872*. London and Basingstoke: Macmillan.

—— (ed.) (1977b) *Papers and Correspondence of William Stanley Jevons Volume IV. Correspondence 1873–1878*. London and Basingstoke: Macmillan.

—— (ed.) (1977c) *Papers and Correspondence of William Stanley Jevons Volume V. Correspondence 1879–1882*. London and Basingstoke: Macmillan.

—— (ed.) (1977d) *Papers and Correspondence of William Stanley Jevons Volume VI. Lectures on Political Economy 1875–1876*. London and Basingstoke: Macmillan.

—— (ed.) (1981) *Papers and Correspondence of William Stanley Jevons Volume VII. Papers on Political Economy*. London and Basingstoke: Macmillan.

Black, R.D.C. and Könekamp R. (eds) (1972) *Papers and Correspondence of William Stanley Jevons Volume I. Biography and Personal Journal*. London and Basingstoke: Macmillan.

Bostaph, S. (1989) 'Jevons' "Antipodean Influence": the Question of Early Influences', with a rejoinder by Michael V. White and a reply by Bostaph. *History of Political Economy* 21 (4): 601–33.

Boulding, K.E. (1971) 'After Samuelson, Who Needs Adam Smith?' *History of Political Economy* 3 (2): 225–37.

Clark, J.B. (1891) 'Distribution as Determined by a Law of Rent.' *The Quarterly Journal of Economics* 5: 289–318.

—— [1899] (1908) *The Distribution of Wealth. A Theory of Wages, Interest and Profits.* London: Macmillan.

Davanzati, G.F. (1995) 'W.S. Jevons: from the Wage Fund Doctrine to the Theory of Individual Supply of Labour.' *History of Eonomic Ideas* III/1995/2: 33–50.

de Marchi, N.B. (1973) 'The Noxious Influence of Authority: A Correction of Jevons' Charge.' *Journal of Law and Economics* 16 (1): 179–89.

Hammond, J.D. (1997) 'Taxonomy in History of Economics.' *HES Mailing List Editorial*, May 1997, http://www.cica.es/ehnet/Archives/hes/may-97/.

Hobsbawm, E.J. [1968] (1984) *Industry and Empire. From 1750 to the Present Day*. Harmondsworth: Penguin.

Hobson, J.A. (1891) 'The Law of the Three Rents.' *The Quarterly Journal of Economics* 5: 263–88.

Hutchison, T.W. [1953] (1966) *A Review of Economic Doctrines 1870–1929*. Oxford: Clarendon Press.

—— (1982) 'The Politics and Philosophy in Jevons' Political Economy.' *The Manchester School* 50 (4): 366–78.

—— (1984) 'Mr. White on Jevons: A Rejoinder.' *The Manchester School* 52 (1): 73–4.

Jenkins, K. (1991) *Re-thinking History*, London: Routledge.

Jevons, W.S. [1865, 1906] (1965) *The Coal Question*. New York: Augustus M. Kelley.
—— [1866] (1965) 'Brief Account of a General Mathematical Theory of Political Economy.' in *The Theory of Political Economy*. New York: Augustus M. Kelley, 303–14.
—— [1871,1879] (1965) *The Theory of Political Economy*. New York: Augustus M. Kelley.
Keynes, J.M. [1936] (1972) 'William Stanley Jevons.' In *Essays in Biography. The Collected Writings of John Maynard Keynes Volume X*. London and Basingstoke: Macmillan, 109–60.
Kolb, F.R. (1972) 'The Stationary State of Ricardo and Malthus. Neither Pessimistic nor Prophetic.' *Intermountain Economic Review* 3 (1): 17–30.
Könekamp, R. (1972) 'Biographical Introduction.' In Black, R.D.C. and Könekamp, R. (eds) *Papers and Correspondence of William Stanley Jevons Volume I*. London and Basingstoke: Macmillan, 1–52.
La Nauze, J.A. (1953) 'The Conception of Jevons' Utility Theory.' *Economica* 20: 356–8.
Malthus, T.R. [1798] (1986) *An Essay on the Principle of Population: First Edition. The Works of Thomas Robert Malthus Volume One*. London: William Pickering.
—— [1826] (1986) *An Essay on the Principle of Population: Sixth Edition. The Works of Thomas Robert Malthus Volumes Two and Three*. London: William Pickering.
Marshall, A. [1890, 1920] (1966) *Principles of Economics*. London: Macmillan.
Mill, J.S. [1848, 1909] (1973) *Principles of Political Economy with Some of Their Applications to Social Philosophy*. Clifton, New Jersey: Augustus M. Kelley.
Mirowski, P. (1989) *More Heat than Light: Economics as Social Physics, Physics as Nature's Economics*. Cambridge and New York: Cambridge University Press.
—— (1998) 'William Stanley Jevons and the Extent of Meaning in Logic and Economics', *History and Philosophy of Logic*, 19(2): 83–100.
Mosselmans, B. (1999) 'Reproduction and Scarcity: the Population Mechanism in Classicism and in the *Jevonian Revolution*', *European Journal of the History of Economic Thought* 6(1): 34–57.
Peart, S.J. (1996a) *The Economics of William Stanley Jevons*. London: Routledge.
—— (1996b) '*Ignorant* Speculation and *Immoral* Risks: Macheaths, Turpins and the Commercial Classes in Nineteenth-Century Theories of Economic Fluctuations.' *The Manchester School* 64 (2): 135–52.
Ricardo, D. [1816–18] (1970) *The Works and Correspondence of David Ricardo Vol. VII. Letters 1816–1818*. Cambridge: Cambridge University Press.
—— [1820] (1970) 'Funding System.' In *The Works and Correspondence of David Ricardo Vol. IV*. Cambridge: Cambridge University Press, 143–200.
—— [1821] (1957) *On the Principles of Political Economy and Taxation. 3rd edn The Works and Correspondence of David Ricardo Vol. I*. Cambridge: Cambridge University Press.
Schabas, M. (1990) *A World Ruled by Number. William Stanley Jevons and the Rise of Mathematical Economics*. Princeton, New Jersey: Princeton University Press.
Steedman, I. (1972) 'Jevons' Theory of Capital and Interest.' *The Manchester School* 40 (1): 31–51.
—— (1997) 'Jevons' *Theory of Political Economy* and the "Marginalist Revolution".' *The European Journal for the History of Economic Thought* 4 (1): 43–64.
Walker, F.A. (1891) 'The Doctrine of Rent, and the Residual Claimant Theory of Wages.' *The Quarterly Journal of Economics* 5: 417–37.

Waterman, A.M.C. (1991) *Revolution, Economics and Religion. Christian Political Economy, 1798–1833.* Cambridge: Cambridge University Press.

White, M.V. (1982) 'Jevons in Australia: A Reassessment.' *Economic Record* 58 (160): 32–45.

—— (1984) 'Jevons in Australia: Response to Professor Hutchison.' *The Manchester School* 52 (1): 70–2.

—— (1991a) 'Jevons' "Blunder" Concerning Value and Distribution: an Explanation.' *Cambridge Journal of Economics* 15: 149–60.

—— (1991b) 'A Biographical Puzzle: Why Did Jevons Write the Coal Question?' *Journal of the History of Economic Thought* 13: 222–42.

—— (1994) 'The Moment of Richard Jennings: the Production of Jevons' Marginalist economic agent.' In Mirowski, P. (ed.) *Natural Images in Economic Thought.* Cambridge: Cambridge University Press, 197–230.

8 Who blushes at the name

John Kells Ingram and minor literature

Terrence McDonough

Introduction

The present volume has invited scholars to address the issue of canonicity in the history of economic thought. In so doing, it has urged economists to draw on and apply the insights of another branch of the academy. Literary theorists are currently embroiled in a heated controversy which seeks to construct and deconstruct, assault and defend the canon of great literature. The course of this debate cannot be rehearsed in the context of the present short contribution.

Nevertheless, posing the problem of the canon in the history of economic thought implicitly urges the importation of this controversy into the field of economic thought. It suggests the questions: who qualifies for entry into the canon of economic thought? and why? Until now these questions have been rarely asked. The list of authors who are accorded extended treatment in the history of thought texts has been looked upon as self-evident. Canonical authors appear to be virtually the same in each of the major textbooks.

A more active examination of the quality of canonicity in the history of economic thought can be entered from two different directions. The standard canonical authors and works can be examined to discover what it is they have in common. Alternatively, we can seek to uncover what attributes result in the exclusion of authors and works from the canon. This essay will approach the question from this latter perspective.

In so doing, I will be drawing on that literary theory which seeks to identify and discuss a body of 'minor' literature. In examining what makes a work minor, this literature addresses the issue of canonicity by looking at the canon, in a sense, through the wrong end of the telescope. It asks what is it that makes a corpus of work unfit for inclusion into the literary canon. In this context, I will examine the quality of minority in the work of the Irish historical economist, John Kells Ingram.

John Kells Ingram appears as the perfect candidate for minority in the history of economic thought. Louis Renza (1984) marks the American author Sarah Orne Jewett for consideration as a minor writer. Her works were 'neither altogether neglected nor significant enough to merit sustained let alone sophisticated critical attention' (p. xxv) This is precisely the position of Ingram in the standard texts in the history of economic thought. His period is not allowed to pass without a mention of his name. Yet he is not deemed worthy of sustained treatment. There is an irony here in that Ingram in his *A History of Political Economy* (1888) is sometimes considered the founder in English of the history of economic thought.

I will first examine the theory of minor literature in order to identify the possible elements which may contribute to exclusion from the canon. I will be paying particular attention to the recent discussion which identifies minority with a kind of refusal of canonicity rather than a straightforward failure to achieve canonic status. I will then try to locate the characteristic of Ingram's work which in a sense excludes itself from the canon of the history of economic thought.

The basic perspective of this essay is that a discussion of what is non-canonical can help throw light on the rules governing admission to the canon. In discussing the work of Kells Ingram, I will be drawing out a self-consciously minor thread in the tapestry, but in the process I hope to unravel a significant part of the question of what constitutes canonicity in the history of economic thought.

The theory of minor literature

A number of literary critics have sought to identify the quality of minority in literature. Unsurprisingly, the dominant tendency has been to see minor literature solely in relation to major literature and as manifesting a primarily quantitative difference from majority. In this view, minor literature can be viewed benignly as a kind of commonplace literary background which sets up and then sets off the achievements of the truly major work. Less benignly, such a perspective can construct minor literature as a set of failed attempts to achieve the status of majority. In this view, minor literature has not measured up in that quality which confers major stature. It has fallen short in innovation, failed to achieve autonomy, submerged itself in collectivity, become debased as a literary commodity, cravenly stood on the sidelines in the oedipal struggle to deny the paternity of literary convention, or cynically fled from great literature's genius, mystery and madness.[1]

There have been a small number of attempts in recent years to approach the question of minority in literature from a more positive perspective. This approach argues that literature achieves minority status by undertaking a role or task which is other than the role played by major literature. If goals other than that of majority are being pursued, minor literature can be seen to be characterized by a refusal rather than a failure of canonicity.

It would be obviously untenable to define minor literature in complete absence of its relationship to major literature. The refusal of canonicity perspective maintains a relationship between the two literatures but radically re-orders that relationship. Seeing minor literature solely in the frame of a failure of canonicity establishes a hierarchical relationship marked by higher and lower places along a posited scale. Identifying minor literature through a refusal of canonicity establishes major and minor literature as two poles in a dialogue about the relationship between literature and the larger culture it reflects.

Establishing a scale along which to measure minor literature's failure of canonicity implicitly and explicitly enlists minor literature in the normative task of raising the canon as a kind of standard. Analysing minor status as a refusal of canonicity, on the contrary, calls the canon into question at least as far as it seeks to establish a universally applicable standard. In searching for minor literature in the history of economic thought, the failure of canonicity approach is unlikely to produce much of great moment almost by definition. We would be reduced to cataloguing minor contributions to schools, nearly endless recitations of normal science, and elucidating grand conceptual schemes which never saw the light of day. On the other hand, the uncovering of a refusal of canonicity could potentially produce a rigorous interrogation of the role of canonicity itself in the history of economic thought.

Deleuze and Guattari (1975) are the first to define minor literature apart from a failure of canonicity in their analysis of Kafka as a producer of minor literature. Deleuze and Guattari identify three characteristics of minor literature. These are first the 'deterritorialization' of the language. By this they mean the freeing of the language of a major literature, for example, the German of official Prague, of the codes implicit in its use in the production of literature and the turning of the language to minority cultural uses. They claim the spare quality of Kafka's style as an example of such a decodification. The second characteristic is an intimate connection between the individual and the political. In a major literature political issues constitute a background against which the individual characters move. In a minor literature these issues are foregrounded along with the characters. The third characteristic of a minor literature is that the works seem to emanate from the collective voice of the minority rather than the authorial voice of a single individual.

As is perhaps clear by now, Deleuze and Guattari are identifying minor literature with the literary productions of a minority group. Specifically, with a minority which is pursuing its own minority project. More specifically, this minority is pursuing a revolutionary, postmodern, anti-majority constitution of its own distinct identity. While Deleuze and Guattari leave the door open to a broad conception of just who might constitute such minorities, the minority ethnic group is clearly the paradigmatic example. The choice of Kafka, a Czech Jewish writer in the German language makes this clear. While Deleuze and Guattari found the analysis of minor literature as a refusal rather than a failure of canonicity, their reading of the concept of literary minority is too literal to be generally useful.

The next critic to take up the refusal of canonicity is Louis A. Renza (1984). Renza trenchantly challenges Deleuze and Guattari's definition of minor literature as being counter-canonical rather than non-canonical. Deleuzean minor literature reflects the critics' desire to mount an assault on the totalizing tendencies of major literature and the formation of the canon. This holds minor literature hostage to the revolutionary political project of the critic and subordinates its non-canonicity in requiring an attack on the canon. This conception of minor literature chains it to the canon in a way which defines it primarily in terms of the existence of the major literature. It also carries the suspicion that a successful overthrow of the canon is perhaps prelude to a canonization of minor literature as the major literature of the minority ethnicity. It is Renza's contention that minor literature must be free to refuse counter-canonicity with almost the same vehemence with which it refuses canonicity. A minor literature which refuses counter-canonicity is all the more definitively minor because of it. While Renza's discussion overturns Deleuze and Guattari's definition of minor literature, it does not really give an alternative conceptualization.

David Lloyd (1987) discusses minor literature in his study of the nineteenth century Irish author James Clarence Mangan. Lloyd begins his discussion with Renza's observation that minor literature can demobilize itself from the counter-hegemonic project without thereby surrendering to the demands of canonicity. Lloyd recognizes Mangan's demobbed status, and goes on to identify Mangan's non- (as opposed to counter-) canonical objectives in the following passage:

> ... the 'failure' of Mangan's work should be seen in terms of its recalcitrance to the demands of nationalist as of imperialist aesthetics for the production of a major writing in conformity with a canon whose function is to produce identity. Mangan's is a minor writing, but a minor writing in the positive sense of one whose very 'inauthenticity' registers the radical non-identity of the colonized subject.
>
> (Lloyd 1987, p. xi)

Lloyd's conception of minor literature builds on the preceding authors in two ways. It recognizes that the status of acanonicity cannot be defined in isolation from the identification of the project of canonicity. At the same time it establishes the acanonical project 'positively' as one which is different from the canonical task but no less valid thereby.

Lloyd develops the task of canonical literature in the bourgeois era by arguing that '... the major work should be in some manner directed toward the production of an autonomous ethical identity for the subject' (p. 19). Canonicity also imposes the parallel requirement that 'the work itself be autonomous' (p. 19). But the autonomous individual so constituted must be reconciled to the social order. The individual must develop 'into the "best self"', that self in which the individual's identifications are with the interests of the state, itself ideally representative of the general interest of the race' (p. 13). By this means an aesthetic is found which can provide 'a means to reconcile the inevitably conflicting and potentially anarchic forces of bourgeois civil society' (p. 17). Minor literature by contrast refuses 'to represent the attainment of the autonomous subjectivity that is the ultimate aim of the major narrative' (p. 22). Minor literature is now free to pursue other aims.

In this way, Lloyd establishes the paradoxically coequal relationship of the major and the minor.

A clever indignant sort of little fellow[2]

Lloyd defines major literature first, in order to discover what it is which distinguishes minor literature, that is, what precisely is the character of its refusal. Nevertheless, there is nothing to prevent the argument from being turned around, from being pursued from the other direction. Lloyd might have ordered his argument as first an analysis of the minor, an analysis whose course discloses as a by-product the essence of majority. This is the route by which I intend to seek the quality of canonicity in the history of economic thought, through examining the minor status of the work of John Kells Ingram. Ingram was born in Donegal in 1823 to a clerical family. He obtained a fellowship to Trinity College in 1846 and held a variety of posts thereafter including the first Professorship of Oratory and English Literature, Regius Professor of Greek, Librarian, Senior Lecturer, and Vice Provost. Ingram's polymathic interests are reflected in the range of his publications. His early articles are largely in the area of geometry, followed by work on Irish economic policy, notes on Greek and Latin etymology, and an article on Shakespeare (Cumann 1907).

He gained a leading position in the English historical school in 1878 with the publication of his address before the British Association for the Advancement of Science, *The Present Position and Prospects of Political Economy* (Ingram 1878). The address was part of a major controversy occasioned by the attempt of Sir Francis Galton to abolish the economics section of the society as unscientific. The address was rapidly translated into German and Danish.

Ingram followed up a number of entries to the *Encyclopaedia Brittanica* with *A History of Political Economy* in 1888. This volume was subsequently translated into German, Spanish, Polish, Russian, Italian, Swedish, French, Czech, Serbian and Japanese. *A History of Slavery and Serfdom*, the first book-length treatment of this subject in English was published in 1895. *Outlines of the History of Religion* followed in 1900 along with a book of sonnets. 1901 saw the publication of *Human Nature and Morals according to Auguste Comte* and a translation of Comte's letters. A sequel appeared in 1904 entitled *Practical Morals*.

Ingram's refusal of canonicity

Ingram grounds himself quite firmly in the historical school of economics and is generally considered, along with fellow Irishman T.E. Cliffe Leslie, to be one of the founding members of this school in Great Britain. Ingram devotes great energy to the critique of 'vicious abstraction' and an overly deductive methodology. He considers Ricardo chiefly responsible for the introduction of these errors into political economy. He advocates a dynamic approach to economics, building inductively on historical comparison. Ingram thus decisively distances himself from the neoclassical tradition.

It might be thought that this abandonment of the mainstream is enough to condemn Ingram to the eddies and backwaters of economic thought. Nevertheless, the heterodoxy of Marx has been tolerated in the history of economic thought and he has been accorded a relatively safe seat in the canon. We must look beyond unorthodoxy to locate Ingram's refusal of canonicity.

Ingram's failure of canonicity can rather be found in his stubborn refusal to constitute economics as a separate science. Viewing society as a living whole, Ingram (1878) argues

> ... we cannot isolate the study of one organ from that of the rest, or of the whole. We cannot break up the study of the human body into a number of different sciences, dealing respectively with the different organs and functions, and, instead of a human anatomy and physiology, construct a cardiology, a hepatology, an enterology. It is not of course meant that special studies of particular organs and functions may not be undertaken ... but ... it is essential to keep in view their relations and interactions, and that therefore they must be treated as forming part of the subject-matter of one and the same science.
>
> (pp. 49–50)

By analogy, Ingram contends,

> There is one great science of Sociology; its several chapters study the several faces of social existence. One of these faces is that of the material well-being of society, its industrial constitution and development. The study of these phenomena is one chapter of Sociology, a chapter which must be kept in close relation with the rest.
>
> (p. 50)

Ingram argues that the then current difficulties of economics can be traced partially to the attempt to consider the economy as the object of a separate science. The problems economics faces will not be resolved 'unless it [economics] be linked in close connection with the general science of society – unless it be, in fact, subsumed under and absorbed into Sociology' (p. 55).

Ingram missed no opportunity to repeat this argument, reiterating it in *Work and the Workman* (1880), *The History of Political Economy* (1888), and the, preface to Richard T. Ely's *An Introduction to Political Economy* (1891). In introducing the Japanese translation of *History*, Ingram hopes it may be found of use 'in helping to preserve the Japanese mind from the narrowness which so long beset our Western labours on this subject' (Cumann 1907, p. 38).

The function of canonicity

If Ingram's refusal to designate economics as a separate science is the key to his failure of canonicity, we can infer inversely that one of the functions that canonical works must serve is the establishment of economics as a separate science. Just as the constitution of the autonomous subject is the subject of literary canonicity in Lloyd's argument, so the constitution of economics as an autonomous science is the subject of the canon in the history of economic thought. Those writers who pursue a different project from the establishment of economics as a distinct science exclude themselves from the canon.

An examination of canonical authors reveals just such a concern with establishing economics as a science. Smith argues that individuals engage in a self-regarding rational calculus in decision-making, weighing benefits against losses. This rational calculation then allows predictions about individual behaviour. These individual actions are then aggregated to produce the economy. In this way, the economy is governed by discoverable laws. An understanding of the economy can then be established on a scientific basis analogous to that of physics or other recognized sciences.

Smith's successors in the canon operate from similar assumptions. Two possible exceptions include Marx and Veblen. Marx would not accept Smith's individualist methodology and would contend that his historical materialism functions as an explanatory theory of more than just economic history. Nevertheless, his canonical work, *Capital*, concerns itself with price theory and the determination of profit in the form of surplus value. While Marx planned to move on to discuss other theoretical questions including the theory of the state, he did not get the chance. Marx's concern with the laws of motion of capital and his theory of the economic base of the other elements of society mitigates the threat his broader view posed to canonicity. Even Veblen, who explicitly disavowed a separate theory of the economy, is primarily focused in practice on the dichotomy between industry and business, between technological progress and ceremonial obstruction.

It can be observed that it is only with the advent of a capitalist economy that it becomes even conceivable to pursue an analysis of the economy as separate from the rest of society. It is only after the market has become disunited from the rest of society that such a project could be seen to be viable (Polanyi 1944). It is only with the analysis of capitalism that canonical writing begins.

Indeed, it may even seem banal to observe that only authors who conduct economics as a separate science would enter the history of economic thought. Yet there is no a priori reason to exclude social scientists with a broader conceptual schema or different disciplinary focus. The enforcement of the view of economics as a distinct science may substantially narrow access to the canon. The elimination of this gate-keeping requirement could conceivably lead to a radical revision of the history of economic thought. Imagine (to quote the late John Lennon) if authors from other social science traditions who addressed economic questions even narrowly defined were encouraged to apply for canonicity and were considered on an equal basis with the 'economists.' The history of economic thought would at minimum have to be reconsidered if not rewritten.

A parallel reality

In *A History of Political Economy*, Ingram (1888) provides an ironic test case of the canonical revisions which could take place under different assumptions and standards. Carl Menger is depicted by the sentence, 'A movement of reaction in favour of the older school is represented by C. Menger, H. Dietzel, and E. Sax' (p. 215). Walras appears as, 'L. Walras . . . has followed the example of Cournot in attempting a mathematical treatment of the subject' (p. 221).

Jevons receives more extended discussion. He is praised for his criticism of Ricardo and his more empirically oriented researches. On the other hand, Ingram is much less impressed with Jevons' 'new theoretical constructions'. He contends strongly that 'the application of mathematics in the higher sense to economics must necessarily fail' (pp. 233–4). Ingram renders the following final judgement on Jevons' system:

> . . . the theorem states that, in an act of exchange, the product of the quantity of the commodity given by its price per unit of quantity (estimated in a third article) is the same as the corresponding product for the commodity received – a truth so obvious as to require no application of the higher mathematics to discover it. If we cannot look for results more substantial than this, there is not much encouragement to pursue such researches, which will in fact never by anything more than academic playthings, and which involve the very real evil of restoring the 'metaphysical ideas and expressions' previously discarded.
>
> (p. 234)

While Ingram is clearly wrong about the future pursuit of 'such researches,' perhaps history will eventually be more kind in regard to the rest of this statement. Ingram and the historicist school have not had the last laugh in their conflict with the followers of Bentham and the deductive school. Beyond being excluded from the mainstream, Ingram has been judged to have excluded himself from the canon of economic thought.

To act as brave a part

Ingram has, however, entered a different canon, the canon of Irish nationalist literature. In his youth, Ingram contributed the ballad *The Memory of the Dead* to the republican paper, *The Nation*. Perhaps more popularly known after its first line as, 'Who fears to speak of Ninety-Eight', the song was published in 1943. It commemorated Irish patriots of a previous generation, participants in the failed rising of 1798. Later in life, Ingram disavowed republican politics, believing that Irish independence, while inevitable, must be postponed indefinitely. There was speculation that he was ashamed of having authored the ballad. But this was not the case. The last time he put pen to paper was to reproduce the song for his daughter in his own handwriting on parchment (Cumann 1907). In one lifetime, John Kells Ingram had occasion to both refuse and embrace canonicity. One verse of *The Memory of the Dead* concludes with hope:

> Alas! that Might can vanquish Right –
> *They* fell and pass'd away;
> But true men, like you, men,
> Are plenty here to-day.

Notes

1   For a comprehensive review of this literature see Renza (1984: 3–29).
2   A characterization of Ingram drawn from Carlyle's diaries (Cumann 1907: 7).

References

Boylan, T.A., and Foley T.P. (1992) *Political Economy and Colonial Ireland*. London: Routledge.
Cumann na Leabharlann (1907) *Bibliography of the Writings of John Kells Ingram*. Dublin.
Deleuze, G. and Guattari F. (1975) [1983] 'What is a Minor Literature', *Mississippi Review*, 11 (3): 13–33.
Ely, Richard T. (1891) *An Introduction to Political Economy*. London: Sonnenschein.
Ingram, J.K. (1878) [1962] 'The Present Position and Prospects of Political Economy', in *Essays in Economic Method*, ed. R.L. Smyth, London: Duckworth.
—— (1880) *Work and the Workman*. London: Longmans.
—— (1888) *A History of Political Economy*. Edinburgh: Adam and Charles Black.
—— (1895) *A History of Slavery and Serfdom*. London: Adam and Charles Black.
—— (1900) *Outlines of the History of Religion*. London: Adam and Charles Black.
—— (1901a) *Human Nature and Morals according to Auguste Comte*. London: Adam and Charles Black.

—— (1901b) *Passages from the Letters of Auguste Comte*. London: Adam and Charles Black.

—— (1904) *Practical Morals, a Treatise on Universal Education*. London: Adam and Charles Black.

Lloyd, D. (1987) *Nationalism and Minor Literature: James Clarence Mangan and the Emergence of Irish Cultural Nationalism*. Berkeley: University of California Press.

Polanyi, K. (1944) [1957] *The Great Transformation*. Boston: Beacon Hill.

Renza, L.A. (1984) '*A White Heron*' *and the Question of Minor Literature*. Madison: University of Wisconsin Press.

9 In search of a canonical history of macroeconomics in the interwar period

Haberler's *Prosperity and Depression* revisited

Mauro Boianovsky

Introduction

It is now widely recognized that pre-Keynesian economic thought did not fit into the mould of what Keynes used to call 'classical economics'. For some decades before *The General Theory*, there had been no simple pattern in the study of economic fluctuations and unemployment, but a plurality of contending explanations. As Terence Hutchison put it, the intellectual situation in economics in the deep depression of the early 1930s 'was one of rather complacent, intellectually messy, confusion, not some rigid, consistent, logically clear-cut, and widely-held "classical" orthodoxy' (Hutchison, 1978, p. 172; see also Sowell, 1972, pp. 210–11; Walker, 1986, pp. 14–15; Backhouse, 1995, part II). It was in that context that the League of Nations set up in 1933 under a five-year grant from the Rockefeller Foundation a programme of research into business cycles in two stages (see de Marchi, 1991, p. 153). In the first stage (1934–6) Gottfried Haberler carried out an analysis of existing theories of the business cycle, followed by a 'synthetic exposition' of the nature and causes of business fluctuations.[1] The outcome was *Prosperity and Depression: A Theoretical Analysis of Cyclical Movements*, published in Geneva by the League of Nations in 1937. In the second stage (1936–8) the theories surveyed by Haberler were supposed to be subjected to statistical testing by Jan Tinbergen (see the preface by Alexander Loveday, Director of the Financial Section and Economic Intelligence Service of the League of Nations, in Haberler, 1937a, p. iv; cf. Tinbergen, 1939).

Prosperity and Depression has since been acclaimed by historians of thought as the authoritative survey of pre-Keynesian business cycle theories (see e.g. Hutchison, 1953, p. 404; Schumpeter, 1954, p. 1123, n. 2; Officer, 1982, p. 151; Pribram, 1983, p. 486; Mirowski, 1985, p. 3; Blaug, 1991, p. 180, n. 10; Laidler, 1991, p. 118; Samuelson, 1996, p. 1682). Succeeding editions (1939, 1941, 1958, 1964) incorporated Haberler's immediate reaction to discussions surrounding Keynes's *General Theory* and his comments on several controversial topics of the 1940s and early 1950s, such as formal post-Keynesian business cycle models, Hayek's Ricardo effect, the so-called Pigou effect, etc.[2] According to Moggridge's study of articles published between 1936 and 1948 and recorded in classes 2.30, 2.31, 2.230, 2.322, and 2.325 of the *Index of Economic Journals*, Haberler's book was third in the individual publication citation rankings (1995, p. 232).

The present paper is set out to investigate the methodological foundations of *Prosperity and Depression* and their influence on Haberler's assessment of theories prevailing before *The General Theory* and of Keynes's impact on macroeconomics. Gottfried Haberler (b. 1900 in Purkersdorf, Austria; d. 1995 in Washington, DC; see biographical information in Chipman, 1987, and Samuelson, 1996) was originally a member of the Austrian school. After graduating at the University of Vienna in 1923, he wrote his habilitation thesis on the economic theory of index numbers (Haberler, 1927). He was, together with Hayek, Machlup, Morgenstern and others, a participant of the famous Mises's private seminar in Vienna in the 1920s and early 1930s (see Haberler, 1981, pp. 121–2; Craver, 1986, pp. 14–15). After holding since the late 1920s the position of 'Privatdozent' at the University of Vienna, Haberler moved to Geneva in 1934 to work as an expert at the financial section of the League of Nations. As Earlene Craver (1986, p. 26) suggests, it was probably the publication in 1933 of his volume on trade theory – where he used the notion of opportunity cost to advance the path-breaking concept of production-possibility frontier – which brought Haberler international fame and led to his appointment in Geneva. He left the League of Nations in 1936 for the department of economics of Harvard University, where he remained until 1971.

One of the regular members of Mises's private seminar was 'the unforgettable Felix Kaufmann' (Haberler, 1981, p. 122), philosopher of social sciences (b. 1895 in Vienna; d. 1949 in New York), who was very active in discussions on methodology (cf. Craver, 1986, pp. 14–15; see also Haberler, [1923–4] pp. 222 and 225). Later on in the 1930s, Kaufmann's 1936 book on the methodology of the social sciences was instrumental in Haberler's emphasis on the distinction between 'tautological' and 'empirical' statements in economics, and on the role of induction in the search for the 'empirical regularities' that are essential for the creation of new hypotheses. I shall argue that Haberler's criticism of Hayek's capital shortage explanation of the crisis (after an initial enthusiasm that showed in his Harris Foundation lecture delivered in Chicago in 1932), as well as his rejection of Keynes's equilibrating mechanism through income changes and his scepticism towards econometric modelling of the business cycle (Tinbergen and others), stem in large part from his views on method.

Analytical framework

The organizing principle of part I of *Prosperity and Depression* is the classification of business cycle theories into groups according to the explanatory

hypotheses deployed (see Haberler, 1946, pp. 1 and 13). This was a urgent
task, since, as Schumpeter put it in his dramatic description of the business cycle literature around World War I (which certainly also applies to
the early 1930s), 'we seem to behold nothing but disagreement and antag-
onistic effort – disagreement and antagonism that went so far as to
be discreditable to the science and even ludicrous' (Schumpeter, 1954,
p. 1125). The purpose of the survey was 'to test the logical consistency'
of the several hypotheses and 'their compatibility with one another and
with accepted economic principles' (Haberler, 1946, p. 1). This would
provide the starting point for the much needed 'synthetic exposition' of
the business cycle in part II. Haberler's methodological standpoint is left
largely only implicit throughout the book, though. We must look at some
of his other writings in order to find out where he stood in the 1930s
controversies on economic methodology.

Most of Haberler's statements on matters of methodology came out of
his criticism of the saving–investment terminology of Keynes and Harrod
(Haberler 1936a, 1937b). He pointed out that the 'neo-Cambridge' terminology had made it difficult to 'decide in this field whether a particular
statement involves a really material assumption about the real world (that
is, about the behavior of individuals), or whether it is a purely "syntactic"
proposition about the definition of certain terms' (1937b, p. 693). This
distinction is, of course, reminiscent of the logical positivism of the 'Vienna
circle', but Haberler had learned from Kaufmann (1933, 1934, 1936) that
one should distinguish between three, not just two, sorts of propositions.
He clarified that in a footnote:

> This distinction is here used in the sense in which it has been made
> quite clear by 'Logical Positivism' (Wittgenstein, Carnap). It should
> be noted, however, that the fact that a proposition has been arrived
> at by purely logical (tautological) derivation from some other propo-
> sition, by no means in itself reduces this derived proposition
> to a tautology, so long as there are 'material' propositions among the
> premises. On all this compare F. Kaufmann, *Methodenlehre der Sozial-
> wissenschaften* (Vienna, 1936), *passim*, and esp. pp. 278–79 (ibid).

The 'Vienna circle' distinction between 'synthetic' statements (verifiable
by empirical evidence) and 'analytic' statements (tautologies) would be
introduced effectively into economics one year later by Hutchison (1938;
but see also his discussion of tautologies in economics in 1933) as a reaction against Lionel Robbins's apriorism (see e.g. Caldwell, 1994, chapter
6). In this connection, it is worth noting that Haberler referred to Hutchison
(1938) in the new chapter on Keynes in the 1939 edition of *Prosperity and
Depression* (see 1946, pp. 194n and 215n). Furthermore, despite the similar
approaches of Kaufmann (1936, part II, chapter 8) and Hutchison (who
referred to Kaufmann; see e.g. 1938, p. 3), the notion, which goes beyond

the Vienna circle, that there are statements that are 'indirectly tested' through the system as a whole cannot be found in the latter.[3]

According to Haberler (1936a, pp. 555 and 559, n. 1, where he referred to Kaufmann, 1936, pp. 32, 43, 48, 257), 'this mistake of treating relationships by definition as causal relationships occurs rather frequently in economics, not only in Cambridge'. As he put it in a letter to Keynes written on 11 April 1936, a relationship by definition is 'exact but does not tell us anything about the real world', while an empirical one 'would tell us something about the world but could not be proved a priori' (Moggridge, 1979, p. 252). Haberler reaffirmed later on in a debate at the 1948 meetings of the American Economic Association his overall anti-apriorism:

> Of course, the difference between experimental and nonexperimental sciences must not be exaggerated. It is a difference in degree only and an anti-empiristic, aprioristic methodology of economics (or any other science) cannot be based on the fact that it is impossible to make laboratory experiments with the economy (or society) as a whole.
>
> (Haberler, 1949a, p. 86n)

In the same vein, there was no straight contrast between the operations of deduction and induction, as Kaufmann (1936, part I, chapter 2; 1934, p. 106; 1933, p. 389) had explained. The premises of deductive reasoning are decided by experience, since they are chosen 'with a view to their empirical applications' (1933, p. 389). Hutchison (1933) made it clear against Robbins that

> it is no comparative justification . . . of the deductive method to attack empirical studies on the grounds of the difficulty of forming successful hypothesis inductively. Quite the reverse. The necessary fundamental assumption of all scientists is that there are some regularities about the facts of the world which allow of successful inductive hypothesis.
>
> (p. 161)

Haberler treated the various explanations of the business cycle (with emphasis on the upper turning point) as empirical statements and called attention to the empirical regularities that could form the inductive basis for the formulation of alternative hypotheses. The first and crucial 'regularity' is the existence of the business cycle itself – that is, cyclical fluctuations in employment and production – which Haberler simply assumed in part I of his report, but went on to argue on empirical basis in part II that it can be divided into four phases: upswing, downswing, upper turning point, and lower turning point (1946, p. 13 and chapter 9).[4] Following that, he suggests that the two regular features of the cycle are (i) the parallel movement between the physical volume of production (and employment) and the money value of transactions, and (ii) the much higher instability in the capital goods sector when compared to the production of consumer goods (1946, pp. 14, 26, 277–8). The last one was not controversial (cf. Schumpeter, 1954, p. 1125), but Haberler was at pains to stress that the former feature is not a tautology, since it is conceivable that prices move in the opposite direction to the cyclical movement of production (Haberler, 1946, pp. 278–9). The statement would be tautological, of course, if prices were absolutely rigid. Haberler later on submitted that this parallelism is suggestive of a causal connection between fluctuations of the money flow ('effective demand') and oscillations in the flow of goods, which, by the way, is consistent with changes in effective demand provoked by autonomous shifts in, e.g., investment (1953, pp. 483–85). He realized that if prices and wages were completely flexible the statement would have to be substantially changed and suggested the concept of 'elasticity of supply' of output to express reactions of aggregate production to changes in the money flow (Haberler, 1953).[5]

In order to explain the business cycle, 'we need either a law about a [cyclical] change in certain data or a dynamic theory' (Haberler, 1946, p. 250; this distinction has a long pedigree in economics; see e.g. Wicksell, 1907, p. 59). This led Haberler to discriminate between exogenous (of which Jevons's 'sunspot theory' is the classical example) and endogenous theories respectively (pp. 8–9). In the first group, the upper turning point is explained by an accidental disturbance, while in the other one the boom itself creates a disequilibrium of the economic system which eventually brings about the crisis. In an article that appeared a couple of months after Haberler finished writing part I of *Prosperity and Depression* in December 1935, he used the distinction between 'logical' (tautological or purely deductive) and 'empirical' propositions to point out that

> From a purely logical point of view, there seems to me to be only a difference of degree between these two types of answers. When it is said that a boom must lead to a crisis, because, say, the expansion of credit is bound to create a vertical maladjustment in the structure of production, this is not to be regarded as a logical but an empirical law. Therefore, exceptions are thinkable and, in fact, we shall see below that it is not difficult to formulate conditions under which the proposition will not hold.
>
> (Haberler, 1936b, p. 4, n. 1)

He further divided the group of endogenous theories into the following categories, according to the reason given for the upper turning point: purely monetary, over-investment (of the monetary and non-monetary types), under-consumption, and psychological theories. With the exception of the purely monetary one (put forward by Ralph Hawtrey), all these theories explain the upper turning point as a result of what Haberler used to call a 'maladjustment in the structure of production', by which he meant 'an allocation of the factors of production in a way that does not correspond to the flow of money' (1936b, p. 4). Furthermore, Haberler's Austrian background showed in his proposition that there are 'vertical' and 'horizontal' maladjustments. If the structure of production does not correspond to 'the decisions of the population as to spending and saving' there is a vertical maladjustment; if it does not correspond to either the 'decisions of consumers as to the distribution of expenditure between various lines of consumption goods' or 'the decisions of producers at every stage as to the distribution of their cost expenditure between different forms of inputs', it is a case of horizontal maladjustment (1946, p. 30; apparently, he introduced this distinction for the first time in 1932, p. 166).[6] Vertical maldjustments are associated with over-investment and under-consumption, while psychological theories are compatible with both types of maladjustment (1946, p. 150).

I shall comment below on how Haberler made use of this scheme to evaluate the explanatory power of alternative hypotheses. Before that, it should be noted that he was critical of the use of the concept of equilibrium in business cycle theory, since it was not empirically framed, but dependent on divergent definitions given by different theories.[7]

> I personally find it advisable to drop the concepts of natural and equilibrium rates ... The concept 'equilibrium rate' suggests, e.g., that there is one definite rate [of interest] ... which ensures the equilibrium* of the economic system as a whole. But this rate cannot be determined even if we agree on the definition of equilibrium, unless we know how the equilibrium can be brought about. Only if we accept as the true conditions of economic equilibrium one of the common theories which proclaim stability either of the level of commodity prices, of factor prices, of some other prices, or of MV in one of the many senses of these terms – only on the basis of one of these theories can we tell what the equilibrium rate is.
>
> [*] What is the equilibrium? It surely cannot be defined by full employment of all factors of production. It is not defined by the condition that 'the market should be cleared'.
>
> (1936b, p. 3)

Haberler repeated his reservations about the use of equilibrium concepts in business cycle analysis when he put forward his own 'synthetic explanation' (cf. 1946, p. 289, n. 1). In the main, he explained the upper turning point as the reaction that follows when – starting from a position of low employment – in the course of a cyclical upswing the economy hits a full employment ceiling. Owing to the operation of the acceleration principle, demand for investment goods will fall abruptly when consumers' goods industries cease to expand. This hypothesis is essentially identical to the one advanced independently by Harrod in his *Trade Cycle* (published in September 1936, when the first edition of *Prosperity and Depression* was already on the press; cf. Haberler, 1937a, pp. 111, n. 4, and 217, n. 1), as Haberler acknowledged in his review of Harrod and in subsequent editions of his book (1937b, p. 695, n. 13; 1946, p. 369, n. 2). It is also part and parcel of Hick's well-known non-linear model of the trade cycle, who referred to Harrod and to Haberler in this connection (1950, p. 99, n. 1). Haberler is here very far from his Austrian heritage, reflecting his critical attitude towards the empirical basis of Hayek's capital shortage hypothesis, as we shall see next.

Money, Hayek and over-investment

In the early 1930s Haberler was quite enthusiastic about Hayek's theory of the business cycle (see 1931a, p. 515; 1931b; 1932). This was in part a by-product of his view that Hayek offered a theoretically superior alternative to both the over-saving hypothesis of Foster and Catchings – 'so harmful and so popular today', as he put it in 1931a, p. 515 – and to the 'traditional monetary theory' (1931b, 1932) represented by Hawtrey. Let us pause for a moment to discuss Haberler's (1946, p. 28; 1936b, p. 4) rejection of Hawtrey's claim that the reason for the crisis is always an interruption of the growth of money supply.

According to Haberler (1946, pp. 20–1 and 362–3), Hawtrey based his theory of the upper turning point on the lag of cash reserves of the banking system behind the expansion of credit, which causes the drain of cash to continue after the expansion of credit has been interrupted. That lag is explained by Hawtrey's assumption that the rise in wages – which largely decides the demand for cash by the public – lags behind the expansion of credit and prices. The upshot is that banks are induced to contract credit – instead of a simple interruption of the expansion – which brings about the crisis (see Laidler, 1991, pp. 104 ff, for a similar account). What Haberler finds particularly unsatisfactory about Hawtrey's explanation is the premise that prosperity could be prolonged indefinitely if only money supply continued to expand, without real maladjustments in the structure of production (especially in the form of the accelerator mechanism described above in connection with Haberler's own exposition of the upper turning point).[8] Furthermore, he did not accept the notion that banks would keep on making the same mistake of underestimating the cash drain in every upswing (p. 363).

Haberler (1946) left only implicit, though, that Hawtrey's pure monetary theory had been falsified by the depression of the early 1930s, which was not preceded by rising wholesale prices. This was the main topic of his 1932 Harris Foundation Lecture, when he argued that the main features of the years 1924–9 in the US were price stability and rapid growth of production, accompanied by increasing money supply and vertical mal-adjustment of the structure of production.

> If we accept the proposition that the productive apparatus is out of gear, that great shifts of labour and capital are necessary to restore equilibrium, then it is emphatically not true that the business cycle is a purely monetary phenomenon, as Mr Hawtrey would have it; this is not true, although monetary forces have brought about the whole trouble. Such a dislocation of real physical capital, as distinguished from purely monetary changes, can in no case be cured in a very short time.
>
> (Haberler, 1932, p. 172)

This is, of course, a description of Hayek's capital shortage hypothesis, which Haberler called a 'more refined monetary theory of the cycle' (1931b, p. 405). What Haberler found especially attractive about this new theory was 'Hayek's convincing proof that "the monetary explanation is not equiv-alent to the explanation through the variations of the general price level". In view of the fact that the present depression in the United States has not been accompanied by serious variations of the wholesale and retail price levels, a theory which does not stress general price changes and yet retains all the obvious advantages and the plausibility of the monetary explanation, should be of considerable interest' (1931b, p. 405). As we could expect from Haberler's application of Kaufmann's framework, it is precisely the investigation of Hayek's ability to explain the American depression that will constitute in *Prosperity and Depression* the crucial test of the capital shortage hypothesis.

It is well known (see e.g. Laidler, 1994; Trautwein, 1996) that Hayek claimed in his *Prices and Production* that it is impossible to bring about a permanent increase in the capital stock of the economy through forced saving. In contrast to voluntary savings, consumers will tend to restore the former proportion between consumption and saving when money income rises during the upswing, with ensuing increase of prices of consumers' goods and abandonment of production in the higher stages. Hayek's reasoning hangs on the crucial assumption that the new roundabout methods of production have not been completed when credit expansion ceases. 'But why must there be any incomplete processes at all when the expansion has to end?', asks Haberler (1946, p. 54). Hayek is not able to show that a steady rate of credit expansion would necessarily bring about unsustainable forced savings.[9] Instead, he argues that credit expansion is halted because of 'a progressive rise in prices and the danger of a complete collapse of the monetary system' (p. 55). The relevance of this conclusion for Hayek's claim that his theory explained the 1929 crisis is pointed out by Haberler:

It seems to follow that [Hayek's] theory does not prove, as it claims to do, that a credit expansion which does not lead to a rise in prices but only prevents a fall in prices must have the same evil effect as the more violent type which brings about a rise in the absolute price level. In a progressive economy, where the output of goods in general grows continuously and prices tend therefore to fall, there is scope for a continuous expansion of credit at a steady state ... The practical importance of this conclusion is considerable in view of the American prosperity in the twenties, a notable feature of which was the fact that wholesale prices did not rise.

(1946, pp. 55–7)

Fifty years later Haberler (1986) reflected once more on Hayek's business cycle theory. He reaffirmed on that occasion his view that there is 'no reason why a steady stream of forced saving, the price level remaining stable, should be unsustainable' (p. 227), but he focused his criticism on Hayek's attempted explanation of the depression as a period of readjustment of the structure of production. Haberler (1946) had already made it clear that this is 'admittedly incomplete and unsatisfactory' and that a general deflationary process (usually referred to as 'secondary deflation') is necessary in order to explain 'why the depression spreads to *all* stages and branches of industry' (p. 58). Later on, he commented on Lionel Robbins belated acknowledgment that unemployment in the 1930s was largely provoked by fall in aggregate demand (and, therefore, that 'Keynesian' measures were justified), which he opposed to Hayek's insistence (in his Nobel Lecture) that the deviation of the actual structure of prices and wages from its equilibrium structure is always the primary cause of unemployment. Haberler's views on the role of empirical testing in economics are apparent in his reaction to Hayek.

[Hayek] ... acknowledges that [his] theory has 'the unfortunate property of not being verifiable by statistical methods'. In his Alfred Nobel Memorial Lecture he argues at length that in economics there are many propositions that in principle – not because of insufficient data – cannot be verified *or, we may add, falsified* ... This is not the place to go into the deep epistemological problems raised by Hayek's Nobel Lecture. The problem at hand is much simpler ... There is sufficient evidence of a general nature to show that Robbins was right.

(1986, pp. 224–5; emphasis added)

Haberler's mention of falsifiability should not be a surprise, for Kaufmann had long stressed that every empirical proposition is 'refutable' (1936, part II, chapter 7; he actually referred to Karl Popper's *Logik der Forschung* in n. 33 to chapter 2, part I, but in connection with probability theory; see also Kaufmann, 1933, p. 399, third paragraph).[10] On the whole, the assessment that 'the high expectations which were originally entertained [in connection with Hayek's theory] have given way to a much more cautious and much more sceptical attitude' (Haberler, 1946, p. 67) seems to apply also to Haberler himself.

Haberler's change of mind about Hayek's approach to business cycles is also visible in the criticism of the notion of equilibrium in *Prosperity and Depression*, which has already been referred to above. In his review of the German edition of Hayek (1933), Haberler had accepted Hayek's view that non-monetary theories of the business cycle are not able to explain their object 'without coming into conflict with the principles of the static system, which is necessarily *equilibrium economics* and has no room for general disturbances' (Haberler, 1931b, p. 405; cf. Hayek, 1933, pp. 85 and 103). In other words, there is no room in Hayek's framework for what Haberler (1946) called 'horizontal' maladjustments of the structure of production and for 'psychological theories' of the kind put forward by Pigou. Haberler stressed, however, that the proposition that the upper turning point is brought about by a 'change from optimism to pessimism' can only be turned into an empirical statement (and, by that, 'make a positive contribution to the explanation of the cycle') if some hypothesis is formulated about how expectations are formed in terms of 'observable factors' (1946, p. 147).[11]

Wrong expectations are also part of the 'non-monetary over-investment theories' of Spiethoff and Cassel, but here Haberler (1946, pp. 32 and 72 ff) was caught in two minds. He tended to play down the differences between these authors and the monetary over-investment theory of Hayek on the grounds that it is largely a matter of the degree of emphasis on real factors (inventions etc.) as starters of the upswing. As far as the explanation of the upper turning point is concerned, Haberler suggested that Spiethoff's diagnosis of the disequilibrium at the end of the boom is 'substantially the same' as that given by Hayek (that is, excess of the production of capital goods and lack of consumers' goods), even though Spiethoff did not draw (as he ought to have) the familiar Hayekian conclusions about the role of the rate of interest (Haberler, 1946, pp. 77–8). However, what Spiethoff contended is that in order for the production of capital goods and the formation of savings 'keep pace with each other, the two processes would have to be adjusted to each other, in mutual knowledge. As such knowledge is lacking, the adjustment is impossible' (Spiethoff, 1953, p. 157; cf. Hayek, 1933, pp. 80–1). In another passage, Haberler seems to realize that Spiethoff's account of the upper turning point was distinct from Hayek's: 'Expansion comes to an end because it is almost impossible to estimate correctly the supply of savings . . . the construction of capital goods must be undertaken in anticipation of demand, which in turn is constituted by saving and cannot be foreseen correctly' (Haberler, 1946, p. 84; see also p. 133, where he shows the ambiguity of classifying Spiethoff's theory as either vertical or horizontal maladjustment).[12] With the publication of Keynes's *General Theory*, however, mistaken expectations – whether money induced or not – and disequilibrium leave the scene, not to mention the business cycle itself.

Under-consumption, Keynes and beyond

How did Keynes's *General Theory* fit in Haberler's classification of business cycle theories? In the first edition (Haberler, 1937a) there are only a few references to Keynes (1936, chapter 22), mainly in connection with the 'psychological theories'. In the second edition (1939) of *Prosperity and Depression* there is a new chapter on 'Some Recent Discussions', which deals basically with the debates that immediately followed the publication of Keynes's book. By then, it was clear to Haberler that Keynes's 'Notes on the Trade Cycle' had little to do with the rest of the book, which was not about mistaken expectations and dynamics, but the application of static equilibrium analysis to the study of unemployment (Haberler, 1946, p. 168; cf. Kregel, 1976, p. 213; and Kohn, 1986).

Haberler's immediate reaction to the publication of *The General Theory* in February 1936 appeared in his methodological criticism of the multiplier, which he submitted to the *Economic Journal* as soon as March of that year. After an acrimonious correspondence with Keynes (who was, of course, editor of the *Journal*), Haberler decided to publish the paper at the Austrian *Zeitschrift für Nationalökonomie* (see Moggridge, 1979, pp. 248 ff). The central points of the article were incorporated into Haberler (1946, pp. 193–4 and 224–7), and the article was reprinted in the American Economic Association 1944 *Readings in Business Cycle Theory*, organized by Haberler himself (Haberler, 1944, chapter 9). Haberler's criticism was aimed at Keynes's (1936, pp. 115 and 122) 'logical theory of the multiplier, which holds good continuously, without time lag, at all moments of time'. After defining the marginal propensity to consume as $\Delta C / \Delta Y$ (measured in wage units), and the multiplier as k in $\Delta Y = k\Delta I$, Keynes argues that, since $\Delta Y = \Delta C + \Delta I$, we can write the marginal propensity to consume as $1 - (1/k)$. Haberler rejected Keynes's claim that the multiplier is, by that, determined by the value of marginal propensity to consume:

> It seems that Mr Keynes has fallen into the trap of treating such a relationship by definition as a causal or empirical relationship between investment and income and that thereby a large part of what he says about the multiplier and its probable magnitude is vitiated. By assuming something about the marginal propensity to consume he assumes something about the multiplier, but this is no more an explanation of the multiplier than pauvreté is an explanation of poverty.
>
> (1936a, p. 554)

Haberler's charge that the relation between the multiplier and the marginal propensity to consume (and between income and investment) in Keynes is a tautology which cannot be used for any causal analysis in the real world has been accepted by many authors (see e.g. Ackley, 1961, pp. 309–12; Kohn, 1986, p. 1208; see also Hutchison, 1938, p. 70, n. 45). He did not convince Keynes, though, who asked Haberler (in a letter of 30 April 1936) 'what has come over you? I am perplexed', to which Haberler answered (2 May 1936) that 'it seems to me that *I* have a right to being perplexed' (Moggridge, 1979, p. 254). Haberler (1936a, p. 556) further criticized Keynes for using two different concepts of propensity to consume: the 'formal' one related by definition to the multiplier (chapter 10 of *The General Theory*) and the 'psychological' (and, by that, refutable) one (chapters 8 and 9), based on introspection and observation. He approved of the notion of a consumption function $C = f(\varUpsilon)$, but insisted that it had no place in the instantaneous multiplier, since 'saving and investment have identically the same meaning' (Moggridge, 1979, p. 251) in Keynes's framework. Consequently, Haberler was not prepared to accept Keynes's claim in the 1937 *Economic Journal* that the 'initial novelty' of his theory lies in the proposition that the equality between saving and investment is assured by changes in the level of income (see Moggridge, 1973, p. 212).

> It is misleading to say that income must change, in order to ensure the equality of S and I. Whatever the level of income may be, S and I must be equal, because they are made so by definition. The change of level of income comes in as a condition only because Mr Keynes takes the 'multiplier' – the 'marginal propensity to consume' – as a constant quantity ... Income must change, not because it is necessary to ensure the equality between S and I, but because we have assumed it by assuming the multiplier.
>
> (Haberler, 1946, p. 193, n. 2;
> cf. 1936a, p. 558)

Haberler's methodological criticism prevented him from realizing that Keynes was driving at the proposition that a decline in output caused by excess aggregate supply will reduce supply more than demand – because of the consumption function – and bring the economy to equilibrium at less than full employment. The equilibrating effect of the contraction in aggregate income has been identified by Don Patinkin (1982, pp. 8–11) and other scholars as the 'central message' of Keynes's *General Theory* (cf. Samuelson, 1996, p. 1683; see also Boianovsky, 1996, for a discussion of the anticipation of the equilibrating mechanism by Frederick B. Hawley). The point was discussed in connection with pre-Keynesian business cycle theory by Lloyd Metzler (1946, 1947), who pointed out that before Keynes a cumulative process of income change was assumed to continue until it was interrupted by some outside force. According to Metzler, the stabilizing influence of consumption upon the cumulative process is the central feature of the 'modern theory of employment', even though he linked Keynes's equilibrating mechanism to the explanation of the turning points of the cycle, instead of the equilibrium level of economic activity (1947, pp. 440–1; cf. Hansen, 1951, pp. 493–7).

Besides Metzler's article, Seymour Harris also included in his book on the *New Economics* a contribution by Haberler which had appeared one year before in the *Review of Economic Statistics* under the title 'The Place of *The General Theory* in the History of Economic Thought'.[13] Haberler did not repeat on that occasion his methodological criticism of the multiplier, but, instead, praised 'the multiplier technique, whose usefulness should not be doubted, despite the crudity with which is often used' (1964b, p. 582). In part III of the third edition of *Prosperity and Depression* he included two sections on 'further observations on the theory of the multiplier' and on 'the foreign trade multiplier' (1946, pp. 455–73) which may help to explain his change of mind. Haberler then distinguished sharply between the 'instantaneous' multiplier of Keynes and the 'successive-spending' multiplier of J.M. Clark and F. Machlup, which uses period analysis to describe the impact on income throughout several periods of a once-and-for-all increase in autonomous spending. It is assumed in this case that consumers' expenditures during one period are determined by their incomes of the preceding one *à la* Robertson. The result is that the total income generated in successive periods can be expressed as a sum of a geometric series, but, in this case, as Haberler pointed out, 'aggregate saving induced in successive periods by any act of investment approaches the amount of the initial investment, implying that S and I are different for any finite period, the differences becoming smaller with the length of the period' (p. 458, n. 1). The final formula for the 'dynamic' multiplier is identical with the formula for the 'comparative-statics' one (cf. Patinkin, 1956, p. 347), but Haberler clearly attached to the dynamic interpretation a non-tautological meaning, since saving and investment differ during the process. Haberler considered Robertson's period analysis as a step in the direction of a 'truly dynamic analysis' and went as far as suggesting in the preface to the Spanish edition of *Prosperity and Depression* that 'there is no doubt' that the future of business cycle research is represented by Robertsonian dynamic sequences (1942, p. xv).[14]

Regardless of Haberler's attitude to the equilibrating effect of income change in Keynes's system, he maintained that an equilibrium with less than full employment could only exist if money wages were rigid (1946, p. 235, n. 1; p. 238; 1964b, p. 584). The point was discussed in an exchange with Keynes in May 1938 (see Moggridge, 1979, pp. 272–3). Haberler asked:

> Would you agree that an equilibrium with involuntary unemployment is incompatible with perfect competition in the labour market? If

namely competition there were perfect, money wages would fall all the time so long as unemployment existed and any conceivably desired level of liquidity could be reached. If that could be agreed upon – and I think you say that yourself in a latter part of your book – most classical economists would agree with you, because nobody denies that unemployment can persist, if money wages are rigid.

He had discussed in the first edition of the book (1937a, pp. 298–9; cf. the corresponding passage in 1946, pp. 403–4 and also p. 242) the positive effects of wage and price reductions on the value of real balances as part of his explanation of the lower turning point. Apart from the introduction of what later became known as the 'Pigou effect', Haberler's description of the indirect effects of a nominal wage fall was quite close to (but written independently of) chapter 19 of *The General Theory*. He submitted, however, that the mechanism was common knowledge (1946, p. 240; cf. the above quoted letter) among orthodox economists such as Pigou, which raised Keynes's objection:

> I am not aware of any passage written before the publication of my book, in which anyone in the classical tradition has said this or anything remotely resembling it ... But you are more learned on this matters than I am, and I await a reference from you to a passage where a classical economist has indicated a theory of wages resembling mine in the above respect.
>
> (Moggridge, 1979, p. 273)

Haberler never provided the references asked by Keynes, though. When Keynes reviewed (anonymously) in the 1939 *Economic Journal* the second edition of Haberler's book, he complained once more that there were no 'precise references to earlier writings' to support Haberler's claim of essential continuity (Moggridge, 1979, p. 275).

We saw above that, in the first edition of *Prosperity and Depression*, Haberler included Keynes in the group of 'psychological theories' on the basis of chapter 22 of *The General Theory*. He also suggested on that occasion (1937a, p. 111, n. 4), that, even though Keynes could not be labelled an underconsumptionist, the concept of the consumption function could be used in support of certain aspects of the underconsumptionist thesis. Haberler was aware that underconsumption theory was, like Keynes's, not primarily about the cycle, but long depressions (Haberler, 1946, pp. 119 and 234; cf. Bleaney, 1976, p. 13). As far as the the explanation of the upper turning point is concerned, his main objections to the over-saving theories of Hobson and Foster and Catchings were, as we could perhaps expect, of an empirical nature: 'There is no evidence that an absorption of savings occurs during the boom or before the crisis ... There invariably exists a brisk demand for new capital, signalised by high interest rates ... There is no evidence for the assumption that the rate of saving rises at the end of the boom . . .' (1946, pp. 123, 126).[15] There is, according to Haberler (1946, pp. 244–5), a distinguished underconsumption flavour to several passages in *The General Theory* where chronic depression is described as a result of the low propensity to consume and vanishing opportunities for new investment. He did not dismiss the possibility of economic stagnation, but, once more, stressed *à la* Kaufmann that 'only the careful scrutiny of a mass of experience and the study of historical processes can make the hypothesis more or less probable' (1946, pp. 246–7).[16]

It is well known that the so-called 'Pigou effect' was brought to the forefront of macroeconomics when Pigou introduced in 1943 the impact of increasing real wealth on consumption as a reaction against Alvin Hansen's secular stagnation thesis. Haberler was, however, sceptical of the empirical relevance of the 'effect' in the actual cycle mechanism (1951, p. 577). He pointed out that the dynamic repercussions of falling prices and nominal wages were far more relevant for the real world:

> What Don Patinkin [1948, *passim*] somewhat pompously enunciates as 'the Pigou effect' . . . is just common sense which must have been in the minds of many writers. At any rate, when I stated it in the first edition of my *Prosperity and Depression*, I thought that I expressed an obvious fact . . . It is true, of course, that all this is not the whole story and that it does not settle all problems of policy. Dynamic repercussions upon the marginal efficiency of capital, changes in the income distribution due to the increased real value of money debts and similar frictions are vastly more important than the mechanics of the static Keynesian system . . . It is high time that Keynesians recognize the inability of the Keynesian system to cope with the problems of wage and price flexibility so that the discussion can be moved out of the dead-end track on which it has been shunted by those writers who take as the last word the static Keynesian system which its author, if he had lived longer and had not been preoccupied with other matters, would have abandoned long ago as untenable intermediate station.
>
> (Haberler, 1949b, p. 571)

The answer to the empirical question 'does flexibility of prices and wages promote economic stability?' was (or should be) according to Haberler (1946, pp. 243 and 491 ff; 1953) the most pressing item in the business cycle research agenda after Keynes. He suggested that Keynes himself (despite a few hints in chapter 19 of *The General Theory*) had no definite answer to that question (Haberler, 1953, p. 485). Formal 'Keynesian' models of the business cycle put forward in the 1940s and 1950s usually assumed rigid wages and prices, and had nothing to say about that.[17]

Epilogue

The early 1930s variety of divergent explanations of the business cycle was largely gone in the 1940s, not because of Haberler suggested 'synthetic' explanations, but because of the proliferation of mathematical models often cast in terms of the multiplier–accelerator mechanism. The 'modern theory' of the business cycle based on Keynes found its 'highest expression', as Haberler (1953, p. 486) put it, in Hicks' 1950 volume, whose explanation of the upper turning point was close to Haberler's, as we saw above. Hicks and others only dealt with the problem of 'capital widening', though, signalizing a 'change in the centre of gravity' of business cycle research when compared to Hayek's emphasis on the problem of 'capital deepening' (p. 490). Haberler pointed out, however, that the accelerator cannot be found in *The General Theory* and that 'it is almost certain that [Keynes] would have rejected modern business cycle theories. He was too much of a business cycle practician and had a deep distrust in complicated mechanical models' (p. 485, n. 2).

Haberler was not fond of 'mechanical models' himself. He had noticed in the second edition of *Prosperity and Depression*, in connection with the work of Ragnar Frisch and Jan Tinbergen, that a dynamic theory of the business cycle 'if fully elaborated in precise terms . . . requires a highly complicated mathematical technique and present formidable problems from the purely formal logical point of view' (1946, p. 254). He discussed the matter further in part III of the book, while commenting on the models put forward by Samuelson, Lundberg, and especially the econometrics of Tinbergen. Haberler compared a 'general dynamic theory comprising the economic system as a whole' to 'Laplace's famous world formula'.

> Given the state of the economic universe at a single point of time (or during a short period) such a formula would enable the human mind to reconstruct the course of economic events into the remote past and to foresee its evolution in the distant future; to an intellect equipped with such a theory 'nothing would be uncertain and the future as well as the past would be present before its eyes' (Laplace).
>
> (Haberler, 1946, p. 478)

Haberler was aware that this is a 'distant ideal', but contended that, in any event, 'some extrapolation, some prediction of the future (or of the past) must be possible, if [Tinbergen's] scheme has any value, not only from the practical, but also from a purely scientific, point of view'. He refrained from pursuing the matter in detail, on the grounds that it would require an extensive discussion of 'fundamental epistemological questions' (p. 479). From the perspective of Kaufmann's philosophical framework (which has many points in common with Popper's) prediction is essential to science. Haberler reaffirmed his position in his 1956 critique of 'certain tendencies in modern economic theory', when he stated that the proliferation of formal models of the business cycle (linear or non-linear) have been so far 'most disappointing', especially because, even if fitting the data well, none of them 'stood up to the test of extrapolation beyond the period from which the data were taken' (p. 464).[18]

One of the corollaries of the econometric approach to the business cycle – whether of the purely endogenous or of the (damped) impulse/propagation type – is that no special theory of the turning point is needed, which was firstly noticed by Tinbergen (1940, p.78). This would render the whole analysis carried out in *Prosperity and Depression* obsolete, but Haberler (1946, pp. 479–80) maintained that, given the 'theoretical stage' of formal models, turning point analysis is necessary for testing and construction of theoretical models, without dismissing the possibility of an eventual general theory 'capable of explaining the cycle in all its phases' (p. 480; cf. Kim, 1988, pp. 61–2). By the middle 1950s Haberler became convinced, though, that the main problem with the formal models produced so far was the neglect of monetary factors, in contrast with their importance in historical episodes such as the Great Depressions of the 1870s and 1930s (see Haberler, 1956). The publication of Friedman's and Schwartz's *Monetary History* in 1963 confirmed that, and Friedman's presidential address of 1967 provided an explanation for the co-movement between money and output in the business cycle. This led Haberler (1980, pp. 605–7) to suggest that the empirical proposition that there is a short-run (not permanent) trade-off between unemployment and inflation formed the basis for a 'Post-Keynesian Consensus' in the 1970s.

Prosperity and Depression has been sometimes described as a history of the development of business cycle theory (see e.g. Mirowski, 1985, p. 3), despite Haberler's explicit disclaimers (1946, pp. 1 and 12). There are a few historical references in the book – such as Marshall's description of the relation between interest and prices (p. 15, n. 2), Wicksell's adoption of Spiethoff's non-monetary explanation (p. 72),[19] Marx on reinvestment cycles (p. 84), Labordère's 1908 elaboration of the capital shortage hypothesis (p. 46, n. 1), Malthus, Sismondi and Lauderdale as founders of the underconsumptionist tradition (p. 118), and a list of the authors who developed the acceleration principle from T.N. Carver on (p. 87) – but they are not pursued. Nevertheless, as Link (1959, p. 186) has shown in his well-known study of theories of economic fluctuations in the first half of the nineteenth century, Haberler's classification scheme can be profitably applied to other periods as well.[20] But is *Prosperity and Depression* the canonical history of interwar macroeconomics? A quick search through macroeconomic textbooks (especially those written in the 1950s and 1960s, the heyday of 'Keynesian economics') shows that Keynes's caricature of 'classical economics' as a straw man to be knocked down still survives (cf. Haberler, 1964b, p. 594).[21] On the other hand, the development of the 'new classical school' in the 1970s has led to the opposite view that Keynesian economics was just a detour in the history of business cycle theories (see e.g. Lucas, 1981, pp. 273–7; Kim, 1988, pp. 2–3), which is also far from the account found in *Prosperity and Depression*. What Haberler has given us is a comprehensive and critical assessment of the complex interwar macroeconomics grounded on a clear methodological standpoint.

Notes

I would like to thank Mark Blaug, Susan Howson and Paul Samuelson for their comments. I am also grateful to Guido Erreygers, Albert Jolink, Michalis Psalidopoulos and other participants at the 1997 European Conference on the History of Economics ('Constructing the Canon') for helpful discussion. Financial support from CNPq (Brazilian Research Council) and a travel grant from CAPES (Brazil) are gratefully acknowledged. (Laidler's (1999) account of inter-war macroeconomics came out when this chapter was already on the press.)

1 According to Moggridge (1995, p. 225, n. 2) the survey was first offered by the League of Nations to Dennis Robertson, who apparently declined the invitation.
2 The first edition of *Prosperity and Depression* was published by the League in 1937 in English and in French with two parts ('Systematic Analysis of the Theories of the Business Cycle' and 'Synthetic Exposition Relating to the Nature and Causes of Business Cycles', respectively). The second edition came out in 1939 with a new chapter 8 added to part I. The third edition enlarged by part III ('Further Reflections on Recent Developments in Trade Cycle Theory') was published by the League in 1941 and reprinted by the United Nations in 1946. The fourth edition (the first by a private publisher) came out in 1958 with a new part III ('Monetary and Real Factors Affecting Economic Stability . . .') and two appendices ('Notes on the Present State of Business Cycle Theory' and 'The Pigou Effect Once More'). Appendix I was omitted in the fifth edition (1964) and a new foreword added. Translations were published in Japanese (1938), Swedish (1940), Spanish (1942), Greek (1943) and German (1948, 1955).
3 Cf. Caldwell, 1994, p. 145, who mentions Machlup's use of Kaufmann's third type of propositions (called by Kaufmann, 1933, p. 392, 'heuristic postulates'; see also Kaufmann, 1942). On the similarities between Kaufmann and Hutchison see Blaug, 1980, p. 94n, who, however, misses the point that Kaufmann (1944) is a revised translation of the 1936 volume.
4 See also Haberler (1932, p. 161), when he assumed 'that we have such a thing as a business cycle' and that 'we have been able to isolate this movement statistically'. As Lucas (1981, p. 274) points out, the 'typical business cycle' analysed by Haberler had been discovered and documented in the well-known empirical studies of Wesley Mitchell.
5 Zarnowitz (1985, p. 535, n. 9) has suggested that the positive correlation of movements in prices and quantities stressed by Haberler 'would indicate that shifts in aggregate demand dominate the shifts in aggregate supply over the business cycle'. There is no doubt that this is quite close to Haberler's meaning (cf. 1953).
6 Haberler (1936b, p. 5, n. 1) further assumed, 'as most cycle theories do, that the money saved flows through the capital market and that the distribution among the various investment opportunities is made automatically in a correct way', that is, he excluded the possibility of divergences between the composition of the supply of capital goods and demand represented by savings.

7 In the same vein, Hutchison (1938, p. 107) contended that the use of equilibrium conditions in economics was only justifiable if the tendency towards equilibrium could be postulated as an empirical proposition. Haberler was critical of Schumpeter's notion that the system passes through an equilibrium position on its way from the lower to the upper turning point (1946, p. 81, n. 1).

8 See also Hawtrey's (1937) reaction to Haberler's criticism. Interestingly enough, he accused Haberler's synthesis of being 'purely theoretical with no reference to practical experience' (p. 96).

9 Haberler had contemplated before the possibility that new processes were already finished when the additional money is spent, but dismissed it in the end (1932, p. 170, bottom).

10 In the third edition of *Prosperity and Depression* Haberler (1946, pp. 481–91) discussed in detail Hayek's attempt in 1939 to use the so-called 'Ricardo effect' to provide an alternative explanation of the upper turning point. According to Hayek's new version, the crisis is brought about not by an increase of the rate of interest, but by the impact of a rise in the price of consumers' goods – and the equivalent fall of real wages – on the entrepreneurs' decision to substitute labour for capital. After a lengthy examination, Haberler rejects Hayek's new hypothesis on the empirical grounds that the substitution of labour for capital is too slow a process to be relevant for short-run fluctuations, and that real wages actually move pro-cyclically. He concludes that 'one cannot help getting the impression that [Hayek] builds his theory on a rather shaky empirical foundation' (p. 491; see also 1986, p. 226, for the same judgement).

11 He went as far as suggesting that expectations are 'non-operational concepts' and that only by asking the individuals we can find out how they are formed (1946, p. 252; cf. Hutchison, 1938, pp. 113–14). The way out could be that 'from a strictly logical point of view, the psychological link between the past and the present consisting of expectations may be dropped and the theory stated in terms of direct relationship between observable phenomena at different points of time' (1946, p. 253, n. 1).

12 According to Haberler (p. 79) Cassel explained the upper turning point as result of a reduction in the flow of savings at the end of the boom, when the production of capital goods increases. I have argued elsewhere that while this is a sufficient condition for the crisis in Cassel, it is not necessary, since the crucial factor is that prices in the market for capital goods are not decided by a *tâtonnement* process (see Boianovsky, 1999).

13 A German translation of the article was added to the 1948 and 1955 German editions of *Prosperity and Depression*. It was reprinted (with a new section on Keynes 'Sixteen Years Later') under the title 'The General Theory after Ten Years and Sixteen Years Later' in a book on Keynes edited by R. Lekachman in 1964.

14 Haberler was not fond of the third approach to investment and saving in the 1930s, that is, the one put forward by the Swedes. 'In spite of the appearance to the contrary, no statements about facts are involved' in the description by the Stockholm school of how the *ex post* equality between investment and saving comes about. It is not a description of a real, causal, process, since 'what actually happens if planned saving and investment differ is *assumed* by way of illustration' (1946, p. 181, n. 2; cf. Ackley, 1961, p. 325, n. 9).

15 Haberler was attracted to another version of the under-consumption theory, based on the effect of a rise in the supply of consumers' goods (instead of a fall in demand) at the end of the boom. He ascribed that hypothesis to Aftalion (who, in his turn, influenced authors such as Robertson and Schumpeter) and considered it to be, when combined with the acceleration principle, the best alternative to and the 'direct opposite' of the shortage-of-capital explanation of

the crisis (1946, pp. 32, 103, 127 ff). He characteristically concluded that only 'extensive empirical studies' could decide which hypothesis was correct (p. 376). Empirical testing is not a straightforward matter, though, as can be gathered from Haberler's reactions to Tinbergen's (1938) negative statistical findings regarding the acceleration principle and, in another context, to Leontief's famous empirical refutation of the Heckscher-Ohlin Theorem (the so-called 'Leontief Paradox'). In both cases, Haberler criticized the tests for lack of correct speci-fication of the respective theories (see 1946, p, 87, n. 13; 1961, pp. 71–2).

16 Guthrie and Tarascio (1992, pp. 402–3) have concluded from their survey of the opinions regarding the interpretation of Keynes's position on secular stag-nation that Haberler (1946) was ambivalent on whether Keynes actually subscribed to that view. Haberler was quite clear about that in his other writ-ings, though (see e.g. 1986, p. 221).

17 The relation between price flexibility and instability has been thoroughly exam-ined by the macroeconomic literature since the late 1980s (see e.g. Blanchard and Fischer, 1989, pp. 546–8).

18 Milton Friedman was also critical of the poor predictive power of macro-econometric models in the NBER *Conference on Business Cycles* edited by Haberler in 1951 (see Kim, 1988, p. 78).

19 While Wicksell was quite positive about Spiethoff's work on business cycles, it is hardly accurate to say that he 'adopted' the latter's theory (see Boianovsky, 1995).

20 Link suggests the following matches: Hawtrey/Thomas Attwood; Hayek/James Wilson and J.S. Mill; Hobson/Thomas Malthus; Keynes/Thomas Joplin and Malthus; Pigou/Thomas Tooke and J.S. Mill (and, one could add, John Mills).

21 See e.g. Ackley, 1961, chapter 5, and Cochrane, 1970, chapter 5. Ackley warns that his model of 'classical economics' is 'historically inaccurate' and is devised for pedagogical reasons only, but his warnings are not always taken into account by students or even by other authors (cf. Cochrane, p. 92).

References

Ackley, G. (1961) *Macroeconomic Theory*. New York: Macmillan.

Backhouse, R. (1995) *Interpreting Macroeconomics: Explorations in the History of Macro-economic Thought*. London: Routledge.

Blanchard, O.J. and Fischer, S. (1989) *Lectures on Macroeconomics*. Cambridge (Mass): MIT Press.

Blaug, M. (1980) *The Methodology of Economics*. Cambridge: Cambridge University Press.

—— (1991) 'Second Thoughts on the Keynesian Revolution'. *History of Political Economy*. 23 (2): 171–92.

Bleaney, M. (1976) *Underconsumption Theories: A History and Critical Analysis*. London: Lawrence and Wishart.

Boianovsky, M. (1995) 'Wicksell's Business Cycle'. *European Journal of the History of Economic Thought*. 2 (2): 275–411.

—— (1996) 'Anticipations of the General Theory: The Case of F.B. Hawley'. *History of Political Economy*. 28 (3): 371–90.

—— (1999) 'Cassel on Cyclical Growth'. In C. Sardoni and P. Kriesler (eds) *Keynes' Post-Keynesianism and Political Economy: Essays in Honour of G.C. Harcourt*. London: Routledge.

Caldwell, B.J. [1982] (1994) *Beyond Positivism: Economic Methodology in the Twentieth Century*. Revised edition. London: Routledge.

Chipman, J.S. (1987) 'Haberler, Gottfried', in J. Eatwell et al. (eds) *The New Palgrave*, vol. 2. London: Macmillan.

Cochrane, J.L. (1970) *Macroeconomics Before Keynes*. Glenview: Scott, Foresman and Company.

Craver, E. (1986) 'The Emigration of the Austrian Economists'. *History of Political Economy.* 18 (1): 1–32.

de Marchi, N. (1991) 'League of Nations Economists and the Ideal of Peaceful Change in the Decade of the Thirties', in C.D.W. Goodwin (ed.) *Economics and National Security: A History of their Interaction.* Durham: Duke University Press.

Guthrie, W. and Tarascio, V. (1992) 'Keynes on Economic Growth, Stagnation and Structural Change: New Light on a 55-Year Controversy'. *History of Political Economy* 24 (2): 381–412.

Haberler, G. [1923–4] (1994) 'Economics as an Exact Science. Translated by P. Camiller', in I.M. Kirzner (ed.) *Classics in Austrian Economics*, vol. II, pp. 215–25. London: Pickering.

—— (1927) *Der Sinn der Indexzahlen.* Tübingen: Mohr.

—— (1931a) 'Irving Fisher's "Theory of Interest"'. *Quarterly Journal of Economics.* 45 (May): 499–516.

—— (1931b) Review of *Geldtheorie und Konjunkturtheorie*, by F.A. Hayek. *Quarterly Journal of Economics.* 39 (June): 404–7.

—— (1932) 'Money and the ·Business Cycle'. Q. Wright (ed.) *Gold and Monetary Stabilization.* Chicago: Chicago University Press, pp. 47–74. As reprinted in A.Y.C. Koo (ed.) (1993) *The Liberal Economic Order: Essays by Gottfried Haberler*, vol. 2. Aldershot: Edward Elgar, chapter 9.

—— (1933) *Der Internationale Handel.* Berlin: Springer.

—— (1936a) 'Mr. Keynes' Theory of the "Multiplier": A Methodological Criticism'. *Zeitschrift für Nationalökonomie.* 7 (June): 299–305. As reprinted in A.Y.C. Koo (ed.) (1985) *Selected Essays of Gottfried Haberler.* Cambridge (Mass): MIT Press, chapter 23.

—— (1936b) 'Some Reflections on the Present Situation of Business Cycle Theory'. *Review of Economic Statistics.* 18 (Feb): 1–7.

—— (1937a) *Prosperity and Depression: A Theoretical Analysis of Cyclical Movements.* Geneva: League of Nations.

—— (1937b) 'Review of *The Trade Cycle: An Essay*, by R.F.Harrod'. *Journal of Political Economy.* 45 (Dec): 690–97.

—— (1942) *Prosperidad y Depresion: Análisis Teórico de los Movimentos Cíclicos.* Translation of the 2nd edn. of Haberler, *Prosperity and Depression.* Mexico: Fondo de Cultura.

—— (ed.) (1944) *Readings in Business Cycle Theory.* Philadelphia: Blakiston.

—— (1946) *Prosperity and Depression: A Theoretical Analysis of Cyclical Movements.* Reprint of the 3rd edn (1941). Lake Success, New York: United Nations.

—— (1949a) 'Discussion'. *American Economic Review.* 39 (May): 84–8.

—— (1949b) 'Further Comment'. *Quarterly Journal of Economics.* 63 (Dec): 569–71.

—— (1951) 'The Pigou Effect Once More'. *Journal of Political Economy.* 60 (June): 240–6. As reprinted in A.Y.C. Koo (ed.) (1985) *Selected Essays of Gottfried Haberler.* Cambridge (Mass): MIT Press, chapter 25.

—— (1953) 'Notes on the Present State of Business Cycle Theory'. *Wirtschaftstheorie und Wirtschaftspolitik, Festschrift für Alfred Amonn.* As translated and reprinted in G. Haberler (1958) *Prosperity and Depression: A Theoretical Analysis of Cyclical Movements.* 4th edn. London: George Allen and Unwin, pp. 483–94.

—— (1956) 'Monetary and Real Factors Affecting Economic Stability: A Critique of Certain Tendencies in Modern Economic Theory'. *Banca Nazionale del Lavoro* 38. As reprinted in G. Haberler (1964) *Prosperity and Depression: A Theoretical Analysis of Cyclical Movements*. 5th edn. London: George Allen and Unwin, chapter 13.

—— (1958) *Prosperity and Depression: A Theoretical Analysis of Cyclical Movements*. 4th edn. London: George Allen and Unwin.

—— (1961) 'A Survey of International Trade Theory'. *Special Papers in International Finance*, no. 1, Princeton University. As reprinted in A.Y.C. Koo (ed.) (1985) *Selected Essays of Gottfried Haberler*. Cambridge (Mass): MIT Press, chapter 4.

—— (1964a) *Prosperity and Depression: A Theoretical Analysis of Cyclical Movements*. 5th edn. London: George Allen and Unwin.

—— (1964b) 'The General Theory After Ten Years and Sixteen Years Later', in R. Lekachman (ed.) *Keynes' General Theory, Reports of Three Decades*. New York: St Martin's Press, pp. 269–96. As reprinted in A.Y.C. Koo (ed.) (1985) *Selected Essays of Gottfried Haberler*. Cambridge (Mass): MIT Press, chapter 26.

—— (1980) 'Notes on Rational and Irrational Expectations'. American Enterprise Institute Reprint no. 111. As reprinted in A.Y.C. Koo (ed.) (1985) *Selected Essays of Gottfried Haberler*. Cambridge (Mass): MIT Press, chapter 27.

—— (1981) 'Mises's Private Seminar'. *Wirtschaftspolitische Blätter*. 4: 121–6.

—— [1986] (1989) 'Reflections on Hayek's Business Cycle Theory'. *Cato Journal*. 6 (2): 421–35. As reprinted in *Wirtschaftspolitische Blätter*. 2: 220–31.

Hansen, A.H. (1951) *Business Cycles and National Income*. New York: Norton.

Hawtrey, R.G. (1937) 'Professor Haberler on the Trade Cycle'. *Economica*. 5 (Feb): 93–7.

Hayek, F.A. [1933] (1966) *Monetary Theory and the Trade Cycle*. New York: A.M. Kelley.

Hicks, J. (1950) *A Contribution to the Theory of the Trade Cycle*. Oxford: Clarendon Press.

Hutchison, T.W. (1933) 'A Note on Tautologies and the Nature of Economic Theory'. *Review of Economic Studies*. 1 (1): 159–61.

—— (1938) *The Significance and Basic Postulates of Economic Theory*. London: Macmillan.

—— (1953) *A Review of Economic Doctrines: 1870–1929*. New York: Oxford University Press.

—— (1978) *On Revolution and Progress in Economic Knowledge*. Cambridge: Cambridge University Press.

Kaufmann, F. (1933) 'On the Subject-Matter and Method of Economic Science'. *Economica*, old series. 13 (Nov): 381–401.

—— (1934) 'The Concept of Law in Economic Science'. *Review of Economic Studies*. 2 (2): 103–9.

—— (1936) *Methodenlehre der Sozialwissenschaften*. Vienna: Springer.

—— (1942) 'On the Postulates of Economic Theory'. *Social Research*. 9 (3): 379–95.

—— (1944) *Methodology of the Social Sciences*. New York: Oxford University Press.

Keynes, J.M. (1936) *The General Theory of Employment, Interest and Money*. London: Macmillan.

Kim, K. (1988) *Equilibrium Business Cycle Theory in Historical Perspective*. Cambridge: Cambridge University Press.

Kohn, M. (1986) 'Monetary Analysis, the Equilibrium Method, and Keynes's "General Theory"'. *Journal of Political Economy*. 94 (6): 1191–1224.

Koo, A.Y.C. (ed.) (1985) *Selected Essays of Gottfried Haberler*. Cambridge (Mass): MIT Press.

—— (ed.) (1993) *The Liberal Economic Order: Essays by Gottfried Haberler*, vol. 2. Aldershot: Edward Elgar.

Kregel, J. (1976) 'Economic Methodology in the Face of Uncertainty: The Modelling Methods of Keynes and the Post Keynesians'. *Economic Journal.* 86 (June): 209–25.

Laidler, D. (1991) *The Golden Age of the Quantity Theory.* Hempstead: Philip Allan.

—— (1994). 'Hayek on Neutral Money and the Cycle', in M. Colonna and H. Hagemann (eds) *Money and the Business Cycle: The Economics of F.A. Hayek*, vol. 1. Aldershot: Edward Elgar.

—— (1999) *Fabricating the Keynesian Revolution: Studies of the Inter-war Literature on Money, the Cycle and Unemployment*, Cambridge: Cambridge University Press.

Link, R.G. (1959). *English Theories of Economic Fluctuations: 1815–1848.* New York: Columbia University Press.

Lucas, R.E., Jr (1981) *Studies in Business-Cycle Theory.* Cambridge (Mass): MIT Press.

Metzler, L. (1946) 'Business Cycles and the Modern Theory of Employment'. *American Economic Review.* 36 (June): 278–91.

—— (1947) 'Keynes and the Theory of Business Cycles', in S.E. Harris (ed.) *The New Economics.* New York: Knopf.

Mirowski, P. (1985) *The Birth of the Business Cycle.* New York: Garland.

Moggridge, D. (ed.) (1973) *The Collected Writings of John Maynard Keynes*, vol. 14. London: Macmillan.

—— (ed.) (1979) *The Collected Writings of John Maynard Keynes*, vol. 29. London: Macmillan.

—— (1995) 'The Diffusion of the Keynesian Revolution: The Young and the Graduate Schools', in A.F. Cottrell and M.S. Lawlor (eds) *New Pespectives on Keynes.* Durham: Duke University Press.

Officer, L.H. (1982) 'Prosperity and Depression – And Beyond'. *Quarterly Journal of Economics.* 97 (Feb): 149–59.

Patinkin, D. (1948) 'Price Flexibility and Full Employment'. *American Economic Review*, September: 38: 543–64.

—— [1956] (1965) *Money, Interest and Prices*, 2nd edn. New York: Harper and Row.

—— (1982) *Anticipations of the General Theory? And Other Essays on Keynes.* Oxford: Basil Blackwell.

Pribram, K. (1983) *A History of Economic Reasoning.* Baltimore: Johns Hopkins University Press.

Samuelson, P.A. (1996) 'Gottfried Haberler (1900–1995)'. *Economic Journal.* 106 (Nov): 1679–87.

Schumpeter, J.A. (1954) *History of Economic Analysis.* New York: Oxford University Press.

Spiethoff, A. [1923] (1953) 'Business Cycles'. *International Economic Papers.* 3: 75–171.

Sowell, T. (1972) *Say's Law: An Historical Analysis.* Princeton: Princeton University Press.

Tinbergen, J. (1938) 'Statistical Evidence on the Acceleration Principle'. *Economica.* 5 (May): 164–76.

—— (1939) *Statistical Testing of Business-Cycle Theories.* 2 vols. Geneva: League of Nations.

—— (1940) 'Econometric Business Cycle Research'. *Review of Economic Studies.* 7: 73–90. As reprinted in G. Haberler (1944) *Readings in Business Cycle Theory.* Philadelphia: Blakiston, chapter 4.

Trautwein, H.-M. (1996) 'Money, Equilibrium and the Business Cycle: Hayek's Wicksellian Dichotomy'. *History of Political Economy.* 28 (1): 27–55.

Walker, D. (1986) 'Keynes as a Historian of Economic Thought: The Perspectives of the "General Theory"'. *Research in the History of Economic Thought and Methodology.* 4: 1–36.

Wicksell, K. [1907] (1953) 'The Enigma of Business Cycles'. *International Economic Papers.* 3: 58–74.

Zarnowitz, V. (1985) 'Recent Work on Business Cycles in Historical Perspective: A Review of Theories and Evidence'. *Journal of Economic Literature.* 23 (2): 523–80.

10 Preobrazhensky and the theory of economic development[1]

Michalis Hatziprokopiou and Kostas Velentzas

Introduction

It is generally accepted that among the three major religions which were developed in the middle east there exists an inner connection. Mohammedanism recognizes the holiness of Jesus as does Christianity with respect to Moses and the Prophets. However it is interesting to note that, first, this kind of recognition only seems to be found in an emerging religion towards an established one and not vice versa and, second, the relation breaks down with the establishment of the new religion. Mohammedanism recognises the holiness of Jesus but largely ignores the Great Fathers. The same is true for Christianity regarding Moses and the Prophets where interest in Judaic tradition ends after Jesus. The consequences of these dissociations are obvious. There is hardly any discourse between different religions or even between exponents of different interpretations of the same religion.

We can find analogies to the above in economics. Specifically, we may observe that Marx recognized his debt to Ricardo and other previous pioneering classic authors but he had a low opinion about the work of their students. Today, in turn, mainstream economists accept Marx's treatises as the last classic works on economics and they comment on his writings, but with a few exceptions they ignore the work of the followers of Marx. It follows that scientific discussion among different schools of thought becomes minimal. As a result different fields of research in economics develop within narrow frameworks of orthodoxy and suppress the possibility of a broader synthesis.

In this paper we are going to analyse the work of Eugene Preobrazhensky, one of the most prominent economists who participated in the industrialization debate of the 1920s in the Soviet Union. Preobrazhensky, who developed a coherent theory related to the issue of economic development, does not belong to the canon. However we shall show that the ideas expressed by Preobrazhensky have not only a historical significance but also they are relevant for the economic reality of the contemporary world. The aim of this paper is to analyse this aspect of Preobrazhensky's work and to show that his work embodies Marxian economic considerations as well as mainstream economic growth theory.

The rest of this paper is organized as follows: in the next section some historical information about politics in the Soviet Union of the 1920s is given. In the third section the ideas of Preobrazhensky are presented. In the fourth section we comment on the relation between his theory and mainstream economics while in the fifth section we comment on the relation between his theory and soviet orthodoxy. Concluding remarks follow.

Soviet ideology and politics in the 1920s

The Soviet Union of the period between the October Revolution and the late 1920s is characterized by a variety of economic systems, the one succeeding the other. The so-called state or controlled capitalism established just after 1917 had two main features. These were, first, nationalization of the land (which at the time belonged to landowners) and its free distribution to the peasants, and, second, control of private enterprise by the state authorities as well as workers' councils. Extraordinary circumstances, however, due to the civil war and foreign intervention, led to the policies of war communism, which lasted from July 1918 until February 1921. The specific policies of war communism were nationalization of big industry and also, later, small industry; application of administrative methods for the concentration of agricultural products and for securing factory discipline; growth of bureaucracy and the parallel development of a centralized system of resource allocation in industry, consumption and the army; and finally, emphasizing exchange in kind and thus restricting the importance and the role of money. The new Economic Policy (NEP) was initiated by Lenin in February 1921 to counter the problems of reconstructing the economy after the end of the civil war at the economic level, on the one hand, and, on the other hand, of restoring, at the political level, the worker–peasant alliance, which had been damaged in previous years by coercive methods used to extract agricultural surplus. The main characteristics of NEP were the revival of market relations and trade, decentralization in the decision-making process of state enterprises and the use of taxation in place of requisitions for the concentration by the state of agricultural products. In April 1929 the first five-year plan for the period 1928–1933, for which work had started much earlier, was approved. The primary target of the plan was the transformation of the Soviet Union from an importer of machines to a country *producing* machines. The plan also prepared the ground for the collectivization of agriculture, which was going to follow soon. In this way the plan secured the resources for investment and industrialization.

Drastic changes in the economic system, like those mentioned above, which were closely connected to significant political issues, caused heated debates among a great variety of people. Party as well as non-party economists, political theoreticians and intellectuals, almost 'everyone who was politically and intellectually articulate in Soviet society', participated in the discussions. In the process of applying Marxist thought to specific economic problems, for which 'the old books could not provide any positive guidance', original ideas and interesting analytical tools were developed. 'This alone makes their debate a singularly exciting chapter in the history of economic doctrines; a chapter which is particularly worth exploring' (Erlich, 1960: xix). One of the central issues of the debate throughout the period but especially during the years 1924–8 was the industrialization issue. The fundamental significance of the issue is justified from the fact that it was inseparably connected to the question of the development pattern which the Soviet Union was to follow.

Industrialization was a political and economic necessity for the Soviet Union of the middle 1920s. There were three main non-political reasons for this. First, in a country in which 80 per cent of its population was dependent on agriculture, the socialist sector in the transitional period should be strengthened and enlarged. Second, the Bolshevik Party had to fulfil its promise to the urban working class as well as to the peasantry for a better material life and higher living standards. And third, in the year 1925–6 industrial production had reached, while agricultural production was very close to, the pre-war levels and so the question of what was going to follow the restoration of the economy was open.

The general agreement existing on the industrialization issue did not prevent disagreements on a number of other related issues, the most important of which were the pace of industrialization and the priority of heavy industry. A great and lively debate developed around these issues, in which there was a close connection and interrelation of the economic and the political element. Fast industrialization had, as a precondition, the priority of heavy industry. The advantages of such a policy were the relatively early appearance of higher productivity, the shortening of the period necessary for the industrialization process and the gradual (but at a high rate) change of class relations in favour of socialism. On the other hand, slow industrialization rates and the priority of light industry had the advantage of imposing a relatively light burden on consumption, which might permit an increase of the consumption of industrial goods in the town as well as in the country and facilitate trade expansion between the two sectors. The main political disadvantage was the reliance for a long period of time on counterrevolutionary elements such as rich farmers, private traders, etc.

Trotsky and the left wing of the Bolshevik Party were in favour of the so-called dictatorship of industry, i.e. fast industrialization which would be facilitated by the central planning mechanism and they declared their position as early as October 1923, criticizing the government for trying to eliminate the disparity of industrial and agricultural prices. The arguments of the Left were systematized and formulated in a coherent theoretical body by Preobrazhensky.[2]

Bukharin and Rykov, who at the time were among the spokesmen for official policy and who were considered as the leading figures of the Right wing of the Bolshevik Party, opposed the policy of fast industrialization on political as well as on economic grounds. They argued that such a policy was going to undermine the worker–peasant alliance and that the expansion of industry should be based on an expanding volume of trade between the two sectors, industry and agriculture, and the lowering of production costs. Capitalist agriculture and socialist industry should aid each other in the process of growth. To reduce the danger of the kulak and the restoration of capitalism they proposed the voluntary progressive expansion of cooperatives, i.e. the gradual promotion of socialist types of organization in agriculture.

The Centre, with Stalin, did not have a clear policy on the issue of the speed of industrialization. Stalin declared his principle for 'socialism in one country', he accepted the need for industrialization, as Bukharin did, but he advised caution and care for the worker–peasant alliance. He was, however, careful to avoid any commitment to pro-peasant positions. Since December 1925, the Fourteenth Congress of the Communist Party had adopted the thesis that industrialization, especially emphasizing the priority of heavy industry, should be the official policy of the country. The Congress stressed the necessity of transforming the Soviet Union 'a country which imports machines into a country which produces machines, in order that by this means the Soviet Union in the midst of capitalist encirclement should not become an economic appendage of the capitalist world economy but an independent economic unit which is building socialism'. This position was, however, supplemented by caution against excessive optimism.

> It is incorrect to take as a starting point the demand for a maximum pumping over of means from the sphere of agriculture into the sphere of industry; for this demand would mean a political rupture with the peasantry as well as an undermining of the home market, an undermining of export and an upsetting of the equilibrium of the whole economic system.

Exactly two years later, at the Fifteenth Party Congress held in December 1928 a new element was stressed. That was the formation of cooperatives in agriculture which should be pursued on a voluntary basis. Nevertheless, one month later, under the pressure of economic reality the coercive methods of war communism to obtain agricultural products were widely used once again. Finally, Stalin changed his position at the expense of the peasant and after the application of the first five-year plan in 1929, he proceeded with forced collectivization, compulsory deliveries of agricultural produce and he increased the relative prices of industrial goods. Thus, Stalin was able to launch industrialization at a 'breakneck speed', which Preobrazhensky never envisaged.[3,4]

The concept of primitive socialist accumulation

As it was mentioned above, Preobrazhensky was in favour of a rapid industrialization process for which a large surplus product was necessary.[5]
This surplus would be directed exclusively to industrial accumulation while
accumulation in the agricultural sector would be desirable only after
'industry can stand on a new technological basis'. He explained his position
taking into consideration both the supply and the demand side. He argued
that during the period of war communism net capital formation may have
been negative and any investment that took place was limited to minor
and the most inexpensive improvements of equipment. Increase in output
up to that time was largely possible only through the intensive use of
existing equipment and its operation at the limits of full capacity. Further
increase in output, therefore, could not be achieved without passing into
a new more advanced state of technology for which a necessary condition was the expansion of equipment. He expected aggregate demand of
consumer industrial goods to be increasing because of the rise of the dispos-
able income of the peasantry – attributable to wiping out of rent payments
and reduction of agricultural taxes. He also expected it to be increasing
because of the improvement in the level of industrial wages, on the one
hand, and the expansion of the city sector and the consequent rise of the
size of urban labour, on the other. Preobrazhensky was aware of the pres-
ence of 'huge disguised unemployment' and consequently of a huge surplus
population in the countryside. This surplus population had to be absorbed
by the city sector (Erlich, 1960: 32–8).

After indicating the reasons for the necessity of large capital requirements, Preobrazhensky had to proceed to the next logical step of his
argument and explain the means by which these requirements would be
secured. To this end, a new analytical concept was introduced, that of the
law of primitive socialist accumulation. The target Preobrazhensky set for
himself was 'to analyse an economic system in which both the planning
principle – within the limits imposed by the degree of organization attained
in the economy – and also the law of value, with its externally-compelling
power, are operating simultaneously' (Preobrazhensky, 1965: 55).

As was mentioned in the previous section, after the application of
NEP the Soviet Union had a dual social and economic character. Two
clearly distinct forms of production existed side by side in the country.
On the one hand, there was a powerful private sector, whose main strong-
holds existed in agriculture, trade, petty production and services. In this
sector, the capitalist form of production prevailed. Its governing principle
was the market and the law of value. On the other hand, there was a
small in size and weak state sector consisting mainly of industry, transport, the banking system and that part of trade which was controlled
by the state. The principle governing this sector, in which the socialist
form of production was present, was the planning principle. The first

analytical difficulty encountered is that 'neither form of production', capitalist nor socialist, 'is present in its pure form'. In any case, the basic tendencies of the planning principle and the law of value 'assumed in the Soviet economy the form of the law of primitive socialist accumulation' (Preobrazhensky, 1965: 55). The second analytical difficulty comes from the fact that economic policy in the new socialist state was aimed to serve not only the economy of the Soviet Union 'but also the domestic and foreign policy, endeavouring to protect the system as it exists, to strengthen it, and to bring socialist principles to triumph in it ... As a consequence of its economic policy the real results achieved in the economic sphere did not follow the optimum line of the law of primitive socialist accumulation' (Preobrazhensky, 1965: 55–6). In Preobrazhensky's analysis, however, emphasis was given on economic rather than political arguments.

The law of primitive socialist accumulation, which was developed in analogy to the law of primitive capitalist accumulation,[6] is the law of extracting surplus from the private sector and channelling it to the socialist sector for the latter's expansion. It is the law of the development of socialist relations of production and the transfer of values from the private to the collective sector of the economy. It is evident that the distribution of labour power and the means of production, as well as the size of investment, depend on this law, which does not work in accordance with but against the law of value. It 'determines in conflict with the law of value both the distribution of means of production in the economy and the distribution of labour power and also the amount of the country's surplus product which is alienated for expanded socialist reproduction' (Preobrazhensky, 1965: 85).

The two laws have some differences and some similarities. The basic difference is that the law of primitive socialist accumulation cannot operate as long as capitalism prevails but only after the socialist revolution has succeeded and a soviet state has been established. By contrast, the law of primitive capitalist accumulation operates in the womb of the feudal society (Preobrazhensky, 1965: 77–81). A basic similarity between the two laws on the other hand is that both of them involve a precondition, the one for capitalism and capitalist accumulation, the other for socialism and socialist accumulation (Preobrazhensky, 1965: 81).

The two laws share also the common assumption that expanded reproduction taking place in the emerging capitalist or socialist economy is based mainly on sources lying outside these economies, i.e. the feudal and the capitalist economy, respectively.

> The transition of society from the petty-bourgeois system of production to the capitalist could not have been accomplished without preliminary accumulation at the expense of petty production ... The very transition presumes, as a system, an exchange of values between

large scale and petty production under which the latter gives more to the former than it receives. In the period of primitive socialist accumulation the state economy cannot get by without alienating part of the surplus product of the peasantry and the handicraftsmen, without making deduction from the capitalist accumulation for the benefit of socialist accumulation.

(Preobrazhensky, 1965: 88)

Socialist accumulation is the use of a surplus product created within the socialist sector for expanded reproduction. Primitive socialist accumulation is the concentration of resources in the collective sector and their use for the expansion of the state economy so that this economy 'achieves purely economic superiority over capitalism'. These resources come 'partly or mainly' from the non-state economy which means that the socialized economy obtains a higher amount of productive resources from the private sector of the economy than it would obtain according to competitive market conditions.

Compared to the agricultural sector, the industrial sector of the Soviet Union of NEP was too weak to support the desirable rapid industrialization process in the state sector. Consequently, any effort 'to count only upon accumulation within the socialist field would mean jeopardising the very existence of the socialist economy, or prolonging endlessly the period of preliminary accumulation, the length of which, however, does not depend on the free will of the proletariat' (Preobrazhensky, 1965: 89). In fact Preobrazhensky was expecting 'the rationalisation of the whole economy, including petty production' to have positive effects on agricultural productivity and on the size of surplus product generated in the private sector. 'The expanded production in industry, its sufficiently quick tempo, the development of railway networks, canals, electrification etc., are indispensable for the peasant economy which cannot without the assistance of a growing industry develop its productive forces ...' (Preobrazhensky, 1965: 89).

The full definition of the law of primitive socialist accumulation is given by Preobrazhensky as follows:

By the law of primitive socialist accumulation we mean the entire sum of conscious and semi-spontaneous tendencies in the state economy which are directed towards the expansion and consolidation of the collective organization of labour in Soviet economy and which are dictated to the Soviet state on the basis of necessity: (1) the determination of proportions in the distribution of productive forces, formed on the basis of struggle against the law of value inside and outside the country and having as their objective task the achievement of the optimum expanded socialist reproduction in the given conditions and of the maximum defending capacity of the whole system in conflict with capitalist commodity production; (2) the determination of the proportion of accumulation of material resources for expanded reproduction, especially at the expense of private economy, in so far as the determined amounts of this accumulation are dictated compulsorily to the Soviet state under that of economic disproportion, growth of private capital, weakening of the bond between the state economy and peasant production, derangement in years to come of the necessary proportions of expanded socialist reproduction and weakening of the whole system in its conflict with capitalist commodity production inside and outside the country.

(Preobrazhensky, 1965: 146)

The next step of Preobrazhensky was to proceed to examine the specific ways the surplus necessary for the primitive socialist accumulation can be extracted. In this effort he attempts to find analogies from Marx to his law of primitive capitalist accumulation. Of course, violent methods for extracting the surplus and directing it to the desirable direction like colonialism, robbery, piracy, etc., which had been used during the period of primitive capitalist accumulation, were rejected without any question. The first among the non-violent methods considered to achieve the same result was direct investment. Preobrazhensky seems to be positive but rather apprehensive about 'concessions' because he feared that they would give grounds for comparisons between the economic superiority of advanced capitalism over the new socialist state established on the foundation of a backward country. Instead, he favoured state borrowing from the capitalist world. State borrowing from abroad despite the interest which would have to be paid 'can serve as a powerful stimulus to the socialist accumulation' (Preobrazhensky, 1965: 90). He thought that the burden of the interest which had to be paid abroad, even if that was above the normal level, would be much less than the benefits accruing from the technically advanced equipment which would be bought with the loans. 'The long-term foreign loan is on the one hand, one of the ways in which foreign capital exploits the new young economy. But on the other hand, it can accelerate the process of socialist accumulation in a most powerful fashion' (Preobrazhensky, 1965: 90). His fear, however, was that foreign capital in the form of direct investment or in the form of long-term loans 'does not intend to flow into an alien economic system on a large scale' (Preobrazhensky, 1965: 90). A different way, according to Preobrazhensky, to transfer resources from the private to the collective economy could be the issue of paper money, i.e., printing inflationary money since the state had the necessary political power and, at the same time, was the owner and administrator of the state's economic sector. 'This accumulation is carried out at the expense either of the incomes of the petty-bourgeois and capitalist elements or of reduced wages of the state's workers and office employees' (Preobrazhensky, 1965: 91).

Another means of financing industrial investment could be exports of agricultural products under the condition that imported goods in exchange would be primarily capital goods. Monopoly control of foreign trade by the state and 'socialist protectionism' would, according to Preobrazhensky, prevent undesirable developments. These developments could have been the destruction of domestic industry under the pressure of foreign competition, and the composition of imports being unfavourable to capital equipment, if free trade was permitted. Direct taxation of the pre-socialist forms of the economy such as the economy of the trader, the capitalist and the kulak (Preobrazhensky, 1965: 89–90) could also be used as a means of extracting surplus product from the non-socialist sector. The disadvantages of this instrument, however, would be economic on the one hand, i.e., the establishment of a complex and expensive apparatus for tax collection, and political on the other, i.e. the negative reaction of the rural population to direct taxation.

Having examined the administrative methods of primitive accumulation of capital, Preobrazhensky continues with what he considers economic instruments. The first of these economic instruments for extracting surplus product from the private economy and transferring it to the state economy was price policy, i.e., the regulation of terms of trade between the state and the non-state economy in a way favourable to the state economy.

> But the concentration of all the large-scale industry of the country in the hands of a single trust, that is in the hands of the workers' state, increase to an enormous extent the possibility of carrying out on the basis of monopoly a price policy which will be only another form of taxation of private economy.
>
> (Preobrazhensky, 1965: 111)

Such a policy is much more feasible for the historical stage of primitive socialist than it was for primitive capitalist accumulation. Because 'the state economy of the proletariat arises historically on the back of monopoly capitalism and therefore has at its disposal means of regulating the whole economy and of redistributing the national income economically, which were not available to capitalism at the dawn of its history' (Preobrazhensky, 1965: 95). Such means, making price policy more feasible, were the transport system, the monopoly of the banking and credit system, the control of internal as well as external trade, and the control of large scale industry by a single trust, the proletarian state.

Preobrazhensky was, however, careful to consider the limitations of such a policy. The state could play with prices but only between certain limits. A minimum would be determined by the cost level, and a maximum determined by demand elasticity and the reaction of the private industry. Prices should not be raised to a level at which demand would shrink and peasants refuse to buy industrial consumption goods (Elrich, 1960: 50). Also, since the state did not have a monopoly over all branches of industry, prices should not be raised to a level which could be attractive for the emergence of competing private enterprises. Such a policy should be combined with a policy of cost reduction, which presupposes technological improvement of industry. The main advantage on the other hand is that the cost of applying price policy compared with other ways of surplus extraction is very low because the setting up of a special mechanism, which would be necessary in the case of taxation, is not necessary. 'Accumulation by way of an appropriate price policy has advantages over other forms of direct and indirect taxation of petty economy. The most important of these is the extreme facility of collection, not a single kopeck needed for any special taxation apparatus' (Preobrazhensky, 1965: 111). Preobrazhensky was not afraid that price policy would be against the interests of the workers and the poor peasants. Both of them could be compensated by the state, the former in the form of an increase in nominal wages, the latter in the form of credit (Preobrazhensky, 1965: 112).

He was very confident in the long-run fruits of primitive socialist accumulation. The effect of new capital formation on the state economy would be an improvement of technology related to the production methods. The use of advanced methods of technology would permit a decline of cost and finally a price cut of industrial goods. The price cut would, other things being equal, raise the real income of the whole population. Higher real income would affect positively the demand of industrial goods. Preobrazhensky believed, however, that cost reductions should only partly be transformed in price cuts in order to speed up the industrial accumulation process. The end of this process would come when 'technological and economic superiority over capitalism' would be secured. At this point of time the socialized sector of the economy would be strong enough and able to fully support its own expanded reproduction process. Leaning on the capitalist sector would not be necessary any more.

Preobrazhensky did not think that his analysis based on the existence of the two laws of primitive socialist and capitalist accumulation and their struggle against each other was applicable only to the specific conditions of the Soviet Union during the NEP period. On the contrary, he believed that his analysis could be generalized and could hold for any case of a post-revolutionary state with the possible exception of the last countries to go over to socialism. The only qualification necessary is that reliance on the capitalist sector of the economy for accumulation in the socialized economy depends on the degree of development of the specific country.

> The more backward economically, petty-bourgeois, peasant, a particular country is, which has gone to the socialist organization of production and the smaller the inheritance received by the socialist accumulation fund of the proletariat of this country when the social revolution takes place, by so much the more, in proportion will socialist

accumulation be obliged to rely on alienating part of the surplus products of the pre-socialist forms of economy and the smaller will be the relative weight on its own production basis . . .

(Preobrazhensky, 1965: 124)

Preobrazhensky and mainstream economics

After what has been said above, a legitimate question to ask is what is the relevance of Preobrazhensky's analysis for mainstream economics and its importance for contemporary economic thought.

As we have seen above, Preobrazhensky's main concern was economic change. From this point of view it may be argued that Preobrazhensky as well as the other participants in the debate that took place in the 1920s in the Soviet Union touched a problem neglected for a long time by orthodox economists. This is the problem of economic growth and development which had been considered by the mercantilists, the physiocrats and the classical economists. It is generally accepted that the introduction of marginal analysis and the genesis of neo-classical economics changed the object of economic science and shifted the interest of economists from the problems of distribution and growth to the analysis of problems related to resource allocation and static equilibrium. Neo-classical economists for a long time ignored macroeconomics, the behaviour of aggregates and their interrelations and they focused their attention on microeconomics, the behaviour of the consumption and production units like the household and the firm. 'With the possible exemption of J.A. Schumpeter, no orthodox theorist, from the 1870s till the 1930s, attempted to develop an integrated theory explaining growth' (Landreth, 1976: 477).

In this sense Preobrazhensky and the other Soviet economists of the 1920s can be considered as pioneers because they tackled issues of economic development and growth which had been neglected by economic theory for a long time. A few years later, in the late 1930s and the early 1940s, there were two important developments in economics. The first development was in the direction of growth theory. The publication of *The General Theory* brought to the surface questions related to the behaviour of aggregates and, hence, macroeconomics re-emerged as a branch of economic theory and policy. After that it was a matter of time for the standard static Keynesian model to be extended and take account of the dynamic aspects of the economy. The work of Harrod heavily influenced the subsequent course in this field. The second development had to do with the emergence of development economics which happened at approximately the same time. In the early 1940s a number of Western economists, Rosenstein-Rodan being probably the first among them, started dealing with problems related to less developed countries and more specifically industrialization and disguised unemployment.[7] What is more interesting is that Rosenstein-Rodan, in his much celebrated article of 1943, seems to be influenced by the Soviet experiment when he explicitly talks about industrialization 'on the "Russian model" (by which we do not mean communism) aiming at self sufficiency, without international investment'.

An interesting question at this point is whether Rosenstein-Rodan was influenced directly or indirectly by Preobrazhensky and his work. The quotation above suggests that Rosenstein-Rodan had been very clear about the Soviet industrialization model when he considered the absence of foreign investment as its main characteristic. As far as we know, however, there is no evidence leading to the conclusion that Rosenstein-Rodan had direct access to the work of Preobrazhensky and the other participants in the Soviet industrialization debate. It is quite probable, though, that Rosenstein-Rodan was aware of what was going on in the Soviet Union of the 1920s, indirectly at least, through Paul Baran, one of his students at Harvard University and an ex-student of Preobrazhensky.[8] In any case it follows that Preobrazhensky and the other participants in the Soviet industrialization debate, independently of their significant contributions to socialist economic thought, have also played an important role in relation to the emergence of mainstream economic development theory.

Preobrazhensky, however, went a step further than just returning to the development issue and the pre-neo-classical tradition of economic thought. He actually developed a rather adequate theory of economic development, which is relevant to a socialist as well as to a non-socialist world. What he is saying in simple words, if Marxian terminology is disregarded and the analysis is applied not necessarily to a socialist country but to any underdeveloped country striving for capital accumulation, can be summarized as follows. An underdeveloped economy consists of a weak industrial and a large agricultural sector. If the development path chosen is a path of unbalanced growth, emphasizing industry rather than agriculture, investment should be mainly directed towards the urban sector. Where are the resources going to be found? Since the industrial economy is small and weak the surplus generated in it is inadequate to secure a satisfactory speed for development so the burden has to fall on the large agricultural sector. There are different ways to extract surplus from agriculture, the most advantageous is the regulation of the terms of trade at the expense of agriculture. Nevertheless, relative prices of industrial goods should not be raised above a level which would discourage peasants to exchange their products for the produce of industry. The corollaries of such a model are: first, expansion of the urban sector; second, raising consumption in both sectors and thus increasing demand for industrial goods; and third, increasing efficiency in the backward sector through the creation of external economies.

It is interesting to note that in the last two decades there has been a serious interest in the issues Preobrazhensky discussed, but disassociating the analysis from the historical context of the Soviet Union and the industrialization debate. On this theme it is worth mentioning the papers by Mitra (1977) and Lipton (1977), who were followed by Sah and Stiglitz

(1984, 1986, 1987a, 1987b), Blomqvist (1986), Carter (1986) and more recently by Baland (1993). The work done focuses on placing the Preobrazhensky model in a modern framework and checking the validity or invalidity of his corollaries. This indicates that the problems considered by Preobrazhensky are of substantial importance for the contemporary less developed world. It indicates also that the theory of Preobrazhensky can be generalized easily and can be incorporated without any difficulty in the main body of mainstream economics.

Preobrazhensky, Stalin and soviet orthodoxy

As it was mentioned above the centre faction of the Bolshevik Party did not have a clear policy for development. It was vacillating, at least until 1928. In early 1928 Stalin initiated a 'Left course' and the next year he applied the first five-year plan, whose central points were industrialization at a fast pace, emphasis on heavy industry and on relying on agriculture for drawing funds for investment. Therefore, the basic points of the theory of primitive socialist accumulation, i.e. high rates of capital formation and reliance on agriculture to draw the required resources, were in fact adopted by the Party leadership; and policy recommendations suggested by it became the official policy of the USSR after 1929. It should be also noted that the theory of primitive socialist accumulation was logically compatible with Stalin's idea about socialism in one country. It seems that Preobrazhensky himself saw the change in the strategy of the Party as a confirmation of his own theory (Deutscher, 1959: 416). Therefore, Preobrazhensky's work seems to be consistent with soviet orthodoxy. Things, however, were not as simple in the Soviet Union during Stalin's rule. Preobrazhensky was expelled from the Party at the end of 1927, re-admitted two years later, expelled again in 1931, arrested in 1935 and executed in 1937 after refusing to confess the false crimes he was accused of. His works were banned by Soviet authorities and the public could not have access to them without special permission. It was an irony of history that official Soviet authorities denied in such a crude way any recognition to the theoretician of industrialization and the price scissor policies.

A number of researchers, however, consider that the work of Preobrazhensky had nothing to do with soviet orthodoxy. They emphasize the fundamental difference between Preobrazhensky and the official policy. Preobrazhensky always advocated indirect means for extracting the surplus: the terms of trade and the market; taxation and tariff policy; credit and central bank policies; he never suggested arbitrary administrative ways and requisitions and enforced collectivization. By contrast, official policy imposed violently the collective solution on the peasantry and used police methods to enforce compulsory deliveries of agricultural products, increasing at the same time, and to an unprecedented extent, the relative prices of industrial goods. Thus,

But it is crucial to understand that Preobrazhensky's conception of industrialisation had nothing at all in common with that finally carried out by Stalin in the Five Year Plans which started in 1928 . . . When Stalin, in blind panic, was forced, under the threat of foreign intervention as well as internal upheaval from the kulaks, to begin a programme of industrialisation, he did so in the most brutal, unplanned manner.

(Preobrazhensky, 1973: x)

Concluding remarks

The main conclusions of this work may be summarized as follows:

1   The law of primitive socialist accumulation can be generalized and can be applied to any less developed country and thus can be incorporated into mainstream economics. The underlying analysis has historical importance but at the same time is relevant for the contemporary world.
2   Preobrazhensky as well as other participants in the industrialization debate may be considered as pioneers of the modern theory of economic development despite the fact that the early writers on development in the Western world had no access to their work. The Soviet industrialization experiment, however, seems to have had a direct influence of a decisive character on these writers.
3   Preobrazhensky was happy to see his basic development model adopted by the Soviet authorities. The latter, however, never accepted their debt to him.

Notes

1   We thank M. Psalidopoulos for constructive comments on an earlier draft of this paper.
2   Preobrazhensky, born in 1886 and shot in 1937, was a prominent economist. He was a founding member of the Bolshevik Party and he was repeatedly arrested and exiled by the Russian authorities during his youth. He was active during the Revolution and the civil war. After the Brest–Litovsk Treaty Preobrazhensky sided with Bukharin and the 'Left Communists'. He co-authored with Bukharin the 'ABC of Communism' and served as one of the three secretaries of the Central Committee of the Bolshevik Party in 1920–1. As early as 1920 Preobrazhensky sided with Trotsky on a number of issues and became a leading figure of the opposition.
3   For the views of the non-communist opposition of the 1920s, which included (bourgeois) republicans, populists of various shades and Mensheviks, see Jasny (1972).
4   For the history of the Soviet Union of the 1920s see Carr (1972), Dobb (1966) and Deutscher (1959).
5   Preobrazhensky's economic ideas about the strategy of economic development in the Soviet Union were expressed for the first time in lectures. They were

published first in the Magazine of the Communist Academy in 1924 and then as a book under the title 'The New Economics' in 1926.

6   The conditions of capitalist accumulation, according to Preobrazhensky are: preliminary capital accumulation sufficient for the application of a higher state of technology, expansion of economic activity and formation of the working class (Preobrazhensky, 1965: 80). Following Marx, however, a fourth condition, the formation of the industrial capitalist class, should be added (Marx, 1967, vol. I, pp. 750–60).

7   See Rosenstein-Rodan (1943) and Warriner (1939, 1948).

8   See Howard and King (1989: 114).

References

Baland, J.M. (1993) 'The economics of price scissors: A defense of Preobrazhensky', *European Economic Review*, 37, 37–60.

Blomqvist, A.J. (1986) 'The economics of price scissors: Comment', *American Economic Review*, 76, 1188–91.

Carr, E.H. (1972) *A history of Soviet Russia: Socialism in one country, 1924–1926*, Harmondsworth, Penguin Books.

Carter, M.R. (1986) 'The economics of price scissors: Comment', *American Economic Review*, 76, 1192–94.

Deutscher, I. (1959) *The prophet unarmed, Trotsky: 1921–1929*, Oxford, Oxford University Press.

Dobb, M. (1966) *Soviet economic development since 1917*, revised, enlarged edition, New York, International Publishers.

Erlich, A. (1960) *The Soviet industrialization debate, 1924–1928*, Cambridge, Mass, Harvard University Press.

Howard, M.C. and King, J.E. (1989) *A history of Marxian economics*, vol. I, Princeton, NJ, Princeton University Press.

Jasny, N. (1972) *Soviet economists of the Twenties: Names to be remembered*, Cambridge, Cambridge University Press.

Landreth, H. (1976) *History of economic theory: Scope, method and content*, Boston, Houghton Mifflin Co.

Lipton, M. (1977) *Why poor people stay poor; Urban bias in world development*, Cambridge, Mass, Harvard University Press.

Marx, C. (1967) *Capital*, vol. I, edited by Friedrich Engels, New York, International Publishers.

Mitra, A. (1977) *Terms of trade and class relations*, London, Frank Cass.

Preobrazhensky, E. (1965) *The new economics*, translated by B. Pearce, Oxford, Clarendon Press.

—— (1973) *From the new economic policy to socialism: A glance into the future of Russia and Europe*, translated by B. Pearce, London, New Park Publications.

Rosenstein-Rodan, P.N. (1943) 'Problems of industrialization of Eastern and South-Eastern Europe', *Economic Journal*, 53, 202–11.

Sah, R.K. and Stiglitz, J.E. (1984) 'The economics of price scissors', *American Economic Review*, 74, 125–38.

—— (1986) 'The economics of price scissors: Reply', *American Economic Review*, 76, 1195–99.

—— (1987a) 'Price scissors and the structure of the economy', *Quarterly Journal of Economics*, 102, 109–34.

—— (1987b) 'The taxation and pricing of agricultural and industrial goods in developing economies', in D. Newbery and N. Stern (eds) *The theory of taxation in developing countries*, Oxford, Oxford University Press.

Warriner, D. (1939), *Economics of peasant farming*, London, Oxford University Press.

—— (1948), *Land and poverty in the Middle East*, London, Royal Institute of International Affairs.

11 Canon and heresy

Religion as a way of telling the story of economics

Albert Arouh[1]

'Church built to please the priest'
(Robert Burns, from *The Jolly Beggars*, 1785)

Introduction

Some people claim that economics is in a state of crisis.[2] Others maintain – admittedly with increasing reluctance – that it is doing just fine.[3] Some argue that economics is not yet a science (Eichner, 1983), others that it is (though in *some* sense, Blaug, 1980). Conflict of opinion, concerning the state of economics and its progress, has always been a characteristic feature of economics. For better or for worse, it was through such perennial conflict, that economics has developed to be what it is. Yet, the question still remains, has this development been for better or for worse?

Traditionally, this question was answered by appealing to rational positivist criteria according to which economic theory progresses from falsehood to truth in a linear and cumulative manner. The state of confusion that besets economics currently, as well as the methodological criticism of antipositivists, postmodernists and others, however, has seriously undermined the positivist view of progress in economics (Dow, 1997a). Despite attempts to reinstate the rationality and scientific progress in economics (Blaug, 1980), none has carried the required conviction (Arouh, 1987).

It seems that economics has been left bereft of the positivist rationality according to which it can assess itself. Especially after the postmodernist assault to positivism, progress in economics became more a matter of faith than of science. If this is true, and progress in economics is a matter of faith, then the most appropriate metaphor for telling the story of economics is not science but religion.

It is not implied that economics *is* religion. Religion is taken as a vehicle (a metaphor) to convey the idea that progress in economics involves much more than rationality and science. A metaphor does exactly that, it transports the context from one situation to illuminate the context of another. A metaphor is a way 'of imposing interpretative order in the buzz'.[4] Economists as religious fanatics is not a representation of reality; just a *parable* in order to make a point. After all, economists have been compared before to 'tribes' (Leijonhufvud, 1981), to actors in markets, power hunters, bureaucrats (Mäki, 1992, pp. 84–6), to magicians (McCloskey, 1991), and to 'philosophers, priests and hired guns' (Goodwin, 1988), exactly to make a point; why not economists as a congregation of believers and bickering practitioners of different religions?

The purpose of this paper is to tell the story of dominance and dissent in economics by using religion as a metaphor. In the first part of the paper, I will try to show some of the problems of telling the story of economics in terms of science. In the second part, I will reconstruct the conflict in economics in terms of contesting systems of religious belief. In the third part, I will give a historical account of dominance and dissent in economics seen from the point of view of religion.

A non-rational reconstruction of the (in)credibility of economics

How to tell the story: through the 'thick and thin' of progress in economics

How is one to evaluate the way economics has evolved to be what it is? The difficulty lies in the term 'evaluation'. There are different ways of evaluating progress in economics. Perhaps, instead, one should not try to evaluate progress, but tell the story of economics pure and simple. Yet, the question remains: how does one tell the story; and does the story have a happy ending?

Different people tell a story differently. As Weintraub says 'there are many . . . ways to tell the story' (1991, p. 114). To begin with, there are those who claim (or used to), that to tell the story of economics has nothing but an antiquarian value, so it is not worth telling.[5] There are those who argue that the story is worth telling because one can appreciate its happy ending better.[6] There are those who, in a spirit of fin de siècle mood of doom maintain that the end of economics as we know it is nigh and it is not a happy one.[7] There are also those who say that one cannot tell the true story, let alone prove that it has a happy ending, except as told, and in the way it is told, by the ones who are the protagonists in it.[8] Finally, there are those who do not care about whether the ending is a happy one or not, but are interested in just telling the story, plain and simple.[9]

Therefore, a taxonomy of approaches to telling a story is required. Many have been duly provided. Khalil (1995), for example, has offered an exhaustive historiographical taxonomy of criteria of progress in economics. Blaug (1990), following Rorty's typology (1980), has provided yet another taxonomy, while also Backhouse (1992a) has contributed to the discussion.[10] I, on the other hand, have no intention of offering another taxonomy; only to classify my own account of conflict in economics, in relation to other accounts, so that salient differences and similarities are recognizable between how I will tell the story and how others have told it.

In pre-postmodernist times, the only way of telling the story of progress in economics was methodology. At first, methodological discussion in economics revolved around logical positivism and instrumentalism. Then it moved on to falsificationism.[11] Credibility criteria were drawn largely from epistemological discussion. Epistemological discussion evolved mostly around physics, and thus methodology in economics has been for a long time dominated by what has aptly been called 'physics envy' (Schabas, 1992, p. 196). Inevitably, this has led to a methodological psychosis among economists more or less alien to economic reality as well as to what economists do in practice. 'I want to stop talking about [correspondence theories of truth]' calls E.R. Weintraub[12] (1988, p.157), a sickness which Mirowski, like another Wittgenstein for economics, resolves to cure (1989).

Methodology, especially modernist methodolgy, eventually lost part of its glamour.[13] Some people now go to the other extreme and argue that theory appraisal is not necessary.[14] According to the critics of positivist methodology, theory appraisal in economics is employed as a means to render its progress credible; in other words methodology is just another hidden agenda for the mainstream cause in economics. Methodology leads to a 'thin' (almost absolutist and timeless) account of economics (what is known as a Whig history),[15] whereas what is required is a contextual (and *almost* relativist) 'understanding'[16] of how the plot in the story 'thickens' (Backhouse, 1992b, p. 271).

Methodology is, however, just one way of telling the story – and one should see it that way.[17] The fact that modernist methodology has not told it particularly well has given methodology in general a bad name. More and more, philosophers, as well as economists, have decried the prescriptive and innocuous character of methodological discussion (see Dow, 1997a). Indeed, in the case of economics, modernist methodology has been more wishful thinking – a sort of scientistic credo – than a realistic view of what economists do when they choose between theories. Positive economics is honoured by economists more in the breach than in the observance (Blaug, 1980).

To add insult to injury, the kind of early methodological discussion that was supporting what Caldwell calls a 'logical empiricist', or hypothetico-deductive, project (1982, pp. 19–32), stumbled upon two major problems of logic that have shaken its foundations: the Duhem-Quine argument and the problem of induction (Dow, 1997, p. 76; Cross, 1984). From a logical and philosophical point of view, such hypothetico-deductive, positivist methodology had, ultimately, to be thrown to the proverbial dustbins of academia, which are the introductions to first year textbooks (see Haas, 1993).

Prescriptive methodological discussion in economics was followed by descriptive methodology. By that I mean methodological discussion which, to some degree or other, makes ontological claims about scientific practice. This type of approach to telling the story can be further broken down into various subcategories.

One subcategory tells the story of scientific progress in terms of methodology, but falls inadvertently into an ontology of science, lest it is accused of prescriptivism. A prime example of this approach is Lakatos's account of theory appraisal and growth in knowledge. Another subcategory approaches methodology as history of science, believing that it forms an ontology of scientific progress, but falls inadvertently into methodology, lest it is accused of relativism. An example of such an approach is Kuhn (see Blaug, 1980 and Kindi, 1995).

Other approaches may claim in an unambiguous manner that they present a clear ontological account of the history of economics. For example, there are those who apply Bloor's (1976) sociology of knowledge, with the aim of generating a realistic (as opposed to a prescriptive) account of the development of economic theory.[18] Here indeed is a prima facie claim for a purely ontological account of the development of economics. There is a problem however. Such account makes implicit assumptions about its philosophical legitimacy, which in effect constitute a hidden methodological agenda (Dow, 1997a, p. 80). It claims that sociology of knowledge is a better approach to science than philosophy. This in itself, however, is a philosophical judgement.

A similar criticism applies to yet another approach, which calls for a non-methodological account of the development of theory, within the context of postmodernism. This approach is known as constructivism[19] and makes the claim that 'a constructivist position on knowledge entails that historical knowledge is constructed' (Weintraub, 1992, p. 274). As mentioned above, constructivism strives to 'understand [not appraise] the way the interpretative community read the economy text and what makes the community more likely to respond to one interpretation rather than another' (ibid.). In other words, one cannot employ objective and external criteria in order to evaluate progress in economics, but one wants to ask why do economists (the interpretative community) say that progress exists.

A 'non-interpretative' account of 'interpretative communities' however, is logically untenable. As Backhouse correctly points out, 'it is impossible for *anyone* to write "neutral" history' (1992b, p. 283 my emphasis). It is untenable even for those who claim that history is not neutral and is constructed. History about non-neutral history is also non-neutral. Thus, there is also a hidden methodological agenda, an Archimedean point, in constructivist accounts of the dominance of an economic theory, such as those of Weintraub and McCloskey (see Schabas, 1993, p. 46). Methodology, alas, is unavoidable.

It is obvious that methodological discussion in economics, as in many other fields, has been caught in the web of postmodernism.[20] Where in literature the god-author has been deconstructed, where in the history of nations, traditions have been de-mythologized, so in economics methodology has been 'de-methodologized'. This is the New Age of discourse and economics has entered it. More and more, discussion on methodology has been baptized in the shifty waters of rhetoric, persuasion and construction, while the devil of appraisal has seemingly been exorcised.

Somehow, however, New Age economics has thrown the unholy water out along with the deconstructed baby. Like original sin, methodology in discussions of the state of economics, as we saw, creeps back. One cannot avoid theory appraisal. This is just a logical and necessary point. Methodology *is* the Archimidean point. The devil of appraisal, therefore, has not been exorcised, it has only been suppressed in the unconscious of economists. (If too much methodology is manic, too little, or none at all, is depressive.)

What follows from the above review is that in telling the story of conflict in economics, both methodology and ontology are important. If methodology, from the point of view of logic, is unavoidable, ontology, from the point of view of reality, is indispensable. Therefore, any account that tells the story of conflict about fundamentals in economics, needs to take both into account.

Yet, in telling the story of conflict in economics, methodology is not to be used as a source of rationality. There is no absolute, i.e. externalist, rationality by which to choose between fundamental beliefs in economics. Nevertheless, there is a logic inherent within each set of fundamental beliefs (a rationalization, but not rationality, as Dow argues in 1997b) within which methodological criteria are defined. Therefore, in the context of these criteria, economists act (methodologically) rationally, or, more to the point, *see* themselves acting rationally. This is independent of whether economists follow these criteria strictly, or pay lip service to them, since they always appeal to them as the ultimate adjudicating authority and as the only source of reason. What matters is that they believe in them.

It follows from the above that a story of dominance and conflict in economics cannot be told by using only methodological rationality. Nevertheless, it cannot be told *without* taking into account the methodological claims to knowledge and rationality made by economists. Such claims then have to be connected to the ontological and ideological context which defines the system of beliefs of economists. Methodology, economic theory and social context constitute an inseparable whole which defines and configures the belief system of economists.

Economics as divine inspiration

The new age of economics

Terminology, as postmodernists argue, is important. The terms employed in any discourse act as metaphors for meaning, overt or covert. Most of the terms used, mainly by mainstream economists, when discussing the credibility of the dominant theory, *signify and magnify* their wish to judge economics in terms of the current model of science. Science is the sole source of rational knowledge, at least that is what modernists (such as Popper) say; and economists want, more than anything, to be rational when choosing among theories (McCloskey, 1983).

Thus, terms such as testing, predictiveness, truth, falsifiability, empirical validation and positivism have been used sparingly in order to persuade the economics profession and the rest of the world (Goodwin, 1988) that what it is doing is credible. When this was doubted and came out of fashion, positivist terms were replaced by terms such as scientific research programme, hard core, protective belt, positive heuristic, novel facts and excess empirical content, in order to acknowledge that though things might not be what positivists say, yet the credibility of economics as science can still be maintained by appealing to some other model of science. When the excess empirical content of mainstream economics was contested, however, economists reverted to scientific paradigms, normal science, anomalies, incommensurability and scientific revolutions to show the discursive and fragmented character of economics yet still preserves whatever modicum of rationality is allowed by Kuhnian science.

Whatever epistemological terms are used, they all convey a belief in economics as rational scientific practice. Reality, however, is different. Mainstream economics dominated and persisted in most of the history of economic thought contrary to major logical inconsistencies and contrary to the reality of which it makes knowledge-claims. McCloskey, who has struck a major blow to the positivist project in economics, emphasizes that 'Samuelson, Friedman, or their followers do not present reasons for adopting such metaphysical position [on methodology]' (McCloskey, 1983, p. 487; see also p. 482). Mirowski, who has struck another blow on the shaky, but unfaltering, neo-classical programme, claims that 'it has been locked in the physics of the 1860s, and persists in this predicament to the very present' (Mirowski, 1989, pp. 393–4). As Routh, finally, despairs, 'The tenacity with which the orthodox faction clings to its view is a monument to the obstinacy of the human mind' (Routh, 1975, p. 340).

Such resilience to logical and real contradictions can be called a positive heuristic or normal science, but this does not make the credibility of economics rational. To begin with, lack of any empirical (let alone excess) content of the 'empty boxes' of the orthodoxy, qualifies it for a continuous and persistent degenerative shift.[21] As McCloskey says, 'The mathematical and statistical tools that gave promise . . . of ending economic dispute have not succeeded' (McCloskey, 1983, p. 514; see also Lawson, 1997). Equally, the lack of any reformation in the fundamental premises of mainstream economics, despite the accumulation of theoretical and empirical anomalies, implies that, though there is a paradigm in economics, it has not gone through a revolutionary science stage, nor is it likely to do so.

The discrepancy between rational scientific criteria and the credibility of mainstream economics has cast doubt on the usefulness of epistemological terminology and science as a metaphor of theory appraisal in economics, as McCloskey's, and in general the postmodernist, critique has shown. Unlike the postmodernist critique, however, which just deconstructs a metaphor in economics (i.e. positivism), I replace one metaphor with another. I use religion instead of science to *re*construct conflict in economics. (In a manner of speaking, the new age of economics, brought about by the postmodernists, cannot be complete without reference to religion.)

Using religion as a metaphor to talk about conflict in the history of economic thought, *signifies and magnifies* the non-rational (though not irrational) belief in the fundamentals of economics. Though it strips away the scientific credentials from mainstream economics, it does not necessarily take away its rationality.[22] Looking at economics as dogma to be believed in a metaphysical sense, divests its justification from any sort of objectivist claim to absolute knowledge. Using the metaphor of religion shows the economist as one that accepts the superiority of the orthodoxy as 'divine' inspiration, like the faithful believe in a superior being on the basis of revelation. 'Divine' in this context, means a belief in certain immutable, unquestionable, untestable, fundamental features of the basic axioms of economics. Orthodoxy, like the word implies, is the 'right opinion' because it has been anointed by the 'right' divinity.

Yet, as was already noted, methodological criteria (practised or not, imagined or real, successful or not) allow the economist to inject this belief with rationality. Looking at methodology from this point of view, therefore, can be compared to Aquinas's attempt to inject Aristotelian logic into revelatory faith. Like in medieval ethics, reason was married to faith, so in economics, methodological criteria have given the economist a rational background for believing in non-rational foundations, prolonging, as it were, his/her suspension of disbelief in the unreality of mainstream economics.

Economics as an article of faith

Looking at economics from the point of view of religion is not without precedent. Many economists have referred before to economics by using terms borrowed from religion. This however was done only as an aside to their methodological or historical proclamations and critiques. Religion was never taken seriously as a metaphor that is central to a reconstruction of theoretical conflict in the history of economic thought.[23]

For example, Bronfenbrenner proclaims (almost as if in prayer) his belief in the credibility of economics that 'Yet we have faith that most if not all such positive disagreements will eventually be resolved' (Bronfenbrenner, 1966, p. 13). Having reviewed the main methodological debates in economics at the end of the nineteenth century, Deane concludes that 'arguments about fundamental principles tend to acquire the bitter and divisive qualities of theological disputes' (Deane, 1983, p. 2). Hahn more recently, referring to theoretical intransigence in economics, touches upon the issue by saying that '[a]fter all in other spheres, say religion, one often encounters increased orthodoxy among some just when religion is on the decline' (Hahn, 1991, p. 49). All this constitutes an echo of Wicksell's earlier comments: 'Within the whole of his [the economist's] science, or what he insists on calling science, no generally recognized result is to be found, *as is also the case for theology and for roughly the same reasons*' (quoted in Deane, 1983, my emphasis).[24] Finally, Samuelson epitomizes the existential angst of the economist by saying, 'we believe in our map because we cannot help doing so' (Samuelson, 1962, p.18).[25]

Perhaps Routh (1975) is one historian of economics who puts relatively greater emphasis on the role of religious belief in the development of economic theory. He says, for example, that 'verification is both impossible and regarded as unnecessary. In effect, then, orthodox economics becomes a matter of faith and, ipso facto, immune to criticism' (Routh, 1975, p. 26; see also p. 12). He expresses his wonder 'that the citadel still stands' (ibid., p. 340) and goes on to give the mystical explanation that '[b]y some mysterious magic, economic thought continued along its traditional channel' (ibid., p. 9). As to the attempts to reform the orthodoxy, '[h]eresy accumulated, but the heretics did not succeed in bringing about the changes they sought' (ibid., p. 1). Wiseman, on the other hand, in a similarly inclined article (1991), thinks that 'heretics grow in numbers, and I become increasingly confident that they will be tomorrow's priests' (ibid., p.149).[26]

It seems clear from the above, that economists have been preoccupied with the religious nature of economics, though in an ad hoc manner. A more systematic analysis might prove a useful insight (no doubt complementary to others) in the understanding of how to tell the story of economics.

Religious affiliations

A good point to start is by replacing any other reference to the foundations of mainstream economics, such as weltaanshaung, paradigm, or hard core, with the term 'canon'. Canon has been used before in economics, especially after Samuelson's celebrated article on 'The Canonical Classical Model' (1978). The term however has been used mostly in its literal sense, which is a rule, a principle or a standard according to which something is evaluated, very much like a paradigm. I want to use 'canon' in its historical sense, in other words as an ecclesiastical decree; a holy order, which has been accepted as the undisputed dogma, and which renders as genuine or 'true' only those ideas, beliefs, or theories that conform to it. Though paradigm or hard core are at times evocative of dogma, they allow a degree of scientificity which demarcate them from religion. Canon, on the other hand, in the ecclesiastical sense, carries a greater weight of immutability and intransigence and implies strict adherence, as in religious belief.

Equally, any other reference to a critique against the canon, concerning fundamentals, should be termed 'heresy', instead of unscientific or anomalous. This is in order to remove from the debate concerning fundamentals in economics any reference to scientific conflict, however this is interpreted, whether in a positivist, Popperian, Kuhnian, or postmodernist sense. The story of conflict in economics, very much like a story of religious dispute, is a story of the conflict between the canon, which dominates, and the heretical attacks against it, which strive to bring about reform.

Canon in economics refers to a metasocial set of beliefs about methodology, ontology and ideology, i.e. the bedrock of the faith. Like metaphysics, the metasocial is dogmatically held, and it is a matter of (implicit) faith. Unlike metaphysics, metasocial refers not to beliefs 'beyond nature', but 'beyond society' ('meta-social' also neutralizes the term 'meta-physic' when discussing beliefs about society, since it does not imply the methodological bias that society is like nature). Heresy also has its own metasocial, which however postulates an opposing faith (equally dogmatically held). A canon, by definition, imposes its dominance by proclaiming that it is the 'true faith', whereas a heresy draws its legitimacy from its protesting reform and its own proclamations of 'true faith'.

Is there a dominant canon in economics in the above sense; Before one answers this question one must ask whether in a discipline such as economics, which is infamous for dissension and unresolved conflict,[27] there is consensus. For instance, Brown warns us that 'there is no consensus in the science of economics' (Brown, 1981, p. 111). However, there is a consensus that dominates. There may be lack of consensus regarding theory and fact in many debates, but as far as certain basic ideas, concerning methodology, ontology and ideology, are concerned – which constitute the foundation of economics, i.e. its metasocial – there is only one dominant canon (and many variations of it).[28] This consensus emerged in the seventeenth century, acquired relative dominance in the eighteenth century and was firmly established in the nineteenth century, after the defeat of the historicists and the diffusion of the methodological and ontological credo of marginalism. As Routh characteristically says, 'Modern economics is a little over three hundred years old' (1975, p. 1), and 'the paradigm that provides the inner core for economic thought has not changed since the seventeenth century' (ibid., p. 27).

As Deane also tells us, by the end of the nineteenth century, after the Methodenstreit, 'suddenly it would appear, there was a consensus' (1983, p. 4). This consensus, in the form of the neo-classical synthesis, was further established, as orthodox economic theory; in the 1920s it survived attacks against it made by all those who criticized the irrelevance and unreality of perfect competition. Later on, it was strengthened by general equilibrium theory, was supported, at both the methodological and substantive level, by the neo-classical synthesis and by monetarism, and was further boosted by new-classicism.[29]

If there is unresolved disagreement in whatever guises it appears in the history of economic thought, it is between the canon and the heresy. The fight is between two opposing faiths. Disagreement also exists within each faith. But, in either case, disagreement is a matter of interpretation of the fundamentals rather than about the fundamentals themselves.[30]

The fight between the canon and the heresy, which appears at various points of time in the history of economic thought, revolves around three fundamentals that define their opposite metasocials: ontology, methodology, ideology. Ontology refers to a view about the nature of social reality, i.e. individualism versus holism, rationality versus uncertainty. Methodology refers to the approach one chooses to study this reality, i.e. deductivism versus inductivism, abstractionism versus realism, instrumentalism versus institutionalism, etc. Ideology refers to the (explicit or implicit) normative tone that colours the theory about social reality, e.g. liberalism versus statism.

The three features of each of the metasocial beliefs are interconnected forming an organic unit, each part supporting and legitimizing the other. An attack on any part of the structure of the belief, jeopardizes the other parts. The metasocial cannot give up any of its parts without giving up the whole. Speaking metaphorically, the methodological, ontological and ideological beliefs constitute a sort of a holy trinity for economics, an inseparable and indestructible triad that forms the basis of the faith, what Polanyi calls the 'catalactic triad' (in Pierson, 1977, p. 77).[31]

For example, the combination of atomistic rationalism (the ontology), deductive abstractionism (the methodology) and market liberalism (the ideology) constitutes the metasocial of what I call the Ricardian canon. This metasocial, which at the fundamental level is accepted to one degree or the other by the faithful, is an organic unit, in the sense that abstractionism is required to support an unrealistic degree of rationalism and individualism, which, in turn, are necessary prerequisites for liberalist conclusions. The ideological implications are then well covered under the slogan of a mythical 'value free' economics, which is abstract and 'pure' and thus distant from ideology.[32]

Despite disagreement as to the exact degree of abstractionism, atomistic rationalism, or liberalism, that is allowed by practitioners of the canon (as for instance in the F-Twist debate or the monetary and 'full cost' debate, or the satisficing versus maximizing controversy), there is nevertheless a strongly built consensus regarding the fundamental character of what economics is, or should be all about, which is anchored in the Ricardian canon. Monetarists and fiscalists may disagree as to the exact number of equations allowed in their models, but they never dispute the usefulness of models in economics. They may disagree on the precise proportions of the micro or macro nature of the economy, but they do not disagree on the validity of this mystical dichotomy. They may disagree on policy, but always as a matter of degree rather than of kind. They may disagree on whether atomistic rationality is a heuristic or a realistic hypothesis, but on the whole they do not question its validity or its necessity. At the end of the day, monetarists or fiscalists, maximizers or satisficers, rational or adaptive expectationalists, instrumentalists or operationalists, agree about the metasocial faith of the Ricardian canon. Their differences have to do with alternative interpretations concerning the appropriate degree of abstractionism, rationalism and liberalism, which form the metasocial of the Canon.[33] They are very much like different monastic orders fighting within Catholicism.

By contrast, the heresy, which I call Keynesian, revolves around a metasocial that is the exact opposite of the Ricardian canon. Its ontology centres on uncertainty and institutional conventionalism, its methodology calls for realism in the formation of theory and its ideology is deeply interventionist. Therefore, the kind of economics that would have emerged, if the Keynesian heresy had succeeded in reforming economic orthodoxy, would have been entirely different from the kind of economics that stemmed from the Ricardian canon. The Keynesian heresy would have been to economics – to carry the metaphor further – what Protestantism was to Catholicism.

The metasocial of the Keynesian heresy is the antipodean holy trinity. God-rationality is replaced by god-uncertainty. It also is an inseparable unit, in the sense that a realistic approach to economic phenomena (the 'son' of uncertainty) recognizes the structural, institutional and disequilibrating character of the economy, does not ignore the role of social conventions and institutions (though there may be disagreement as to their exact role), emphasizes unknowledge, imperfections and rigidities in economic decision-making, and views the economic agent as part of an organic whole that is more than the sum of parts. (Interventionism, finally, is the 'holy ghost' of the Keynesian heresy and is of the same 'substance' as its divine progenitors.)

I refer to the metasocial of economic orthodoxy as the Ricardian canon because Ricardo, unlike Smith,[34] was the abstractionist par excellence and the symbol of what we consider to be orthodox economics (or what Keynes had in mind when he referred to the 'classicals'). The orthodoxy goes back to Ricardo, Mill and the marginalists in the past and extends to the general equilibrium theorists and the rational expectationalists in the present. In a sense, though Smith was Adam, the original sin was committed by Ricardo.

The Keynesian heresy, on the other hand, is called Keynesian, even though as a tradition it precedes Keynes, because, like Ricardo is the symbol of orthodoxy in economics, so Keynes is the symbol of heresy.[35] The heretical tradition in economics, goes back to Smith, Malthus, Sismondi,[36] the historicists and the institutionalists, all the way to Keynes who affirmed it and to the post-Keynesians and evolutionists who reaffirmed it. Keynes, however, constitutes the epitome of heresy in economics, both because he is seen as such by the orthodoxy, in relation to what is known as the Keynesian revolution, as well as because his real critique (and not the one imagined by so-called bastard Keynesians) does shake the metasocial foundations of economic orthodoxy in a radical manner.

The three hundred year war in economics

Reformation and counter-reformation

If one looks at the major debates in the history of economic thought, one will see that most of them are manifestations of the same dispute between the metasocial faiths of the Ricardian canon and the Keynesian heresy.[37] This dispute extends to debates even before Ricardo, when enlightened liberalism crusaded against pragmatic mercantilism. The Ricardian canon had one of its first victories in the battle between the bullionists and the banking school. It further established its 'truth' after the debates concerning the corn laws in the beginning of the nineteenth century. By the mid nineteenth century, Ricardo's abstractionism had become holier than Malthus's profane realism. It is on the battleground of these debates, that the apostle Ricardo built his church.

The church of Ricardo grew and flourished and acquired a multitude of followers as industrial capitalism grew and flourished and acquired a multitude of followers. The return to the gold standard and the repeal of the corn laws were not only a victory for *laissez-faire* capitalism, but also 'god sent miracles' that sanctified the 'truth' of the Ricardian canon. It was in the debates between Ricardo and Malthus in which deductive abstractionism, rationality and liberalism were crystallized as the dominant methodology, ontology and ideology of economics. From then on the Ricardian canon revealed its truth in the thought of most economists up until the last quarter of the nineteenth century, including Senior and Mill.

By the late nineteenth century, however, heretical voices protesting against the Ricardian canon became louder and louder. A new dispute about the 'theology' of economics erupted and the first attempt to reform the premises of the Ricardian canon became known as the Methodenstreit. The debate may have been mainly on method; given however the organic and holy unity of the Ricardian canon, its indestructible oneness as it were, it extended also to its ontological and ideological premises (holism versus individualism, interventionism versus *laissez-faire*).

The marginalists were the new apostles of the Ricardian canon. In their fight against the historicists, defending the metasocial faith of the Ricardian canon, as the new jesuits of economics, they perfected its form and rendered its 'theology' purer. At the methodological level, they established deductive abstractionism as the sole source of truth in economics. At the ontological level, they made a strong case for a utilitarian atomistic rationality for economics. Though utilitarianism was accepted as the ontology and ethics of the Ricardian canon since Bentham's and James Mill's time, it was just an awkward appendix to the overall conception of the economy. Given the way the paradox of value was interpreted by political economists of the eighteenth and early nineteenth centuries, utilitarianism was never properly integrated into the fabric of classical political economy. Neither was individualism. The assumption of atomistic rationality was taken as a background hypothesis. Classical analysis, as for example Say's law, Smith's development theory and Ricardo's theory of distribution, was in terms of aggregates. Atomistic rationality was assumed to be a background principle applying to the organization and coordination of the economy.

The proper integration of utility, and, by extension, atomistic rationality, was in effect achieved by marginalism. But this was done at the expense of the labour theory of value. The dispensing of the labour theory of value did not in effect undermine the metasocial foundation of the Ricardian canon.[38] One might even say that the labour theory of value was always an embarrassment to the Ricardian canon, as it led neither to a satisfactory profit theory nor to a theory free from the – dangerous to the Ricardian canon – socialist implications related to exploitation. Thus, also, at the ideological level, the marginalists 'purified' economics from any heretical interpretations of the labour theory of value that would compromise liberalism. (It is interesting to note in this context that Smith's 'inability' to transform his 'crude' labour theory of value into a sophisticated one, accounting for capital and land, has more to do with his uncompromising sense of realism – especially where aspects of the division of labour are concerned – than with his so-called analytical inadequacy compared to Ricardo.[39])

According to the above, the Ricardian canon can be seen as continuing through the nineteenth century, asserting and perfecting itself with the marginalists, rather than being replaced by them. Most conventional accounts see the end of the nineteenth century as either a shift of focus, or even a scientific revolution in economics.[40] The way I see it is, that marginalists confirmed and reaffirmed the metasocial of the Ricardian canon, by excluding any elements that were alien or threatening to it and absorbing anything that strengthened the canonical faith.

Economics in an empty box

By the twentieth century, after the victory of the Methodenstreit, the Ricardian canon further established itself as the dominant orthodoxy through Marshall's influence at the ontological and ideological level, and through J.M. Keynes's influence at the methodological level (see Deane, 1983, pp. 3–4). By the 1920s, however, there were two more attempts, after the historicists, to reform the Ricardian canon. Both attempts came mainly from the (ever protesting) Cambridge University environment, which at the time was dominated by the apostle (literally) J.M. Keynes.

As has already been suggested, protestations against the orthodoxy existed well before the late eighteenth, early nineteenth century, but, as Routh argues, they 'went unheeded' (1975, p. 8). In a sense, while the canon maximized utility, the heresies maximized futility. The attempts to reform economics in the early twentieth century threatened the Ricardian canon in a more fundamental manner, as compared to any other attempt, including that of the historicists, since, among other things, they attacked directly the logic and consistency of its metasocial assumptions. One would think that, if economics developed along the lines of science, then these attacks would have shaken the foundation of the Ricardian canon. They did not. At the beginning they did cause disturbance, but they were eventually absorbed and neutralized by the neoclassical synthesis' counter-reformation.

The revolution against the Ricardian canon in the 1920s relates to the so called 'empty-box' controversy. In this controversy, the reality and logical consistency of the perfect competition assumption of the theory of the firm, and the possibility of equilibrium for the whole economy (and by extension the rationality assumption as well as abstractionism) was questioned.[41] Logically, the church of Ricardianism would have to crumble when it was confronted with the reality of imperfect competition and the logic of increasing returns. In the end, the church did not crumble.[42] As Hillard says, 'the citadel of equilibrium economics has remained impervious to the heretical onslaught of the twentieth century' (Hillard, 1992, p. 60).[43] Imperfect competition became a special case of the general equilibrium model, the legacy of the Ricardian canon. Reality had to be adjusted to fit the theory and one more epicycle was added onto the firmament of the Ricardian canon.

And so, the first most important heretical attempt to reform the foundations of the Ricardian canon in the twentieth century, and achieve a 'protestant revolution' against the 'catholicism' of the Ricardian canon, was ultimately aborted. In time, monopoly was rendered a harmless subcase of perfect competition, an embarrassing example of reality, whose moral worth, nevertheless, was still measured against the purity of pure competition.[44]

Economics on the Hicksian cross

The second most important attempt to question the dominance of the Ricardian canon in the twentieth century and reform economics, was Keynes's heretical attack on all three aspects of the metasocial foundations of orthodox economics. Like the first, however, it also was aborted. In the context of this paper, where the Ricardian canon is seen as a metasocial dogma,[45] that has almost the quality of a religious encyclical that carries the papal bull, Keynes must then be interpreted as the Galileo of economics.[46] Keynes saw himself, however, more like Einstein fighting against Newtonian and Euclidian economics rather than Galileo (Routh, 1975, p. 18).

Still, Keynes could be more successfully compared to Galileo, rather than to Einstein, or to Luther for that matter. His desire to give his theory a palatable form which would be more digestible to the faithful of the Ricardian canon detracted from his reformist zeal. As Routh says: 'Keynes, [played] two roles: one as destroyer of graven images, the other as preserver of the temple' (1975, p. 2). Much like Galileo, Keynes also had to compromise his ideas in the face of the intransigent resistance and opposition from the mainstream economics of his day. Keynes's willingness, however, to have his economic policy reform widely spread, led him to compromise and thus avoid excommunication, by underplaying the methodological and ontological threats that uncertainty meant for the Ricardian canon (see Johnson and Johnson, 1978; Skidelsky, 1983).

Nevertheless, Keynes's message, as witnessed by chapter 12 of *The General Theory* and the *QJE* article of 1937, as well as the *Treatise on Probability*, was radical and damaging to the Ricardian canon.[47] By recognizing that decision-making cannot be rational, since the consequences of decisions cannot be known with any degree of certainty, it postulated an alternative ontology. Though there may be many interpretations of Keynes, it is abundantly clear that Keynes regarded irreducible uncertainty as the most fundamental characteristic of the behaviour of economic agents (Dow, 1997a). A rational agent is rational because s/he has full knowledge of the conditions in which s/he makes a decision, as well as s/he knows exactly, or with some degree of probability, the future consequences of such decision. But in the context of total ignorance such knowledge is not available. Therefore, decisions, in the face of uncertainty, cannot be determined a priori to be rational.[48]

Behaviour that is predicated on such uncertainty is incompatible with the assumption of rationality, which constitutes the ontological foundation of the Ricardian canon. Attempts to accommodate uncertainty within the context of rationality, such as equating uncertainty with risk, or ornamenting behaviour with all kinds of expectations (adaptive, rational, etc.), that assume some knowledge of the future, cannot evade the consequences on rationality from the fact of total ignorance (Dow and Dow, 1985, pp. 55–7). This has repercussions for the corollary of the rationality assumption, which is individualism. There is no such thing, at least in the context of the ontology of the Ricardian canon, as collective rationality. Rationality is predicated on the individual. However, once rationality is replaced by uncertainty, then the individual is lost in the mass of convention, tradition, group behaviour, herd instinct, animal spirits and institutional complexity. Such holistic behaviour is not necessarily irrational. Collective rationality is a cumulative and institutional response to the vagaries of uncertainty, whereas individual rationality is based on certitude (probabilistic or not). The institutional complexity of the economy, the sociopolitical parameters that surround the economic agents, and all those elements that economists belonging to the Ricardian canon ritually ignore are functional ingredients of the economic process.[49] To blur them out of the picture, however, not only is unrealistic but also is somehow paranoid; as in religion, a large part of reality is either blocked out or distorted to suit the believer.

But unrealism is the sine qua non methodological foundation of the Ricardian canon. At Keynes's persistence to take into account uncertainty as a necessary and unavoidable piece of economic reality, as well as, therefore, to call for a more realistic – admittedly less precise or quantitative – approach to economic theory, the faithful of the Ricardian canon would have to revert to instrumental unrealism (Friedman's heuristic constructs), or naive sociology (Robbins's means–ends distinction), endow the agent with clairvoyant-cum-scientific characteristics (Lucas's rational expectations), or, as in the case of McCloskey, accept orthodox economics on the basis of its 'introspective congruence with reality'.[50] Such ingenious circumlocutions may have saved the metasocial foundation of the Ricardian canon from reform, but they have lost the substantive soul of economics by rendering it, once more, just an 'empty black box'.

These attempts to accommodate ignorance, uncertainty, institutions, in fact the actual society itself, and protect the canonical assumption of unrealistic rationality from the heresy of realistic uncertainty, are what I call the epicycles of Ptolemaic economics.[51] Though the epicycles form complex structures that cast doubt on the relevance, and thus credibility of economics, the economics consensus constructed them in order to maintain the credibility of the metasocial of the Ricardian canon. As Mirowski remarks 'economics has been the most rigidly doctrinaire of all the social sciences' whatever intellectual challenges have appeared, defenders of the mainstream have been remarkably successful in 'either coopting the rival metaphor or else amputating the new offending doctrines as unsound and unscientific' (Mirowski, 1989, p. 368).

Keynes's message, like Sraffa's critique in the empty box controversy, was finally neutralized by some of his revisionist disciples (Hicks, Harrod, Hansen, Samuelson et al.), who effected a largely innocuous, but necessary for the evolution of the Ricardian canon, (textbook) revolution in economics. By expunging from Keynes his uncertainty principle (damaging to the orthodox metasocial), and reducing his critique to a rigid wage assumption in otherwise classical labour markets within a hydraulic economy, the cause of the Ricardian canon was furthered. In the neo-classical synthesis, the Ricardian canon found a way to bear the Hicksian cross more cheerfully.[52]

In the light of the above, the history of modern economic thought, at least in the last three hundred years, is a history of the continuous struggle between the Ricardian canon and the Keynesian heresy. After classical orthodoxy was established, protesting rebels such as the historicists, Keynesians and other heretics, attempted to reform economics, but without success. Economists, as modern-day jesuits, mounted a counter-reformation, first with the neo-classical synthesis, then with monetarism (Friedman is Loyola to Keynes's Galileo) and lastly with new classicism, which established the continuing dominance of the Ricardian canon. It is very much like the history of any religion, which strives to dominate by excluding, absorbing and at times suppressing dissent stemming from heresies protesting for reform.[53]

Conclusion

So, how a story is told, and who tells it, matters. As I myself cannot be outside the conflict of the two metasocial faiths in economics, but I am very much a part of (and partisan in) it, I cannot tell the story neutrally. It is obvious that my metaphor, i.e. the way I choose to tell the story, undermines the credibility of economics, which does not wish to see itself as religion but as science. Therefore it betrays my protesting and heretical bias.

In contrast to the Keynesian heresy, however, I do not postulate an alternative methodology for doing economics properly, (as Lawson does in 1997 calling for transcendental realism in economics). Belief in the heresy is of the same nature as belief in the canon, i.e., adherence to metasocial dogma. I see the history of conflict in economics as a conflict between a religious canon and a heresy which strives to reform it. It a story of the battle between two dogmas fighting for power.

This position betrays my own methodological bias – that economics is more like dogma and less like science. I have told a story about conflict in economics by using religion as a metaphor. Very much like an involved observer of the seventeenth century would have told the story of a religious war by using a metaphor so as to put himself outside the conflict, yet be part of it. I cannot avoid the postmodernist predicament. Like everybody else, I have a hidden *methodological–ontological* agenda. I have told this story with a methodological bias in heart and an ontological purpose in mind.

So how does the story end? The story of course does not end. It will keep going on as long as some economists claim that economics progresses from one stage to a better one, requiring no radical reformation, while others claim that economics does not progress at all and that it requires radical reformation. The story cannot end as long as some claim that it has ended very happily, and some that it has ended unhappily. If economic theories are more like a religious belief than science, connected to a historical point in time, the story indeed cannot end, in the same way that history cannot end. The story will simply be told differently by different people in different historical settings.

Notes

1 I would like to thank the American College of Greece-Deree College for their financial and other support. I would also like to express my gratitude to professor S.C. Dow for inviting me to the University of Stirling. Many thanks also to professor Brian Loasby. My gratitude to Stavros Drakopoulos, Vasso Kindi, Albert Jolink and Gregory Kafetzopoulos for their valuable comments. Of course the usual disclaimer applies. Finally, I would like to thank B. Togia for assisting me in my research, but most of all C. Alevizou for her constructive criticism, understanding, patience and technical assistance.
2 See, in chronological order, Ward (1972), Blaug (1980), pp. 253–6, Wiles and Routh (1984), and Dow (1997a).
3 McCloskey for instance, says (or used to say) that 'Economics . . . is in reasonably good health' (McCloskey, 1983, p. 482). See also Friedman, 1991.
4 Coats, 1993, p. 273.
5 See Blaug (1990).
6 See for instance, Stiglitz, (1991, pp. 134–5), Friedman (1991, p. 37) and Blaug (1990, p. 30).
7 For example, Hahn (1991), Wiseman (1991).
8 Weintraub (1991 and 1993), McCloskey (1983).
9 See especially Schabas (1992).
10 See also Mäki who discusses systematically the various, so called, 'context' theories of knowledge, (1992), p. 67.
11 For the changing moods in methodological discussion in economics, see the excellent review article by Dow, 1997a, p. 74.
12 See also Weintraub (1982–3), where he says that 'it is not fruitful to argue methodologically' (p. 295) but also reply by Dow (1982–3).
13 For the 'end of methodology' discussion, see McCloskey (1983, pp. 322 and f. 1).
14 See for example Weintraub (1992, pp. 274), but for a clash of this view see Backhouse (1992b).
15 See Samuelson (1987, p. 52) and for a critique, among others, see Kurdas (1988).
16 Weintraub (1991), and Dow (1997a, p. 97).
17 For a similar position see Backhouse (1992b, p. 281).
18 Mäki (1992), Eagley et al. (1964), Cole et al. (1983), Hands (1994).
19 See Weintraub (1991), Klamer et al. (1988), Samuels (1990), Rossetti (1992), McCloskey (1994a) and Dow (1991b); and for a hermeneutic approach to economics see Benedeto and Solari (1997).
20 See Coats (1993, p. 271).
21 See for example Dow, (1982–3, p. 306, 1991 p. 182), Arouh (1987), Loasby (1989), Mirowski (1993, p. 314) and Wiseman (1991).
22 This is unlike McCloskey's indictment that 'moderns . . . know well that . . . any of the canonized methods of persuasion . . . have been used as methods of deceit' (1983, p. 510).

23 Talking about economics from the point of view of religion must be distinguished from connecting economics to religion, i.e. looking for a Christian political economy, as in Waterman (1991).

24 Wiles refers to neo-classical atomism as the 'sacred proposition' (1983, p. 70). Hillard says that 'this whole issue is more a matter of faith than reason' (Hillard, 1992, p. 74). Talking about contradictions in economics, Samuelson also says that 'Like the Bible, the canon of classical political economy contains passages that seem to assert and to deny the same thing' (Samuelson, 1978, p. 14, f. 290). Also Gee uses similar terminology when he says: 'in fact, the orthodox economist would regard the type of economics taught as being definitive, rather than as belonging to a particular school among alternative equally valid schools ... The neoclassical school is a broad church offering a methodology and paradigm embracing many sects. The high priests of the church are well versed in mathematical techniques' (Gee, 1991, p. 71).

25 Mirowski affirms this angst by saying that 'orthodox neoclassical economics is experiencing severe pangs of self-doubt at the moment' (1993, p. 310).

26 'In so far as ... mathematical economics continue[s] to exist at all, [it] will occupy the kind of academic niche enjoyed by endowed chairs of Divinity' (Wiseman, 1991, p. 155).

27 For a theory of unresolved controversy in economics see Arouh (1978); see also Cole et al. (1983).

28 As McCloskey says, 'The extent of disagreement among economists ... is in fact exaggerated' (1983, p. 514).

29 'There can be no doubt that the neoclassical school of economics is the dominant school of economics' (Gee, 1991, p. 71).

30 See Wiseman (1991, pp. 150–1).

31 See also Dow (1982–3, p. 305); Gee (1991, p. 72).

32 See Deane, (1983, pp. 5–6)

33 Deane refers to the same thing when she says that after the dispute on method settled, and consensus was formed, debate still went on 'on whether pure economics should become an essentially mathematical science' but the debate never questioned 'the foundations of the discipline' (Deane, 1983, p. 6). See also Brittan (1973). For a discussion of economics as 'orthodoxy and heterodoxy', see Samuels (1980).

34 Samuelson (1978) classifies Smith as one of the founders of 'canonical classical economy'. However, this is disputed by Kurdas (1988) who argues that 'Smith's ideas on division of labour sit ill with the most basic premise of mainstream economics' (ibid., 20) and therefore there is 'conflict between the "canonical" view and Smith's actual discussion' (ibid., p. 19). See also Wiseman (1991, p. 151) and Hollander (1980) who argues that 'the canonical model is a Ricardian construction ... and should not be attributed to Adam Smith' (p. 573).

35 As Hillard says, 'Keynes adopted a habit of mind in approaching the subject-matter of economics which was profoundly different from the canonical stereotype' (1992, p. 66).

36 See Routh (1975), pp. 3–7.

37 See Brown (1981, p. 111).

38 In fact, neither did the dispensing of the labour theory of value undermine the classical conception of the economy, as was shown by Sraffa (see Samuelson, 1987, p. 55).

39 Kurdas for instance claims that 'Smith recognizes institutional constraints to accumulation – but these are not fit for Cartesian space' (1988, p. 19); see also Samuelson (1962).

40 See, for example, Bronfenbrenner (1971, pp. 137–8) and Coats (1969, pp. 292–3), but for a different view which sees marginalism as an extension of classical

political economy, see Routh (1975), and Hollander (1984), who argues that there had never been a marginal revolution in the 1870s, and there was no fundamental break in the history of economic thought between classical and neo-classical economics.

41 Routh, (1975), p. 15 and Deane (1983), p. 9.

42 Ward (1972, pp. 34–48) also wonders why such important criticism did not have any major impact on the essence of economics. Once one sees this in the context of religion, however, it is no wonder.

43 This tenacity of equilibrium economics has been described by Joan Robinson as 'mumpsimus' (see Arouh, 1987). See also Katouzian (1983, p. 51); and Coats (1993, p. 274).

44 As Cole, et al. say, 'economic theory never completely displaced values in the pew' (1983, p. 71).

45 As Georgescu-Roegen says, 'standard economics, by opposing the idea that the economic process may consist of something more than a jig-saw puzzle with all its elements given, has identified itself with dogmatism' (quoted in Hillard, 1992, p. 59).

46 For a discussion of the need for a Galileo for economics, see Wiseman, 1991 p. 150.

47 See Arouh, 1987; Dow, 1995; O'Donnell, 1989; Lawson and Pesaran, 1985; and Loasby, 1976.

48 See Dow and Dow, 1985, Wiseman, 1991.

49 Atomistic rationalism allows a kind of mechanics of society, with market forces, equilibria and paths, which is very much connected to the ritual of quantitivism (Dow and Dow, 1985, pp. 57–8; Leijonhufvud, 1981, pp. 350–5), whereby the uninitiated are baptized in mathematics by the priests, while the ones refusing to accept the faith are (literally) marginalized.

50 'we like the metaphor of . . . the selfishly economic person as calculating machine on grounds of its prominence in earlier economic poetry was plainly successful or on grounds of its greater congruence with introspection than alternative metaphors' (McCloskey, 1983, p. 508).

51 See Dow and Dow, 1985, pp. 62–3.

52 On the Hicksian cross and its role in the aborted attempt by Keynes to reform economics, see Dow, 1982–3.

53 For the many forms of suppression in economics, see Wiseman, 1991, p. 150, and Katouzian, 1983, p. 63.

References

Arouh, A. (1978) 'Towards an Explanation of Persistent Controversy in Economics', Research Report, Department of Economics, University of Edinburgh.

—— (1987) 'The Mampsimus of Economists and the Role of Time and Uncertainty in the Progress of Economic Knowledge', *Journal of Post-Keynesian Economics*, vol. IX, no. 3, Spring 1987.

Backhouse, R.E. (1992a) 'How should we approach the History of Economic Thought, Fact, Fiction or Moral Tale?', *Journal of the History of Economic Thought*, vol. 14, no. 1, Spring 1992.

—— (1992b) 'Reply: History's Many Dimensions', *Journal of the History of Economic Thought*, vol. 14, Fall 1992.

—— (ed.) (1994) *New Directions in Economic Methodology*, Routledge.

Benedeto, E. and Solari, S. (1997) 'Levels of Description in the Hermeneutics of Economic Theory', in Salanti, A. and Screpanti, E., *Pluralism in Economics*, Edward Elgar.

216 *Albert Arouh*

Birner, J. (1993) 'Neoclassical economics as Mathematical Metaphysics', in de Marchi, *Non-Natural Social Sciences: Reflecting on the Enterprise of More Heat than Light*, Duke University Press.

Blaug, M. (1980) *The Methodology of Economics*, Cambridge University Press.

—— (1990) 'On the Historiography of Economics', *Journal of the History of Economic Thought*, vol. 12, no. 1, Spring.

Bloor, D. (1976) *Science and Social Imagery*, London, Routledge and Kegan Paul.

Brittan, S. (1973) *Is there an Economics Consensus?*, Macmillan.

Bronfenbrenner, M. (1966) 'A "Middlebrow" Introduction to Economic Methodology' in S. Krupp, *The Structure of Economic Science*, Prentice Hall: Englewood Cliffs.

—— (1971) 'The "Structure of Revolutions" in Economic Thought', *History of Political Economy*, vol. 3, no. 1.

Brown, E.K. (1981) 'The Neo-classical and Post-Keynesian Research Programs: The Methodological Issues', *Review of Social Economy*, October 1981, no. 2.

Caldwell, B. (1982) *Beyond Positivism: Economic Methodology in the Twentieth Century*, Allen and Unwin.

—— (1984) *Appraisal and Criticism in Economics*, Allen and Unwin.

Coats, A.W. (1969) *Is there a 'Structure of Scientific Revolutions' in Economics?*, Kyklos, vol. 22.

Coats, B. (1993) 'What Mirowski's History Leaves Out', in de Marchi, N. (1993) *Non-Natural Social Sciences: Reflecting on the Enterprise of More Heat than Light*, Duke University Press

Cohen, B. (1993) 'Analogy, Homology and Metaphor in the Interactions between the Natural Sciences and the Social Sciences, especially Economics', in de Marchi, N. (1993) *Non-Natural Social Sciences: Reflecting on the Enterprise of More Heat than Light*, Duke University Press.

Cole K., Cameron J. and Edwards C. (1983) (1991) *Why Economists Disagree: The political economy of economics*, Longman.

Cross, R. (1984) 'The Duhem-Quine Thesis, Lakatos and the Appraisal of Theories of Macroeconomics', in Caldwell (1984) *Appraisal and Criticism in Economics*, Allen and Unwin.

Deane, P. (1978) *The Evolution of Economic Thought*, Cambridge University Press.

—— (1983) 'The Scope and Method of Economics' *Economic Journal*, vol. 93, no. 369.

de Marchi, N. (1992) *Post-Popperian Methodology of Economics: Recovering Practice*, Kluwer Academic Publishers.

—— (1993) *Non-Natural Social Sciences: Reflecting on the Enterprise of More Heat than Light*, Duke University Press.

Dobb, M. (1973) *Theories of Value and Distribution since Adam Smith: Ideology and Economic Theory*, Cambridge University Press.

Dow, S.C. (1982–3) 'Substantive Mountains and Methodological Molehills: A Rejoinder', *Journal of Post-Keynesian Economics*, vol. V, no. 2.

—— (1991a) 'The Post Keynesian School', in Mair, D. and Miller, A.G., *A Modern Guide to Economic Thought*, Edward Elgar.

—— (1991b) *Are there any Signs of Postmodernism in Economics?* Methodus, vol. 3, no. 1.

—— (1995) 'Uncertainty about uncertainty', in Dow, S.C. and Hillard J. (eds) (1995) *Keynes, Knowledge and Uncertainty*, Edward Elgar.

—— (1997a) 'Mainstream Economics Methodology', *Cambridge Journal of Economics*, 21.

—— (1997b) 'Rationalization in Economics: Theory, Methodology and Action' in draft form.

Dow, S.C. and Dow, A. (1985) (1989) 'Animal Spirits and Rationality' in Lawson, T. and Pesaran, H., *Keynes' Economics: Methodological Issues*, Routledge.

Dow, S.C. and Hillard, J. (eds) (1995) *Keynes, Knowledge and Uncertainty*, Edward Elgar.

Eagley R. (1968) *Events, Ideology and Economic Theory*, Wayne State University Press, Detroit.

Eichner, A.S. (1983) *Why Economics is not yet a Science*, M.E. Harpe.

Fine, B. (1980) *Economic Theory and Ideology*, Edward Arnold.

Friedman, M. (1991) 'Old Wine in New Bottles', *Economic Journal*, vol. 101, no. 404.

Gee, J.M. Alec (1991) 'The Neo-classical School', in Mair, D. and Miller, A.G., *A Modern Guide to Economic Thought*, Edward Elgar.

Gellner, E. (1982) 'The Paradox in Paradigms', *TLS*, 23 April, p. 451.

Gerrard, B. and Hillard, J. (1992) (eds) *The Philosophy and Economics of J.M. Keynes*, Edward Elgar.

Giddens, A. (1995) *Politics, Sociology and Social Theory*, Polity Press.

Goodwin, C.D. (1988) 'The Heterogeneity of the Economists' Discourse: Philosopher, Priest, Hired Gun', in Klamer, A., McCloskey, D.N. and Solow, R.M. (1988) *The Consequences of Economic Rhetoric*, Cambridge University Press.

Haas, D.J. (1993) 'A Historical Narrative of Methodological Change in Principles of Economics Textbooks', *Journal of Economic Issues*, vol. 2, no. 1.

Hahn, F. (1991) 'The Next Hundred Years', *Economic Journal*, vol. 101, no. 404.

Hands, D.W. (1994) 'The Sociology of Scientific Knowledge: Some Thoughts on the Possibilities', in Backhouse (1994) *New Directions in Economic Methodology*, Routledge.

Henderson, W. (1994) 'Metaphor and Economics', in Backhouse (1994) *New Directions in Economic Methodology*, Routledge.

Hillard, J. (1992) 'Keynes, Orthodoxy, and Uncertainty', in B. Gerrard, and J. Hillard (eds) *The Philosophy and Economics of J.M. Keynes*, Edward Elgar.

Hollander, S. (1980) 'Paul Samuelson On the "Canonical Classical Model"', *Journal of Economic Literature*, June 1980, vol. XVIII, no. 2.

—— (1984) *Classical Economics*, Basil Blackwell.

Hutchinson, J. and Smith, A.S. (ed.) (1994) *Nationalism*, Oxford University Press.

Johnson, E.S. and Johnson, H.G. (1978) *The Shadow of Keynes*, Basil Blackwell.

Katouzian, H. (1983) 'Towards the Progress of Economic Knowledge', in Wiseman J. (1983) *Beyond Positive Economics?*, Proceedings of Section F (Economics) of the British Association for the Advancement of Science, Macmillan.

Khalil, E.L. (1995) 'Has Economics Progressed? Rectilinear, Historicist, Universalist, and Evolutionary Historiographies', *History of Political Economy*, 27:1.

Kindi, V. (1995) *Kuhn & Wittgenstein*, Smili, Athens (in Greek, forthcoming in English: The University of Chicago Press).

Klamer, A., McCloskey, D.N. and Solow, R.M. (1988) *The Consequences of Economic Rhetoric*, Cambridge University Press.

Kurdas, C. (1988) 'The "Whig Historian" on Adam Smith: Paul Samuelson's Canonical Classical Model', *History of Economics Society Bulletin*, vol. 10, no 1, Spring.

Lawson, T. (1997) *Economics and Reality*, Routledge.

Lawson, T. and Pesaran, H. (1985) (1989) *Keynes' Economics: Methodological Issues*, Routledge.

Leijonhufvud, A. (1981) *Information and Coordination*, Oxford University Press.

Loasby, B.J. (1976) *Choice, Complexity and Ignorance*, Cambridge University Press.
—— (1989) *The Mind and Method of the Economist*, Edward Elgar.
Mair, D. and Miller, A.G. (1991) *A Modern Guide to Economic Thought*, Edward Elgar.
Mäki, U. (1992) 'Social Conditioning of Economics', in de Marchi, N. (1992) *Post-Poppesian Methodology of Economics: Recovering Practice*, Kluwer Academic Publishers.
McCloskey, D.N. (1983) ' The Rhetoric of Economics', *Journal of Economic Literature*, vol. XXI, June.
—— (1991) 'Voodoo economics: some scarcities of magic', *Poetics Today*, 12 (Winter).
—— (1994a) *Knowledge and Persuasion in Economics*, Cambridge University Press.
—— (1994b) 'How to do a Rhetorical Analysis, and Why', in Backhouse (1994) *New Directions in Economic Methodology*, Routledge.
Meek, R. (1967) *Economics and Ideology and other essays: Studies in the Development of Economic Thought*, Chapman and Hall.
Mirowski, P. (1989) *More Heat Than Light: Economics as Social Physics, Physics as Nature's Economics*, Cambridge University Press.
—— (1993) 'The Goalkeeper's Anxiety at the Penalty Kick', in de Marchi, N. (1993) *Reflecting on the Enterprise of More Heat than Light*, Duke University Press.
O'Donnell, R.M. (1989) *Keynes: Philosophy, Economics and Politics. The Philosophical Foundations of Keynes's Thought and their Influence on his Economics and Politics*, Macmillan.
Pierson, H.W. (ed.) (1977) *Karl Polanyi, The Livelihood of Man*, Academic Press.
Robinson, J. (1962) *Economic Philosophy*, Watts.
Rorty, R. (1980) *Philosophy and the Mirror of Nature*, Basil Blackwell.
Rossetti, A. (1992) 'Deconstruction, Rhetoric and Economics', in de Marchi (1992) *Post-Poppesian Methodology of Economics: Recovering Practice*, Kluwer Academic Publishers.
Routh, G. (1975) (1989) *The Origin of Economic Ideas*, 2nd edn, Macmillan.
Salanti, A. and Screpanti, E. (ed.) (1997) *Pluralism in Economics: New Perspectives in History and Methodology*, Edward Elgar.
Samuels, W.J. (1980) *The Methodology of Economic Thought*, Transaction Books.
—— (1990) *Economics as Discourse, an Analysis of the Language of Economists*, Kluwer Academic Publishers.
Samuelson, P.A. (1962) 'Economists and the History of Ideas', *The American Economic Review*, vol. LII, no. 1.
—— (1978) 'The Canonical Classical Model of Political Economy', *Journal of Economic Literature*, vol. XVI, 4: 1415–34.
—— 1987) 'Out of the Closet: A Program for the Whig History of Economic Science', *History of Economics Society Bulletin*, 9.1, Fall.
Schabas, M. (1992) 'Breaking Away: History of Economics as History of Science', *History of Political Economy*, Spring, vol. 24.
—— (1993) ' What's so Wrong with Physics Envy', in de Marchi, N. (1993) *Reflecting on the Enterprise of More Heat than Light*, Duke University Press.
Skidelsky, R. (1983) (1992) *J.M. Keynes*, vols. 1 and 2, Macmillan.
Stiglitz, J. (1991) 'Another Century of Economic Science', *Economic Journal*, vol. 101, no. 404.
Torrance, T. (1991) *The Philosophy and Methodology of Economics*, in Mair, D. and Miller, A.G. (1991) *A Modern Guide to Economic Thought*, Edward Elgar.
Ward, B. (1972) *What's Wrong with Economics?*, Macmillan.
Waterman, A.M.C. (1991) *Revolution, Economics and Religion*, Cambridge University Press.

Weintraub, E.R. (1982–3) 'Substantive Mountains and Methodological Molehills', *Journal of Post-Keynesian Economics*, vol. V, no. 2.

—— (1988) 'On the Brittleness of Orange Equilibrium', in Klamer, A., McCloskey, D.N. and Solow, R.M. (1988) *The Consequences of Economic Rhetoric*, Cambridge University Press.

—— (1991) *Stabilizing Dynamics: Constructing Economic Knowledge*, Cambridge University Press.

—— (1992) Comment: 'Thicker is Better', *Journal of the History of Economic Thought*, vol. 14, Fall.

—— (1993) *Stabilizing Dynamics, Constructing Economic Knowledge*, Cambridge University Press.

Wiles, P. (1983) 'Ideology, Methodology and Neo-classical Economics', in A.S. Eichner, *Why Economics is not yet a Science*, Macmillan.

Wiles, P. and Routh, G. (eds) (1984) *Economics in Disarray*, Macmillan.

Wiseman, J. (1983) *Beyond Positive Economics?* Proceedings of Section F (Economics) of the British Association for the Advancement of Science, Macmillan.

—— (1991) 'The Black Box', *Southern Journal*, vol. 101, no. 404.

12 The neo-classical synthesis in the Netherlands

A demand and supply analysis

*Henk W. Plasmeijer and Evert Schoorl**

Introduction

The theoretical and canonical foundation of the internationalization and homogenization of postwar Dutch economics was the neo-classical synthesis. This is the canonical view which at first gave rise to the belief that 'we are all Keynesians now', and which not much later was disqualified by Joan Robinson as bastard Keynesianism. The Dutch economists who developed a dislike for schools in economic thought, considered both the neo-classical and the (bastard) Keynesian toolboxes as important instruments for economic policy and in the 1960s they had strong doubts about the practical relevance of the destructive criticism which came from Cambridge (UK). Indeed, as one would expect, in the Netherlands the neo-classical synthesis was welcomed as an invitation for a Dutch treat.[1]

For more than 35 years after the second world war the neo-classical synthesis was the core of university education in economics. Generations of Dutch economists have started their studies with Marshallian micro and Hansen's $Y = C + I$ and Hicks's IS/LM macro. Samuelson's *Economics*, although not much used at economic faculties, was acknowledged as the standard textbook treatment.[2] Even until the mid-1970s the students were told that there is no basic conflict between the Keynesian and the neo-classical conclusions; the former apply to the short and the latter to the long run (see Pen 1965, 1971).

It is not only interesting how canonical views originate, are developed, criticized and eventually dismissed by the global community of scientists, i.e. how this community has struggled intellectually to arrive at internal theoretical consistency. It is equally interesting how a canon functions socially in specific geographical or cultural circumstances, both within a national community of scientists and within society at large. This is among others the story about how the profile of the economic profession in a society is shaped, about how economic debates are organized and about what problems the profession is supposed to deal with or what problems are likely to be considered relevant by the profession itself. Particularly when canonical views are admittedly eclectic, as was the case with the neo-classical synthesis, we may expect that a national scientific community with a high research profile evaluates theoretical debates somewhat differently from one with a high policy profile. In the Netherlands, the central issues in most theoretical debates are the consequences for economic policy and, although all Dutch economists informed themselves very thoroughly about the doctrinal debates abroad concerning the neo-classical synthesis, very few of them and none of the eminent ones felt the temptation to engage in them. In the 1970s they held the opinion that the proof of the monetarist pudding could only be found in the eating.

In this paper we discuss how the profile of the postwar Dutch economist, largely although not exclusively characterized by a policy-oriented macroeconomics, was shaped by concentrating upon the forces of demand and supply in the Dutch markets for economists and economic ideas. To economists it may be obvious that the social functioning of the postwar canon can be studied from the perspective of market forces. In the history of economic thought, however, it is not very common and even controversial (see for a counter-example Kadish and Tribe 1993). However, recognizing this influence seems essential for an understanding of the appreciation of the neo-classical synthesis, particularly in the Netherlands where this appreciation was the outcome of a gradual shift in the basic outlook of the economists. The shift started in the early 1930s when the Dutch Austrian school lost its intellectual appeal and declined (see Haan and Plasmeijer 1997; Plasmeijer 1998). It is true that for the Dutch economists, joining the international mainstream was a most natural thing to do; they always considered themselves members of an international intellectual community. But postwar eclecticism contrasted sharply with the prewar hairsplitting of the Austrian schoolmen.[3] The sudden topicality of the theory of economic policy in 1945 was also eyecatching. Indeed, notwithstanding the fact that Dutch economists have always taken a great interest in policy matters, and particularly in monetary policy, it may be said that their prewar and postwar policy outlooks differ remarkably.

The profile of the Dutch economist had drastically changed. The new profile came hand in hand with the neo-classical synthesis and a change in the social functioning of canonical views. To explain what happened to the social functioning of the canon we take a look at the market for economic knowledge. It is a striking fact that in the prewar period this market, although not negligible, was very small. After 1945 it expanded rapidly because of a demand shift. This was mainly the result of a rather drastic change in the Dutch economic order. A collective bargaining economy was created in which the most recent changes in economic variables were discussed at all levels. This historical change boosted the labour market for policy-oriented economists, and the institutions educating them.

The main argument of this paper is bold Marshallian economics: in order to gain an insight into how the neo-classical synthesis was put to work in the Netherlands, it is essential to deal with the supply reactions of Dutch universities to the autonomous demand shift. We certainly do not argue that consumers' sovereignty is all that matters and that society gets the economists it wants. What happened in the Netherlands to the other blade of the Marshallian scissors, i.e. the supply side of the market for economic expertise, was twofold.

- The institutional change offered – or seemed to offer – to academic economists the possibilities of testing and applying the most recent developments in economic theory, in particular in macroeconomics.
- With a view to the practical career of most students at the universities, the academic profession engaged in a debate about values and instrumentalism of economic theory, about the personal involvement of a scientifically educated policy advisor, in short about the theory of economic policy.

These supply reactions created the profiles of the Dutch academic economists and the policy advisors. During our period a Dutch economist is someone who combines a strong belief in value-free scientific economics with a permanent policy-orientedness; who as a moderate eclectic concentrates upon the tools of macroeconomics offered by the neo-classical synthesis; who strives for consensus when discussing the effectiveness of policy instruments; and who cherishes a large interest in monetary economics, the first decades in the specific version of 'Dutch monetarism' (see Fase 1992; Vanthoor 1991).

Stressing the social functioning of the canon seems to be directly relevant for recent debates about a 'European economics', in the background of which are suppressed suspicions about an 'Americanization' of economics (see *Kyklos* 1995, vol. 48, no. 2; Coats 1996). It goes without saying that no such thing as a European or American science can exist. What may differ is the social functioning of the canon, for good or for bad. But what is in this respect 'typically' European? Our demand and supply analysis of the functioning of the neo-classical synthesis in the Netherlands suggests that giving too much weight to the stickiness of social beliefs or cultural heritage may not be wise.[4] Between 1933 and 1950 the profile of a 'typical' Dutch economist changed very rapidly and there is absolutely no reason why this could not happen again. Indeed, nowadays the policy-orientedness of the economists is – as everywhere on the continent – to an increasing extent seen as a hindrance to academic success. Although the widening gap between policy advisor and scientist gave occasion to complaints (see Van Bergeijk et al. 1997), recent changes in the academic incentive structure have made a record of outstanding publications the core university business. Moreover, in the 1980s a reorientation upon microeconomics was clearly discernible. We are witnessing a 'European' process of an ever more narrowing academic profile.

First we deal with the amazing quantitative changes in the market for economists. Section one reviews the institutional changes that from 1945 onward boosted the demand. Section two presents some figures about this 'golden age' for economists. Next we deal qualitatively with the supply reactions to the new institutions of the consensus and welfare economy. The third section discusses how the neo-classical synthesis was put to use: it presents some material about the conversations among economists. Since both eclecticism and consensus were seen as foundations for a well-considered policy advice, we discuss in section four how the consensus concerning the theory of economic policy came about.

Postwar institutional change

Supply does not create its own demand. The huge postwar demand for policy-oriented economists had little to do with autonomous developments in the economic sciences. On the contrary, the demand came to a large extent from newly built institutions for economic and social policy. In this section we discuss the origins and the type of the institutions. It is our claim that the postwar demand for economists depended to a large extent on political and demographic developments.

From a general perspective the Dutch situation is perhaps not unique.[5] An important point to note, however, is that the subtle system of institutions and advisory councils was largely a postwar construction, erected between 1945 and 1955. Obviously, in 1945 most European countries confronted similar economic problems. At the time, most continental economists accepted the challenge and racked their brains over blueprints of a new institutional framework for economic policy. The unique national systems are to a large extent the results of – at the demand side – the unique political situations in each European country and – at the supply side – the economists' theory of economic policy.

The prelude

The foundations for the new postwar Dutch institutions were laid in heated political debates, which had been going on for decades before the second world war. The main participants in the debates were the supporters of the confessional and socialist parties, each arguing for the type of government interference they preferred, and the liberals, arguing for an unhampered functioning of the market economy. Mainstream economists had chosen the side of the latter. Elsewhere (e.g. Haan and Plasmeijer 1997) the story is told how in the early 1930s an increasing social acceptability of government interference was accompanied by increasing doubts about mainstream arguments. This eventually resulted in the decline of the Dutch Austrian school. Indeed, by 1935 it seems that economic theory in the Netherlands was at the crossroads. Notwithstanding many continuities, particularly in the fields of monetary theory and policy (see Plasmeijer and Schoorl 1999), a remarkable new feature of the post-war profile of Dutch economists is the consensus with respect to the applicability of the theory of economic policy in the new Dutch institutional setup.

The postwar demand for policy-oriented economists can hardly be detached from a peculiar aspect of postwar institutional change. Dutch society rapidly became a collective bargaining economy. This was mainly the result of the political clash between confessional corporative ideals and social-democratic ideals of planning (see Dullaart 1984). Already at the beginning of the century, the confessional parties had stressed the need for some protection of industry and the need for organizing enterprises and workers at the industry level, which would reduce wage bargaining to bilateral negotiations. At the time the socialists strongly believed that the concentration tendencies of the 1920s were a step towards the social-ization of capital, and since this tendency was expected to improve economic stability as well as productivity and profits, they argued for a nationalization programme to improve wages. When faced with mass unemployment in the 1930s, the confessional parties modified their corpo-rative views a little by their 'subsidiarity principle', which is the idea that government should not interfere when lower level institutions can do better. This principle however led to rather centralistic ideas about wage and price policy, which were not too far removed from socialist ideas about achieving a fair income distribution.

What institutions boosted the demand for political economists? Our account here is necessarily incomplete. We hope it gives the reader an impression of the direction of institutional change.

The Central Planning Bureau

In 1935 the socialist party and the socialist labour unions published a memorandum, *Strategy for Labour* (Plan van de Arbeid), of which Jan Tinbergen and Hein Vos were the main architects. The memorandum developed new ideas about planning. Planning should only interfere in free enterprise when private interests conflicted with social ones. This was, according to the *Strategy*, clearly the case where investment is concerned. Since investment behaviour was considered essentially erratic, the *Strategy* proposed an institution for the socialization of investment, which was called the 'Central Business Cycle Bureau'. Among its foreseen tasks were super-vision over the capital-widening and the capital-deepening of each and every existing and newly founded firm.

After the war, the newly founded Dutch labour party PvdA had a broader base – including many formerly confessional politicians, such as the monetary economist and finance minister Lieftinck – and had an even more reformist character than the prewar SDAP. In the first postwar administration, Vos became the minister of economic affairs. In order to speed up postwar economic reconstruction he asked Tinbergen to organize provisionally a so-called 'Central Planning Bureau' in anticipation of the passing of a bill on the subject. Equipping the Bureau with legislative powers as proposed in the *Strategy* was clearly politically unfeasible, so in the proposed bill the Bureau was assigned the task of advising government about the socialization of investment. Unfortunately for Vos and Tinbergen, the confessional parties won the 1946 elections before the bill was passed and although the new administration was once again a coalition of confessional and socialist parties, Vos had to leave office. The new minister of economic affairs, the roman catholic politician Huysmans, amended the bill. Instead of being the central agency of the managed economy, the role of the Central Planning Bureau was confined to economic forecasting (see Passenier 1994).

Statutory industrial organization

In 1950 in a sequel to a prewar amendment of the constitution, a bill was passed which granted legislative power to trading organizations, which were to be founded according to corporatistic ideals. The bill identified two kinds of trading organizations, in which we recognize Marshall's dual definition of an industry:

* product organizations or 'vertical' bodies defined over the industrial column;
* trading groups or 'horizontal' bodies of similar activities.

An example of the legislative power of the vertical bodies was the compulsory sale by auction of certain primary products (such as fish, flowers and vegetables) and levies in order to finance the commodities which had to be withdrawn from the market because of minimum price arrangements. The horizontal bodies engaged in re-sale price maintenance, cross subsidies (now forbidden, but in the book market still winked at), etc., and the enforcing of the 1954 establishment act for firms. Both the confessional corporatistic ideals and the socialistic ideals of codetermination were reflected in the executive committees of most trading organizations; employers and employees were equally represented.

An important aspect for the economic profession of the 1950 act on statutory industrial organization was the formation of the 'Socio-Economic Council' (SER). This tripartite council of 45 members appointed by employers' organizations, labour unions and the Crown (i.e. government) got two tasks. These were supervision of the trading organizations and advising government on socioeconomic matters. The Council was the centre of the Dutch collective bargaining system, in which the claims of the 'social partners' were confronted with the experts' assessments of 'sound' economic policy. For economics professors, the so-called Crown appointed membership was a prestigious (part-time) job, because in this role they could combine economic theory with their insights of the 'ordinary business of daily life' and even of politics. The Council also offered quite a few job opportunities to the rank and file in economics. For its work soon proliferated and a lot of it was delegated to temporary or permanent committees, such as the Committee for Consumers' Affairs, founded in 1965.

The Labour Foundation (Stichting van de Arbeid)

This organ was founded in 1945 by the employers' organizations and the labour unions. The main argument was that the postwar economic reconstruction required social harmony. This private initiative was so much appreciated by the government that the Foundation for a long period became an important advisory board in socioeconomic matters. Central wage negotiations started in the Foundation. In the 1950s and 1960s, it was regular practice that whenever in a particular sector an agreement had been reached which was not too irresponsible in the eyes of the CPB and the SER, the minister could declare it binding for the whole sector. The final evaluation of the agreement was laid in the hands of another institution, which advised the minister about declaring it valid. This was the so-called Council of State Mediators, founded in 1954.

Further demand effects

We are certainly not at the end of the story of the new institutions in the Dutch bargaining economy. We could easily go on with the tripartite 'Council for Social Security', and even continue beyond that. But we end our enumeration here. The main point is that institutionalization of the collective bargaining economy led to a huge demand for policy-oriented economists. This demand came not only from the newly formed institutions with its many committees, but also from the existing ones such as labour unions, employers organizations and ministries. Each and every one of them had to evaluate the proposals of the 'social partners' and the Crown-appointed SER members. Economic knowledge became the precondition for engaging in collective bargaining.

On top of this institutionalization came two developments which boosted the demand for political economists even further.

*   The European integration, starting with the Benelux in 1944 and really taking off with the Coal and Steel Treaty of 1953 and the Treaty of Rome in 1957, multiplied the institutions and the jobs for economists at the international level.
*   At some very popular secondary schools, general economics (Marshallian micro and Hansen's $Y = C + I$ macro) was taught as a separate subject, distinct from bookkeeping and commercial knowledge.

Between 1958 and 1963 the postwar baby boom arrived at this level, which led to an expansion of secondary education. This was the beginning of a steady shift in demand for teachers, for when average income rose many parents put their children on the path of intergenerational upward mobility.

We do not deny that the economists played a very active role in the debates about the new postwar Dutch economic order – as we will discuss in the fourth section. The driving force, however, was politics. So we may safely conclude that the demand for policy-oriented economists was mainly determined by political developments.

The golden age of the economists: excess demand

A remarkable difference between the prewar and the postwar period concerns the number of people wishing to be an economist. This is, of course, a matter of incentives. Staffing the institutions for economic policy, government departments, European institutions and the offices of the 'social partners' with economists led to a tight labour market for economists. In this section we present some figures about the quantitative effects on this market. The least we can take from these is that both the employers of economists and the younger generation seeking a career had the impression that they were being served by the educational system. Although the number of graduate economists increased rapidly, as can be expected with excess demand, the growth in numbers of jobs was even faster. For lack of reliable figures about labour unions, employers organizations, committees of the Socio-Economic Council and so on, we give an impression in Table 12.1 of the postwar demand growth as compared with the prewar period. It presents the number of economists who got a job offer in two important agencies and three ministries during the indicated time interval.

At the supply side of the labour market are mainly those with a recent 'doctorandus' degree (comparable to a MA) in general economics. In order to interpret the figures for five universities in Table 12.2 it should be kept in mind that the Dutch economics departments educate both business students and general economists. Since the MA is in economics and since the number of students specializing in business or general economics are not always registered, reliable figures about the supply of general economists are hard to come by. Notwithstanding this difficulty, Table 12.2 gives an idea. At the same time the market for business economists was booming too. Changes in the social convictions of the students may have influenced the choice, so it seems reasonable to assume that in the wake of the 1968 events general economics was very popular.[6] For the period between 1950 and 1970 we assume that the distribution between the specializations was relatively stable and that across all universities the

Table 12.1 New positions accepted by economists

	< 45	45–49	50–54	55–59	60–64	65–69	70–72	Total
Central Bureau of Statistics	7	9	26	20	24	22	13	121
Central Planning Bureau	0	37	23	24	21	28	17	150
Ministry of Economic Affairs	43	94	29	33	38	42	7*	286
Ministry of Social Affairs	5	5	6	9	24	26	15	90
Treasury	8	40	21	12	15	38	38	172
Total	63	185	105	98	122	156	90	819

Source: *Bemelmans-Vide, Tabellen en Bijlagen*, 1984: 1

Note: * The researcher could only identify (and contact) seven economists, although the real number must be somewhere around twenty to twenty-four.

Table 12.2 Master of Arts (doctorandus) degrees in general and business economics

	EUR	UvA	KUB	RUG	VU	Total
1916–1920	33					33
1921–1925	128	9				137
1926–1930	148	57				205
1931–1935	186	58	46			290
1936–1940	270	130	100			500
1940–1945	228	65	101			394
1946–1950	640	157	258	1	1	1057
1951–1955	724	330	346	36	68	1504
1956–1960	534	294	203	78	128	1237
1961–1965	664	331	301	73	176	1545
1966–1970	1047	472	713	304	309	2845
1971–1975	1608	795	788	563	462	4216

Source: *Bemelmans-Videc, Tabellen en Bijlagen*, 1984: 185

Notes
[1] Econometricians are not included in these figures; until the 1980s they graduated in the so called interfaculties, cooperative ventures of the economics and mathematics departments.
[2] The universities are the Erasmus University of Rotterdam (EUR), the University of Amsterdam (UvA), the Catholic University of Brabant (KUB) in Tilburg, the State University of Groningen (RUG) and the Free University (VU) in Amsterdam.

Table 12.3 Total numbers of students at the economics departments in the Netherlands

	EUR	UvA	KUB	RUG	VU	Total
60–61	1966	808	685	280	504	4243
61–62	2187	893	794	323	529	4726
62–63	2162	1039	927	377	563	5068
63–64	2325	1163	1075	413	627	5603
64–65	2561	1357	1112	571	698	6299
65–66	2767	1581	1210	647	778	6983
66–67	2990	1770	1354	728	869	7711
67–68	3298	1902	1511	766	961	8438
68–69	3610	1959	1577	832	1045	9003
69–70	3972	1992	1681	902	1176	9723

Source: *Statistiek van het Wetenschappelijk Onderwijs* (CBS)

percentage of students specializing in general economics was between five and fifteen per cent.

The tight labour market for both business and general economists had an enormous impact on the career choices of the younger generation. For the word rapidly spread that business economists were very often offered high salaries in industry. General economists were relatively well paid in, for example, the banking sector and Brussels; and those applying for a job in the civil service, where the starting salaries were not that good, could expect to achieve a rapid career progression. Economics departments expanded enormously, even more than the rest of higher education. Although Table 12.3 also reflects the postwar baby boom, which started to arrive at the universities in 1964, and the relative increase of adolescents seeking higher education, it gives an impression of the impact of excess demand in the labour market on the economic departments.

Summing up: the first twenty-five years of the postwar period were really the golden age for the economists. The labour market was very tight. This produced a flood at the economic departments, where the number of academic positions multiplied accordingly.

The neo-classical synthesis: the Dutch balance between theory and policy

Perhaps we ought to ask what this enormously expanding rank and file in economics was talking about, but we think that the better question is how the neo-classical synthesis was put to use. In this section we discuss the main areas of interest of the Dutch economists between 1960 and 1970.[7] These interests were very broad and clearly reflect a deep concern for both (macro and micro) policy issues and international theoretical developments. In organized discussions about policy matters much importance was attached to approaching problems from different angles, which together with a desire to reach consensus about a reasonable economic policy led to rather eclectic evaluations. The attention for macroeconomic theory and policy, however, is significant.

It seems to have been true that the macroeconomic toolbox was the important thing in policy matters. One of those arguing this has been J.E. Andriessen, who between 1955 and 1965 was first an Amsterdam academic and simultaneously a civil servant at the Ministry of Economic Affairs, and later the minister of this department. At the time the Ministry employed about 200–240 economists (see Table 12.1). Recalling from the period what these economists were doing Andriessen records, with some feeling for drama:

> Macro-economics was everything and micro-economics almost nothing. . . . In economic policy business life was a somewhat shadowy phenomenon, which largely could find its way under its own steam.

The former professors could excel in their strongest point: juggling with macro-economic variables for an economy without serious disturbances.

(Andriessen, 'Het Economisch Eldorado 1955–1965', in Knoester 1987: 190)

Indeed, a main concern for those engaged in economic policy at the Central Bank, at the ministries or at the Central Planning Bureau, or for those dividing their time between academia and the Socio-Economic Council, was to keep the economy on its path to prosperity (with annual growth rates of 5 per cent), applying the Keynesian instruments of macroeconomic policy. But this is certainly not the whole story for the academic economists, and the reason indicated by Andriessen for the predominant preoccupation with macroeconomics – i.e. the interests of the former professors – seems rather coloured by his own experiences.

The debates within the Royal Netherlands Society for Economics (KVS) can immediately verify that the economists' interests were rather diversified. Preparatory to the annual meeting the Society publishes the *Preadviezen*, which almost always deal with a particular subject in economic policy. The subjects for the period between 1960 and 1970 are summarized in Table 12.4. We can take from this that the conversations about economic policy where definitely broader in this Society than they were, according to its sometime minister, at the Ministry of Economic Affairs. The topics certainly reflect important problems of the day. It seems significant for the academic influence in the Society, that the economics of education is discussed in 1968, a year before the student unrest at the Dutch universities dramatically reached its highest point with the temporary shut-down of the university in Tilburg. Although the articles in the *Preadviezen* were traditionally not too technical – in the Netherlands the annual meeting of the Society is not the place for the professors to excel with their models – no instrument of the economic toolbox was left unused. For how can you discuss house rents without a fine piece of Marshallian tax-bounty analysis?

In order to find out more about the academic interest we took a look at what was published in two scholarly journals between 1960 and 1970.[8] The results are presented in Figure 12.1. From this we may certainly conclude that the interest in macroeconomics was rather strong. What cannot be read from the figures is that the theoretical articles on macroeconomics are analytically (mathematically) much more refined than the other ones, except for a few articles in which econometric techniques are used. As expected, we also found a strong interest in international matters. European integration is the subject of many articles. *Maandschrift Economie* published a special issue on the GATT treaty. The interest in the problems of underdevelopment is increasing. And finally we found many descriptive country analyses. When the focus of interest is compared with

Table 12.4 The subject matter of the annual KVS papers (Preadviezen)

1961	International coordination of economic policy
1962	Economic growth in the Western hemisphere, in particular in Western Europe
1963	Public expenses in the Netherlands. The volume and structure of government expenses in relation to the main goals of socioeconomic policy
1964	Pensions in the private sector. The possibilities of realizing inflation-proof and welfare-indexed pension claims
1965	The problem of house rents. The analysis of a desirable long run policy with respect to rents, subsidies and allowances
1966	The European economic integration. What institutions are necessary in order to have the common market functioning according to the Treaty of Rome?
1967	Raising the savings rate
1968	The economics of education
1969	The economics of spatial planning
1970	Agricultural policy in the European Community

that of the period 1945–55 (see Plasmeijer and Schoorl 1999), no remarkable differences can be found.

When the articles on macroeconomics are subdivided, we find the same interests that we found for the period between 1945 and 1955. Figure 12.2 gives the subdivision for the period between 1960 and 1970. The number of theoretical articles increased in both journals. The number of articles on macroeconomic policy is rather modest. The enormous number of articles on monetary theory and policy in *De Economist* reflects the traditional interests of the Dutch economists in monetary economics. It should be noted that at the end of our period (1960–70) it became customary to discuss monetary theory within an advanced IS/LM framework, which makes our subclassification rather arbitrary. The articles on public finance are mainly about the government budget, although at the end of the period public choice makes its entry.

Figure 12.3 shows an impression of the interests in microeconomics. It should be noted that in our period it is not the microeconomics one would expect nowadays. We have, of course, found a few little gems. In most cases, however, the use of analytical instruments is highly tentative. Only a few examples of econometric analysis were found. Very often the analyses of imperfect competition, price policy and the economic order are purely descriptive and by present standards would hardly qualify for this category. Most of these are intended to discuss policy matters. It should be

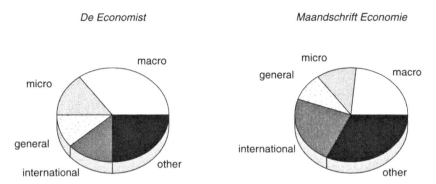

Figure 12.1 Subjects of articles in two scholarly journals between 1960 and 1970

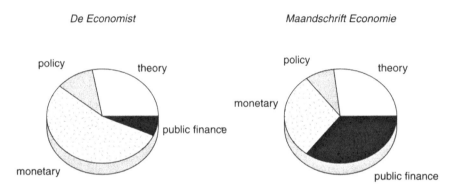

Figure 12.2 Macroeconomics in two scholarly journals between 1960 and 1970

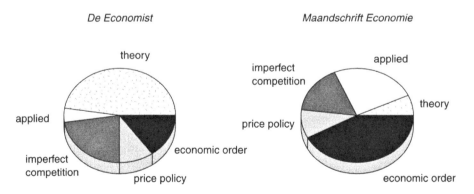

Figure 12.3 Microeconomics in two scholarly journals between 1960 and 1970

noted that our main category 'other' in Figure 12.1 contains many sector studies, of which quite a few are about the health care system and agriculture, which are equally descriptive and serve the same purpose. Since by including the articles in this or that category no rational choice was involved (except perhaps for the criterion that the author at least engaged in some discussion of market functioning) we present our Figure 12.3 rather hesitantly.

The most remarkable thing to note about the two journals is the changing quality during the period. In macroeconomics the use of mathematical techniques seems to become an essential requirement for getting your article published. What we classified as 'general' in Figure 12.1 were in the period between 1945 and 1955 almost always broad stories (How to be a catholic economist and so on). These kinds of stories can still be found between 1960 and 1970, but they are gradually substituted by very good essays in methodology, the history of economic thought and economic history. Particularly *Maandschrift Economie* changed in this respect. It is true, we have found at least three stories about the financial problems of the Roman Catholic church, a most pressing problem in Tilburg of course. But during the decade the parochial character of the journal decreased and the last volumes we examined were quite readable (one single issue even for a Marxist reader). This could be indirectly explained by the growth of the economics departments. For it seems that the supply of articles had reached such a critical mass that the editors could engage, at least more than they did before, in selecting by quality.

We may conclude that the interests of the academic economists were certainly very broad. The predominant interest in macroeconomics, which ruled the roost in the Ministry of Economic Affairs, is not unambiguously reflected in the *Preadviezen* and in the scholarly journals. The academic economists went their own way and, although we found a strong overlap between the problems on the economists' and the politicians' agendas, they discussed the topics they considered relevant. Their attempts to arrive at consensus in policy matters are remarkable. We certainly found an enormous interest in refining the tools of macroeconomic and monetary analysis.

The expert in politics: on the theory of economic policy

An amazing new feature of the social functioning of the postwar canon is the striving for consensus in policy matters within the profession itself. We think it is far too easy to refer merely to social circumstances, i.e. the consensus in society about postwar reconstruction. As in the prewar period many economists were deeply involved in one or the other political party. In this section we argue that the theoretical foundation of the postwar consensus was laid in an academic debate about the theory of economic policy. The basic arguments were formulated by Pieter Hennipman,[9] who defined the theory of economic policy as a branch of the political theory of democracy. This starting point allowed all economists to combine their increasing policy-orientedness with a strong belief in a value free economics.

The theory of economic policy can be seen as a supply reaction to the demand shift in the market for economic knowledge. The shift changed the role of the economists in society, which brought along an obvious academic problem. In the prewar period the academic economists, and in particular those of the old Dutch Austrian school, had insisted upon a value-free science. For the leading Austrians this meant that they were impartial spectators, in which capacity they did not hesitate to disqualify socialist and confessional economic ideas as anachronistic (see Plasmeijer 1998). For the academics the postwar demand shift, and in particular the new institutional set-up, was in fact an invitation to participate in shaping the economic order (or to educate the people who were able to do so). When their role changed accordingly and it was clear to them that they were no longer merely critics but had become participants in social policy, the Pontius Pilatus trick did not work any more. The core of the theory of economic policy is a very rigorous division between theoretical and political social policy debates. For economists of different persuasions this was the theoretical foundation of striving for consensus in the former, while differences of opinion could be respectfully discussed in the latter.

In the Netherlands neither Hennipman nor Tinbergen was the first to stress the need for such a theory.[10] In November 1945, however, Hennipman descended from his beloved ivory tower to address the problem of postwar economic recovery in his inaugural lecture on *Theoretical Economics and the Postwar Reconstruction*. In three sections he managed to discuss the theoretical notion of economic policy, the problem of unemployment and the problem of shaping the economic order. Already at that time Hennipman was reputed to have read everything, and apart from Dutch authors he quotes just as many German language authors as Anglo-Saxon ones. Quite significantly, however, when dealing with unemployment he does not mention Keynes, but Beveridge. And even more significantly, when dealing with the economic order he does not hide his admiration for the theoretical contributions of the German Ordo-Liberals, such as W. Eucken, W. Röpke and F. Böhm. Coming to his conclusion he brings up the competence of the economic theorist to evaluate social ideals about the economic order:

> When one wishes to maintain in principle the so called capitalist or liberal system, it will be necessary to take a whole of finely furcated and differentiated measures in order to remove its deficiencies. Whether one takes as a point of departure the socialist or the liberal ideal, in any case it turns out that one is forced upon the road leading to a synthesis of freedom and restraint, and where the market

mechanism is deliberately employed as an instrument of government policy. Only theoretical considerations could point out the road to such a solution.

(Hennipman 1945: 22)

Hennipman left no doubt that according to him only a value free theory is able to produce suggestions for these 'finely furcated and differentiated measures', because only such a theory can impartially evaluate the objective economic consequences of the socialist and liberal ideals.

The Keynesian revolution offered no solution to the fundamental question which Hennipman addressed. The answer it came up with is that economic theory is able to develop policies which benefit everyone. As useful as this may seem, a theory of economic policy which is confined to such policies was soon evaluated as too restrictive. Still, Keynes's work impressed the younger generation of economists, if we may believe Zijlstra's recollections:

[The General Theory] had an enormous influence and in many respects completely overturned traditional economic theories. During the war, and even more thereafter Keynes's message came to the Rotterdam Hogeschool (Economics Polytechnic, the present Erasmus University) and from the start we, the students, were enthusiastic. It meant that an economic crisis no longer was such a thing as pneumonia, where you just had to wait whether or not the patient would recover. No, the economic penicillin had been discovered. Only able and energetic politicians were needed to build a new world, free from want and unemployment. In 1945 after the liberation, that was the gospel. Especially the younger generation of economics students felt an almost missionary zeal to contribute to such a world.

(Zijlstra 1992: 13)[11]

Zijlstra's phrasing betrays the social engagement with the real world problems of poverty and unemployment, an engagement he shared with many if not all Dutch economists. Indeed, as Zijlstra notes, the concern with the needs of the day led to a strong belief in the instrumentality of economic theory. It should be noted, however, that the economists' social engagement was fueled by rather diverging belief systems. It is easily seen that at the time it must have been impossible to reach a consensus about the instrumentality of economic theory on basis of the mere willingness to 'better the world'. For when it comes to social justice we may expect a confessional economist like Zijlstra to hold a rather different vision of a 'new world' than a socialist colleague like Tinbergen.

Although Tinbergen's *On the Theory of Economic Policy* (1952) is a masterpiece on its own, it hardly addresses Hennipman's fundamental question. It is in fact a superior tract in instrumentalism, which clearly betrays its background in ideas about planning. Tinbergen's argument is sufficiently known: when the goals of economic policy are given, the empirical model enables the economic expert to define 'instrument variables' with which 'target variables' can be influenced. It is, of course, absolutely true that at the time Tinbergen's combination of instrumentalism and a deep personal political engagement and concern with the poor (both in the developed and the less developed world) was and still is (Van Dalen and Klamer 1996) a shining example to the Dutch economics profession. But notwithstanding this admiration it was equally felt at the time that Tinbergen's *On the Theory of Economic Policy* had carried the scientific econometric model beyond scientific purposes. It is also true that Tinbergen repeatedly stressed that the goals of economic policy are a matter for politicians to determine, although he never hid his personal opinion that a fair income distribution ought to be among them. However, he equally stressed that an economist designs an econometric model not only for isolating 'targets' and developing 'instruments', but also for testing the consistency of the goals of economic policy. We will see that the objection to that was not that when testing the consistency of political aims, social values necessarily come in, but that Tinbergen had left the matter inconclusive. Social values do come in – and the cherished value freeness of the economic sciences is left behind – when the experts' debates about the consistency of political objectives are not sufficiently distinguished from the social debates about political priorities.

Hennipman fought the battle for a value free economics mainly on his own grounds, which were Paretian welfare economics. For Hennipman the real scientific question in economics was the employment of scarce resources which have alternative uses. Economics is, according to him, neither about the ends, nor about the origins of individual material and political preferences. This being the case, Paretian welfare economics is by all the criteria of what is called Hume's guillotine (Blaug 1992) a positive science, for a statement that an allocation is economically optimal is quite different from one which says that it is desirable. Quite the contrary, the optimal allocation depends on the original distribution of resources and may evidently be highly undesirable by criteria of human rights. Hennipman explicitly denied that normative statements are involved in welfare economics. For more than one generation of Dutch economists, Hennipman's essays epitomized the creed of value free economics, meticulously documented from the entire history of economic thought. In 1992, when criticizing Blaug on the subject, Hennipman referred to the actual agreement among Dutch economists as follows:

> When in 1962 I criticized the ethical conception of welfare economics in a Dutch study I could refer not only to Archibald but also to a number of other like-minded economists. Since then the same view has been briefly voiced by, among others Buchanan and Ferguson. . . . It has gained wide support in The Netherlands.
>
> (Hennipman 1995: 125)

The Dutch article Hennipman refers to was his tremendously influential intervention in the debate on the theory of economic policy. For a long time it was considered to be the definitive statement on the topic.[12]

Although presented with many subtleties, Hennipman's position was a straightforward application of his ideas about value-free economics. Economic theory is about arriving at a goal, never about the goals themselves. Especially in economic policy the theorist should realize that the policy maker has his own utility function. For this implies, according to Hennipman, that the economic advisor can only be of help when maximizing this function, and not when defining it.[13] Although it is impossible to discuss Hennipman's position at length, the following observations he made give an impression.

• The goals of economic policy are not necessarily consistent from an economic point of view. Indeed, Hennipman believed they seldom are. These goals, however, are items in the politicians' utility function. The economic theorist can, of course, draw attention to these inconsistencies, but, according to Hennipman, he should not try to remove them by engaging in a political priorities debate. The task of the policy advisor is to show how the politicians' utility function can be optimized. Hennipman's point is that a solution to the politicians' problem which is 'second best' from the economists' point of view may be an optimum for the policy makers. With impeccable logic Hennipman pointed out that the politicians' and hence a Paretian optimum may depend on finding this 'second best' solution.

• A personal engagement of the scientist in policy matters is, according to Hennipman, unavoidable. But in all circumstances, any scientist should make clear whether he is presenting scientific results or a political opinion. Moreover, he should try hard to produce his scientific results by scientific reasoning alone. For the academic debate this does not mean that the socially engaged economists should try to hide their diverging belief systems from one another. It meant that the common ground for these debates is not the instrumentality of economic theory, but the robustness of the value-free scientific results alone.

Hennipman considered his 'theory of economic policy' a solution to the Weberian *Wertfreiheit* problem. Although he did not mention it, he arrived at his solution by defining this theory as branch of political theory. Basically Hennipman dealt with an old fundamental problem in the social sciences, which is: since the purpose of social science is to enable control of the world, scientific success may endanger democracy and can lead to scientific (or philosophical) authoritarianism. In fact, Hennipman came up with a rather familiar solution to that problem. The basic tenets are well known. The first is that the differentiation of the social sciences puts each specialization in a modest place. The economic expert can say fine things about improving the world, but so can the sociological expert. The second is the distinction between scientific advice and political decision, which Hennipman interpreted as the division of labour between policy advisor and policy maker. Expertise is invaluable, but it is for society itself to take decisions about its future. The third is that the expert should stick to the rules of social decision making, even when the outcome is different from his personal or scientific point of view.

Although Hennipman's solution to the *Wertfreiheit* problem was certainly not new, its importance for postwar economics in the Netherlands can hardly be underestimated. In the prewar period one could present oneself as a socialist or confessional economist, although the academic economist, of course, tried to pronounce himself in the name of value free science. Politically, value-laden statements were accepted because at the time Dutch society itself was compartmentalized along confessional and sociopolitical lines. After the war the religious and sociopolitical barriers in Dutch society were breaking down. We presume that among economists the political purport of the solution to the *Wertfreiheit* problem rapidly made a compartmentalized scientific community an anachronism. Before the war Tinbergen was perhaps a socialist economist, but after the war he definitely was – in his professional life – a highly respected economist and – in his personal life – an inspired social-democrat.[14]

Final observations

When discussing the social functioning of the neo-classical synthesis in the Netherlands we relied upon a demand and supply analysis of the market for economic knowledge. We are, of course, aware that applying the economic toolbox to the history of economic ideas is deliberately metaphorical. But with the framing of the story of our Dutch case we have tried to bring into the limelight some essential characteristics of the development of canonical views. In the Netherlands no such thing as Say's law of markets for economic knowledge existed and the social functioning of the neo-classical synthesis can be described by a *tâtonnement* process in which the Dutch community of economists reacted to demand shifts in this market.

During the postwar reconstruction drastic changes in the Dutch economic order, which were basically a political compromise, boosted the demand for policy-oriented economists who were able to discuss the most recent changes in macroeconomic variables at all levels of the collective bargaining economy. The reactions of the academic community were scientifically guided and relatively autonomous. Indeed, a policy-oriented and a moderately eclectic macroeconomics was the main stamp of all Dutch economists. The improvements in the tools of analysis were significant. But it was certainly not an exclusive stamp. The increasing policy involvement of many economists provoked a debate about the theory of economic policy, in which the roles of the economic scientist, the economic policy advisor and the economic policy maker were more or less clearly delineated. This is perhaps what characterizes a 'typical' Dutch economist most: he knows when he trespasses over one of these borderlines. Still, there is very little 'typically' Dutch about this profile. As we told, in 1945 it was relatively new. In 1945, when Europe lay in ruins and everyone believing in a better world knew he had to start from scratch, the burden of tradition could not have been less. There is no reason why this profile could not change in the near future. In recent times the collective bargaining economy is gradually being broken up. The demand for policy-oriented economists may after all those years shift back. It is much too early to speculate what can happen with the social functioning of canonical views in economics. We have not collected figures about the conversations among economists as we did for the period between 1945 and 1970. But modern Dutch economists are successfully trying to increase their academic profile.[15] We would not be surprised at all if it turned out that the *tâtonnement* process in the market for economic knowledge has started to work the other way around.

Notes

* The authors would like to thank Willem Drees, Jan Jacobs and Harro Maas for useful comments.

1 In an earlier paper we sketched the postwar internationalization and homogenization of Dutch economics. Our conclusion was that there has been a strong internationalization of Dutch economics since 1945, but not only at the receiving end. Through the influence of Tinbergen and the 'brain drain' of people like Theil, Tj. Koopmans and J.J. Polak, the Netherlands have been at the transmitting end as well, so it is even possible to speak of a certain 'Tinbergenization' of Anglo-American economics (Plasmeijer and Schoorl 1999).

2 Samuelson's textbook was translated in 1968. The reasons for not adopting the book were various, but one of them certainly was that the book was considered too wordy. The textbooks written by the Dutch professors themselves tell basically the same story on often less than half of the number of pages.

3 For example, when in 1936 Jan Tinbergen presented at the annual meeting of the Royal Netherlands Economic Association the first econometric macro-model ever made, the dean of the Dutch Austrians, C.A. Verrijn Stuart, criticized Tinbergen for circular reasoning. Economic phenomena can, according to him, only be explained by relating them causally to essentials which organize economic life in each and every society. Tinbergen, of course, dealt most adequately with this criticism (see Knoester and Wellink 1993: 16–19).

4 Van Dalen and Klamer (1996) have recently presented such a cultural approach for the Netherlands. They reduce both the profile of the Dutch economists and the consensus among them to the influence of Jan Tinbergen. In this paper we stress that this profile resulted from collective efforts and that its foundation was the consensus among economists about the tasks of the economic sciences. It also makes no sense to attribute national differences in the continental systems of economic policy exclusively to cultural differences. These reflect to a large extent the historical differences in both the political environment and

the economists' theory of economic policy. It is not very difficult to recognize in the more academic profile of the highly influential German *Sachverständigenrat* (Council of Experts, whose tasks are similar to those of the Dutch Central Planning Bureau) the ideas on economic policy of the economic architects of the *Soziale Marktwirtschaft* (social market economy), the so-called Ordo-Liberals.
5 According to Van Dalen and Klamer (1997) the Dutch situation is typically European:

> The Dutch economists appear to fit the European image. They have produced a remarkable number of prominent politicians and they take an active part in the numerous advisory councils that characterize Dutch politics. Yet nowhere in Europe do we observe the influence that one single research institute is having on policy, as that of the Central Planning Bureau (CPB) in the Netherlands.

Van Dalen and Klamer are, of course, right about the CPB's influence. However, in our opinion it is worth stressing that the CPB is a part of a rather subtle system of economic policy. To a large extent the Bureau derives its acceptability and hence its influence from the interplay within that system. Moreover, its access to the most recent economic data is excellently organized, as are the contacts with ministries on policy debates. This clearly enhances the status of its computational results. In the formative years it was Tinbergen's authority that gave the Bureau its status. Under his successors, its authority was unchallenged for many years. It is true that in the early 1970s the Bureau took the lead in criticizing Keynesian policies, but also in that period it rapidly had to adjust its model to academic monetarist criticism. However, also in this respect things are changing rapidly. Since the Lucas critique the Bureau's influence is challenged by an increasing distrust of both policy makers and academic economists in large econometric macro-models.
6 From 1971 onwards the student administration of the economic department in Groningen has collected figures about the specializations of the 'doctorandus' degrees (see figure 12.4). It should be noted that in the 1970s and 1980s the time-lag between the students' choice and the awarding of the degree was about four or five years. In the academic year 1971/2, 8.8 per cent of all awarded degrees in economics was in general economics. Changes in the social convictions of the students in the wake of the 1968 events are reflected in a steady increase in the percentage of students getting a degree in general economics. This percentage reached its peak of 27 per cent in 1979/1980 and went down to 8 per cent in 1994/5. These figures should be treated with care. (1) Some differences in student population may exist between the universities. (2) Econometricians are not included. (3) The figures do not tell the whole story about the weakening of the boom which started in the 1970s and which was probably the result of the students' revolution. In the early 1980s a new Department of Business Studies opened its doors. This department, which nowadays equals the Department of Business Economics in size, attracts many students who otherwise would have chosen business economics at the Economic Department. When these three provisos are taken into account, it seems safe to say that about 5–15 per cent of all economic students specialize in general economics.
7 Our sources are the discussions at the annual meeting of the Royal Netherlands Society for Economics and the published articles in two Dutch scholarly journals, *De Economist* and *Maandschrift Economie*, which at the time were both in the Dutch language. At the time *Maandschrift Economie* was a journal edited by and almost completely filled by scientists at the Economics Polytechnic of Tilburg, the later Catholic University of Brabant. We also inspected the studied texts

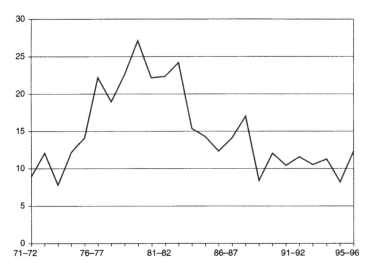

Figure 12.4 Percentage of students in economics getting a degree in general
economics in Groningen

in undergraduate studies in order to find out what toolbox was handed down
to the younger generation that came to the universities. This led to the conclusion that the curricula were everywhere highly conventional, although we
found a lot of amusement (in Amsterdam, Rotterdam and Groningen) at the
peculiar manner of model building in Tilburg. Most texts were written by Dutch
professors.

8 We classified the articles in a few broad categories and subcategories. We tried
the classification of the *Journal of Economic Literature*, but too many articles did
not fit in. We counted the number of pages devoted to each subject. In Plasmeijer
and Schoorl 1999 we give a detailed account of the figures used in this and our
earlier paper.

9 As a professor at the University of Amsterdam, Pieter Hennipman (1911–94)
was an influential teacher to many generations of economists. As a scholar in
welfare economics he was not a prolific author, but apart from his monumental
thesis on savings he produced a number of extremely influential essays on
economic methodology and competition policy. He could be viewed as the
typical ivory tower economist. In our opinion he epitomizes the gradual transition from Austrianism to the neo-classical synthesis that was typical of the shift
in canonical views in the Netherlands in the 1940s and 1950s.

10 In 1944 W.L. Valk had devoted his contribution to the *Festschrift* for F. de Vries
to the subject. Willem Lodewijk Valk was mainly known for his contributions
to Walrasian theory, from which perspective he criticized Austrian theory (see
Plasmeijer 1998). In the 1920s and 1930s François de Vries (1884–1958) was a
leading member of the Austrian school in the Netherlands. In 1952 he turned
his back on Austrian theory (see Plasmeijer and Schoorl 1996).

11 Jelle Zijlstra (1918) is well known for his work on monetary theory and public
finance. In the 1960s and 1970s he was respectively prime minister and director
of the Central Bank. He also was a professor at the Free University in Amsterdam.
As a prime minister he was extremely popular. He is perhaps the only economist

in the world about whom a song has been written. The song hit the charts and at a carnival (Mardi Gras) it was sung in the streets: Jelle will take care ('Jelle zal wel zien'). Although Zijlstra's recollections are not very different from those expressed by J. Tobin (when interviewed by M. Blaug for a video on Keynes's legacy), in the Netherlands there was no sect of converts of the type described so well in Colander and Landreth's *The Coming of Keynesianism to America*. There was no a radical turn to Keynesianism in macroeconomics. It came gradually in the format of the neo-classical synthesis.

12 The title was 'The ends and criteria of economic policy' (Doeleinden en criteria der economische politiek', in Andriessen 1962; 1–106). It is partly republished (omitting most references to Dutch literature) as 'On the theory of economic policy' in Hennipman (1995: 1–58). In the Netherlands the main point was the desirability of a value free economics, not the possibility. In later studies in the English language Hennipman criticized Mishan (*Welfare Economics, Ten Introductory Essays*) and Blaug (*The Methodology of Economics*), who both had argued that Paretian welfare economics are necessarily normative (see Hennipman 1995).

13 This, of course, does not mean that the policy process cannot be studied scientifically. At the time a Dutch debate went on between Jan Pen and his Groningen colleague Floor Hartog, on the role of the economist in explaining economic policy. Pen saw a role for the profession here, even when economists would venture outside the boundaries of their discipline when engaging in this kind of discussions. Hartog was afraid that an economist would be playing the dilettante in such efforts. Although siding with Hartog, Hennipman admitted to Pen that: 'the economist need not necessarily always abstain from taking factors into account that are outside his domain in the strict sense.' A little later one of Hennipman's pupils, H. van den Doel, was to publish his influential text on the subject, *Democracy and Welfare Economics*.

14 In reality the theoretical distinction between an expert's advice and the political belief of the economist was and is not always clear. This gave rise to the rather funny 'hat problem' (pettenprobleem). Since in policy debates an economist is not supposed to be wearing two hats, he always has to make clear whether he is talking as an economist or as a politically engaged citizen. A Dutch economist can change 'hats' rather rapidly. His famous trick to make his political point is to change the 'hat' in such a way that nobody, except a colleague, notices it.

15 A clearly discernible change in the social functioning of canonical views is the change in academic competition. Academic esteem increasingly depends upon the record of international publications. The change seems to have brought along a reorientation of microeconomics. The costs seem to be (1) a declining policy-orientedness, (2) a loss of eclecticism and (3) a marginalization of heterodox schools and of historical, methodological and other 'fringe' subjects. But in the research assessment, organized in 1995 by the Dutch Universities Association VSNU, the Dutch academic economists are doing rather well.

References

Andriessen, J.E. and M.A.G. van Meerhaeghe (eds) (1962) *Theorie van de Economische Politiek*, Leiden: Stenfert Kroese.

Bemelmans-Videc, M.L. (1984) '*Economen in overheidsdienst, 1945–1975*', PhD thesis Rotterdam.

Bergeijk, P. van, Bovenberg, A. L., Damme, E. van and Sinderen, J. van (eds) (1997) *Economic Science and Practice, the Roles of Academic Economists and Policy-makers*, Cheltenham: Edward Elgar.

244   *Henk W. Plasmeijer and Evert Schoorl*

Blaug, M. (1992) *The Methodology of Economics, or how Economists Explain*, Cambridge: Cambridge University Press.

Coats, A.W. (ed.) (1996) *The Post-1945 Internationalization of Economics*, Durham and London: Duke University Press.

Dalen, H. van and Klamer, A. (1996) *Telgen van Tinbergen, het Verhaal van de Nederlandse Economen*, Amsterdam: Uitgeverij Balans.

—— (1997) 'Blood is thicker than water: economists and the Tinbergen legacy', in Bergeijk et al., (1997) *Economic Science and Practice, the Roles of Academic Economists and Policy-makers*, Cheltenham: Edward Elgar, pp. 60–91.

Dullaart, M.H.J. (1984) 'Regeling of Vrijheid, Nederlands Economisch Denken tussen de Wereldoorlogen', PhD thesis Rotterdam.

Fase, M.M.G. (1992) 'A century of monetary thought in the Netherlands', in J. van Daal, A. Heertje (eds) *Economic Thought in the Netherlands*, Avebury, pp. 145–81.

Fase, M.M.G. and Zijpp I. van der (eds) (1992) *Samenleving en Economie in de Twintigste Eeuw*, Leiden/Antwerpen: Stenfert Kroese.

Haan, M. and Plasmeijer, H.W. (1997) 'On the decline of an intellectual empire, the paradigm shift in the Netherlands', in H. Hagemann (Hrsg), *Die Deutschsprachige Wirtschaftswissenschaftliche Emigration nach 1933*, Marburg: Metropolis Verlag, pp.459–78.

Hennipman, P. (1945) *De Theoretische Economie en de Wederopbouw*, Amsterdam, Noord-Hollandse, inaugural lecture.

—— (1995) *Welfare Economics and the Theory of Economic Policy*, edited by D.A. Walker, A. Heertje and H. van den Doel, Aldershot: Edward Elgar.

Kadish, A. and Tribe, K. (eds) (1993) *The Market for Political Economy: the Advent of Economics in British University Culture, 1850–1905*, London: Routledge.

Knoester, A. (ed.) (1987) *Lessen uit het Verleden, 125 Jaar Vereniging voor de Staathuishoudkunde*, Leiden/Antwerpen: Stenfert Kroese.

Knoester, A. and Wellink, A.H.E.M. (1993) 'Tinbergen and the Royal Netherlands Association', in Knoester, A. and A.H.E.M. Wellink (eds) *Tinbergen Lectures on Economic Policy*, Amsterdam.

Passenier, J. (1994) *Van Planning naar Scanning, een Halve Eeuw Planbureau in Nederland*, Groningen: Wolters Noordhoff.

Pen, J. (1965) *Modern Economics*, Penguin: Harmondsworth.

—— (1971) *Income Distribution*, London: Allen Lane.

Plasmeijer, H.W. (1998) 'Early Walrasians in the Netherlands', in J. Glombowski, A. Gronert and H.W. Plasmeijer (eds), *Zur Kontinentalen Geschichte des Ökonomischen Denkens/History of Continental Economic Thought*, Marburg: Metropolis Verlag, 261–82.

Plasmeijer, H.W. and Schoorl, E. (1999) 'Postwar Dutch Economics', in A.W. Coats (ed.) *The Development of Economics in Western Europe Since 1945*, Routledge: London.

Sinderen, J. van (ed.) (1990) *Het Sociaal-Economisch Beleid in de Tweede helft van de Twintigste Eeuw*, Groningen: Wolters Noordhoff.

Tinbergen, J. (1952) *On the Theory of Economic Policy*, Amsterdam: Elsevier.

Vanthoor, W.F.V. (1991) *Een Oog op Holtrop, Grondlegger van de Nederlandse Monetaire Analyse*, Amsterdam, NIBE Series, no. 75.

Zijlstra, J. (1992) *Per Slot van Rekening: Memoires*, Amsterdam: Contact.

Index

Page numbers in italics refer to tables and figures.

Dante 18
de Marchi, N.B. 113–14, 136
Deane, P. 203, 205
debasement, practice of 11
Debreu 74, 75
Deleuze, G. and Guattari, F. 148, 149
Demosthenes 7, 29
Denzer, H. 55
depression (1930s) 156, 163, 164
deregulation 75
development
    Aristotle's concept of 2, 5–6, 11
    and Ibn Khaldun 11
    and Latin scholastics 17
    new concept of 4
development economics 94, 95
    emergence of 190–1
Dionysio-Hadriana 40–1
division of labour 60, 208
Dow, S.C. 200
Dufour, A. 55
Duhem-Quine argument 198
Dutch Austrian school 221, 223, 235
Dutch economists *see* Netherlands
dynamic theory 93–4, 94–5, 96

eclecticism 223
economic development and
    Preobrazhensky 191–2
economic growth 92–105
    canonical model 92–3, 93–6, 97, 98,
        99, 104, 105
    closed and open models 96
    and decreasing returns 97–8, 99,
        103
    differences between Malthus and
        Ricardo 104–5
    and dynamics theory 93–5
    and Harrod 94
    long time in establishing of in
        economic discourse 93
    Malthusian system 93, 96, 97,
        99–105
    and 'progress of wealth' 96–9
    Ricardian system 93, 96, 97, 98–9,
        100, 101, 102, 105
    and Soviet economists 190
economic policy, theory of 234–9,
    239–40
economics
    as an article of faith 202–3
    conflict of opinion concerning 196
    consensus in science of 204–5
    developments in 190–1

as divine inspiration 201–7
and 'empty box' controversy 209,
    211
history of conflict in as conflict
    between Ricardian canon and
    Keynesian heresy 205–7, 210,
    212
and methodology 198–9
new age of 201–2
non-rational reconstruction of
    (in)credibility of 197–200
and science 201–2
telling the story of 197–200
and theory appraisal 198, 199, 200
three hundred year war in 207–12
Economist, De 232, 233
economists 196–7
Einstein 122
Elements of Law, The (Hobbes) 47
Eltis, W. 100
'empty box' controversy 209, 211
energeia 5
Enlightenment 1
Epicureans 3
equilibrium
    in business cycle theory 157, 161,
        165
    see also general equilibrium theory
Ethica Nicomachea see Nicomachean Ethics
Eucken, W. 235
exchange relations
    and Aquino 15–16
    and Aristotle's economic canon 7–8,
        13, 15, 18, 31
    and Buridan 18
expansionary monetary policy 111
Ezekiel 28, 31, 34

F-Twist debate 205
Fable of the Bees, The (Mandeville) 61
falsificationism 198
Franciscan scholars 17
free market 69, 74, 75
free trade and scarcity 129
French humanists 18
Friedman, M. 211
Friedman and Schwartz *Monetary
    History* 172
Frisch, Ragnar 171

Gadamer 73
Galileo 210
Galton, Sir Francis 150
Garin, E. 20

For Product Safety Concerns and Information please contact our EU representative GPSR@taylorandfrancis.com Taylor & Francis Verlag GmbH, Kaufingerstraße 24, 80331 München, Germany

T - #0009 - 230425 - C0 - 234/156/15 [17] - CB - 9780415191548 - Gloss Lamination